TELECOM
WARS

ADVANCE PRAISE FOR THE BOOK

'The smartphone revolution which happened over the same time as the liberalization of the economy is a fascinating chapter in the history of modern India. Deepali Gupta is the ideal person to bring this story alive. She has followed the ins and outs, ups and downs of the developments, the rivalries, the successes and the failures in this saga, telling us about who is who, and what they had to do to be part of the globalization of the economy. This volume is a mine of information, a gold mine. If you wish to follow the Indian story, here is your invaluable guide'—**Lord Professor Meghnad Desai, economist and Padma Bhushan awardee**

'A fascinating account of the evolution of the telecom industry in India. From waiting nearly eighteen years for a landline connection to getting a mobile in the hands of a billion people is nothing short of a revolution which has acted as a great leveller, irrespective of the level of education, literacy, size, wealth and position. Deepali has done painstaking research and has gathered data and information to weave a story with a lot of drama and suspense to keep alive the interest of the reader. It has all the ingredients of a Wild West adventure—ruthless corporate rivalries, close relationships going sour and the vagaries of government policies—which did fluctuate and play favourites but often brought clarity and uniformity. Also excellently covered is the innovation in the selection and use of technology and sales and marketing to match those in the FMCG industry, especially the sharp focus on penetration, where the ultimate winner is the customer! This is a must-read, as what the book reflects is true for all industries in many countries'—**Ravi Kant, former managing director, CEO and vice chairman, Tata Motors**

'The most compelling stories are told by those who have lived them from the front row. Only a few understand the telecom sector as deeply as Deepali Gupta, and this book offers an insightful look into a complex industry. But what sets it apart is how it goes beyond the data and policy to capture the human stories that shaped its biggest moments, making it an engaging and memorable read'—**Anish Shah, group CEO and MD, Mahindra Group**

'*The Telecom Wars* is a captivating account of India's telecom sector evolution from a state-controlled monopoly to a private sector-led oligopoly, connecting over a billion people. The book took me through the long wait for landlines in the 1980s to the privatization boom of the 1990s, with the emergence of major players like Bharti Airtel, BPL and Reliance. Deepali's insightful narrative covers the political challenges, policy reforms and the 2G spectrum scam that reshaped the industry. What stood out to me was her thorough research, particularly on Airtel's rise, the "Batata" saga and the Hutchison–Max–Vodafone journey. The book also sheds light on RCom and Idea–Vodafone's struggles, which I saw playing out. A highlight is Reliance Jio's groundbreaking 2016 move to offer free voice calls and ultra-cheap data. As India moves toward 5G and a digital future with AI, IoT and smart cities, this book provides a detailed understanding of the sector's growth and challenges'—**Ashu Suyash, founder, Colossa Ventures, and former MD and CEO, Crisil**

TELECOM WARS

The Race to Capture a Billion Voices

DEEPALI GUPTA

PENGUIN
VIKING
An imprint of Penguin Random House

VIKING

Viking is an imprint of the Penguin Random House group of companies
whose addresses can be found at global.penguinrandomhouse.com

Published by Penguin Random House India Pvt. Ltd
4th Floor, Capital Tower 1, MG Road,
Gurugram 122 002, Haryana, India

Penguin
Random House
India

First published in Viking by Penguin Random House India 2025

10 9 8 7 6 5 4 3 2 1

ISBN 9780143467595

Typeset in Adobe Caslon Pro by MAP Systems, Bengaluru, India
Printed at Thomson Press India Ltd, New Delhi

www.penguin.co.in

Author's Note

This book is based on information obtained from various sources, including documents available in the public domain, press reports, many hours of interviews, and several interactions and email exchanges with the parties involved and those with a ringside view of events. I reached out to nearly a hundred people for my research. They include current and former employees of the various companies, promoters and government officials mentioned in the book.

The quotes in the book are verbatim from press reports and interviews. For the purposes of narrative flow, certain events unfold in dialogue form and must not be treated as representing word-for-word transcripts. Rather, they have been reconstituted from the memory of people present or as recorded in documents.

The journey of writing this book started with reaching out to the companies and individuals seeking comments and clarifications on their perspectives. Many were forthcoming. Equally, many refrained from comment or expressed their inability to cooperate. This book is not intended to support any party. Nothing in this book is intended to defame or disparage the persons involved or hurt their sentiments. It is a dispassionately observed view to portray the events neutrally as they unfolded.

To my boys,
Dev and Darsh

Contents

Part Six

Part Seven

Dramatis Personae

Sunil Bharti Mittal is the founder of Bharti Enterprises and the mastermind behind Bharti Televentures, the parent company of the mobile service provider Airtel. Hailing from Punjab, Sunil partnered with Siemens of Germany to manufacture push-button landline phones, which marked his entry into the telecom world. Sunil built a strong management team, starting with his elder brother **Rakesh** and younger brother **Rajan**. His leadership style emphasized hiring top talent and empowering them to take charge, fostering an environment where innovation could thrive.

Mukesh Ambani is the second-generation chairman of Reliance Industries, renowned for its leadership in petrochemicals, energy, textiles and retail, and its second avatar of the telecommunications business, Jio. Mukesh is the eldest of four siblings in a close-knit family that saw its fortunes transform when his father, **Dhirubhai Ambani**, became an entrepreneur on his return from Aden, where he served as a gas station attendant.

Mukesh and his younger brother **Anil Ambani** rose from living in a chawl (or lower middle-class housing) to leading one of India's largest corporations. After Dhirubhai Ambani's demise, the two parted ways in 2006, splitting Reliance Industries under a family settlement. Anil controlled the telecom business, while Mukesh was excluded from it under a non-compete clause, which was annulled in 2010. Mukesh then launched a competing telecom arm, Jio.

Kumar Mangalam Birla is the chairman of the Aditya Birla Group, an influential conglomerate rooted in Indian family values and etiquette and Western business principles. He ascended to this role after his father's untimely death and inherited with it a nascent telecom venture, which later morphed into Idea Cellular. During this journey, he counted on his lieutenants and, for a while, on the advice of the Tata Group's leader, Ratan Tata. The telecom business led to a falling-out between the two groups.

Mahendra Nahata is the founder and chairman of the Himachal Futuristic Group. He started out as a tea trader and ventured into early telecom cabling businesses in partnership with Vinay Maloo and Deepak Malhotra. Their mainstay was to provide domestically produced technology at a fraction of the cost at which it was being imported. Nahata's outlandish bid for telephone service licences and an alleged bailout from following through on it put his company at the heart of a corruption scam with former telecom minister **Sukh Ram**. Nahata settled as a telecom vendor partner and business solutions provider but never entered the mobility business. He made a phoenix-like reappearance when he assisted Mukesh Ambani in initiating his re-entry into telecom in 2010.

Arun Shourie served as the minister of disinvestment and later as the minister of communications and information technology under Prime Minister **Atal Bihari Vajpayee**. Before his political career, Shourie was the editor of *Indian Express* newspaper. He was voted 'The Most Outstanding Minister' in Vajpayee's government shortly after successfully resolving a significant stand-off among mobile phone operators by introducing a universal licensing system instead of one that distinguished between various technologies and platforms.

Known for his flamboyance and outspoken nature, **Siva,** or **C. Sivasankaran,** was an original winner of the mobile service licence in New Delhi, which he sold. The Chennai-born businessman forged a relationship with Ratan Tata and became a negotiator for the Tata Group's telecom business. He later launched the mobile service operator Aircel, which he sold to Malaysia's Maxis in 2005. His investments included minority stakes in Airtel, Idea and Tata Teleservices.

A. Raja, a member of the Dravida Munnetra Kazhagam (DMK) political party based in south India, was appointed as the minister of telecommunications in 2007. The DMK was a coalition partner to the ruling Congress Party, led by Prime Minister **Manmohan Singh**. Raja's nomination came after M. Karunanidhi, DMK Party leader, relieved Dayanidhi Maran from his ministerial position due to insubordination. Raja, as the new telecom minister, was accused of improperly favoring his associates in the allocation of telecom licences, which paved the way for the infamous 2G scam investigation. Ultimately, Raja was cleared of these allegations.

Part One

1

Mittal Meets Sanchar Bhavan

In 1982, when Telecom Minister C.M. Stephen was defending the failings of India's only phone service provider with angst and a hint of indignation, Sunil Bharti Mittal had already ploughed through several business ventures. Mittal had even become ensnared in the crosshairs of India's big businesses that were prospering under the 'licence raj', which was at least in part responsible for the deplorable state of communications in the country.

The government was the only licence holder that could provide phones, and that meant midnight queues at phone booths to make calls in the morning, innumerable outages and technical issues. Such was the state of affairs that if the paperwork for a phone line were completed for a newborn baby, the child would likely receive the connection on their eighteenth birthday.

The poor quality of service was not lost on its users, who, as a result of the paucity, tended to be influential people. On one occasion, the crescendo reached the corridors of the parliament. The conversation went something like this:

Parliamentarian: My phone is always dead, and still, I get bills.

C.M. Stephen: Last year, in the monsoon, 18,000 telephone lines were disrupted. This year, the number is only 2200. My own phone is down.

Another parliamentarian: I get 'wrong number' calls in the middle of the night.

Third parliamentarian: I make calls that get connected to someone else, and then I have to disconnect and call again. I have to pay charges for two calls rather than just one!

C.M. Stephen: A wrong number is not a disease injected by me.[1]

Stephen then narrated an incident from a book where a lady got the US President on the other end of the line instead of her laundry.

Stephen valiantly defended his ministry. The country had 2,00,000 phones, of which under 4000 were out of order, and the general level of accuracy was high to an unspecified number. Stephen even let it slip that if customers were unhappy, they were welcome to surrender the lines allocated to them so that the telecom ministry could accommodate others from the over 1,00,000 pending requests. He later retracted his statement.

Sunil Mittal was not following this commotion. Destiny would soon make him walk the halls of Sanchar Bhavan, the building that was home to the telecom ministry. He had decided that the sweet spot for a new venture with limited competition had a captive market in India, required a licence, and did not interest deep-pocketed big business.

Sunil Bharti Mittal's father, Sat Paul Mittal, was a politician from Punjab affiliated with the Indian National Congress party. He was best known for his low profile and ability to get things done. As youngsters, Sunil and his brother Rajan showed a flair for table tennis. The Sunil–Rajan Mittal duo had upset the lead competitors of the tournament at Punjab University.

They were on a winning streak when the rug was pulled from under their feet. A new regulation prevented brothers from forming a doubles team. Only one of them could continue in the league. As sons of a politician, they were in a position to influence the table tennis association, allow an exemption or even have the rule changed, but that was not how the Mittals rolled. They followed the rule and changed their course. Rajan Mittal said, 'You've got to move on. The challenges teach you how the future will be.'[2]

In the 1970s, when Sunil Mittal and his brothers were coming of age, Ludhiana, Punjab, was an industrial city bustling with businessmen. The steady stream of visitors and living in the public eye were never unfamiliar feelings. As the brothers, Rakesh, Sunil, and Rajan, recall, theirs was never a lavish household, but they also never went wanting for anything. As they watched babus[3] and guests go in and out of their home, the seeds of entrepreneurship were sown.

His potential table tennis career stymied by politics, eighteen-year-old Sunil turned his focus to business and made a successful run. Even his brushes with bankruptcy were complemented by phoenix-like re-emergence.[4]

Sunil Mittal set up a factory in 1976, not the least driven by his lack of interest in academics. In a time when licences and government permissions tightly controlled production and technology, this alone was a mark of accomplishment. Sunil Mittal's factory manufactured bicycle components and was powered by a loan of Rs 20,000 from his father.

The initial phase was difficult. Money ran short. Mittal approached a family friend, Brijmohan Lall Munjal, for a further loan of Rs 5000 to keep the bicycle crankshaft production going. He was accorded the loan but with a distasteful warning not to make a habit of such borrowing. Mittal did not.[5] Soon, the factory's products caught on and sales picked up. Over the next three years, Mittal expanded into yarn manufacturing and cold-rolled steel, a fast-emerging segment seen as critical to industrialization.

Sunil travelled to the cramped bazaars (markets) of Mumbai by train or truck to sell steel sheets from his factory, living in low-cost accommodations. Busy markets have often been good learning grounds for wide-eyed, savvy young sellers—Mumbai was it for Sunil. Before he knew it, he was charming his way to higher credit with bankers, building loyal customers and creating a friendly ecosystem among competitors.

* * *

At the turn of the decade in 1980, India set up an Indo–Japanese trade corridor to attract some of the leading Japanese brands to tap the Indian mass market while also bringing technology and innovation to India. Japan's Suzuki was keen to participate and found its way to New Delhi under the bilateral scheme.

Suzuki tasked a representative with signing dealerships for its mini power generator that was the rage in its home market. Japan had abundant home electricity, but its power generators found buyers among ice cream trucks and street food vendors. That was the market Suzuki chased in India, only to find that the gas-wielding chaat makers on Delhi's streets found a generator irrelevant. For a moment, it appeared that the Suzuki's generator had no local appeal until one Suzuki representative met Sunil Mittal.

Mittal's perspective differed vastly. He saw an opportunity at small stores and homes in a nation struggling with power insufficiency, which contrasted with rising aspirations and spending capacity. He signed a dealership agreement with Suzuki. The Japanese partner had doubts about Mittal's enthusiasm. For Mittal, this fit squarely with his strategy to identify a protected business in which large enterprises were disinterested.

Sunil Mittal's generator business was soon roaring. In its reimagined usage, demand for the product shot through the roof not just in Delhi but also in other regions. Sales were still dominant in north India, and Mittal would have perhaps considered expansion when a very successful two-year run abruptly ended. Rajan Mittal recalls that the government suddenly banned the import of generators in 1983, creating a whole host of troubles for Mittals.

Licensing under the government tended to be mercurial. The success of the generators prompted the government to issue manufacturing licences for groups like Birla and Sriram. This also meant that Mittal's import business came into direct conflict with the local makers. The Mittals were considering producing generators for Honda and Suzuki, but the ban, followed by intimidating regulatory enquiries, forced the brothers to look elsewhere.

Out of adversity came opportunity, one that brought Sunil Mittal to the halls of Sanchar Bhavan. Mittal first wound up the generator business and then packed his bags in search of the next venture. With Suzuki, he tested the foreign partnership model. Mittal decided his new venture would entail technology, funding, and a market need among Indian consumers.

The hunt led him to a trade fair in Taiwan, an emerging centre for electronic manufacturing. With him was his old teammate and brother Rajan Mittal. A few business options stood out. They eliminated them based on regulations and market opportunity in India, and the final selection came to the wire between Timber and Resin, an emerging epoxy business that could upset traditional manufacturing in several verticals and Kingtel Corporation, which made push button phones.

The first could turn into a commodity business, thought the brothers. It would soon fall prey to pricing pressures. The push-button phone, on the other hand, fascinated the young Mittal brothers. 'I have always wanted to be the first to do things,' said Mittal.[6] Telephones were not a priority for the

Indian government, and the import of phone instruments was prohibited.

Yet, the Mittals felt changing winds among Indian consumers, who were maturing and ready to dump the large, analogue instruments for a sleeker push-button model. Thus began their unsuspecting romance with telecommunications. Mittal started importing components of the instruments to be assembled at a facility in Ludhiana. The instruments were then sold to the telecom ministry that packaged them with phone landlines it provided to its customers.

2

Wireless Is Only a Value-Added Service

In 1981, Sam Pitroda had a meeting scheduled with Prime Minister (PM) Indira Gandhi. The Orissa-born, US-educated engineer had recently sold off his telecom switching venture, Wescom. He was there to pitch for the digitalization of phone exchanges.

Indira Gandhi was running late for the meeting. To get the meeting started, Pitroda was greeted by the PM's younger son, Rajiv Gandhi, who spent a long time understanding Pitroda's research work and ideas for India. Indira Gandhi spent merely a short while with Pitroda, but between mother and son, he had been able to convince the leadership of the need for a revamp.

A bolder and broader programme to expand the country's communication infrastructure, with homegrown solutions was on the cards. In early 1984, the government launched C-DOT (Centre for Development of Telematics), a digital foundation for communication systems native to India. However, political turmoil and then the sudden assassination of Indira Gandhi later the same year adjourned progress. Rajiv Gandhi was elected as prime minister in 1984 and again in 1986, he revived the communications programme to increase and digitize exchanges, laying extensive cabling and completing C-DOT.

Three years later, the country established its Telecom Commission to guide the Department of Telecommunications, or DoT, the single authority and service provider for the entire country. It was housed in the prime administrative district of Delhi, in a building aptly named 'Sanchar Bhavan', meaning 'Communication Centre' in Hindi.

The DoT was a powerful and coveted institution. Its expansion plan was grand, but funds for it ran short as they did for most government objectives at the time. As the next two years played out, it became evident that the country had empty coffers, forcing it to rethink its licence regime. For the DoT, the dilemma was severe as it lagged behind the developed world, which was already moving to a much more capital-intensive technology—mobile services.

In 1991, India was on the verge of bankruptcy. The protection of the Indian industry had slipped from knowledge and technology gathering to complacency. Indian products were obsolete in the global market and inaccessible domestically. The ambitious and upwardly mobile were leaving the country for foreign education, causing one of the country's biggest brain drains.

The vicious cycle became so severe that the government found industry increasingly dependent on its support. The government's ability to do so was falling so sharply that the finance ministry literally faced selling the family jewels. Gold is precious to the government. Instead of paring the country's gold reserves, the finance ministry that was handed to recently appointed technocrat Manmohan Singh, drew up a plan to open the economy, taking cues from global experience. The government sought ways to invite participation from international industry to finance and add technical knowledge to key sectors.

Telecom was a fitting sector, and Sam Pitroda's US connection made it possible. Pitroda had already urged global

Indians to come home. He offered an opportunity to bring in foreign partnerships to further India's communication network. However, selling a stake in the national telecom operator or allowing a new private competitor still appeared fraught with risks.

Rather than disinvestment, the DoT formed a five-member committee headed by the chairman of the Telecom Department to identify global patterns and formulate a privatization agenda that would suit India's objectives. The committee was as diverse as the nation and comprised three members representing southern states. At the time, the adoption of computers and technology was higher in south India than in other parts of the country.

Elsewhere in the world, telecom had been a natural monopoly of the state. The initial investment in setting up the network was high, and the returns on it were unclear. Only government agencies less concerned with return on investment could indulge in such a market. India followed the global pattern for a different reason. The government did not allow private operators to undertake a network buildout. The Department of Telecommunications owned the only telecom network of landlines and the only network landing stations that connected India's phones to the rest of the world. It was also the only provider of dial-up internet connectivity in the country. Pitroda was pushing for an even stronger landline network based on C-DOT technology. To that end, keeping control of the government was advisable, but wireless was another story. It was seen as less central to the future.

Wireless service depended heavily on the landline network and could not survive independently. Even if the last mile were privatized, the state-owned operator would retain control indirectly. Wireless was a value-added service on top of telephones operated by the Department. The regulator decided that mobile telephony licences could be offered to interested private players to conserve Department funds while still opening up a mobile service across India.

The technologists at Sanchar Bhavan set to work, researching the solutions, processes and standards India would exact from a private operator. The technology deployments around the globe were still ad hoc and emerging. Western countries had developed varying protocols and technologies as private companies poured financial and human resources into building market-specific solutions. Three key technologies were prevalent, of which two were in a race for supremacy. The third, already on the path of obsolescence, although easier to deploy with existing networks, was an analogue protocol.

Established and already cost effective this analogue technology was the standard that all neighbouring Asian countries were deploying. The DoT committee, however, had the foresight to press for something more futuristic.

As it delved into global standards and practices it found that thirteen countries in Europe had set up a detailed new digital standard called Global System for Communication or GSM. Europe was in the early stages of moving to GSM from analogue communication platforms. Trials for GSM were being conducted in pockets of the Western world. In contrast was the more nascent American technology, Code Division Multiple Access or CDMA. To the best of their understanding at the time, it appeared that GSM was more apt for dense areas with high populations.

Indian bureaucrats, looking to set rules of engagement for private mobile operators, eventually ruled in favour of GSM. Technology developers had compiled a detailed manual, over 5000 pages long, explaining the nuts and bolts of GSM, which made it easy for adopters and the regulator to proceed.

Hoping to pole-vault an entire generation of technology, this was the standard the Department decided Indian bidders would need to follow if they wanted to offer mobile services.

The Department proceeded cautiously. At the outset, it was prepared only to allocate licences in four metro cities—Mumbai, Delhi, Kolkata and Chennai. In keeping with the GSM manual, some spectrum in the 900MHz band was vacated by the Indian armed forces for two potential carriers in four cities.

The Department then advertised guidelines seeking bids in newspapers in 1991. The application process was divided into two parts: the technical bid and the financial muscle. The first required an in-depth understanding of the GSM standards, deployment capability, equipment requirements and a promise of job creation. Special emphasis was placed on procuring Indian equipment or manufacturing it locally. The second part was called a 'Beauty Parade' to show what kind of foreign partnership and funding a bidder could attract.

The country's objective of privatizing mobile telephony was to invite foreign investment and technology transfer. Keeping this in mind, the Department of Telecommunications set out a marking system for bids. For the Beauty Parade applicants did not need to fork amounts out, merely demonstrate the backing of an international partner.

The DoT was learning on the fly and therefore, modified the criteria during the process, making exemptions and inclusions. The telecom committee explained that these tweaks were intended to foster competition.

For the technical document, the applicant operator needed to show the design and details of the final rollout. Since this was an exploratory phase for everyone, technical details were accepted as long as they were in accordance with the GSM guidelines.

The more aggressively contested part was the financial bid. An applicant could secure up to fifty marks for its proposed service rental. This was the top criterion in the financial bid. The Department set a service rental range between Rs 150 and

1000 for bidders. This would be the fixed cost a customer would pay for a wireless connection. The committee believed that this would be the key to the adoption of wireless services.

The next criterion was project finance, which was subdivided further. It measured the operator's ability to raise money through the rollout stages and required a clarification on the proportion that would come from foreign exchange. A bidder could score up to eight marks for this. They could secure another ten marks based on the amount of equipment the operator would source locally compared with imports and the degree of investment from the foreign partner, including technology transfer, to make in India.

Bidders could secure fifteen marks based on their and their partner's telecom experience. The minimum requirement was the deployment of 1,00,000 phone lines. It was meant as a filter to invite experienced foreign partners rather than cash contributors since no Indian company had any experience, barring the state-run company. The committee later added an alternate option for experience enabling any mobile operator with 80,000 GSM phone connections to partner with an Indian bidder. As an emerging technology standard, the committee felt that expertise in mobile deployment would be a valuable asset to potential bidders.

Finally came the financial strength of the domestic applicant. If pockets were deep, the staying power and an extended return on investment cycle would be more palatable. For this, companies could receive up to twelve marks.

Oddly enough, the total marks tally amounted to ninety-five rather than 100. It is unclear why. Some believe it may have been due to a criterion which was dropped at the last minute. A successful application was made for multiple submissions each time fulfilling the old and new criteria and revised forecasting for the market.

3

Goa to London

Sunil Mittal was on vacation. The entire family was holidaying with him on the beachfront in Goa. He sat there during his morning ritual of reading the newspaper and drinking chai when he spotted the advertisement. It was with some excitement that he had heard talk of a tender in the corridors of the DoT as he struck deals with the ministry for push-button phones upgraded from the analog dialing instruments that were prevalent. In the last few years, he and his two brothers had done well in business.

The Taiwanese Kingtel Corp's phones were well received in export markets in Africa. Soon thereafter, the government allotted fifty-two licences to make more such phones and devices in the country. The instrument branded 'Mittbrau', a Germanization of Mittal Brothers to give the device an international feel, caught Siemens' attention. Bharti Ventures, a company named after Mittal's middle name, forged a tie-up to manufacture their push-button phones in 1986. They launched India's first push-button phone instrument in 1987.

Bharti then expanded into answering machines with Japan's Takacom Corp., cordless phones with South Korea's Lucky Gold Star International and Sprint to export phones to America.

The relationship with Siemens expanded into a joint venture in 1995 to market telephone instruments branded

Beetel and Siemens, and dominated the Indian market for the next decade. The Mittals also forged a relationship with Casio to make pagers in 1994, which at the time seemed like a promising mobile communication technology.

As he read it in Goa, the newspaper advertisement for mobile services made Mittal's entrepreneurial senses tingle. The business fit in smoothly with his general philosophy of market selection, and in his opinion, wireless was the next big thing.

Sunil Mittal left the flourishing factories with his two brothers, Rakesh and Rajan Mittal, and relocated to London, United Kingdom, to learn a new trade: mobile telephony. Here, he splurged on specialists to learn a new trade and make 'a bet of a lifetime'.

'Extensive work was required in sixty days—find partners and bid. I took leave of absence from my small company, and told my brothers, "Don't ask me where I am or how much money I'm spending." At that time, spending a crore*—20 per cent of our profits—was huge. We actually spent more than that.'[1]

On his return, he took up a small office on the top floor of Devika Tower, Nehru Place near Sanchar Bhavan in Delhi, in a building that also housed a competitor, the Max Group, headed by a young but more established businessman, Analjit Singh. One of the executives recalls using runners between the Bharti and Max offices in the form of a camaraderie between competitors to navigate the complicated application process.

Two desks, several runners, three or four secretaries, lots of chai and Black Label after 7 p.m.! That was the two-month run-up to the submission of bids for Mittal.

---

* A unit of counting equivalent to ten million.

4

Filing Finish Line

Sunil Mittal may have been the most excited bidder, but reaching the finish line to apply was arguably the most arduous for Bharti. The millions spent on consultants in London had given Mittal a sound technical understanding. Like a pupil ready to fill one answer sheet after the other, Mittal had loaded box after box of pages for the technical specifications of Bharti's mobile business Airtel, under the company Bharti Televentures.

It started with helicopter rides for aerial photography of the four metro cities. He was applying for all four. Then came satellite photography. He had a model application, and the GSM standards guided him to include the smallest detail in the most graphic form. As the document became longer and longer, time lapsed quickly.

In the financial bid, Bharti's steam ran low. While the brothers had done well in the business, their pockets were hardly deep, and the Bharti brand was practically non-existent. It had been a business-to-business supplier rather than a consumer-facing organization. The lack of a prominent Indian business name hampered Bharti's search for a foreign partner.

The hunt took Mittal to Mauritius to meet a friend, Bashir Currimjee, who ran the local mobile service network, Emtel. Mittal was exporting phone instruments to the African island, giving him access to Mauritius' telecom ecosystem. Sunil Mittal made his pitch to partner Emtel, but the pact was not forthcoming. Mittal's persistence was his strongest asset and even that seemed ineffective. Yet, as the car rode to the airport for Mittal to catch his return flight, he continued to whisper the promise of his company and Indian mobile telephony. Something he said on the journey moved Currimjee to sign a pact in that car. It was a win for team Bharti, but its bidding prospect was not out of the woods yet.

Emtel was a small, nascent Mauritius operator. It fell short of the Indian bid requirement for foreign participation.

Mittal now sought further advice from his new partner. Currimjee offered to introduce Mittal to the French ambassador to India, Phillippe Petit, who then introduced Mittal to French operator SFR[1] that would have cleared the foreign partner criteria set by India because it had a GSM-based mobile service deployment. SFR was state-run and therefore, could be considered an extension of France Telecom although it was an independent organization specializing in mobile telephony while France Telecom owned the landline and other communication networks of the European nation.

The catch—SFR had never heard of Mittal, nor was the company too wedded to the idea of tapping the Indian market. Since Mittal's introduction had come from an ambassador, Michael Villaneu, an executive at SRF condescended to meet him for merely half an hour on a Saturday, at a deserted office, Mittal recalls. Mittal was afraid that he had a tiny window to convince Villaneu. He turned on his charm. That would do handsomely on that afternoon. The half-hour meeting continued for over an hour, spilling into the lunch. Villaneu invited Mittal to join him for the meal. They wound the conversation up and the French executive told Mittal to have lawyers draw up a document and send it for signing on Monday.

A tenacious Mittal preferred not to wait. He requested time with an office secretary to complete documentation on the spot. The Frenchman was alarmed, given that Mittal lacked any legal background, but possibly also appreciated Mittal's dedication. So, Mittal drew up a memorandum of understanding that would back his bid and it was signed on the spot.

When work resumed on Monday, another bidder (rumour has it this was Rajeev Chandrasekhar's British Physical Laboratories [BPL]) called SFR for a similar agreement. While SFR said it had already signed a partner, Villaneu was shaken by the lack of visibility and scale of Bharti Televentures. He decided to annul the pact with Mittal.

'There was something you felt at that time when I saw you, and you signed the same day. Stay with the same instinct. What is there to lose?' pleaded Mittal, along with a promise to give the company a dignified exit as soon as possible.[2] Villaneu was still unsure but respected the contract he had already signed.

On the day of the application submission, Rajan Mittal arrived at the Department of Telecom with several loaded cartons. On his way to the thirteenth floor of Sanchar Bhavan to submit the application, Rajan spotted Tata Group executive Zaid Baig. Baig was seemingly empty-handed. 'Where's your application?' asked the young Mittal. The Tata executive drew attention to a file tucked between his body and arm, tapped it and said, 'This is it.' That took Rajan by surprise. *What was Sunil thinking putting all these cartons of pages together?* He thought. Anyway, this was it. He filled out the application receipt and left the pages with the clerk . . . waiting for a verdict in good time.

Part Two

5

Ratan's Search for a Gem

When Telecom Minister C.M. Stephen was defending the lacunae in India's communication network in 1983, Ratan Tata was busy restoring purpose to Tata Industries, which he had been deputed to head in what appeared to be a punishment posting.

Ratan bore the family name, but his induction into management at the prestigious Tata Group was done ardently and from the grassroots. After an architecture degree from Ivy League Cornell University, he turned down a job offer from International Business Machines (IBM) for a blue-collar role at the sprawling steel factory in Jamshedpur, where among other things, he shovelled coal into a furnace.

Founded over a hundred years ago, most of the Tata Group's profits were directed towards charitable endeavours. Between 1919 and 1945, Tata Group's founders donated nearly 75 per cent of the holding company Tata Sons' shares to charitable trusts, modifying the Tata Group's mission statement which overlooked profit in favour of attracting scientific innovation, technology, research and the best international talent to Indian shores.

In keeping with this, the group launched many firsts for the country: an aviation venture—Air India—which was taken over by the Indian government after India's independence and economic reform in 1953; an automotive venture that fuelled India's logistics capabilities; and a technology launchpad, Tata Consultancy Services (TCS), which spurred India's technology service industry. It fell upon the group's leader to continue the rich legacy.

When J.R.D. Tata was set to retire after nearly fifty years at the helm, the successor he chose was not the frontrunner. While leading group executives believed they would secure the role, it was as if J.R.D. had been grooming Ratan.

Until 1991, when J.R.D. Tata nominated Ratan Tata to the chairmanship of the Tata Sons and the group, Ratan Tata had received tough love from the group's stalwarts who never failed to remind him of his lack of experience or success.

He was first entrusted with turning around the loss-making National Radio and Electronics Company Limited (NELCO), which made electronics, including radio equipment. The company was shuttered after PM Indira Gandhi declared a state of Emergency in 1975, which led to curfews, blackouts and an indelible dent in India's corporate image.

Ratan was then sent to the group's genesis point, the Mumbai-based Empress Textile Mill. The proposal to modernize equipment and reduce worker salaries sparked unionized protests. J.R.D. chose to deploy the Tata Group's Rs 50 lakh elsewhere, and the textile operation languished.

In the run-up to his nomination, Ratan Tata was assigned to head Tata Industries, once a financier company for all new ventures, had fallen by the wayside as regulation and access to money markets changed in India. Here, Ratan Tata proposed a vision of a transformed and younger Tata Group heading into a transformed Indian financial market.

The Tata Group was ageing; Ratan pointed this out to his mentor when he proposed a management restructure to include more youth at the top to ideate and lead the group into the digital age. Ratan Tata delivered a proposal to transform the many floating companies birthed by Tata Sons to be bound together, tightened and redirected. J.R.D. parked Ratan Tata's proposal, but Tata Industries became an incubator for the group to launch into new verticals.

When he was nominated to lead the Tata Group, Ratan Tata had more than one detractor, who believed this was a mistake on J.R.D.'s part. The mood within the group was rife with expectations of a power struggle.

The old guard had taken to the press. Russi Mody, chairman of TISCO, now Tata Steel, announced his candidature for the top job. Ratan was like the rabbit that a magician pulled from the hat. The direction that the young Tata would turn the group towards was being closely watched.

As he fought off the old guard and took charge of Tata companies' fate, Ratan Tata took refuge in the technology ventures he had promoted earlier. Among them, financial and equipment design and manufacturing services stood out. This was Ratan Tata's first tryst with the telecom sector when he started Tata Telecom to make equipment at facilities in south India.

Tata started a communication equipment-making facility for telephone exchange switches in Bangalore. The group partnered with American Telephone & Telegraph's (AT&T) Bell Labs, widely credited with engineering telephone systems as we know them today. Ratan Tata hoped that large-scale manufacturing would reduce equipment prices and lead to technology transfer from Bell Labs to his group. The partnership between Bell Labs and Tata was founded on the understanding that the Indian salt-to-software conglomerate would get access to and contribute to building intellectual property.

Already piqued by the telecom sector, when Ratan Tata saw the invitation to mobile service licences, he believed it could present the group with an opportunity alike TCS. Cellular technology and its exploration was a refreshing change from the steel and hotel boardroom battles, for the Bombay-based conglomerate. None of the other comparable business houses has shown any interest in the sector. Mobile telephony had the potential to cement Ratan Tata's legacy as a young and forward thinker.

Given their history, the partnership between the Tata Group and AT&T for cellular licences could have been a foregone conclusion, but as allocations in India faced a myriad of delays, AT&T's financial footing in its home market was shaky. The American company was not ready to risk the Indian mobility market. Besides, the application was a cakewalk for the Tata Group. It already had exposure to a universe of foreign partners and on every other count the group far exceeded requirements.

The Tata Group scouted and met several investors. Eventually, it forged an alliance with Canada's Bell Canada Enterprises (BCE) for its cellular telephony bid.

6

The Others

The government and the Telecom Department were happy to give away licences for wireless services because they were sure it would not dent state-run services. Leading business houses agreed. For Sunil Mittal, this was good news because large, deep-pocketed players like Reliance Industries, the Birla Group and Godrej were not interested. Tata was the only aberration.

Mobile telephony appeared to be a thankless business with a long gestation period and high upfront capital expenditure. The lack of interest from big business was a dampener for the DoT. The government hoped to raise at least some finances from the sale of these licences and to get private participation in expanding the country's infrastructure.

The DoT had to court more bidders for the eight licences, two in each metro city. After it became clear that it could not interest large conglomerates, the DoT had little choice but to entice entrepreneurs already walking the corridors of Sanchar Bhavan as vendors or niche radio companies that were setting up pager services.

The short-lived pager service comprised a wireless digital device with a single-row electronic screen, a bit like a calculator. It could receive text messages, which usually had to be written in telegram format given the character restrictions.

Sanchar Bhavan had awarded licences for this service, which
was reasonably well-penetrated in the US, Europe and Japan.
Small pager assembly factories were slowly mushrooming in
India in partnership with foreign players. Department members
thought these would be the most suitable candidates to bring
foreign investment into mobile telephony. Investors may more
readily accept them as partners, thought the DoT, because many
of their network components, including signal emitting towers
and switches were common to mobile services.

   '*Aap toh humare damad jaise hain* [you are like our son-in-law],'[1]
said a general manager at the DoT to Analjit Singh, promoter of
the Max Group. Singh, along with his chief executive officer for
telecom, Ashwini Windlass, was there to demonstrate the newly
launched pager service of the Max Group. The general manager
slid the tender forms for a mobile licence across the table. 'This
licence application has been issued just for you,' he said as if
offering Singh a present.[2] Singh slid the papers closer to himself
with a nod of acknowledgement but quickly moved on to what had
put a smile on his face that morning. He brought out the pager and
placed it on the table.

   This was Max's debut in the pager business across five cities.
The deployment was one of the maiden wireless attempts in India.

   The general manager smiled in appreciation, picked up the
device, toyed with it for a bit and twisted and turned it in his
hands. Then, he quizzically looked up and asked, 'So, where do
I speak into this?' That was a telling question and potentially
a decisive moment for Analjit Singh, whose telecom bid
eventually morphed his firm into one of the country's largest
cellular players.

   Analjit Singh, the youngest son of Bhai Mohan Singh, was
shortchanged of his legacy. The family's flagship pharmaceutical
company Ranbaxy that was fast becoming a leader in exporting
medicines, was handed to his elder brother, Parvinder Singh.

Analjit Singh had proven his business acumen by getting US Food and Drug Administration (FDA) approvals for chemical and bio plants in his company Max India, which at the time was a subsidiary of Ranbaxy. Yet, like a true entrepreneur, he had simultaneously diversified, first into plastics and then Max Electronics, which had become one of the largest importers of components. The branching had brought Singh face-to-face with leading tech manufacturers of the time—Motorola, Hewlett Packard, Toshiba and Advance Micro Devices Inc. (AMD).

When the family business was handed to the next generation, Max India was spun off from Ranbaxy without the FDA licences or the cash-positive medicine business. Analjit Singh was handed the spun-off entity. The ambitious Analjit Singh hoped to build an iconic empire in a new vertical.

Of course, having the family name and financial backing helped open doors. After securing licences to launch a pager service, Singh's Max partnered with Motorola, a mobile device and infrastructure company, to launch services in Chandigarh, Bangalore, Pune and Ahmedabad.

Singh and his company, and his company, Max, had proven to be reliable local partners to global businesses. He seemed to have the political muscle to move things forward and the polish to deal with the developed world. Motorola chose Max as its partner to offer paging services in north India. Max was also a vendor to Motorola that saw great potential in the Indian market.

As Singh and Windlass walked out of the DoT after that meeting, they were nearly sure that the future of communication lay in mobile telephony and not pagers. Now, the two returned to their office near Nehru Place in Delhi and analysed the papers that the general manager had slid towards them.

They combed through the mobile licence application requirements, and found Max was more than halfway home.

They called on Amit Sharma, who was leading Motorola's India operations. Motorola may have been willing to partner, but as an equipment maker, the company did not qualify as a partner with experience in running a network. The company did, however, have a client in Hong Kong that may have been interested. The Motorola team introduced Analjit Singh to Li Ka-shing and Canning Fok, the founder and executive head of Hutchison Whampoa.

Windlass and Singh quickly caught a flight. Along with them, they brought their chief of paging, Sandip Das. Das later became the head of the company's cellular business.

Hutchison Whampoa had a diversified portfolio across ports, real estate development, hospitality and cellular telephony. The company recently emerged as Hong Kong's first cellular operator. Its success was so stark that the move doubled the group's revenue in just two years. As a business port, Hong Kong had high appetite for mobile services and Hutch had garnered more subscribers than needed to back a licence bid in India. Moreover, it was interested in the unpenetrated Indian market.

The Max team was welcomed to Hong Kong with much fanfare and in five-star style. They were ushered into a lavishly furnished room and then uniformed service executives brought each one a box on a salver. On unboxing them emerged mobile phones. At least for some of the Indian contingent present in the room, this was a first and rather exciting moment. Then came Li Ka-shing with his team led by Fok. They shared some insights they had gathered but mostly heard Max's plans.

Outside the room awaited executives from the Tata Group to scope the same partnership.

While Singh and his team chased Hutchison, the Tatas presented a more reassured face. Why wouldn't they? They knew that they were by far the strongest bidder and needed a partner to fulfil the criteria but had the wherewithal to go the full distance alone. Perhaps it was this that disconcerted the risk-taking Li. Hutch backed Max's application, making it a top contender for the prime markets.

The DoT, meanwhile, urged others to make a run. They successfully aroused the curiosity of Harsh Goenka of the Rama Prasad Goenka (RPG) Group.

Regulatory changes in India forced large companies like IBM and Coca-Cola to abandon their Indian arms in 1977. The exit of IBM from the country proved to be a boost for local technology hardware manufacturer International Computers and Tabulators (ICT). The British company had a manufacturing subsidiary in Pune, India. It manufactured personal computing products. IBM's departure from the country left a space in the market for ICT to occupy, along with competitors Wipro and HCL. In 1988, the Harsh Goenka-led RPG Group acquired a significant stake in the Indian arm of ICT.

Along with the stake, RPG found a Japanese partner, Fujitsu, which was ICT's joint venture partner globally. ICT, at the time of RPG's acquisition, was in the midst of a transition from being a hardware company to a software maker. The outfit in Pune was therefore suitably placed to contribute to the Department of Telecommunications efforts to build an indigenous telecom software protocol for C-DOT telephone exchanges spearheaded by Sam Pitroda.

The project also brought the RPG company to the attention of American telecom service provider Sprint. The two formed an equal joint venture for paid messaging and software to enable message-based services. This gave the RPG Group know-how on the wireless process and backend systems.

RPG then partnered with an arm of Japan's Nippon Telephone and Telegraph (NTT) to start a paging service in

India. The Japanese company had already seen and deployed successful paging services in its homeland. It was looking to outsource software development for its international platform and naturally extended that relationship to back RPG's paging service bid.

His group was at the forefront of technology, and Harsh Goenka was keen to tap all forms of communication. He was already working on starting a satellite communications firm. When the DoT invited applications for mobile licences, Goenka was negotiating a tie-up with Iridium Satellite Communications, one that never fructified, even though RPG later formed a satellite communication company on its own.

It did not take much convincing for Harsh Goenka to apply. The partners would not be difficult to find, and the service would certainly fit in their portfolio. Still, Goenka was wary of what it would entail, and therefore, RPG was not gunning for the top spots of Mumbai and Delhi. The group preferred to test waters on their home ground, Kolkata.

Now, if Goenka and Singh were willing to bid, then their competitor, B.K. Modi would join the fray too. Modi's partner was a competitor to Motorola—Alcatel. Modi frequented the halls of the DoT to sell switching systems that his company manufactured using Alcatel's technology. The equipment was an intermediary to connect an emerging call to its destination. The Department always needed these systems as it expanded its network and bolstered its numbers. Modi's licence allowed manufacturing of the technology in India, rather than importing directly from Alcatel to control the price and premium the DoT was paying. The Department was constantly squeezing Modi's margins.

Modi's profits soared from the private sector as companies that were setting up intercoms and internal phone systems, some of which used wireless radio frequencies. Modi aced the list of vendors to such organizations.

Modi's company seemed to have the necessary infrastructure to make a successful wireless services application. Competitive motivation was in place. Egging this company into offering mobile services seemed logical and natural for the Department that gave a gentle nudge in the right direction.

Having worked with Xerox and Alcatel in joint ventures to manufacture equipment for India, Modi's credentials led to an easy relationship with Australia's Telstra for the mobile service launch.

The DoT then turned to Sunil Mittal's more established competitor in the push-button phone market, Crompton Greaves. Founded pre-Independence in the 1970s, Crompton Greaves was finding its Anglo–Indian roots as it expanded its portfolio beyond motors.

The wave of telecommunications was taking over India, and as a developing company in the consumer electronics space, the imminent change was not lost on the Thapars of Crompton Greaves. They were one of the fifty-two licensees to make phone instruments and one of the dozens that actually implemented production. They, too, partnered with Siemens, like Sunil Mittal, to manufacture push-button telephones.

In 1990, Crompton Greaves was setting up a rural telecom equipment manufacturing unit near Bangalore. The unit would make data-receiving terminals similar to pagers, power supply units for computers and telecom equipment, and a rudimentary communication switch, which were being embraced by the Indian armed forces and private sector companies. The knowledge of radio frequency technology and participation in deployments made the company a suitable bidder. The existing relationships with foreign companies gave it a better chance of success.

By the time Crompton Greaves readied its application, the excitement among potential partners had reached a crescendo. Crompton Greaves received interest from too many partners who were complementary to each other. As a result, the company entered the race with three other partners—Mauritius-based Emtel (also Sunil Mittal's partner), US-based BellSouth and another Indian partner, Sawant Singh-owned DSS. Could 'too many cooks spoil the broth'? That was yet to be ascertained. In the moment, the Thappars chose this as their best option.

7

Unexpected Entrants

There were two other prominent additions among the applicants for the first mobile telephony licence.

The first was Rajeev Chandrasekhar, who got invited to the corridors of Sanchar Bhavan ensuing a series of coincidences.

Chandrasekhar left India to study in the US after graduation and shortly after completing his engineering degree, landed a job at Intel, the world's leading computer chip maker. He took a professional break after working with the team designing Intel's transformative personal computer processor, the Pentium Chip. As he mulled what he would do next, staying in the US seemed inevitable. A parallel opportunity to work at the cutting edge of technology research hardly existed in India. Only Chandrasekhar had met a girl. For her, he would need to be India-bound. He hoped to marry T.P.G. Nambiar's daughter, Anju. Bangalore-based Nambiar owned one of India's most loved consumer electronics brands, BPL, known most popularly for television sets.

Given the little wealth to his name, Chandrasekhar thought his chances of acceptance by Anju's family were slim. Luckily, the senior Nambiar valued education over personal fortune, and Chandrasekhar was welcomed into the family. That said, Chandrasekhar needed a project that tied in with his education.

In 1991, Chandrasekhar on a visit to a temple in Kerala, was still in two minds about whether his calling was in the US when he stood at his hotel's reception to make a call to Delhi. A phone call was something routine in his life at Intel. Here, however, it seemed to have raised eyebrows, connectivity issues and a huge bill. The call had to be booked. A call at a standard rate would be connected after a longer wait and the caller was expected to stay near the phone till it was. An urgent call would be processed in a couple of hours and a lightning call, which Chandrasekhar chose, was immediate but exorbitant.

It played on Chandrasekhar's mind. A few weeks later, when his father, a retired air force pilot, introduced the young techie to Rajesh Pilot, who had served as a squadron leader under Chandrasekhar's father, the US-returned engineer could not pull his punches in criticizing the state of communication infrastructure in India. Pilot was the minister of communications under Prime Minister P.V. Narasimha Rao.

It is not as if Rajeev Chandrasekhar was expecting Pilot to remedy the situation, but the response he received made him introspect. 'You Indians should come back; we are opening up the country. Things are going to change,' said Pilot. 'You should try and do something.'[1]

'I was obviously a very serious chip designer. Frankly, I didn't know anything about the telecom sector,' Chandrasekhar recalls. He was familiar with networking and that is how, not long after his chat with Pilot, Chandrasekhar found himself in Sanchar Bhavan discussing a potential bid for a licence. A regional connect with three committee members—U.V. Naik, S.K. Nayar and B.R. Nair—who hailed from south India 'took a paternal interest' in Chandrasekhar. They urged and encouraged him to join the race. Chandrasekhar understood the technical aspects of the deployment, but with what backing?

The committee members assured him of help when the time came, and BPL's Nambiar was willing to endorse to his application. Armed with his father-in-law's trust and technical knowledge, Rajeev Chandrasekhar decided to take the plunge headlong into the race.

The technical document was right up his alley. One step at a time, he compiled the network plan. The document ran into over a thousand pages. It detailed radio frequency utilization charts, telecom towers, and even protocols by which a call would be handed over to the user's instrument, recalls Chandrasekhar.[2]

He then continued to build the company's financial plan from marketing to subscription. There was one major catch. Chandrasekhar did not have a foreign partner. Foreign investors were circling the market to meet potential, but the questions he was being asked stumped Chandrasekhar, practically to the point of offending his US-returned sensibilities about governance.

At a meeting in the Belvedere, the elite club run by hospitality chain Oberoi, Micheal Chow of BellSouth asked him, 'How many MPs (members of parliament) do you know?'[3] Hesitantly or otherwise, Chandrasekhar said he could get a reference letter from the Bangalore MP, but that was not the answer Chow was looking for. The filing date came nearer and nearer. The application still lacked a backer, and it would have all but failed without an introduction from U.V. Naik. Naik listened patiently to Chandrasekhar's dilemma, then pulled out a visiting card from a drawer in his desk. The name read Brian Mackay; the company was France Telecom. Naik told his visitor that this company was scouting for a partner and offered to introduce the two of them to explore. That introduction culminated in a short-lived backing for BPL's cellular bid.

Chandrasekhar's international pedigree and BPL's brand both played a role. In hindsight, Chandrasekhar felt that France

Telecom came on board partly because it believed that he might be more suggestible to do things the way the international partner wanted. At the time, it was a foot in the door for Chandrasekhar.

The second prominent entry was that of C. Sivasankaran, or Siva, as he became popularly known. He believed in the power of connectivity. More than anything else, he was interested in the internet. Mobile telephony was a step towards it. He had no backing but had emerged as a businessperson in the knowledge industry on his own steam.

The son of a local schoolteacher, Siva was considered the king of personal computing in south India and was quickly gaining visibility in the North too. He made a name for himself selling personal computers at almost a third of the prevailing price for computers made by IBM and other global brands like Fujitsu.

One way he reduced cost was to import components of computers, keyboards and other peripherals—which in assembled form would incur import duty—and assemble them locally. The other, of course, which famously brought him close to the Tatas in the early 2000s was his ability to strike hard bargains. The reaction to Siva among businesspeople and government alike was either love or hate owing to his brusque and flamboyant personality. Yet, all said and done, he knew how to get his way.

Siva grew his business with flair and fearlessness. Detractors dubbed his methods as illegal. Supporters called them creative.

Siva was found in the corridors of the DoT's Delhi and Mumbai arm, Mahanagar Telephone Nigam Limited (MTNL), for a contract to print the Yellow Pages—the sole directory of numbers of businesses across the country—a prized property in the early 1990s. The assignment went through the regular tendering as any other material contract would undergo. Siva was excellent at low bids, a quality that arguably won him the MTNL contract. That raised questions over corruption at MTNL during the selection process. It was even followed by an enquiry from the Central Bureau of Investigations, which would later haunt Siva's attempt at securing a mobile licence.[4]

When he saw the mobile telephony licence advertisement, Siva perceived this as a good opportunity to connect with global business partners, which made him an enthusiastic bidder. On finding the legal mire Siva was shrouded in, securing a foreign partner must have been challenging. A US-based company, Cellular Communication International Inc (CCII), elected to become Siva's partner in his India mobile bid.

Eventually, some other companies filled out applications too, including Ashok Leyland, Onida, Jubilant and a DoT company called Telecommunications Consultants India Limited (TCIL).

8

Selection Begins

By the date of submission, the DoT had thirty applications. An eight-member team—the Tender Evaluation Committee—perused through filings to select final winners. To everyone's dismay, twenty-two applications were rejected, eighteen mostly because they failed to submit adequate engineering details and another four for miscellaneous reasons. The four were Rajeev Chandrasekhar's BPL, RPG Group's company, Siva and one of the entities formed by B.K. Modi. All prime candidates, all well connected and now an integral part of the race. Eliminating these companies would leave too few in the selection pool.

The government formed a higher body to reconsider all candidates. It was called the Selection Committee and was headed by the telecom minister and the chairman of the Telecom Commission. The committee chairman overruled objections raised on the four prominent names that were disallowed and reversed their rejection from the selection pool. He argued that a larger number of bidders was required to create competition. After their inclusion, the Department felt it had adequate bidders for eight licences and twelve bidders. Two more companies, Ashok Leyland and Jubilant, were eliminated from the race because of technical glitches in their applications, leaving fourteen contenders for slots in the metro cities as of September 1992.

The fourteen were invited to submit financial bids for rental and the per-minute price of a call, incoming and outgoing, in sealed envelopes. The next step in the process was a grand and public revelation of these closed submissions in a meeting room at Sanchar Bhavan. That October morning, sealed envelopes were stacked on the oval wooden table to be opened one at a time in front of all the examining eyes.

Suspense hung densely in the room as the bids were opened. The first brown envelope was opened. After the initial few bids were opened, a pattern emerged. People at the edge of their seats slunk back a little. In Mumbai and Delhi, the expected rental landed somewhere near Rs 300 and in Kolkata and Chennai, it tended to be higher, closer to Rs 600. Then Siva's unexpectedly bold bid came out of its envelope: 'zero rental'. For a split second, time stood still as the call resounded. It was followed by a gasp from the operator's end, an 'awww' from the middle of the room and claps from the Department officials sitting at the other end. This was outrageous and anti-competitive, clamoured the attendees. They left the room wondering who would finally get licences and would thus need to activate their foreign partnerships. Analjit Singh, with the backing of Hutchison Whampoa from Hong Kong, was a favourite; Siva, too, stood a good chance of securing a spot. The rest was all conjecture.

The Department issued a provisional list of winners and then a final one. But the second one came as a shock because it upset the expectations set by the first. Analjit Singh's Hutchison Max came at the top of the pack in the provisional list. A week later, headlines read that Analjit Singh was out of the telecom race. It appeared that Siva too was out despite his eye-popping bid![1] A public sector company that had provisionally won the licence was sent packing. Instead, Bharti and Chandrasekhar topped the list. Bharti got licences for all four cities, and BPL won in Mumbai and Delhi. That left one slot for Tata Cellular in Kolkata and one for Skycell, the Crompton Greaves entity in Chennai. The clamour for explanations that day at Sanchar Bhavan resembled children gathering around the teacher's table, fighting for that half-mark wrongly deducted in the final exam.

While they knew the broad marking structure, the actual breakdown of the marking system had not been disclosed to the bidders. Why? Asked the companies that had been left out. They argued for themselves, questioned the integrity of the selectors and sought transparency. The most persuasive argument came from Siva, who said the government was not doing justice to the subscribers by leaving him out of the race. He had been omitted because of the CBI enquiry over the order he received from MTNL to print the Yellow Pages. Max argued that it did not meet the requirements because of a clerical error, it was not in the interest of the government for it to be left out.

Sanjay Dalmia's India Telecom was also left out because the foreign investor partner Malaysia Telecom overlapped with Usha Martin. Since in the overall ranking, Usha Martin scored higher, India Telecom was eliminated.

A month later, the process was coming to its first anniversary with no end in sight. The minister decided that the process owners must be changed to expedite the process. So, yet another selection committee reviewed the applications and applicants. This time, Minister Rajesh Pilot and the chairman of the Telecom Commission made some changes to the selection criteria. First, only one licence could be given to a company. Second, an even higher emphasis would be laid on the rental and foreign inflow components of the bids. The updated criteria for foreign exchange requirements now cut Bharti, Modi and RPG from the race along with three other companies for a variety of reasons.

Siva also remained out of the race but was granted an exemption to participate till the outcome of the enquiry on him. Given the other rental bid for Chennai was Rs 960 per month, which was extremely high, the committee decided to reintroduce Siva to the mix in the interest of competition. The aim was to at least lower the rental to Rs 600, which would be the same as Kolkata, explained the minister, while allowing Siva's bid to stand. He also allowed B.K. Modi to participate on an exemption and issued yet another list of winners.

Mumbai's winners—Bharti and BPL—both had French partners. Why was one not dropped as per the policy? Questions were bound to be asked.

Analjit Singh was cutting a sorry figure with Hutchison. His sudden elimination from the race would have been disconcerting for any investor, let alone one that could have partnered with one of India's oldest conglomerates. Singh was not going down without a fight. Lobbying through the corridors of Sanchar Bhavan was now a common sight. It was time to aim higher. Singh wrote of his 'great shock' with the system to India's prime minister. The first letter did not receive the desired welcome, and Singh wrote again. This time, he explained, that his company and his partner would not have gone through the trouble if they did not intend to submit a proper bid. Hutchison had assumed that winning with Singh's pedigree was a given. Eventually, the DoT caved under pressure and the telecom chairman gave Singh an audience. He explained that Max's error was purely clerical. In the excitement of the application, the chief financial officer of Max had forgotten to sign a form. That signature was costing the company elimination from the race.

The chairman then, for the third time, had a revised winner table in mind. But amid this hectic ping-pong match between the Department and the players involved, work took him out of town briefly on an international trip. While he was away, wheels within the DoT seemed to have churned faster than before and a reformed list was presented to the minister to approve . . . in the interest of time! Within the day, it was also approved.

Once again, Bharti topped the chart to win in Mumbai along with BPL Mobile. Delhi went to India Telecom of Sanjay Dalmia and Tata Cellular. Kolkata went to RPG and Usha Martin and Chennai went to Siva's Sterling and Thappar's Skycell.

Between the provisional, first and second allotment, there were now three versions of winners and ground was rife for a no-holds-barred fight. Finger-pointing at the Department for playing favourites became the flavour of the season. Four petitions were filed in the Delhi High Court in which everyone involved was a party. It was a free-for-all when it came to taking potshots at each other as companies scrambled to secure a spot.

After they were admitted, the court in its wisdom, combined the cases to reduce the overhead of repeating itself in each. There was much to-and-fro. Over the next year, the petitions were heard in Delhi and escalated to the Supreme Court which tossed it back to the Delhi High Court for an outcome.

The accusations against the government's decision-making process to allot licences were that it was biased. Plaintiffs argued the Department had invoked hidden conditions to enable this bias. To further this end, it inserted irrelevant considerations to tweak the grading of bidders. Eventually, when even that did not work, the Selection Committee was bypassed to hurriedly approve the list of final winners, who would otherwise have been disqualified. Worst of all, the Commission was accused of manipulating criteria in the marking system to determine a winner. It was tailor-made to knock off losers and favour Bharti!

Bharti Airtel had so far steered clear of examining eyes but was now the cynosure of everyone's attention. Not to the comfort of its owners. This small company without notable backers had topped the list in every circle every time. It had also secured the most coveted Mumbai circle each time. Bharti's partners did not have experience with 1,00,000 phone lines. It was SFR's over 80,000 GSM connections that allowed Bharti to bid. The acceptance was an outcome of a round of rule modifications. 'The criteria was changed to favour Bharti,' accused the others. Bharti chose to remain silent. The Department defended vehemently that the relevance of a lower number of GSM lines was higher than analogue or landline networks in the current context. India was adopting a new technology and the burden of rediscovery to shift from a legacy network must be recognized.

The other winner of the most coveted spot in Mumbai was BPL and this company was on the list of ineligible ones to begin with. The issues with BPL were mounted sky-high in legal arguments. It had an overlapping France Telecom partnership with Bharti. Thus, BPL should be eliminated, said the other contenders, like the public sector company that lost a bid in Kolkata because its partner was the same as Usha Martin's. Winning exemption after exemption for BPL was the outcome of corruption, they alleged. At the centre of this accusation was B.R. Nair, a fellow south Indian and Selection Committee member. If there was a desire to implicate others, the remaining aspirants could not find ground to implicate them. Nair, however, had a son employed at BPL since the company decided to apply for a licence. To the other potential operators, this was adequate reason for Nair to favour Chandrasekhar. Nair had also been instrumental in ensuring that the financials of the rental remained a key criterion with the most weightage. This had played to BPL's strengths.

BPL lost one of its foreign partners, McCaw, midway through the process. Fortunately, since it still had France Telecom, it was safe on its foreign partnership requirements. The question over BPL's eligibility, given the change in application status, was raked to eliminate the company from the race. As if this were not enough, BPL's competitors found more charges to pursue. They said BPL had failed to show commitment from a foreign partner as it had not applied for foreign investment clearance as was required in the financial bid document.

Explanations came rolling out from BPL's defence. As an investor, France Telecom was indirectly related to SFR's Talkland, the arm which was investing in Airtel. On corruption, BPL explained that it had advertised the vacancy in a newspaper. Chandrasekhar said that when recruiting Nair's son, the company did not know of the bureaucrat's involvement with the licensing committee or that the candidate was Nair's son. On his resumé, his father's name was mentioned, but not his profession, argued BPL.

More importantly, Nair made no final decision. He only made recommendations on selection criteria, which were later vetted twice. The Department seconded BPL's argument; if this was corruption it was ineffective, said the lawyer justifying the DoT's actions.

The regulator found proof that BPL had applied for foreign exchange approvals to the Reserve Bank of India. The Indian central banker had redirected BPL to the secretariat for Industrial Assistance. It was still permissible for the company to apply to the Foreign Investment Promotions Board, said the Department.

As it turned out, exemptions favoured the two most influential bidders, Tata and Max. Singh needed the technical error in his application overlooked. The Tata Group, which had merely submitted bids for Kolkata and Chennai, wished to modify its application to include Mumbai and Delhi. Concessions were at the Department's discretion and allowing it to correct its mistake would form part of that, the two entities argued alongside BPL and the DoT.

Then, the operators began to question the marking criteria before the court. Siva led the race based on his rental bid, but was eliminated, then brought back and now was once again in the line of fire. He had received higher marks for foreign exchange inflow than his competitors. However, his means to attract foreign inflow was merely based on international tourists using his mobile network and paying roaming charges. He made no specific commitments on amounts or time frames. His competitors argued that official communication from their foreign partners confirming they would fork out the dollars when needed should have outweighed Siva's proposal.

The two-member bench led by Justice D.P. Wadhwa in Delhi High Court listened to all the sides and soon came to its conclusion: 'We reject the allegation of the petitioner that the criteria so laid were in any way irrelevant, irrational, arbitrary or whimsical.' The two proceeded to rule on each issue individually.

In the case of Max, the bench said, 'It appears to us that the department has been rather hyper-technical in its approach . . . The basic idea was to get the best operator for the job and when this defect came to the notice of the Department, it could have asked the petitioner to correct the error and not to reject the tender altogether on a ground which appears to us to be rather flimsy. No public interest would have suffered by that process.' Max was thus allowed to amend its application.

In the case of BPL, the court found no reason to suspect corruption. 'When we examine the minutes of the Telecom Commission in the DoT, we do not find even an inkling that Nair in any way tried to favour BPL . . . Whatever policy decisions were there that were of the minister and Nai, had no role to play. It is difficult for us to see from the notes as to how even it could be suggested that Nair could influence the decision-making process in the case.' With that, Chandrasekhar's place among licensees was secured.

The court agreed that Siva, too, should be allowed to participate. Sterling Cellular, Siva's company, would be awarded a licence on a provisional basis and should the company steer clear of allegations cast upon it, the licence was Siva's to keep. 'There was no FIR (First Incident Report) and no preliminary report adverse to the company and we feel the ghost of CBI has been unnecessarily brought into play,' said the order. 'The company appears to have been punished for no sin of its. However, since the company has not complained we will leave the matter at that.'[2]

With that, the court dismissed the case and asked the Department to reconsider its decisions. Now, with its marking system validated, the government merely had to score and rewrite the allocations, including Max. Thus, followed yet another reshuffle: Max and Bharti were winners in Mumbai. BPL and Dalmia received the licence for Delhi, RPG and Usha Martin in Kolkata and Siva's Sterling in Chennai.

'It was a lottery. There were criteria about which we heard so many stories that one didn't know what to believe. Besides, who would pay for a call at Rs 16 per minute? So, there was no saying what the business case would be,' recalls RPG's chairman Harsh Goenka.[3]

9

Tata Fights On

In this new scheme of things, the Tata Group had been left out. It had been two years since the process began, and in that time, Tata had gone from being the favourite to being eliminated. Ratan Tata would at least challenge this omission. Who would be better to further India's technology cause than the Tata Group? In fact, its plan for a wireless network was already in the works. The anticipation of a major metro licence had been set up by the regulator in its various lists before the Delhi High Court's intervention.

As was its right, Tata Cellular went to the Supreme Court to further question this outcome and once again delayed the allocation of licences in an attempt to expose the arbitrary grading by the Department of Telecom. For instance, the Tata Group had received lower scores on its financial abilities even though it was apparently more flush with cash than any of the competitors.

Under pressure to conclude the matter quickly—in the interest of allowing a public service that was already delayed by two years—the apex court took up the matter. To Tata's dismay, the judges decided not to interfere or propose changes to any of the grading criteria or award points.

Instead, they decided that they would delve into three issues to decide whether the process was flawed. The first was whether the licences were issued in bad faith, with an intent to trick those who did not win. The second was whether there was ostensible bias among decision-makers distorting the outcome. The third was whether it was reasonable for the Department to issue licences at all.

Naturally, none of the parties were interested in arguing that the licensing process should be cancelled. Tata was keenest to win the Mumbai licence and therefore strategized its arguments to point out the personal involvement of committee members with bidders to show bias.

Yet, when it came to argument, it was merely a new name for a repeat of what was raked up in the Delhi High Court.

Competitors were happy to detail their innocence before this court with as much zeal as they displayed on the last occasion. Tata, represented by eminent lawyer Soli Sorabjee, led the charge, pointing fingers at loopholes in the grading system that had eliminated it from the race. Other companies defended it. The final judgment came soon enough. It concurred fully with the Delhi High Court's conclusion, adding only that the Department should once again hear Tata and consider their application afresh and reconsider the allocations in that light.

The Department considered, graded and spent a little while. It created a little flutter with some change. A new list of winners was published, but it still did not include the Tata Group among the final eight licensees. After all was said and done, companies were allowed to proceed with rollouts once and for all in November 1994.

Going head-to-head in Mumbai were Analjit Singh and Rajeev Chandrasekhar. In Delhi, Sunil Mittal and Siva were ready to compete. In Kolkata came Usha Martin and B.K. Modi and Chennai were RPG and Skycell.

Siva struck a $105 million deal with Shashi Ruia to sell the precious Delhi licence under his company Sterling Cellular to shipping major Essar. He remained the chairman of the company till Essar transferred money and completed deal formalities, and thereafter, the Essar Group took charge. It directly competed against Bharti. The Essar Group appointed T.V. Ramachandran as Sterling Cellular's chief executive. Fortunately for both competitors—Bharti and Essar—at this stage, business was more about creating a larger market than cannibalizing each other. The Essar-led company did so by running half-page advertisements in newspapers to educate potential subscribers about the upcoming service. It was a successful strategy.

Growing public euphoria and rising interest from foreign investors hooked bigger Indian businesses to the prospects of mobile telephony. So much so, that despite the high price, a Sony mobile instrument that came with the connection at Rs 80,000 a piece, Sterling had to shut pre-registrations after around 36,000 people presented cash to buy the phone even before a service launch. The foreign partner, Cellular Communication International, insisted that subscriber induction needed to be paced out even though the network capacity was projected at 1,00,000.

Globally, investors were salivating at revised outlooks for the Indian market. They still preferred to secure partnerships with large Indian business names as they egged established business houses to the lure of valuation increase in telecom companies that loomed large even if returns were distant.

10

Race to Take Off

It took over three years to get the licence, but once it was in hand, the clock was ticking. The licence condition stated that a network must be up and running to cover over 10 per cent of the city's population within a year. More importantly for the businesses, each passing day without a service incurred licence fees and a lost revenue opportunity. Even so, the nervous excitement that followed was not for these mundane business concerns; it was the heady, scary feeling of starting something new. Everyone wanted a piece. Local politicians wanted credit, and operators found the early adopters waiting eagerly for their services.

There were vendors to deal with and partners to find. It was a time when the strongest interpersonal relations were built, shrouded in an air of uncertainty and enthusiasm.

Sunil and Rajan Mittal decided to take an international trip to discover who would make equipment suitable for Bharti's needs. They were invited by the entire clutch of GSM equipment makers. A populous city like Delhi would surely need a multimillion-dollar rollout and give the vendor access to a nation with unchartered mobile penetration.

Motorola literally rolled out the red carpet. A private plane to ensure a comfortable journey to the US. A motorcade awaited at the airport from where the brothers were taken into meeting rooms for presentations with flourish and royal treatment. Impressed though they were, they chose to research some more.

France's Alcatel felt surer than others of winning the Bharti contract. After all, Bharti's bid was backed by long-term client SFR and as first-timers, the Indian founders would lean in. They did to some extent.

The Mittals decided to complete their research anyway, stopping in Sweden next. Here, they were to meet the equipment-making company Ericsson. After the presentations ended, the Ericsson and Bharti teams headed to a lavish lunch at a local restaurant. The anticipation, as with other vendors, was that Ericsson would foot the bill. In the traditional Indian style of courtesy, Mittal offered to pay, expecting that the offer would be turned down. To his surprise, Kurt Hellström, chief executive officer, agreed, and Mittal was in a spot. He did not have a credit card, which was not the norm in India at the time, and inadequate foreign exchange. He requested a colleague from Mauritius, who was carrying a card, to settle the bill on his behalf.[1]

The meal was a pretty penny but worth it. It helped loosen some of Mittal's inhibitions the next day when he told Hellström that Bharti would only pay 15 per cent of the initial equipment cost upfront. Ericsson had estimated an order of $27 million for equipment for an initial launch.

Naturally, Hellström asked if the company were to proceed when Ericsson could expect the remaining payment. Mittal's response was 'on happiness'. Perplexing as that answer was, he then went on to explain. When customers are satisfied with the experience and happily pay for Bharti's services the operator would repay Ericsson on a revenue share basis. The onus of a good network would fall as much on the vendor as securing the right customers on Bharti. It's unclear if Mittal offered the same to any of the other companies, but Ericsson accepted the challenge.

Then, when Ericsson proposed to kickstart the network with around thirty signal-emitting sites, or telecom towers, Bharti responded with a request for 108 to cover the region meaningfully. Mittal built Delhi's network with an upfront investment of merely $3 million. Along with that, he also set a precedent for free sampling of the network for Airtel's subscribers.

Post-retirement in 2004, Hellström joined the board of Bharti. When asked why he had accepted what seemed like a dubious proposal at the time, Hellström said he had conviction in Mittal's passion to make a go at telecom. Perhaps, losing a sure-shot contract in Kolkata also had a role to play.

The Ericsson experience with B.K. Modi's Modi Telstra, which had a licence in Kolkata, was opposite to Sunil Mittal's experience.

Telstra, Modi's Australian partner in the mobile licence bid, was a big client of Ericsson. Executives from Australia leaned on Umang Das, chief executive officer, of Modi Telstra, to select the Swedish equipment maker for its Kolkata network rollout. To the supplier, selection was almost a foregone conclusion.

While Das and his team appreciated Telstra's experience, they preferred to decide based on competitive vendor bids rather than allowing any 'preconceived favouritism'. Das and the Modi Telstra team travelled to Australia for a business review meeting to decide on the company's next steps to deployment. It was here that, Das recalled, the Indian delegation met a gentleman named Hanu Karavitta, who was designated Australia business head for Nokia. Das asked Karavitta to participate in a competitive bid for Modi Telstra's network against Ericsson.

To the team's dismay, when they contacted Nokia, Ericsson's biggest competitor, not only was the company unwilling to participate in the bidding process, but its executives were not even forthcoming about organizing a meeting with Das and his team.

'Why are you not interested in at least making a proposal?' asked Das.

Turns out Karavitta was reluctant to spend time and effort on this because 'he saw no chance for Nokia'.

Das reassured him that bids would be considered on merit. Even so, the Nokia executive visited India reluctantly. 'It was our sheer persuasion and professional approach that built up Nokia's confidence to decide to participate in the India business opportunity.'[2] So when the company finally decided to present to Modi Telstra, Nokia came prepared to upend a competitor.

In sharp contrast, the Modi–Telstra team found that the detailing offered by Ericsson was complacent. They seemed confident that the cat was in the bag.

In the final analysis, Das found that Nokia's technical bid was superior to Ericsson but at a higher price than the Swedish equipment maker. Modi Telstra persisted with Nokia and asked the company to match the cost structure proposed by the competitor. Nokia obliged. The contract was closed in February 1995. Karavitta relocated to India and opened Nokia Network's India Office as its head, said Das.

Nokia did not know at the time that the deployment deadline had been ticking for the entire time, and it was about to face an unexpected challenge.

A little before the final licence allocation, in November 1994, Modi and Das set up a meeting with West Bengal chief minister, Jyoti Basu, to test the kind of political support they could expect.

Basu was charming and, for the most part, did not give away his intentions as Modi and Das elaborated on this new opportunity that Kolkata had.

'When will all this happen?' asked Basu, still not letting on what he made of it but polite enough to encourage his presenters. Modi continued on the transformational power of the mobile phone. Then the meeting wrapped up, and the two—Modi and Das—began to rise to leave.

'Still, you must have some idea of when you expect to bring service to the people,' Basu pressed for a final date.

A moment's awkward silence was broken by Das, who meanwhile mentally calculated that an aggressive launch could be completed in one year.

'31 July,' said Basu, a definitiveness that had been missing in the leader's demeanour so far. 'You'll get all the support you need for this date,' he added, bidding adieu to his guests.

Modi himself was hung up on being the first to make India's first mobile phone call, so the date did not fall foul with him, but now there was no time to lose.

With Nokia on board, the 31 July deadline loomed large. Team Modi dangled the deadline over Nokia's head. There was only time to meet the government imposed minimum rollout obligations. To be fair, the government machinery worked quickly enough.

Nokia set up a network comprising just eleven cell sites to cover the metro region of Kolkata. When the testing and connectivity checks were complete, the team dicovered a new problem. For an official mobile call, the connection had to pass through the Telecom Department's network.

That came with its own bureaucracy. By now, the Department had started viewing mobile services with some degree of scepticism. Were they stoking a competitor, asked the bureaucrats. For Modi Telstra's first call, the political pressure was sufficient to get permissions to route a call through the state-run operator's network by 27 July.

Bharti and Analjit Singh's Hutchison Max were also in the same race, following similar timelines and were pipped by a couple of days in these permissions to switch into and through the Department's network.

The moment was celebrated at The Grand Hotel in Kolkata. On one end was Chief Minister Jyoti Basu, and on the other, newly appointed Telecom Minister Sukh Ram. They only had pleasantries to exchange as the call went down in India's history. Within a week, pilot networks in Mumbai, Delhi and Chennai also booted.

It had been a game of snakes and ladders. India's mobile revolution had begun.

11

Unlocking the Value of Population

Hong Kong-based Hutchison was an ideal partner for an Indian telecom company. It was at close quarters to India making travel, time zone and general liaison easy. Its management was aware of Asian cultures, but since Hong Kong was still a British colony, Hutchison's best practices reflected European openness and social structure.

Analjit Singh's team, led by Ashwini Windlass and Sandip Das, designated head of cellular from heading the pager business, had proven their efficacy as they began to run the Mumbai operations in competition with BPL Mobile. Their logical partners for the equipment were Motorola and Ericsson. Singh considered the venture a success even though, from its inception, he believed it was cash-crunched, especially in contrast with the competition. Singh's Hutch Max spent Rs 15 crore on marketing. In Singh's opinion, BPL was spending several times that amount and therefore captured a larger chunk of the market share.

To compete with a moneyed opponent, Singh and Windlass decided to take a different path to network planning. Max launched the cellular service in Mumbai with around sixty-five base stations or points of signal emission and reception (Delhi's Airtel started with 108 and ramped up quickly). The network covered only the posh South Mumbai up to a fairly central suburb, Santacruz.

Hutch Max, the joint venture between Analjit Singh and Hong Kong-based Hutchison, launched a service under the brand Max Touch in a campaign titled 'Hello Bombay'. From there, instead of focusing on expanded coverage, the company brought its attention to indoor coverage.

The move was designed to attract more high-paying corporate users. They required network inside the building in fixed locations rather than long distances in the outdoors. The capital expenditure on it was higher to cover a smaller footprint compared with outdoor coverage. Hutch charged a premium for the service. It was successful in capturing its target market but later came under pressure when competitors started adopting predatory pricing, meaning they were offering customers call rates below the cost of carrying one to stem the cash deficit from licence payments rather than aim for profitability.

The uptake from the urban rich peaked within a couple of years, and the middle class was still too conservative to spend on mobile phones. Airtel in Delhi, for instance, had a static customer base of around 1,00,000 for a year with no additions and high churn. The back debts, too, ballooned because people would not pay.[1] In Mumbai, Hutch Max was watching the growing trend with trepidation even though it enjoyed a significantly higher per-customer revenue each month than its competitors. Singh felt the company was falling behind the competition from BPL Mobile. Hutch Max saw the need to unlock a bigger market.

As the team discussed the country's advantages, it awakened to the micro economy of India's mega population. This was a market for shampoo sachets and single cigarette sticks sold by the corner store to daily wagers at a price of Re 1, much like the chocolate eclair toffee, for which there were many takers. How could Hutch unlock this segment of subscribers?

Hutch Max decided to launch a service called prepaid, which would be sold for a nominal charge, but receive cash up front, and when the amount ran out, while its owner could not make or receive calls, a ring would land on the instrument—a missed call. There were scant studies to suggest the use of the prepaid internationally; none that had sustainably or successfully worked. The Indian market proved unlike others.

The early adopters of prepaid mobile technology were small and medium companies with large field staff. The offering capped bill shocks and still delivered the connectivity. This was the turning point of mobile connection sales to the fast-moving consumer goods model.

The operator faced a dilemma: What would offering the phone service to a low-income group mean for the premium customers who saw social status in their mobile phones? Moreover, the cost structure of a high-end marketing organization would never justify a low-revenue product.

Windlass and Das elected to distinguish the services in both brand and technology back-end. Hutch Max prided itself in its Motorola and Ericsson network, but the company bought a system from Nokia for prepaid. At the time, Nokia's representative for Hutch Max was Rajeev Suri, who later ascended to the global CEO position of the Finnish equipment maker. Nokia agreed to a low-cost, per-customer billing structure so that Hutch Max paid a revenue share from the subscribers using the system instead of an upfront capital cost. Its concern now was how to lure the customers.

The company created a twin structure with a parallel marketing outfit. It rented a new office in Prabhadevi, Mumbai. It was close to the existing one, but not in the same building. 'We didn't want the cultures to mix at all,' Das recalls. No high-end marketing budgets, no high-profile hires, and staff in the new office comprised largely of an on-ground sales force with the ability to get its hands dirty. Salaries that were rich and fixed for the Hutch Max post-paid service offering were commission-based for the new team onboarded for prepaid card selling. Nearly three-fourths of the wage bill here was success-based with very low fixed salaries. For the team selling post-paid connections, this would have been blasphemous because the industry was already stagnating, and sales for some months ran in the hundreds and not more.

The new sales team was selling a distinctly different product under a new brand name—'Ace'. It was intentionally designed to avoid any correlation between the premium post-paid service. Hutch Max, the post-paid service, bore an orange-and-black logo, while Ace had a green one.

The eight metro city operators had formed a cosy group, knowing that none was truly competing with the other and joining forces made them stronger as part of an industry voice when dealing with the regulator. It had become common for founders to exchange ideas, and good relations between Sunil Mittal and Analjit Singh pre-dated even the licence applications.

When Bharti Airtel realized Hutch had already launched a prepaid service, Bharti Airtel's Sanjay Kapoor along with his colleague Deepak Gulati travelled to the Mumbai headquarters of Hutch Max to learn from its prepaid strategy and experience. Then, Bharti replicated a similar model for Delhi under the brand name 'Magic'.

With low-budget billboard advertising, Ace SIM cards were distributed in a van that would set out from the southern end of Mumbai and drop them off point by point as it travelled northward. Hutch offered credit to distributors to stock and push the SIM cards, and soon stockists began to see the value. If they were able to sell the SIMs before the next stocking, they could create a cash flow and profit without putting any of their own money on the line. A new market opened and brought a fresh boost to mobile sales.

Hutch Max then elected to use the distributors of Cadbury, India's most popular chocolate brand by multinational Fast Moving Consumer Goods (FMCG) company Unilever, called Hindustan Unilever at the time. They also onboarded the Colgate Toothpaste distribution channel. Sellers of these products were well penetrated in every corner of India, and their supply chain was already in place. Since SIM cards were low-volume items, tagging them along with the remaining goods being moved was a win-win for all parties involved. It helped the telecom company that sellers of these goods were typically respected and had personal connections with the local clientele.

Sunil Mittal's team in Delhi first tried to tap chemists to stock chips for mobile connections—the SIM cards. It then came to the conclusion that Hutch's approach was more effective. The rest of the industry followed closely on the heels of Hutch.

An FMCG approach to selling mobile phones requires a mirrored marketing approach. Companies explored celebrity endorsement to add a glamour factor to mass-market mobile telephony.

Bharti Airtel's Magic brand had the first line of star endorsements. Sunil Mittal's operator hired advertising agency Leo Burnett to curate a new sub-brand with similar values but a distinct physical personality from Airtel's premium brand. The company went on to engage contemporary Bollywood movie star Shah Rukh Khan coupled later with Kareena Kapoor, who has a family legacy in the industry. The deal with Shah Rukh was fairly straightforward, recalls an executive. The order of negotiation with him was limited to numbers. Bharti kept the relationship professional and while he may have had requests from fans among family and friends, Sunil Mittal never let on. The company did, however, host star-studded channel partner events and awards to build trust and loyalty among the sales channels.

The new prepaid format revived demand to some extent, but most of all reduced the burden of outstanding bills for the mobile phone operators and improved cash flows.

Over four years had passed since the preparation of the first launch. Hutch Max had lost out on bids for service areas outside of Mumbai. Competitors were struggling, largely because there were no takers for calling rates pegged at Rs 16 a minute and a receiving rate of roughly half that. So, operators who had paid or were due to pay licence fees were raking up a daily bill without commensurate revenue. To top that off, the Department created numerous hurdles in interconnecting phone calls. If a mobile phone could not successfully call a landline, its use to a subscriber dropped infinitely. A war between operators and the Department had erupted on this issue.

The Department was both the regulator and chief competitor for the industry. From the private operators' perspective, it dismissed any complaints made if they were detrimental to the state-run telecom service. 'Any different moves would be thwarted with a change in regulation,' one of the telco chiefs from that time said.

Singh and his family elected to exit rather than ploughing in more money. In 1998, Analjit Singh decided to capitalize on the company's relatively strong position compared with its peers and sell his stake. The deal he struck demonstrated the potential value in the sector still to be unleashed.

A restructuring was brewing at Sanchar Bhawan, where the telecom network operations were being spun off from the ministry to separate the company—Bharat Sanchar Nigam Limited (BSNL). It was done to allay concerns and increase the government's objectivity in decision-making.

Hutch thus assessed India's potential differently from Singh's. The big collision between the private industry and government could end in bigger business opportunities. Hutch still had faith in the millions of potential users of the service in India. It, therefore, proposed an offer that made everyone in the industry salivate. His contemporaries recall that perhaps Singh himself had not estimated the value that Hutch assigned the deal. Analjit Singh turned over 41 per cent in the company and walked away with a whopping Rs 561 crore.

While Hutch acquired economic interest, it required Indian participation in the transaction to comply with foreign direct investment norms. Uday Kotak became a joint venture partner who held equity on Hutch's behalf. Indian rules also required Indian control of the board which Kotak and Singh held.

Hutch then strengthened its presence within the company. It took on a management restructuring which led to the appointment of Asim Ghosh. After stints at Procter and Gamble and Pepsi, Ghosh had settled in Hong Kong into the role of managing director and CEO of A.S. Watson Industries, the consumer goods division of Hutchison.

Hutch also looked at expanding the operation. It searched for other telecom potentials willing to do an equity swap and merge operations. Essar emerged as the deal clincher. Essar's arm ran service in Delhi competing with Bharti Airtel. There was an equity exchange deal stitched up by Ghosh and Essar's owners Ravi and Shashi Ruia.

Many things could have torpedoed these negotiations. For starters, if the original licensing norms were to be considered, the value of a licence in Mumbai was higher than the value of one in Delhi. Yet, in the interest of time and simplicity, the partners chose to treat the per-subscriber valuation of Mumbai and Delhi more-or-less at par.

Then, an even more surprising turn in this deal structure raised the hopes of aspiring telco giants further. At the end of the transaction, Essar would have been required to front around $250 million. The Indian shipping group instead negotiated that Hutch loan money to Essar to buy its share in the combined entity. Hutch also went on to finance another nearly $100 million for Essar to expand the network. By the turn of 1998, as the sector flirted with a new regulatory regime, Hutch Max was ready to fire on all cylinders.

Part Three

12

A New Opportunity

The bitter and prolonged court battle for licences that lasted from 1992 to 1995 had an unexpected side effect. It allowed foreign interest to build, raising a number of potential investors to circle the Indian telephony market like hawks. The technology could unlock the potential of India's billion voices, a magnitude unheard of in Western geographies.

Study after study suggested that telecom was to be the first true unleashing of India's population advantage, economies of scale and consumption story. Leading business houses too began to see merit in the sector. So, groups like Essar and Tata lobbied to further open up the sector. Still, this was not a business for the faint-hearted. Investors egged bigger local groups to dip their toes in the telecom pot. Partnering with little-known companies presented risks international organizations found difficult to justify to their shareholders.

The Indian government saw gold! In true 'yeh dil mange more [the heart wants more]' style, the government readied more licences to sell under Telecom Minister Sukh Ram and Prime Minister P.V. Narasimha Rao.

The government had set a target to provide phone connections on-demand to anyone in the country by 1997. The Department of Telecom was in no position to achieve this.

Representatives from foreign telecom operators like France Telecom, Swiss PTT, Telia from Sweden, British Telecom, Vodafone, Telecom Italia, AT&T and BCE from Canada became a common occurrence at the Department of Telecommunications since the tender of private cellular licences. There was euphoria that the valuations in this business would soar. Everyone wanted a piece.

So, in a move that seemed like killing two birds with one stone, the government mooted the idea of launching an auction for landline service licences in 1993. Yet, offering such a large platform to a private sector company could not be done without legislation. Thus, for the first time in over a century, regulators formed a Telecom Policy in 1994.

As part of the policy, the country was divided into twenty zones, called circles. The circles were further categorized based on their urbanization. Category 'A' was for places with higher population and spending power, 'B' for mid-tier zones and 'C' for remote, rural and low-revenue potential service areas. The Department envisaged that the cash and expense requirement in 'A' circles would be higher, but the revenue opportunity would also be commensurate. Therefore, to apply for each 'A' circle, the applicant's net worth had to be Rs 300 crore. If the company were to apply for two 'A' class service areas, its net worth had to be Rs 600 crore. The requirement for a 'B' circle was Rs 200 crore and a 'C' was Rs 50 crore. Thus, to apply for one 'A' and one 'B' circle, the applicant's net worth had to be Rs 500 crore.

The net worth eligibility requirement included the value of the foreign partner based on its most recent audited financial results. This time, a licence bidder needed to service 5,00,000 subscribers or telephone lines to be considered. However, there could be any number of partners in a bidding consortium and their experience and net worth would be accumulated as long as they held over 10 per cent each in the final entity. The bidding for licences was opened in the first quarter of 1995.

There were those bidding to cash in on a quick valuation jump of the licences and those who planned to deploy networks and offer services. Tractor makers Escorts partnered with First Pacific from Hong Kong while Mahindra and Mahindra allied with BT (British Telecom). From Uttar Pradesh, Vinay Rai who had just returned from an academic stint overseas created Koshika Telecom, a venture backed by his family steel business, Usha Ispat.

Essar was ready for round two having tasted success in Delhi. Even more so was Siva, who won last time. The eight operators in metro cities were also keen to participate, most of them hoping to secure a big footprint across India. Their partners were already lined up and experience in the domestic market was most relevant in the selection criteria.

Many emerging business groups saw an investment opportunity and the unions that emerged to bid were complex. For instance, in one combination of foreign partners, Thailand's telecom operator—Jasmine—and Sweden's Telia along with Indian promoters Rajamohan Rao, the Parasrampuria family and the Sanmar Group. They founded JT Mobile. Or the Thapar family-led electronics maker Crompton Greaves with telecom partners Daljit Singh of DSS Enterprises, US Millicom and BellSouth.

These were attempts to match the financial strength of India's established conglomerates Tata, Birla and Reliance, which were dropping their names in the hat this time around.

13

Kumar Mangalam's Nascent Adventure

Even as a sixteen-year-old, in 1983, Kumar Mangalam Birla was dealing with stardom and the weight of his business empire due to land someday on his shoulders. While his friends hung out after school, Kumar Mangalam Birla had already spent a year involved with the family business. It was his grandparents who had convinced him of the need for this early induction into the sprawling empire that he would come to own.

Where his friends squandered time talking about the nothings of daily routine, Birla was being groomed to wield a fork and knife, ride horses and face the paparazzi with poise and grace. As such, the world could get lonely on some days. He learnt to take recourse in quiet alpine mountains during holidays. In later years, as holidays dwindled, his passion for shooting emerged. He frequented a range in Worli, Mumbai not far from his home.

The Birla business was an uncommon mix of Indian family values and Western work ethic. It was one of the few business powerhouses that believed in giving back to the community, creating a meditative oasis in the form of 'Birla Mandirs' across the country among many initiatives post-Indian independence to cultivate local culture and arts. This philosophical melding of worlds was emulated in the group's corporate culture.

While he worked in the halls of the family firm, Kumar Mangalam was expected to achieve suitable educational qualifications to succeed in his managerial role. The road ahead was long. He studied commerce, then chartered accountancy and then management, all the while maintaining watch on the group's core focus, the pillars of the industrial revolution, steel and cement.

Kumar Mangalam enjoyed the patronage of his father, loving encouragement from his mother and exploration of his persona.

However, in 1995, when new telecom licences were being auctioned, Aditya Birla, Kumar Mangalam Birla's father, was struggling with poor health. After an education at the highly acclaimed Massachusetts Institute of Technology (MIT), Aditya Birla had taken this eminently Indian group global with joint ventures in the core sector across Asia. It was his track record and global outlook that attracted AT&T, a US-based cellular company, which had otherwise been hawkish on Indian entrepreneurs and investment prospects. AT&T, after having passed up the first round, now acknowledged that telecom in India was worth a second thought. The Birla chairperson was not entirely convinced of a future in telecom, but AT&T's backing softened his view. Lore has it that it was M.C. Bagrodia, an advisor to Birla, who helped cement the decision to participate in telecom.

Aditya Birla passed away the same year, 1995, at the young age of fifty-one, succumbing to health complications due to cancer. Kumar Mangalam ascended as group chairperson, under the watch of his grandfather, until he was ready to take full charge. He had been groomed for the role his entire life. Still, little was known about Kumar Mangalam's business acumen or style.

Birla Communications, the group's telecom venture was probably one of the last businesses Aditya Birla signed off on. It was left as a newborn baby in the arms of twenty-eight-year-old Kumar Mangalam Birla. A joint venture with AT&T was formalized in December 1995 a couple of months after Aditya Birla's passing.

Kumar Mangalam's immediate attention was needed in core industries for the conglomerate ranging from aluminium to textile.

His father's shoes were big ones to fill, and Kumar Mangalam had to do it retrospectively. Tata's Ratan 'uncle's' ascension was an ascension Kumar had seen and likened to his situation.

When Ratan Tata took over the Tata Group just four years earlier, in 1991, his competence had been called into question. Both Ratan Tata and Kumar Mangalam were taking over from successful and well-respected predecessors. The small Bombay industrialist community watched their every move. The pressure to perform was immense, and the desire to do so even higher.

By the time Kumar Mangalam assumed leadership of the Aditya Birla Group, Ratan Tata's actions were already beginning to bear fruit. Kumar's management was seemingly styled after Ratan Tata. Kumar Mangalam introduced a retirement age to rejuvenate the executive cadre at the Birla Group. 'Soon after he took over he introduced a retirement policy, a very scientific policy and he had planned well in advance. Around 350 very senior people had to leave,' Kumar's grandfather B.K. Birla told a newspaper in 2005 about his grandson. 'In retrospect, till 1994 or 1995, we hadn't noticed anything especially exciting about his business acumen. But the change was almost overnight and within a few months, it was very obvious.'[1]

This seemed like an uncanny echo from Ratan Tata's ascension when he introduced a retirement policy taking out Tata veterans from Russi Mody to Ajit Kerkar—who were competitors for the top seat at one point. They were very likely to slow Ratan Tata's agenda for reform.

Kumar Mangalam and Ratan Tata shared more than common circumstances. There was also the deep intertwined history of the Birla and Tata groups. Both were instrumental in ushering in the Industrial Revolution in India. While the Tata Group tried its hands at all things new, the Birla's had stood by the Tata flagship, Tata Steel, for long. The trust Ratan Tata and Aditya Birla, Kumar's father, shared was deep. During the 1990s, when Ratan Tata tasked himself with consolidating the equity of Tata Group companies to protect them from hostile takeovers, Tata Steel remained an exception. The Birla Group remained Tata Steel's largest shareholder, with Tata Sons, the group's apex company, holding as little as 2 per cent.

On the subject of telecom, Kumar trusted Ratan Tata for good advice.

Birla's telecom venture with AT&T was well-funded and in the hands of trusted lieutenants and AT&T experts. Initially, the venture functioned on auto-pilot mode. Bagrodia, Raghuvir Bhandari, who held a financial post, and Rajan Mathews were among the founding team of Birla AT&T. While decision-making at this company was quick, the knowledge bank had to be built from scratch, starting with plans and maps and even a decision on which regions to focus on. In the Maharashtra service area, competition deployed in on populous cities like Pune and Nagpur. In contrast, AT&T explored the challenging topography of Goa. There were some things the company learnt the hard way. On one occasion, the team rented office space in a building along with around 5000 square feet for a switch to be provided by Ericsson. The floor height of the building was ten feet, seemingly adequate to house the switch, but its deployment required nearly a foot of height for cabling and 'under-cooling'. The container with the switch lay outside for a while before a suitable alternative could be found. The operator's first telecom tower was installed on top of a building in Pune. There was a party that evening. Pune became the centre for the group to pilot initiatives in times to come, including a bio-fueled power generator for towers and signal emitting stations.

14

Mukesh and Anil Take a Dip

The entry into telecom was a more measured family decision for Reliance. When the first telecom licences were offered in 1991, Reliance was caught up with its Hazira unit to make integrated polyester. Or perhaps it wasn't ready? In any case, the first round of cellular licence bids did not stimulate any curiosity.

Four years later, however, US-returned Anil and Mukesh Ambani looked outward, beyond the traditional businesses of Reliance, as the next step to building an empire. The corporate image of the group was far from ideal, and the buzz it had once generated from its public listing was on the wane. Its integrity was openly questioned in the media and had the potential of becoming a ground for the political positioning of Reliance's allies and foes. The deepening equity markets and the infamous trading scam by Harshad Mehta in the 1990s had diverted attention from Reliance. As Reliance thrashed out its future course, it seemed clear that entering a consumer business should be next on the cards. But which one?

Led by their father, Dhirajlal Hirachand Ambani (popularly known as Dhirubhai), the brothers were happy to explore telecom alongside financial services. However, the group was still busy expanding the core petrochemical business and the attention accorded to any new venture would need to factor that in.

Mukesh Ambani may not have completed his course at Stanford, USA but in his limited time in Silicon Valley, he had wisened to the transformative power of technology. Even when the big personal computing wave of the late 1980s swept through India, Mukesh had an eye on it. However, that was a crucial decade for Reliance's backward integration from a polymer maker to a petrochemical company. Reliance could not be distracted. So metaphorically, the company had missed the bus. This time, with telecom, it planned to keep options open as Mukesh and Anil Ambani steered the group into a new era.

As the eldest of four children of a savvy businessperson, Mukesh Ambani vividly remembered the family's rise from limited means to a sprawling empire. Dhirubhai's was a true romantic, rags-to-riches story. From an attendant at oil fields in the Middle East, the Reliance patriarch had built a polymer trading business.

Reliance was publicly listed on stock exchanges in 1977. At that time, Mukesh was named to the board of the company but was expected to earn that position over the years. He completed his chemical engineering degree from Mumbai University and then headed off for a management degree at Stanford University, California, USA. He was in the class of '81.

In 1980, Dhirubhai secured a licence for polyester filament yarn. The polyester production business could not wait for Stanford to award Mukesh a degree, said Dhirubhai, who generally thought differently from his peers on such matters.[1]

Mukesh Ambani recalls his father telling him to return to build this opportunity of a lifetime. But what about completing the degree? Dhirubhai left it to his son to choose between learning as he built or waiting for the next opportunity, which may or may not arise. Put in that perspective, a twenty-two-year-old Mukesh dropped out of his class and joined his father in building the company.

In 1983, it was time to welcome Anil Ambani, two years younger than Mukesh, back into the fold as he returned with his MBA from the University of Pennsylvania's Wharton School.

It was a tight-knit family. Mukesh remembered an occasion that had brought the brothers together. Dhirubhai was upset with them for acting rowdily in front of guests. The two were punished to live in the garage for two days. They were only given roti and water. It brought adversity, but also 'bonded the two brothers', Mukesh said in a later interview.[2]

The two were almost opposites and complemented each other. Mukesh was introspective and analytical while Anil was flamboyant and fast. Combined with their academic experiences, this contrast cast Mukesh in the role of the builder and Anil into the face of the company. The 80s were golden years for Reliance, and the brothers worked through it together. Late nights at the office often ended with pav bhaji, a typical Mumbai street food item, at a budget restaurant in Tardeo, a predominantly lower-middle-class area of the city.

In 1986, Dhirubhai Ambani suffered his first stroke that left him paralysed in one arm. In the face of adversity, the brothers worked like two sides of a coin. Anil said when it came to business it was not a question of senior and junior. 'Mukesh being an engineer leads the technical decisions, I take finance decisions,' said Anil in another interview. 'We work as two bodies one mind.'[3]

Almost a decade later, as the father and sons considered entering telecom space, they first decided to test the waters with a small bucket of capital allocation.

Soon after, Reliance invited technology consulting firm Booz Allen to discuss the prospects of telephony and what a full-scale deployment would entail. A presenter who impressed the Ambanis was Praful Gupta. The consultant had a larger-than-life image. One executive remembers that

he lived on a farm he owned and flew to Denver, US on his
plane to catch the nearest connection further. The Ambanis
decided it would be better to hire him for the telecom venture
than pay merely to get arms-length consultations. Gupta was
a game for the opportunity and joined Reliance to build the
company's foray.

Gupta's opinion was that any new hyper-competitive
industry would fail to yield a financial return for the investor.
In line with this principle, he delivered a licence-buying charter
to Mukesh Ambani that the business scion would adhere to for
the next couple of decades. In 1995 this meant Reliance would
steer clear of hotly contested regions.

Reluctant to bid at all amid such euphoria for telecom
licences, Gupta directed Reliance's bid for mobile licence to a
clutch of service areas that interested very few other bidders.
Reliance did not bid for basic or landline service licences like the
other major players and, therefore, staved off getting embroiled
in the political confusion that followed.

Perhaps as a corollary, this was not a business that was
as important to Mukesh Ambani who was immersed in an
expansion project at Hazira, Reliance's petrochemical unit.
The telecom business came at an estimated investment of
$100 million. An executive said Dhirubhai Ambani left the
decision to his younger son, Anil Ambani, about whether he
wanted to head the business or appoint a professional chief
executive. Anil chose the latter and got the ball rolling with an
old friend of the Reliance Group, Akhil Gupta.

None of Tata, Birla, or Reliance anticipated what was to
follow in telecom licensing. Amid this much stronger line-up
of bidders, a little-known entity called Himachal Futuristic
Communication Ltd (HFCL), with a recorded net worth of
Rs 4622 crore, including the value of foreign partners, placed

bids totalling well over Rs 85,000 crore! This was more than double that of the next competitor.

Mahendra Nahata's HFCL had applied in partnership with Thailand's Shinawatra Group and Israel's Bezeq. Competitors had considered this company a red herring because HFCL itself only had a net worth of Rs 62 crore, and much of it was built in the halls of Sanchar Bhavan.

15

Surprise from Himachal

Tea trader Mahendra Nahata met his nephew and son of RPG's chief financial officer Bane Chand Maloo, Vinay Maloo, at a family wedding in 1987. They got talking about the big shift Sam Pitroda was pushing for in telephony. In Mumbai and Delhi, the government was struggling to keep up with the demand for phone lines. For each connection, a massive cable laying project had to be undertaken.

Nahata and Maloo thought there might be an opportunity here. Then the talk evolved into more, a resolution of sorts to enter the sector together. They partnered with Deepak Malhotra to add to the management depth.

The venture began with manufacturing optic fibre cables, which the Department was entrusted to swiftly lay across the country. Then Nahata came across a technology company, Seiscor Technologies, that had developed a protocol called frequency-division multiplexing to allow the use of a cable for more than one phone connection.

The Department was happy to get any help it could, so Nahata was welcomed into its specialized wing, called the Telecommunications Engineering Center (TEC). Here was definitely an opportunity, it was the need of the hour. To be able to enter the sector, however, they would need a licence.

The state of Himachal Pradesh had one but could not hand it to Nahata. Under the protectionist regime, Nahata entered into a 49:51 joint venture with Himachal Pradesh State Electronic Development Corporation. Seiscor Technologies was a tough negotiator and tight-lipped when dealing with Nahata. The telecom tech research company charged high royalties and the products were imported. Nahata's company proposed adapting the technology and manufacturing the product locally.

It may have made business sense, but securing an order from the Department proved extremely challenging for Nahata. He travelled from Amritsar to Delhi to attend prearranged meetings at the Department of Electronics, which were not at Sanchar Bhavan, but in a building adjacent to Delhi's posh Khan Market. When he reached the venue, he was turned back empty-handed because the officials delayed the appointment to another day.

'There was no money for flights,' he remembers. Without communication media, being stranded in Delhi was uncomfortable, unproductive and frustrating.

On one such occasion, he exited the government office and stood in a typist's queue to print a letter to send to the Department. His turn was after a well-built elderly gentleman who was dictating a letter about a shortfall in the pension he had received. He complained that he had written to the government earlier, but the mistake had not been rectified. Once the letter was done, the gentleman paid the typist Rs 2, under much protest from the worker who had expected Rs 5. After he was gone, Nahata asked the typist who the gentleman was. The answer shook him. This was Mirza Hameedullah Beg, former chief justice of India.

'If a Chief Justice can be reduced to waiting like this, I should not take affront to being made to wait by government officials,' Nahata reasoned. He swallowed his pride and persisted with the Department. Eventually, the company won a tender of Rs 18 lakh from MTNL—a company that was spun off from the DoT and listed on public stock exchanges because of which it had more funds to build Mumbai and Delhi's telephone network. The order was followed up by another worth just under Rs 3 crore by the Department for the same equipment.

HFCL then chanced on a German technology company to add capacity and automation on the exchange end. The tie-up was all but completed when the Indian government forced it shut, because it was keen to further develop its indigenous platform C-DOT. Stymied by the state and its majority partner, HFCL appeared briefly to stagnate until 1991.

This is when the company got its biggest breakthrough and split from its government parenthood to enjoy some independence.

The government floated a tender for companies that could use radio equipment to connect various district headquarters to the block headquarters. Keen to capture this market, Nahata's team tried partnering with global companies that could share the technology to be deployed. HFCL, however, was too small and too unknown to find willing partners. It did not help that it was now a private company since it floated a capital raise, which was subscribed to by Nahata's friends and family and not the government.

Eventually, with about eight months to spare, Nahata boldly decided to enter into a research and development contract with a Canadian company. He recruited and sent ten engineers to develop a suitable radio solution. The research project overran its deadline, and when he went to the ministry to ask for an extension, Nahata vividly remembers the push-back he faced. He suspected that vested interests may have influenced the government's hesitation towards his request, but all said and done, the request was granted.

A month later, the radio solution developed by the team was tested at small locations in Bihar, where hub offices were connected to the main building using wireless. When the final submission of bids came in, Nahata recollects his bid was a sixth of the competition. He proposed to sell radios at Rs 6 lakh a piece compared with the next most suitable bid at Rs 36 lakh a piece. For this rather economical offering, the government gave Nahata an order of Rs 100 crore, which was huge for the Himachal Futuristic Group. Over the course of the next year deployments of the radios worked successfully, cementing Nahata's reputation within the electronics department. This contract was followed up with another worth Rs 90 crore.

The profits financed Himachal Futuristic's entry into optical transmission, a telecommunication technology that involved laying optic fibre cables and passing multiple signals on a single backbone with minimal data loss. The company proposed solutions at a lower price than those offered by multinational companies and won another contract worth around Rs 40 crore.

However, success came at a price. Nahata was accused of receiving a favour to get this order from Telecom Minister Sukh Ram, who also hailed from Himachal. Sukh Ram had taken office midway through the process of selecting the vendor partner for the radio contract.

Nahata contested this claim from his competitors. His pricing for any contract to the government was a fraction of the established global challenger and the quality was comparable, he said. Yet, it was an odd coincidence that Punjab-based Nahata set up shop in Himachal and thereafter prospered under Minister Sukh Ram.

That said, dreaming small was never for Nahata and his superlative Rs 85,000 crore bid for telecom licences was its latest testament. This bid was so far from all the competition that it not only shocked business leaders but also threatened to scuttle the process for the Indian government by becoming the only other player than the DoT.

16

Let the Scams Begin!

The tension and decibel levels in the Indian Parliament were numbing as the opposition hurled accusations at Telecom Minister Sukh Ram, who found himself reassuring both the upper and lower houses of Parliament that he would not allow a private monopoly in India's telephony.

Himachal Futuristic's bids had created a furore about who would win what service area licence. Nahata led the bid in nine service areas—most of them prime markets. The nearest competitor for each of them seemed unlikely to match the price, a prerequisite to getting a second licence in the region. This would mean HFCL would be the only private player. Anyhow, Nahata who was used to quoting in exponents of competitors, seemed shaken too. Perhaps HFCL had expected to lose in some regions but had bitten off more than it could chew.

No one was keen to see HFCL win all of those licences. So, the Department of Telecommunications announced some new conditions and a list of licence winners after what would eventually be challenged as manipulation of the process.

A new diktat from the Department of Telecom said that a bidder could win licences in at most three service areas. Himachal Futuristic was given a choice among the nine areas where it had emerged as the highest bidder. The company was smart to pick regions where its bid seemed less out of whack compared to the competition.

Himachal Futuristic net outflow after the selection was merely Rs 10,000 crore for access to Delhi, Haryana and Uttar Pradesh West. If the government had chosen to select its highest bids HFCL's bill would have been closer to Rs 45,000 crore.

The stakes were high and a precedent of questioning the affiliation between Sukh Ram and Himachal Futuristic already existed. This was enough grounds for an upheaval in Rajya Sabha or Upper House of Parliament on 6 December 1995.[1]

Sukh Ram: We are looking to finalize licence allocation by 15 January. I had reassured the house that I would not allow for private monopoly, so the number of licences has been limited to three. We gave an option to bidders to select which final three circles they wanted. If we had imposed our choice, there was a risk that they would take just one and leave the others. That would be bad for the government.

Mahajan: It (the rule about limiting licences to three circles) isn't written anywhere. HFCL (Himachal Futuristic Communications Limited) should be given the three it has bid highest. For one circle, HFCL has bid Rs 15,000 crore while Birla AT&T has bid Rs 11,000 crore but for its next highest circle, it has bid five times the amount of AT&T. Under the guise of preventing monopoly, you are saving HFCL . . . This is a scam of Rs 1,00,000 crore!

Digvijay Singh: It is a scam. It is a loss of Rs 20,000 crore for the government!

Sukh Ram: Scamsters can only see scams everywhere!

Digvijay Singh: There must be an enquiry.

Sukh Ram: We have followed uniform guidelines for all bidders. I promised there would be no monopoly. If I gave licence to one company for nine circles we would take the monopoly from the Department of Telecom to the private sector. This is not a question of money.

Mahajan: Why did you allow such bidding?

Nilotpal Basu: There should be an enquiry!

Digvijay Singh: How will you make up for the Rs 20,000 crore loss for the government?

Sushma Swaraj: Why did you take preferred options from bidders? The licence should have been given for the highest bids.

Sukh Ram: This is the tender condition. We have gone by the rules. We had the right to do that.

Digvijay Singh: He has just confirmed enabling the theft of Rs 20,000 crore. We just heard him saying that Rs 20,000 crore of the government is gone!

Sushma Swaraj: Why did you make this decision?

This was followed by an incomprehensible uproar as ministers awakened to the possible magnitude of this event.

Overall of this, comes the emphatic voice of Sukh Ram: The capping was for all.

Drowned quickly by protests.

Jaipal Reddy and Digvijay Singh: Institute a house committee to investigate.

Jaipal Reddy: The Minister must resign![2]

The debate was once again drowned out by an uproar as the speaker requested members to maintain decorum. Not that anyone was listening. Shortly after that, the Parliament session abruptly ended, and it did not convene for three more days in protest.

Had HFCL bid too high without realizing it and was bailed out by Sukh Ram? That question disintegrated quickly into a

political debate. Vested interests egged politicians on in various
directions. The Congress Party, to which Sukh Ram belonged,
demanded that the minister remain adamant about his stance to
avoid raising further suspicion or seeming guilty. There was the
odd minister lamenting that they were not the ones to raise the
question in session because Mahajan cashed in on the opportunity.
The next three days, however, were busily spent among the Delhi
politicos as the ruling United Front coalition under Prime Minister
Deve Gowda canvassed to reverse its opponents' stance or at least
remain quiet on the matter. Eventually, that equilibrium was found.

There was no evidence against Sukh Ram at the time,
but after this furore, a corruption investigation was launched.
Politicians prompted the Delhi Science Forum to file a lawsuit
challenging the government's authority to licence telecom
services to private enterprises. The outcome of the two cases,
however, could not have been more disparate.

When the Central Bureau of Investigation (CBI) raided
Sukh Ram's residence, they found money in the mattress, which
was seized. Less than a year later, the minister was once again
central to a Parliamentary discussion.

> Nilotpal Basu: On 16 August, CBI raided the residences of
> the former communications minister, Shri Sukh Ram. There
> have been widespread reports that apart from the huge sum
> of liquid cash which has been recovered from the residences.
> CBI has also found a huge property disproportionate to his
> sources of income and the income tax filings.

A shouting competition among the House representatives
began.

> Surrinder Kumar Singla: Have you seen his income
> tax returns?

Indecipherable clamour interrupted the conversation.

Basu: Madam, I feel sorry for some of my friends on the Congress benches because . . .

'Why,' arose a chorus from across the room.

Basu: Only for some of my friends.

A clamour interrupted again and the deputy chairman urged 'Congress benches' to settle down.

S.S. Ahluwalia: Do not instigate. Otherwise, you will be in trouble.
Basu: Madam, some of the honourable members are disturbing . . .
Deputy chairman: Mr Basu, address the chair, not other members! Do not look here and there.
Basu: The honourable member interrupted me; that is why I feel sorry for him.
Deputy chairman: You do not [need to] feel sorry for anybody. You just speak.
Pranab Mukherjee. Nobody requires his sympathy.
Basu: Thank you for the advice. We were charged at a point in time that we were unnecessarily attributing malafides to a particular minister. Now, what has happened has corroborated what we had been saying over the years. All the tender procedures for the purchase of telecommunication equipment to the tune of Rs 20,000 crore, over the last four years, had been violated and flouted. So far as dealings with the Hyderabad-based company ARM are concerned. Other companies are also there such as HFCL, Shyam Telecommunications and NATALCO. I would like to

congratulate this government because the CBI, it appears,
is taking on the leads and the CBI director himself has gone
to Dubai because some hotel has been traced to his [Sukh
Ram's] son.[3]

Sukh Ram went to London for some time but was eventually
arrested and jailed for corruption. Even the incumbent Finance
Minister, Manmohan Singh, who later served two terms as
prime minister, found mention in the Sukh Ram scandal.
It would still never be clear if HFCL bid too high only to
realize later and ask the minister for a bailout. Did Sukh Ram
make policy changes to help HFCL? Or perhaps HFCL had
genuinely hoped for a monopoly. Either way, this was the first
of several occasions when the word 'scam' would be twinned
with the telecom sector. On this occasion, it formed one of the
straws that led to a BPJ-led government in 1998 which had
started with a thirteen-day stint for Atal Bihari Vajpayee as
prime minister in 1996.

* * *

The Delhi Science Forum's case in the Supreme Court
challenging the allocation of the licences was resolved far
more speedily and to the satisfaction of the Department. The
judgment was announced in February 1996, within a couple of
months of its filing.

Judges shot down key issues raised by the plaintiff, Delhi
Science Forum. The first was that the government could not
allocate licences in the interest of national security. To this,
the judges pointed out that the government was well within
its rights as per the 1885 Telegraph Act, which envisaged a
situation when the government would need to defer the right to
build telecommunications to other agencies. The order further

said that the decision to allocate licences was approved by the Parliament and it was not the place of the courts to intervene in such decision-making.

The court's role was purely to ensure that the rules were followed and bereft of corruption.

The plaintiff raised the issue of Himachal Futuristic, which had a skewed capital value in favour of its sponsors and had been favourably treated in the options it was given.

The court ruled in favour of the defendants, the DoT because submissions made by Himachal Futuristic were in line with the tender requirements. The implication was that if a sponsor expected less equity for a higher monetary contribution, this was a business agreement that did not concern the judicial body. As for favouritism, the judges said that if the rules set out by the DoT were questionable, it is the Parliament that must intervene to change them.

With that, the entire issue fizzled out. Licences were awarded to a host of applicants at exorbitant prices, fragmenting the service throughout India over many operators. Bharti received a cellular licence for Himachal Pradesh and a landline, not cellular, licence for Andhra Pradesh. Birla received licences in prime markets Gujarat and Maharashtra (excluding Mumbai). Reliance did not win any prime licences but contented itself with a cellular licence in the seven north-eastern states of India, in which the government decided to grant it licence at a nominal fee due to a lack of interest from the bidders. The Tata Group received a cellular licence for Andhra Pradesh.

No one was satisfied, but the bid amounts had run up and the companies needed to launch service within a year, so the entrepreneurs put their heads down and got to work.

17

Steering Clear of Trouble

Some companies that bid in a bet to exit quickly at a high valuation found themselves cornered. They overpaid for the licences and became over-leveraged. As a result, they were too cash-strapped to roll out services. Vendors such as Ericsson and Nokia now understood and had captured the Indian market. They were less inclined and more guarded when offering vendor credit as they had done with Bharti. The capital cost of setting up a telecom site, or tower, by 1996 had hit Rs 1 crore, and the number of towers required for long-distance deployment in the states was expected to be much higher than in the dense cities.

Licence winners soon found that foreign partners were unwilling to plug the financial gap. The waffling, assignment and reassignment of licences, as well as the tweaking of regulations mid-process made many mid-sized foreign investors cagey and afraid of the regulatory environment. The tag of 'scam' raised governance alerts in many of their home countries and they risked investigations if corruption charges were levelled against Indian partners.

Even worse, damning reports from consultancy firms like McKinsey suggested that there was no room for business growth in India's telecom sector. McKinsey said that India had reached its capacity of premium subscribers, and the state-run landline service would prevent expansion beyond a point.

The subscriber numbers seemed to validate this hypothesis. After an initial spurt in subscriber additions, business for the initial eight metro operators had plateaued. In mid-1996, a major business news fortnightly magazine wrote a detailed report on the subscribers of the eight metro operators' networks. Most of the companies had around 24,000 subscribers except for the glaring deviation of Bharti which had just clocked 11,000. The story ranked the companies based on their depth of funding and brand recognition of the parent. BPL led the chart and there was no surprise that Bharti trailed.

Seeing Bharti's name at the bottom of the list was a shocker for Sunil Mittal and the Bharti team. It did not matter that the predominant opinion, including that of the magazine, was that Sunil Mittal would be forced to sell the company to a cash-rich partner. That was not on Mittal's mind and certainly not the operating premise of Mittal's team.

It called for a huddle in the conference room of Bharti's office in Mehrauli, New Delhi. This was a farmhouse converted into an office. On one side of the office space was carved out for heads of departments, and on the other was the remaining office staff. Here, from a meeting room with one large table at the centre and a window overlooking the Qutub Minar sat the core team writing the early tenets of Airtel.

In that room, as the underdog of the industry was being rubbed into the ground by deep-pocketed competitors, the group decided to use 'the blessing of nothing'. No expectation to live up to and nothing to lose.

'Were we doing this right?' was the big question on the table. This was no longer a small company based in Ludhiana. At the same time, it was not a cash-rich entity that could spend its way to supremacy. It was critical to identify focus areas.

The team made a very important decision. Its capital would be deployed towards the product rather than branding. 'We'll please people with the product,' said Sunil Mittal.[1] For the rest, decisions taken at the company would remain as they were, growing with economic prudence.

In addition to the technology, Bharti spent even more time and effort on team building and training. Leaders were trained to foster empathy, and sales were trained not to oversell, said Anil Nayar, CEO of Bharti Airtel. In one instance, a Danish expatriate called the Bharti call centre saying she was stranded and in need of medical attention, but her mobile recharge had run out. Instead of simply crediting a sum of money to allow a call, the call centre executive, a girl from Himachal Pradesh, took the initiative to manage logistics and ensure the Dane was rushed to the hospital. These were instances that were celebrated internally and courtesies that were encouraged even among colleagues.

SFR had deigned to partner with Bharti, but having got cold feet was an unlikely partner to infuse funds, or for that matter contribute massively to the know-how of the company. Emtel, now with vested interests apart from Bharti, could offer the experience of merely a small deployment, but Mittal needed to find another partner who would not only bring money but also technology.

Meanwhile, the lines of credit from Indian banks were drying because of a thorn in Mittal's image.

Bharti Overseas Trading Company was already reeling from a CBI enquiry into its business after 1993 equities scam-accused Harshad Mehta had named Sunil Mittal as the one who had introduced him to Congress leader Rajiv Gandhi. After the meeting with Gandhi and his assassination in 1991, Mehta maintained a relationship with the Congress Party. He met with Prime Minister Narasimha Rao, shortly before Mehta's equity market manipulation was unravelled. The banks were under fire over the lack of scrutiny and excess trust when lending to Mehta. They feared any association with the Harshad Mehta scandal, as the CBI was still formulating its charges and could rope any official in. Sunil Mittal's public outing with Mehta made bankers wary of the rub-off effect of lending to Mittal's businesses.

The CBI eventually charged Bharti Overseas a fine of around Rs 53 million (Rs 5.3 crore) for flouting import rules, naming Rajan Mittal personally in the case. The Mittals suspected that the equity case was fostered by motivated competitors, but the proof was scarce and pointless. The financial implication was small, but the social toll from the CBI enquiry was much higher.

When Sunil Mittal went to the banks to get the required ten-year guarantee against the licence payments for Himachal Pradesh cellular licence, which he won in the 1996 allocation, banks resisted approving it beyond the three-year mark. The initial request made to the Bank of Baroda fell through. Eventually, it was the State Bank of India, which had some history and familiarity with Bharti Telecom, the phone manufacturing unit with Siemens. SBI stepped up so Bharti could complete its paperwork to get its second licence.

Sunil Mittal knew he needed a sponsor to remain in the telecom race. It came as a big relief then when Italy's Telecom Italia showed interest in Airtel just a few months later. 'It was not love at first sight for them,' recalls an insider.

The fiasco with fixed-line licence bidding had also left several interested foreign investors groping for a reliable partner. Among them were Italy's STET and the UK's British Telecom (BT).

Telecom Italia, under STET Group led by Biagio Agnes, was due to sign a deal with Himachal Futuristic, the Mahendra

Nahata-led consortium that also included an Israeli technology company, Bezeq. An industry insider recalls that Nahata had introduced STET's team and Sunil Mittal ahead of the 1995 bids for telecom licences. Bharti was not considered a competitor for companies bidding to get landline services. At the time, it may even have been considered synergistic as a player that could be acquired.

In the end, however, Nahata's consortium was pushed out of the race, but STET still wanted entry into India's telecom market. The Italian company eventually redirected its plans to partner Himachal Futuristic to land as a backer for Bharti's bid for cellular licences in Himachal Pradesh.

Similarly, British Telecom had partnered with the Mahindra and Mahindra Group, an established business house in Mumbai, known primarily for tractors and heavy vehicles. That partnership eventually morphed into a technology outsourcing company—Tech Mahindra. However, for the telecom business, M&M had missed securing the telecom licence that BT was interested in. BT's preferred option was to stay in Mumbai, India's most lucrative market. A version of the story goes that BT sought access to network switches to validate the subscriber and traffic recorded in diligence documents. BPL declined to open up while Bharti agreed to reveal its network. That tipped the odds in Bharti's favour.

The Delhi service area was seen as less prestigious than Mumbai, but Bharti came to own it. The players in Mumbai—Max and BPL—had already secured international backers and thus negotiated from a position of power. For BT, Bharti was a company willing to pare with a bigger chunk of equity.

Armed with interest from both European telecom firms, Sunil Mittal did something few Indian entrepreneurs of his time did. He addressed a meeting of department heads at Bharti's Mehrauli office.

Mittal asked the executives their opinions. Then he told them that in addition to opening the books, investing companies would be given access to Bharti's department heads. 'Feel free to share your views on the company and interpretations of its market dynamics,' Sunil Mittal told the team.[2] There was only one alert he raised and emphasized: any information shared with STET should be consistent with that given to BT. This set the ball rolling for an open culture that stood Bharti well in the decade that would ensue.

The diligence and evaluation teams of both Telia and BT were invited on the same dates.

The Italian operator was first to buy a 20 per cent stake in Bharti Tele-Ventures, which was a subsidiary of Bharti Telecom but held all its telecom business. The money that came in funded the launch of services in Himachal and powered an agreement with the Essar Group to provide services in Punjab—Mittal's home state. Essar held rights to the Punjab licence.

Mittal leveraged the STET relation to make representations to the Indian government. In December of 1996, for instance, Bharti organized a seminar for bureaucrats and senior politicians in the finance and telecom ministries in which the foreign trade minister of Italy and the secretary of the Ministry of Industries addressed Indian officials on their commitment to invest further in Indian telephony.

The intangible benefits soared, but money ran out fast.

Fortunately, quick at its heels came BT's offer. Adept at negotiations by now and vindicated by previous success, Mittal was in a better bargaining position, but the relation with BT was different. The British operator was keen to invest in the parent company, although at the moment it made little difference. It also requested to nominate some key executives to keep a closer tab on the ground. Where conventional entrepreneurs may have been bound by ego, Sunil Mittal used this as an opportunity to increase management depth at BT's expense. The discussion was about how much ground to give and what we expected in return, recalls a former department head at Bharti.[3] BT repatriated a financial officer who would work under Akhil Gupta, a chartered accountant who had come to be known as the fourth Mittal brother, and a technology head, a department that had so far not been entirely carved out at Bharti.

Sir Iain Vallance, chairman of BT said, 'Close cultural and historical links between India and the UK make our relationship with India special for BT. India is a key market for BT as it is one of the largest emerging markets for telecom services.'

This was a relationship of equals. The first two officers deputed by British Telecom struggled to enmesh with the entrepreneurial culture of Bharti. 'They worked nine-to-five and focussed more on reporting back to headquarters than contributing within the organisation,' said an executive. When the feedback was shared with BT, the investor was sympathetic and deputed a better-suited pair. Among them was Saravjit Singh Dhillon in the finance department. He integrated like one of their own and stayed on at Bharti even after BT exited its investment.

The corporatization of Bharti in the face of an overall failing industry highlighted the organization in global eyes. Towards the end of 1996, global investment bank Morgan Stanley invited Akhil Gupta to speak at a telecom conference about India's cellular telephony market. As Gupta presented his paper on the potential of the country, investors watched the company as an aberration from others who were reeling under licence debts.

Investors remained unconvinced of India's potential in the mobile sector. Sunil Mittal's Bharti was low on the list of companies that would survive the overall political mayhem, but it had successfully consolidated its position as one that would skirt licence cancellations that appeared to be looming for many competitors struggling with rollout requirements and licence payment deadlines.

In the lull that followed over the next couple of years, Mittal saw an opportunity outside India. In 1998, the Indian telecom business was cooling its heels amid licence pressures and regulatory uncertainty. Sunil Mittal used the window to apply for and win a licence in Seychelles. Here, Bharti received a licence for basic or landline services as well as mobile. The rollout followed by regular services mirrored Bharti's experience in India.

Part Four

18

Clip Their Wings

The Department of Telecommunications predicted that in ten years until 2007, India would have to add capacity for around twenty-three million phones. Of these, merely two million would be mobile or private sector service users. The rest would be catered to by the state operator. Around the time of this report, in mid-1996, the country had one phone for every 150 people. Calls needed to be booked in advance, and the delivery schedule moved at the behest of the local BSNL official.

The emergence of private mobile operators was shaking the Department's grip on customers. In barely a year, the cumulative subscriber base of mobile operators was touching 2,00,000. The waiting lines for landline services seemed to shrink commensurately. The Department's monopoly was certainly collapsing. It seemed imminent that either mobile callers would outstrip the state-run services, or that the Department's offering would need a serious overhaul to serve more demanding customers.

Subservient to customers? Never. In self-preservation mode, the DoT did something that would fragment it.

The Department retaliated with an increase in pricing for mobile users. A Public Switched Telephone Network (PSTN), or landline-to-landline call, cost Rs 1.4 per three minutes.

It included the cost of connecting and carrying the call. A new order was issued in December 1996 for rate revision of mobile callers. Under the new regime, a call to a mobile phone from a landline would cost as much as Rs 32. This was the DoT trying to dissuade landline users from calling mobile phones. It also made an outgoing call from a mobile phone unviable.

Not only was this price imposed on incoming calls from mobile phones, but the Department also levied a much higher carriage charge on long-distance calls from mobile phones. The further the distance, the higher the price. A mobile call between Mumbai and Delhi would now cost Rs 50, and one between Delhi and the US would cost Rs 90. At the contemporary exchange rate, this was equivalent to $2 for one call. The sharp price rise threatened the viability of mobile businesses.

Any appeal operators made to roll this back was routed back to Sanchar Bhavan, and the veto was guaranteed. The DoT had become the judge, jury and executioner for private operators. With the privatization of basic or fixed line services already in the doldrums, this would have been the failing of the sector altogether, except for speedy intervention from the Delhi High Court.

The Cellular Operators' Association of India (COAI), formed by the eight metro operators rushed to court. They found support from leading business houses like Tata and Reliance, which were affected by this order too. As a combine, the unit was almost as strong as the government itself.

The COAI argued vociferously against the move and against the Department being a competitor and a regulator all at the same time. The judge listened to the emerging but eminent lawyers argue and perused the piles of submissions each made and then asked a telling question: These are matters a specialist panel should be looking at. Why had one not been formulated yet?

The answer to that was tricky. The proposal to initiate a Telecom Regulatory Authority of India, or TRAI, had been languishing for almost as long as the existence of privatized cellular telephony. A new authority would dilute the powers of Sanchar Bhavan, and the political and bureaucratic will had aligned to stall it.

A parliamentarian said in 1994 that his party had 'pleaded and pleaded' for the formation of the TRAI to no avail. He then ascribed inaction to the widespread corruption within the Department.

To the judge's question, the Department reverted to the proposed but unfinished plan to initiate a quasi-judicial authority with expertise in telecom and neutrality from vested interests. As arguments proceeded, pressure increased on the Department to separate its conflicting roles as India's largest telecom service provider and regulator increased. So much so that lawyer Abhishek Singhvi, who was representing the government, turned to his own client and nudged it into conceding to form TRAI.

The case melted away quickly with two major outcomes. The first was an expeditious beginning of a three-member TRAI and the second was a complete spin-off of telephone services from the department into a company called Bharat Sanchar Nigam Ltd, or BSNL. The TRAI Bill was passed in the Lower House of Parliament in February 1997. TRAI was formed with a 'mission to create and nurture conditions for the growth of telecommunications in the country in a manner and at a pace which will enable India to play a leading role in emerging global information society'.

Work at the TRAI began in March with its first three-member panel. At a big press conference in Delhi, the three-member panel that formed the TRAI was announced to the press and industry. Justice S.S. Sodhi was appointed the panel's

chairman. Sodhi, after serving as chief justice of Allahabad
High Court, had retired only to receive a sort of superannuation
assignment as Lokpal of Punjab. The Lokpal Bill of Punjab
was revoked ending Sodhi's term in December 1996, perfectly
timed with the vacancy at the TRAI, which needed a head who
would not be bullied and held an incorruptible image. Sodhi
was joined by former Indian Administrative Services officer
B.K. Zutshi as vice chairman. The third member and telecom
specialist on the panel was the former managing director of
Mahanagar Telephone Ltd, the government telephone operator
in Mumbai and Delhi, N.S. Ramachandran, who had retired
just a day before business at TRAI began.

Sodhi's first statement at this conference was that the
TRAI would not work under the shadow of the Telecom
Department. As a measure of confidence, the first action of the
TRAI would be a hearing on the most recent charges imposed
by the Department on mobile calling. The cynics may have said,
'This is all for show, an agreement between bureaucrats will take
place behind closed doors.'

To that, Sodhi had an answer. All hearings were open, and
anyone willing to listen was welcome. The TRAI would have a
single-minded focus to resolve disputes between operators and
address consumer concerns. Arguments that had been presented
to the Department were repeated before this panel.

The industry argued that BSNL or VSNL did not incur
any additional cost to carry a mobile call over a fixed-line
call. The operators also argued that longer distances in digital
call transmission were not synonymous with higher costs. A
multifold increase in charges was a vindictive move to crush
competition.

BSNL's approach seemed shaky. It spoke of infrastructure
but with no specificity. It spoke of state funding, but companies
were building their networks. A month later, Sodhi and his

panel agreed with the private operators. The TRAI panel ruled that the increase in charges was to be reversed. In the next major order, the authority allowed companies to increase rental tariffs above Rs 156 a month, which the Department had earlier imposed.

The TRAI added that the ability to interconnect with BSNL's network was a base assumption paired with government-issued licences. Therefore, the state-run telecom company must allow other licensees to interconnect networks.

The assertion of TRAI began to change the world view on India's potential. After making a last-minute bid for state licences under a company called Koshika, Vinay Rai from the Usha Group travelled to Geneva for a conference. Rai had won licences in the populous but less developed regions of Uttar Pradesh and Bihar. The morale of Indian mobile operators and bidders was low. The importance accorded to the mobile sector was still insignificant. 'They had one junior director in charge for all of mobile,' recalls a telco founder. Despite that, global telecom companies circled seeking investment opportunities in the sector.

Rai met with the chairperson of AT&T. As they discussed the prospects of Indian telephony, the AT&T chief reassured Rai that India's population would salvage telcos from the bleakest prospects. Partly, it vindicated Rai's decision to bid only for 'B' and 'C' class circles—as the less urbanized centres of India were graded. Partly, it told of the telco's need to reduce price and leverage scale. But how?

Rai and his team travelled to the hinterlands of Uttar Pradesh and Bihar. Parked beside farms and rural lands in these areas Rai found Mercedes cars, which were a sight for sore eyes even in the leading cities of the country. 'Forget the main cities, focus on growth,' Rai remembers telling himself. To that end, Koshika slashed call rates to as low as Rs 2.75 per call in off-peak hours when competing operators offered the same service at Rs 16. Moreover, instead of offering it as a personal service, Koshika launched public phone booths based on mobile technology. There was a significant uptake, but this was a violation of licence norms and ate right into the Department's main revenue stream.

Moreover, each call came at a cost for Rai's network and his competitors resented the aggressive, profit dilutive move. He was forced out of the COAI in the heat of the moment. Most companies were incurring large losses to the extent that by 1997, several of them were unable to pay licence fees. The Department was in no mood for mercy and decided to invoke bank guarantees for companies with defaults. Koshika and Himachal Futuristic were among these. Not only did this affect the ability of these companies to operate, but the Department also initiated proceedings to cancel licences.

Even leading names like Essar and JT Mobiles fell foul of the government regulator. Companies fell short of network rollout obligations as they deferred plans due to financial stress. A worry loomed large: Was telecom privatization a failure?

19

Complementary Revenue Streams

The Department did not have the time to evaluate the health of the private sector. It needed to compete in a market with an offering that paralleled its new competitors. Yet, as per the licence agreement, the state-run company could not offer mobile telephony.

In 1986, to improve the terrible situation of Indian telephony, the networks needed funding for sourcing materials and laying cables across the country. The DoT had at the time spun off Mahanagar Telephone Nigam, a company that ran telecommunication networks for Mumbai—India's financial capital, and Delhi—the national capital, where the service was most in demand. The capital investment required in the company was extraordinary, so the government listed the company publicly to raise money.

A better-funded MTNL grew its operations, but demand always exceeded supply . . . until the launch of mobile services in Mumbai and Delhi. It began to shrink the waiting lines for phone connections. What had been envisaged as a value-added service to landline telephones was eating into MTNL's customer base.

MTNL struggled to compete because the time and capital it took to connect each phone over a wire was several times that of offering the same service over wireless communication. Privatization or not, MTNL wanted to win in its marketplace and the only way to do so was to also go wireless. Good thing it was joined with the regulator at the hip.

The government issued licences to new fixed-line service bidders in March 1996, before the formation of the TRAI. The DoT also issued MTNL an updated Fixed-Line Service Provider (FSP) licence to offer services in Mumbai and Delhi. But MTNL wanted more.

The two licences sold for mobile services so far came along with around 10MHz in the 900MHz band, a frequency that had good propagation and was best suited for GSM technology. MTNL executives, all bureaucrats with seniority, began canvasing with the defence and broadcast ministries to release more airwaves. The defence ministry accorded the request and vacated some more airwaves towards the end of the 800MHz band. Armed with the airwaves and a competitive spirit, MTNL approached the Department of Telecommunications for a mobile licence. The Department was happy to oblige with one in October 1997.

Naturally, when mobile operators got wind of this, they rightly feared for their survival. After all, one of the licence conditions was that there would be a private duopoly in the two cities. They stirred against the Department's move. The newly formed quasi-judicial body the TRAI needed to be consulted before the government could issue such a new licence to MTNL, said the COAI.

TRAI came to the private operators' rescue. It stayed the allocation of the mobile licence awarded to MTNL. The company was rearing to launch mobile services if it could get an interim order permitting launch even as the issue was thrashed out in court. Unwavering in its pursuit, MTNL questioned TRAI's decision in the Delhi High Court.

The battle lines were drawn before Judge Usha Mehra between Additional Solicitor General C.S. Vaidyanathan and Deepankar Gupta on behalf of MTNL, while the TRAI appointed K.K. Venugopal and Gopal Subramaniam to represent them. Occasionally throwing in their hat were lawyers of mobile operators, including senior advocate V.P. Singh, arguing for BPL Mobile in favour of the TRAI.

'The idea behind the introduction of TRAI Act 1997 Act was to curtail the exclusive and arbitrary powers of the Central Government in the grant of licences,' said Singh as he chimed in with the arguments of Venugopal and Subramaniam. The TRAI's role is to guide the government, said the two, especially when it sets out to issue a new licence.

Gupta countered: 'How could an amendment to license terms for MTNL be deemed as a new licence? This is a state-operator that has existed before even the creation of the license regime.'[1]

Venugopal stepped in and rebutted that MTNL was never a wireless operator. In fact, there was no wireless operator until the government allocated licences. So, this new permission for MTNL to offer mobile services must be deemed as new.

Vaidyanathan aimed at higher ground. The government is the licensor, while TRAI is merely a consultant. The government supersedes TRAI and while the opinion may be desired, it is not imperative.

The to and fro came at a high time cost. The operators refused to take cognisance of MTNL's mobile licence. The case lingered in court.

MTNL continued to canvas its options. It discovered a newer wireless technology, CDMA. The technology had limited deployments, primarily in the US, and the receiving instrument was large, like a fixed-line phone. Qualcomm the maker of this technology looking to expand its royalty collection by getting in on the Indian action. So far it had been left out because of India's GSM selection. The infrastructure services unit of the American technology firm jumped at MTNL's interest to demonstrate higher spectral efficiency and lower cost of CDMA deployment than GSM. The only catch was that the consumer was tied into a single CDMA device, unlike GSM, in which a SIM card could be plugged out of one instrument and put into another.

The state-owned operator had found its peg. It went on to convince both operators and the government that a CDMA launch, with a short-range wireless broadcast, could not be deemed as mobile service. Yet, it addressed the high cost and in some cases, logistical problems MTNL faced in laying cables to provide phone connections. As such, it would be able to reach consumers as quickly as mobile service operators, preventing users from adopting mobile technology as a means to cut short the waiting time to get a landline. The service was called Wireless in Local Loop (WLL) technology.

The day 17 May 1997 was a unique World Telecommunications Day celebration for both MTNL and Qualcomm. 'We are pleased that the DoT and MTNL have launched the first CDMA digital system in India, introducing state-of-the-art technology to this dynamic marketplace and allowing Indian consumers to benefit from CDMA's many advantages,' said Marshall Towe, regional vice president for operations in Asia for Qualcomm's Wireless Infrastructure Products Division. 'With Qualcomm's network equipment, fixed telephones and portable handsets, MTNL's customers will experience improved levels of service, including exceptional voice quality and greater call security. MTNL and other Indian operators who introduce CDMA service to India will benefit from reliable systems, decreased maintenance and operational costs, and high-capacity systems that can keep up with subscriber demand.'[2]

Portable handsets? Other Indian operators? Incumbents were worried. So were their investors. At a meeting between the COAI and the DoT in March 1998, the industry recorded its dissent even as litigation endured.

There is no provision for WLL in the licence conditions of a Fixed Service Provider, said the COAI. MTNL's lawyers drew attention to a clause that would allow 'limited mobility', which is how it termed its CDMA offering. The elite were looking at this solution potentially to use as car phones. It was a large instrument, but calls were clearer and more reliable.

By July 1998, the Delhi High Court was ready with a verdict. It ruled squarely in favour of MTNL, vacating the interim order the TRAI had passed and allowing mobile services by the government-owned entity.

Mobile operators challenged it in a higher court but the competition from MTNL mounted even as they waited. Private operators also had problems brewing on the financial front. The licence fee burdens were becoming unsustainable. In an effort to limit competition private players sought to restrict the range of a WLL phone to 100 metres, along with a written reassurance from MTNL that it would not issue small or mobile handsets.

Meanwhile, two deep-pocketed players began to toy with the idea that 'if you can't beat them, join them'.

20

Reliance Changes Direction

Arun Sur was an Indian civil servant at the DoT when he was deputed to the United Arab Emirates. Here, he got an opportunity that would have tempted any engineer—to turn an analogue telecom system into a digital one. It came from the local telecom operator, Etisalat. As an engineer at heart, Sur could not refuse and was therefore committed to living in Dubai as he took on the role.

Over the years, new technology and dynamic changes kept Sur on his toes. In 1993, Etisalat crowned him head engineer and assigned him the project to implement a GSM system for its mobile services. Three years passed, the project was completed, and Sur began to feel restless and a little homesick. Then, one day he received a meeting request from Reliance's telecom chief executive officer, Akhil Gupta, who had been introduced to him by a telecom equipment vendor.

Gupta was negotiating with Motorola and Ericsson, both bidding as vendors to start Reliance's network in the seven service areas it had won licences.

He and Sur met in Abu Dhabi. Here, Gupta presented the lure of an initial opportunity to connect the eastern part of India over GSM service. For Sur, this was all well but there was little to choose between being a two-hour flight away from home in

Mumbai or Abu Dhabi. Both Gupta and Sur trod on eggshells. Could Reliance's operation be headquartered in Kolkata? It was not a deal breaker. So saying, the two agreed that Sur would meet the Ambanis for more.

In Mumbai, Sur was greeted by Dhirubhai Ambani and his son Anil Ambani. After some pleasantries and a traditional welcome Sur expressed that if he joined, he preferred to be based in Kolkata. Gupta had already alerted the younger Ambani and recommended that Reliance acquiesce to this request. Anil Ambani had mulled it over. Given the licences, most of the project was going to be in the North-east, so staying close to the business in Kolkata could work.

With an initial outlay of about $100 million, the company began operations. At the close of every day, Anil would receive a list of hurdles and approvals. At 5 a.m., he would shoot off communication to key people about things that had been dealt with and curate a checklist for the day. For a few decisions, he waited to get his elder brother Mukesh's opinion or asked one of his lieutenants to do so.

Then one day, at a joint meeting Dhirubhai Ambani told the team, 'The price of a call should be the same as a postcard.' The others were incredulous of this over-ambitious goal, but one person believed—Mukesh Ambani. His father had set seemingly impossible targets before, and he had executed them.

On one such occasion, Dhirubhai Ambani had told his son to treble the oil refining capacity of the company in just eighteen months. Questions were raised about whether this was possible, and forecasts were made on the erosive impact of such an influx of capacity. It could tank the prices of the final product disastrously for Reliance. Yet, over that din, Mukesh saw the project through, and Reliance reaped the benefits.

For the telecom team, this seems to coincide with the inflection point of Mukesh's interest in the business and Anil's involvement waned. Mukesh checked on what top executives perceived as the biggest challenge standing in the way for Reliance Telecom to become successful. It had by this stage been nearly two years since licences were awarded and reports of ailing licence buyers were peppering newspaper headlines.

Yet, unlike the others, Reliance's problem was not over-indebtedness or a lack of expansion funds. It was potential competition from mobile operators using Wireless in Local Loop. The wireless airwaves were being awarded to basic, or landline, licence holders to connect areas where laying cables was difficult. The only silver lining for GSM was the mandatory use of CDMA technology for WLL. Where others saw a threat, Mukesh saw an opportunity.

The engineer in Mukesh Ambani set out to find the best way forward for the telecom business. As he dug deeper and saw more of the Western market, it seemed clear to him that the future did not lie in cellular or landline service.

The political and economic commotion and confusion in the telecom sector that ensued gave Reliance the time to fully research its venture before taking any decision, not that it would have rushed into one had the environment been faster moving.

Mukesh Ambani sponsored a paper on how critical data capacity would be the differentiator for communication networks. In the search for answers, Mukesh found the world was veering towards a converged offering. The thought emerged from US-based AT&T which had adopted CDMA technology and spoke of capturing the multi-screen experience—phone, computer, television—of consumers. This approach promised scale and longevity in an emerging India where Mukesh was prepared to plunge with the massive capital expenditure.

The group set out to make a digital box—like a set-top box—that would deliver data, video, and voice to the home on a 'triple play' platform called Canopy that was also in use by

AT&T. Reliance placed an order estimated at $100 million—still considered an extremely large amount in the India of the late 1990s. The vendor partner was eager to please.

Reliance attempted to deploy the tech over its GSM network in the north-eastern states, but the outcome was unsatisfactory. Motorola at the time also promoted a move to Wireless in Local Loop.

The system developed for Reliance had two prickly points. The first was that it was a one-way system of entertainment. It could not create interactive experiences, including telephony. Second, the system was designed over CDMA technology protocol but needed a lot more spectrum than the Indian government was allocating.

Reliance did not have any licence at all to launch, but there was a sense that a wave of change in regulation was on the anvil.

'I have always believed it is important to do what is right and not important to do what I want. And when you do what is right, everybody agrees and falls in line,' said Mukesh when asked about business arguments with his brother.[1]

When it was time to decide on the key technology that would power Reliance's network, they disagreed.

Anil Ambani wanted to pursue a business in cellular services using GSM technology from the beginning. He saw the great returns early cellular licence holders made in financial markets. He watched Bharti Airtel's rise with some scepticism. In 2001, investment bankers recalled Ambani following Sunil Bharti Mittal's attempt to tap the public markets closely.

A first-generation entrepreneur from a relatively small location, growing the business from scratch and now going public—this was oddly reminiscent of Dhirubhai Ambani. Anil Ambani believed that Reliance should have been fighting on this battlefield. Unlike other operators, Reliance was not scouting for a foreign partner or funding.

The channels that Anil was interacting with forecasted the demise of CDMA and its substitution with 3G or third-generation GSM mobile technology, which adopted similar technology protocols for connecting and switching calls as CDMA. CDMA technology was led by the US, its biggest deployment by AT&T and supported by South Korea. With one eye on the public image and stock impact, Anil Ambani kept crunching the numbers for return on investment, and the picture looked dissatisfying.

Yet, Mukesh stepped in. A key competitor, Tata, was forging a start of a CDMA technology service using equipment from Lucent, which was later bought by Alcatel.

The right thing in Mukesh's opinion, for Reliance, was to adopt CDMA which the opposing lobby admitted was a more stable technology.

Jyotaindra Takkar, commonly referred to as JT, said in an interview many years later that Reliance's engineering excellence arose from its planning. 'We spend a hell of a long time in planning, planning, planning. Sometimes you go crazy asking why are we engineering and re-engineering, but what Mukesh bhai loves is to get that 80-85 per cent right and order all that material for 85 per cent in one go.'[2] That philosophy he has held fast since the beginning.

21

Tata's Dual Play

AT&T spun off its research and manufacturing business into Lucent Technologies in October 1996. Lucent comprised the coveted Bell Labs that has been at the forefront of telecom research for several generations. Ratan Tata, who was already toying with a manufacturing partnership with Bell Labs, found an old friend at the top of Lucent. The newly demerged equipment manufacturing arm appointed Henry Schacht as its CEO during the transition. Tata had transacted with Schacht as the leader of Cummins Engines for Tata Motors, a company Ratan Tata held particularly close to his heart.

Tata Telecom was already working with AT&T manufacturing before it became Lucent, and Ratan Tata was quick to solidify an alliance with Lucent. Lucent had three entities in India, which made and sold network equipment. In January 1997, the two groups combined efforts into a joint venture that comprised Tata's equipment manufacturing facility in Bangalore and the three Lucent companies.

Lucent that championed CDMA technology, introduced the standard developed in the US and South Korea to the Tatas. Having lost out on the metro city licences of 1995, the Tata Group had a little more time to do its research. CDMA was more stable as a mobile technology than time division multiple access used in GSM. The key difference was that GSM split a second of data collection on its towers between all the callers, causing only fragments of what was said to be heard on the other end. When there were many callers, this resulted in staccato voices and call drops. CDMA, on the other hand, assigned a code to each call and transferred all the data over multiple mobile channels, delivering higher clarity and continuity in conversation.

So, when Tata bid for licences in 1996, it sought both cellular and basic service licences. In the end, it only got one state, Andhra Pradesh, but got both licences. On one it ran GSM mobile services and on the other, it launched landline services. At the time, the plan was not cast to use CDMA as a mobile technology. Tata Teleservices had two operations, viewed as synergistic for the Department. Along with the basic licence, it received airwaves for CDMA service over short distances where connectivity over cables was unavailable.

Unfortunately for the Tata Group, Schacht left Lucent in October 1997 and gave up the chairmanship of the board in February 1998. He pared his connection with Lucent, encashing all his stock options when he left the board. Lucent then entered into a gradually deteriorating spiral as competitors overtook it on its own technological foundations. For the Tata Group, this dwindled the hope for technology transfer and the India manufacturing unit was phased out.

While the Tata Group was exploring telecom, the Birla Group too was finding its feet in the sector. It had secured cellular licences in the states of Maharashtra and Gujarat—both wealthy and prime telephony markets. Moreover, AT&T was back in the Indian market and allied with Birla.

As all telecom companies ailed, both Birla AT&T and Tata paid their licence fees. When cheques from other companies were bouncing and the Department was invoking bank guarantees, these two groups stood fast on their promise even when their financial position was no better. Synergies between the two, both strategically and culturally, were clear, but it wasn't until the regulatory environment cleared up that the groups made their move.

22

Policy Decision

The survival struggle of companies unfolded in times of great political unrest. In 1996, for the third time in the history of independent India, the Indian National Congress, a dynastic political party, fell short of forming a majority government. Its loss, however, turned out to be no one's gain as a United Front formed by a mélange of much smaller outfits with arm's length support from the Congress party took office. Political partnerships were short-lived, and the government collapsed in merely two years, making way for a fresh election. In 1998, the government that succeeded was led by the Bhartiya Janata Party, but it was still a coalition. With each ally came a new set of demands and the agendas of the government shifted.

One among the list of mandates was to course correct telecom. 'All the big wigs were involved by this time,' recalls a promoter. But the industry still needed its share of canvassing. This was the golden goose that had not laid its egg yet.

Airtel had reached 1,00,000 subscribers nearly a year ago and was unable to break past that barrier. In view of rising defaults, the Department had foregone its Rs 1200 per subscriber licence charge in metro cities. To convince the government this was not a private sector ruse, a report was written under the watch of K.V. Kamath, chairman of India's largest private sector bank,

ICICI Bank. The report portrayed a bleak picture and said in its current state, the industry would not survive. This was followed by a study conducted by the Bureau of Industrial Cost and Pricing. Foreign direct investment in the sector, which had risen from a mere Rs 2 crore in 1995 to Rs 4000 crore at the start of 1998, had plateaued, and urban teledensity (number of phones per 100 people), which spurted from under 4 per cent to nearly 7 per cent was languishing.

Armed with these reports and a slew of payment defaults, the Department chairman, A.V. Gokak, approached the minister in September 1998.

His representation was thus: The sector was in free fall and projections made at the time of bids were clearly too optimistic. Big businesses endorsed and reinforced the message Gokak was passing.

The reasons included: the demographic did not pan out as expected; the Indian middle class, which was pegged as the most prolific user of the service, still treated the phone as a luxury expense and even among landline users, many paid basic rentals but made few calls and therefore contributed limited call income. In the case of private telecom companies, lower rentals were a grading criterion and came with a lock-in price of just Rs 156 a month, so companies could not increase rentals to offset losses.

The network rollout conditions were another hurdle for companies. Even for the state-run company 80 per cent of the revenue came from 20 per cent of customers. The figure for mobile operators was even more skewed. The equation balanced itself out partly for Mumbai and Delhi, but even Kolkata and Chennai did not see an inflow of users as expected. In states with greater expanses and population, paying customers were limited to one or two major cities and the cost of deploying a network across the remaining space was capital-intensive with limited returns.

Gokak did not mention the brewing concerns over network interconnectivity or the piling disputes. Since incoming calls were also charged on mobile phones, wrong numbers remained a common occurrence. Sales calls were on the rise, and many subscribers disputed bills, leading to massive bad debts in the books of telecom companies and undoubtedly a cash crunch.

Perhaps financing was the answer. Gokak represented to the government that the industry should be allowed to collateralize its licence to raise funds. Emanating from this, a lender should be allowed to acquire the licence like any other mortgaged asset. The telecom already bore 'infrastructure' status. By extension, enabling such finance made logical sense.

'A resolution must be found to revive the sector,' Gokak told rule-makers. A new and more comprehensive regulation was due. However, a backlash was to be expected if licence conditions were changed, Gokak warned. For starters, those who bid but did not win could litigate if, two years after the fact, rules were modified. A possible solution to that was to allow bidders to buy troubled companies along with licences. As a state official, Gokak's recommendations could not overlook the angst the rising competition was creating in the ranks of BSNL and MTNL. He also suggested including a third licence across India for the state operator to maintain competitive pressure on private companies.

Much to the industry's relief, the new administration was listening. In fact, it was doing more than listening. Prime Minister Atal Bihari Vajpayee, who took office for 13 days in 1996 and then again from 1998 to 2004, decided to oversee matters himself. It helped that mobile phones had, by this time, taken off around the world. India was trying to position itself on the world stage of technology. Software had become a pillar for export income and telecom infrastructure promised to be another tipping point. Telecom also found its day in the sun as it rose to the second contributor to secure foreign funds after the fuel sector. The opposition wanted to score a win. Manmohan Singh, an opposition leader who later went on to serve as prime minister, raised a question in Parliament as to why this inflow in the telecom sector had stagnated.

Industry participants recall the Vajpayee government truly supporting privatization and foreign investment. Not long after, the PM announced the need to revisit the National Telecom Policy, which was last written in 1994.

Jaswant Singh took the chairmanship of a sub-panel— 'Group on Telecom'—created under a newly formed panel for infrastructure reform. The overarching infrastructure panel comprised industry representation by leaders including Ratan Tata. Likewise, in the telecom one, the ministers invited four sector leaders to sit in: Sunil Mittal, Rajeev Chandrasekhar, B.K. Modi and Analjit Singh. It was a busy couple of months for the committee. The group was agile. A first draft of a recommended new regulation for the telecom sector was ready by February 1999. Then, more industry feedback was collected. Meetings were held either in a twenty-people meeting room at Sanchar Bhavan or at the planning commission's conference room, or for larger gatherings at hotels surrounding Raj Path in Delhi. Montek Singh Ahluwalia, Surendra Kulkarni, Jairam Ramesh and Somnath Chatterjee were some of the people the industry recalls finding at these meetings. There was a conspicuous absence of bureaucrats at these meetings, although MTNL unflinchingly canvassed for a mobile licence.

At least two of these meetings were chaired by Prime Minister Vajpayee himself. He opened the meetings with general comments on the need to revive the sector and then elaborated his understanding of the pain points with an emphasis on discussing resolutions the state could offer.[1] Then Vajpayee sat listening for over two hours only to ask short questions at the end. These questions were mostly rhetoric. As he asked them, he tasked ministers present individually to arrive at a solution within a week. As he closed the meeting, Vajpayee told operators and other private sector participants that for this policy to work, everyone's consensus would be needed. Vague as that may sound, what he meant was that all parties with vested interests must work together, refraining from future litigation due to political hurdles that may arise and promise that change will be accepted in spirit, not just the letter.

'There was some serious canvassing to be done and it all happened at breakneck speed,' recalls Umang Das, chief of Modi Telstra, the leading operator in Kolkata.[2] There were some murmurs of 'scam' since a new telecom policy was to be passed within months, but opposers quietened quickly, possibly because of the strength and depth of companies canvassing for change. 'The new telecom policy framework is required to facilitate India's vision of becoming an IT superpower and develop a world-class telecom infrastructure in the country,' read the purpose statement of the policy. The implementation of the National Telecom Policy of 1999, till today, is remembered as the turning point of telecom in India.

The first step was to establish a distinction between the roles of government bodies. The policy clarified that the TRAI was the governing authority on pricing and quality of telecom service. The Department of Telecom remained the licensor. The state operators, BSNL and MTNL, would function at arm's length from the DoT. They would need to pay licence fees like other private operators.

The new regulation changed the way licence fees were charged. Instead of lump-sum payments upfront per subscriber, operators now had to pay a one-time settlement along with a revenue share from future earnings. This came much to the sector's relief—it linked the industry's fate to earnings and ensured there was cash flow before they needed to pay. It also doubled the licence period from ten years and allowed for a ten-year extension on mutually agreed terms.

To maintain competitive pressure on the sector, BSNL was awarded a licence to offer cellular service as the third operator everywhere, and a fourth cellular spot was to be sold when the time was right. This significantly changed the business case of a duopoly but now was not the time for the struggling promoters to worry about that.

For fixed-line players, the policy lifted a cap on the number of licences any applicant could secure a permit. The high capital requirement of the business was a barrier enough for aspirants. Operators were happy to accept this. Any new entrant would need time and investment to catch up with incumbents.

It was only a matter of a year. Incumbents who had survived the previous couple of years were excited to further their journey under the new revenue-sharing regime.

Other aspects of this policy that seemed less important at the time. For instance, it ascribed value to spectrum, or airwave frequencies, on which mobiles would function. The policy spoke of wiser allocation of this resource. An earlier Frequency Allocation Plan from 1981 was being revisited and revised so that four operators could be accommodated across India.

It also included allocating airwaves for WLL to fixed line operators. The intent was to kick start operations in regions unconnected by cable. Yet, operators would need to pay an additional charge apart from the licence fee to get these airwaves. The amount of additional fees and their payment conditions were left to be determined by the TRAI.

Nonetheless, the most immediate change spurring on-ground deployment was that now operators could also bypass

BSNL's network to make calls. New rules said they could connect calls directly within their own network, strike deals with other private or public infrastructure owners, and even connect to long-distance carrier Videsh Sanchar Nigam Limited (VSNL) without involving BSNL. There was also a charter to allow operators to set up their own long-distance networks. The policy banned the use of voice over the Internet (VoIP) but opened up the option for private players to start offering Internet which till then was restricted to VSNL.

The state-run communications company, VSNL, still maintained a monopoly over international traffic, both voice and data. Once again, it was not a leading concern for the sector and players chose their battles. As long as liberalization of domestic infrastructure was on the cards, they chose to let international monopoly remain unchallenged. It laid the foundation for the eventual divestment of VSNL and for a battle of supremacy on account of interconnect.

23

Call Incomplete

'*Is* route *ki sabhi line vyast hai. Kripiya thodi der baad call karein* [All lines on this route are busy, please call again later].'

There may have been a larger number of private phones, but BSNL was about to teach the new operators a trick that would prove handy to some a decade and a half later. The bulk of phone calls still had to pass through BSNL's network and often terminated on one of its landlines. The threatened state-run company had one more trick up its sleeve—restricting interconnect.

For a call to connect from an outgoing mobile phone to the landline, it had to travel through the BSNL port which would accept and forward it to a switch to route it correctly. Each operator has a limited number of ports to support the interconnection of calls at a given moment. These ports can be dedicated to sending calls outside the network or accepting ones coming into the network. Typically, the distribution of which function a port performs is governed by the nature of traffic on the network.

As the number of private phone connections rose, the interconnect port capacity BSNL allocated to accept calls overflowed and incomplete calls were turned back, giving the caller a 'busy line' message. Once again, this was frustrating for mobile callers and perhaps an accidentally discovered competitive trick for BSNL.

The state-run company had allocated the bulk of its capacity to calls initiated on its own network and sometimes it remained underutilized. Private operators pleaded that at least this could be redesigned to receive external network calls.

When it failed to yield results, private sector operators turned to the TRAI for help. The regulatory authority realized it could make a timely intervention because the National Telecom Policy had liberalized the laying of cabled infrastructure but interconnectedness between networks was the only way for the country to reap the benefits of the infrastructure expansion. Mindful of the DoT's sensibilities and politics, initially, the TRAI issued an advisory that all the operators should sign mutually agreeable 'interconnect agreements', adding that if they could not come to a negotiated agreement within three months, TRAI would be forced to intervene.

To help negotiations the authority issued a paper that established a link between an increased number of ports, payment structures to fund expansion, rentals, and call charges as per the licence agreement. Negotiations between operators—primarily the state-run company and private players came to nought. So, TRAI issued a mandate forcing all the players including BSNL to sign the agreement to provide capacity on ports to each other.

The rule maker had made a new rule. The industry heaved a sigh of relief. But as history bears witness, the letter and spirit of rules can often find themselves at cross purposes. Any phone that could not call BSNL's network was still useless. Private telephony was fast diluting BSNL and MTNL's stronghold and company officials were only too aware of this. If call prices and licence fees would not make private operators unviable, there were other ways.

TRAI's first verdict mandated BSNL to play nice with the new players. It may even have opened minds at the top echelons of the Department, but the true power of the company, BSNL, lay in its spoke offices. 'At the senior levels meetings were very cordial. In principle we agreed on what needed to be done,' recalls a senior executive. So hands were shaken and dotted lines were signed. And executives returned to their home states, only to sit in waiting rooms outside the local deputy general managers' cabins.

Theoretically, BSNL was obliged to give the operators what was needed. But, BSNL had not learnt customer centricity. So, from the bottom up, there was never any sense of urgency. In contrast, the private sector was counting pennies from day one because licences were rich and set to lapse in ten years. A senior executive recalls standing in long queues in the Uttar Pradesh West service area just to get an audience. In Allahabad, a conversation, loosely constructed from memory, went something like this:

Executive: Sir, we now have many more connections, but there is no capacity at the exchange for lines to connect.

BSNL Representative: Yes, yes. We also want to give you capacity but there are others also in line.

Executive: Capacity needs to be expanded.

BSNL: We have put it up for approval.

Executive: So, when do you think it will be done?

BSNL: Oh, it is hard to say. I have sent it from my desk. Now someone at HO (Head Office) will look at the proposal to approve it. Then it will go to budgeting. Then, as you know we will make a tender. We have to be fair to the manufacturers also. Then we will get the equipment.

Executive: And once the equipment is here, it will be done?

BSNL: Yes, we will work as fast as we can. We will need to wait till an engineer gets assigned to set up the equipment. And your work will be done!

The executive thanked the gentleman and left. What he had just heard was that it would take over a year to get the job done. This of course was a rare case of plain speak, generally, private operators would at best be hosted to tea, a few pleasantries would be exchanged, and then they would be sent packing.

Along with this arose the question of who would bear the cost of equipment. Who would then go on to deploy it? After the licence fees, this was going to be the next implosion point for the telecom sector.

The folks at BSNL were rightly spooked. The National Telecom Policy gave options to all operators to bypass it completely, to lay their own cables and set up their own exchanges. The access to its own network was still in BSNL's control, and it was only fair that operators should spend the years BSNL had to build its base. The industry could not afford this wait.

Operators returned to the TRAI seeking relief. Its outcome: an even greater enhancement to the earlier proposal: Calling Party Pays. This would end charges for incoming calls and the cost would be paid by the caller. Representatives at TRAI agreed that this was the eventual direction all telephony needed to head. It perhaps did not factor in that this stance would spark a power struggle between the Department and the Authority.

In September 1999, TRAI issued an order to be implemented by November. The authority fixed rates for different services, such as the cost of terminating a call on another network and that of using a network for transit of the call and said the caller would need to pay for the entire call. This meant mobile operators could reassure subscribers that they would no longer rake up a bill unless they were making phone calls, especially useful when it came to redundant sales calls. It also forced BSNL, which offered lower call rates to its subscribers to increase them, particularly if the call was made to a mobile phone—for which the termination charge was higher than a landline. Bureaucracy, unused to such mandates, was taking no orders from the authority. The panel had been established to give opinions, not orders, they said.

This was betrayal! While the beginning of the TRAI came with a bang the DoT believed that the TRAI was simply an extension of the government. The Department was not going to take this lying down. So, Mahanagar Telephone Nigam, MTNL, BSNL's counterpart in Mumbai and Delhi took to the Delhi High Court a plea that the TRAI was overstepping its mandate. In a face-off between lawyer Harish Salve on behalf of MTNL and Abhishek Manu Singhvi from the TRAI, Salve scored as the court ruled that the Authority could not instruct the government, only advise it. 'Telecommunication Interconnection Charges and Revenue Sharing (First Amendment) Regulation, 1999 (3 of 1999) issued on 17 September 1999, stands quashed,' ruled the court. TRAI officials made an exit in an 'I'll be back' moment.

In addition to quashing the TRAI recommendation, the Delhi High Court raised several lacunae in the authority of the quasi-judicial body. TRAI's mandate was to give recommendations, the bench said. As such, TRAI could not ascertain price or financials or get involved with commercial negotiations. In any case, if an operator were to challenge a TRAI order, the panel responsible for the order was also its appellate body. There was something unconstitutional about this.

In this turf war, TRAI was losing, and it seemed that the state-run operator that now also had mobile licences was going to win at the cost of private mobile players. 'Rush to a higher court,' was the knee-jerk reaction at TRAI. After all, TRAI had been set up by the government as a demonstration of fair play to private investors. Apart from a continuing need to invite investment for the country, TRAI now also had the support of some of India's largest corporate houses. Still, swaying the administrative will differed significantly from moving the political will. TRAI, which had floundered in its effectiveness since Justice Sodhi's early positioning, needed a rethink.

Despite the urge to file an appeal in a higher court, the body refrained. If it could not change the outcome, it would have to change the game. Thus, the TRAI filed for an amendment to its founding Act. It was passed quickly. By end of January 2000, the TRAI had a new form and set of powers.

Much of the Act's changes included the creation of the Telecom Disputes Settlement and Appellate Tribunal (TDSAT). This judicial panel heard appeals to TRAI's orders. It was also a faster method of addressing inter-operator disputes and customer complaints. The body had the authority to offer commercial suggestions and rewards.

Part of the amendment also differentiated the hierarchy between the Department and the TRAI. It clarified where TRAI's mandate was restricted to an advisory role and where its regulatory powers kicked in, validating once again that the licensor was the ministry. This time, however, it was clearer than before that all operators, including BSNL, would need to follow TRAI's decisions on the pricing of services. Slipped in the middle of the clarification was Clause 2, Section 11, which said TRAI was responsible for the execution of interconnections between operators.

Following this, TRAI mandated full disclosure of interconnect agreements between operators and proposed to publish the more meaningful ones—namely that of BSNL— to ensure complete transparency. Alongside this, it also revived talks of free incoming calls or CPP (Calling Party Pays).

In 2002, TRAI finally made another move. It issued a prototype interconnect agreement draft with broad commercial guidelines and mandated all operators, including BSNL, to sign slightly altered versions of this among themselves. The final negotiated terms were to be submitted to the TRAI for approval. The Authority would then publicly publish the agreement, scuttling any chance of further discretion. BSNL saw red. It once again turned to the courts.

The private sector cheered! BSNL fought this for almost a decade, but its immediate sight had turned elsewhere. As its penetration and mobile subscriber base began to rise, private operators found themselves doubly disadvantaged. A BSNL mobile user had access to calling landlines at much lower prices than the competition. Private players had to route calls through the BSNL network, so in addition to paying a charge to BSNL's mobile division for terminating a call, they had to pay a pass-through charge to BSNL's landline division.

The National Telecom Policy of 1999 allowed operators to use their own infrastructure or connect with each other without using BSNL's network as a pass-through. Although that sounded simple, building infrastructure to accommodate the heavy influx of customers would take years. The connectivity with BSNL was still an essential part of the service requirement. The industry continued to peck at the hold-ups through the TRAI, mutual agreements and gradually building infrastructure. For a large part within concentrated service areas, operators dispensed with physical infrastructure in favour of wireless technologies to connect nodes or towers. It created issues of call drops or unclear voice transmission but was more cost-effective than the alternative.

Compounding their woes was a problem with the rising awareness of the correlation between cellular transmission and health and business. Municipal bodies, local authorities and property owners had all wizened up. Between the Department of Telecommunications, the local government, municipal body and rent agreements, promoters of mobile companies vaguely recall needing between eighty and 100 permissions to set up one telecom tower from which a signal could be emitted. Laying cables to connect them was an even longer saga. Nevertheless, leaders in the telecom space recognized that owning cables to connect the network was a means to future-proof the business from uncertainty.

Bharti chose a path to set up a cable alliance as it deployed long-distance infrastructure slowly. Reliance and Tata pinned their eyes on VSNL, the owner of India's long-distance cable network and the point of interconnect from international operators.

24

Backhaul Becomes Private

'I think the privatization of VSNL was a really hotly contested one. The Tatas, I think, won by just Rs 90 crore in a bid of about Rs 1,400 crore. That established our credibility because this is the first instance in which even Reliance could not find out what was happening!'[1] former telecom minister Arun Shourie reminisced of a time when the telecom vortex drew him in.

The Vajpayee government faced all the same problems as its predecessors and needed to raise finances. The move to sell stakes in state-owned companies had been put in place since 1991, but its success had been limited. Unlike Western economies that had chosen to privatize at an early stage, the Indian political class was hesitant to hand over control to private businesses. The decision to do so at this late stage resulted in naming the process 'disinvestment'. The proposal was to start by selling small stakes in state-run businesses. In the last decade of the millennium, the companies raised finances by overseas listing of shares through global depositary receipts or GDRs. VSNL was one such company.

In the 2000s, the situation needed to change. The government created a new arm, the 'Department of Disinvestment' under the finance ministry, only to shortly thereafter elevate the unit to an independent ministry. Minister Arun Shourie was put in charge of it because of his understated, crystal-clear articulation which could draw investors. Working with him on disinvestment on the bureaucratic side was IAS officer Pradip Baijal.

The policies published by this duo mimicked global privatization more than its predecessors, primarily because the new plans involved dissolving monopolies under trade agreements and allowing the private sector some autonomy. The policy proposal was geared to unlocking development on the ground while simultaneously lowering the government's cost burden to do so. Shourie and Baijal were on a short timeline to conclude disinvestments. Repeated messaging in annual budget speeches about its imminence and ire from the opposition on its delay, pressed for action before it could be stymied.

Among the companies on the anvil was VSNL. It comprised the national long-distance cables running across state lines throughout the country. They were largely used by BSNL and MTNL to route long-distance traffic. VSNL also had a monopoly over international connectivity landing in India. As such the company had agreements with 240 territories for landing traffic into India and porting it out for international calls and internet connectivity. This, therefore, was the only company that could connect India to the world over the phone and the Internet.

In 1994, when India signed the General Agreement of Trade of Services, VSNL's monopoly was in violation. The government placed a sunset clause on VSNL's monopoly in ten years, set to conclude on 31 March 2004. In view of the 1999 National Telecom Policy, the government also moved the end of VSNL's monopoly up to March 2002, because it was liberating the laying of national long-distance infrastructure as part of the 1999 policy.

VSNL was mammoth. In addition to its massive infrastructure, it owned over 1400 acres of land and a cash reserve of over Rs 4600 crore. Bidding was not for the faint of heart. On the block was 25 per cent of the company out of the government's 53 per cent stake, which would trigger a mandatory open offer from the buyer to mop up 20 per cent from retail shareholders, a portion of which was VSNL's employees. Since VSNL's GDRs were listed on the New York Stock Exchange, the buyback was needed to comply with exchange regulations.

Stepping up to the plate were Mukesh Ambani's Reliance, Ratan Tata-led Tata Group and Sivasankaran's Sterling when bids were launched for groups to express interest by 10 April 2001. For Reliance, this plugged in nicely with the plan to launch a home and mobile solution for customers. To Tata, this would compensate for the late entry by reducing the time to market that the group had already lost in the licence jugglery of the 90s.

Modi Corp, the Kolkata-based company that won the race to the first mobile call in the country, realized it had missed a chance to get ahead in November 2001. The group went to Delhi High Court to become a late entrant in the bidding process. The Modi group argued that subsequent to the bids, VSNL had issued dividends of 1250 per cent to the tune of Rs 3918 crore and moved to hive off the land deflating VSNL's value from Rs 10,000 crore to merely Rs 3500 crore. The new valuation seemed far more palatable and biddable for Modi Corp.

The ministry opposed the challenger, as introducing a new bidder would delay the already late process. The court overruled Modi Corp and allowed bidding to proceed between the three competitors.

As telling as Shourie's comment on the government's discretion on VSNL's bidding process is, for the Tata Group, corporate espionage was a palpable threat, recalls a person familiar with the group's dealings. The biggest threat was a leak from the ministry, but there were also others within the business environment. The Tatas held a board meeting and agreed to quote Rs 185 a share for VSNL. Then, away from the crowd, Ratan Tata sensed something off. At the last minute, when it came to putting the final number on paper, Tata upped the bid to Rs 202 a share. When the bids were opened, it turned out Reliance had bid around Rs 190 a piece and had been pipped. Folklore has it, that Tata feared there was a mole in his own company. Whatever the case may be, the Tata Group was now the proud owner of VSNL, which the group later renamed Tata Communications.

The trouble with VSNL's divestment process began at its inception. In October 2001, Shourie and his team met with resisting VSNL executives and the telecom department to iron out the technical and administrative hurdles that had held the process hostage. Then, they went on to efficiently conclude the dividend issuances and finally drafted the segregation of the land.

During his run at divestment, Shourie had learnt to partner with business leaders. In states where getting a meeting with a minister spurred corrupt practices, Shourie imposed an unusual 'tax' on his visitors. This tax was mostly advice or solutions to problems with no fee. On one occasion, when Anil Ambani was visiting Shourie, the minister put forth a problem that was plaguing the bidding process for many of the companies on the block.

If the valuer was asked to fix a floor price after the opening of bids, the consultant was influenced by bid amounts because their fee was dependent on the success of the transaction. On the other hand, if the reserve price became known, bidders would limit themselves within a slim range.

Anil Ambani suggested that the process be broken down into four steps. First, the valuer should undertake the diligence process but not fix the reserve price. Second, the government should solicit bids from companies in sealed envelopes. Third, the valuer should now set a floor price. Lastly, the bids should be opened. Those below the floor price should be disqualified, and the highest bidder should win. Shourie used this methodology. 'It was a simple trick, but it worked. We would receive the bids in front of all the competitors. Everybody would sign on the other fellow's envelope at the back, cross sign it to make sure, and it would be opened only in front of them all,' Shourie said.[2] This was the process followed for VSNL.

At the start of 2002, the move to privatize VSNL was expedited. Financial bids were opened on 1 February and Tata was allocated 25 per cent in VSNL with fanfare on 13 February. It didn't take long for dissent to boil over. In barely four months, Telecommunications Minister Pramod Mahajan questioned the integrity of the transaction with the Tata Group. He accused Shourie of siding with the conglomerate to shortchange the telecommunications department, which Mahajan said had been left out in the process of selling the asset. He also raised concerns over Tata's administration of the company.

As Tata restructured alignment with Tata Teleservices, Mahajan accused the group of stripping VSNL of its cash reserves. The Tatas said they had spent around Rs 1200 crore from VSNL's reserves on buying a stake in Tata Teleservices, which would give VSNL a permanent tie-up with a telecom operator.

By the time it had gained control of the company, Tata's best clients, like Bharti, were turning competitors by laying long-distance communication cables across the country. Margins were eroding; business began to dilute. Tata Communications quickly became over-leveraged and strapped in capital expenditure, which would be its key differentiator against the competition, because the Tata Group could not infuse more equity until the gains from land separated from VSNL were not dealt to other existing shareholders. It took over a decade to get that approval from government authorities.

The Tata Group tried to appeal to the Bombay High Court to capture funds in compensation to stymie VSNL's monopoly by two years. Tata Communications argued in court that the government was liable to pay Rs 2560 crore as compensation for the two additional years of monopoly. The suit languished in court for eight years, until it was redirected to TRAI which had jurisdiction over the matter.

The Tata Communications backbone garnered some lucrative corporate clients for Tata's telecommunications service, but the company's integration with its other businesses remained elusive.

Meanwhile, Mahajan's corruption accusation, even though he was part of the ruling Bhartiya Janta Party (BJP) was bringing a bad name to the entire political regime. Shourie decided to end the matter with approval from other senior leaders. In a rather chaotic press conference for which journalists were first sent off to the Press Information Bureau (PIB) office and then recalled to Yojna Bhawan, the headquarters of the divestment ministry, Shourie, with finality, clarified that VSNL's sale was above board, and Tata was in the clear to administer the company. 'Corporate warfare,' Shourie said was bringing the government and the country a poor name. He alluded to Mahajan's messaging being on behalf of a competitor.[3] Mahajan's comments belied his pro-divestment philosophy, which lent weight to Shourie's suggestion.

In an environment of immense pressure and lobbying, Shourie and his team, led by Baijal, established themselves as incorruptible and solution-oriented. More importantly, with the respect he had built within the corporate sector, Shourie soon became the ideal fit for the telecom ministry, where Mahajan's views increasingly appeared to be leaning in favour of Reliance Industries. The incumbent operators like Bharti Airtel and Hutchison were at loggerheads with Reliance and Tata over the permission of limited mobility. There appeared to be few leaders who could successfully preside over both without accusations of corruption. Shourie had risen to the occasion and was soon reassigned to the telecommunications ministry. He took with him the trusted bureaucrat Pradip Baijal as the TRAI chief.

25

International Calling at National Rates

VSNL tied into Reliance's global vision, but its loss was not going to slow the massive onslaught it brought on market players. A UK-based global undersea cable company, Flag Telecom, declared bankruptcy in 2002. A global cable network on distress sale, which made no sense to international players as traffic had become a low-yielding commodity, shone like an opportunity at the Reliance headquarters.

In October 2003, Reliance Infocomm acquired the Nasdaq-listed Flag Telecom for around Rs 1000 crore. The company had already splurged on laying an optic fibre network across India and only needed a domestic port to land international traffic.

That was the one aspect VSNL still controlled, and the formerly state-run company was in Tata's hands. Reliance reached out to the relevant constituents in the telecom ministry. The Ambani-led company argued that the entire point of divesting VSNL was that the long haul of telecommunications would no longer be the vestige of a singular firm. Before long, Reliance received permission to create its own international landing infrastructure. Thus, the sunset of VSNL's monopoly arrived all too fast for the Tata Group.

Not to be left behind, the Tata Group, under the leadership of Kishore Chaukar, also found a distressed global undersea cable system: Tyco Global Network (TGN). Tyco International, which built TGN, had been beleaguered by employee fraud for several years after it launched the project and was all set to report a loss in 2003 when the Tata Group swooped in to secure TGN at Rs 585 crore.

Tata bought TGN for just a little more than half the amount RIL paid for Flag, but the backing of VSNL helped it secure international clients bringing data traffic into India quickly. The global presence opened doors for both companies to tap the Indian diaspora in foreign locations as a more profitable business that could alleviate the competitive stress on pricing that had brought Flag and TGN to the brink of bankruptcy.

Tapping the Indian diaspora was one such cash-accretive opportunity. Both Tata and Reliance decided to compete. The customer was the winner as a price war between the two diminished calling costs.

Indian students in the US and Australia, there were so many, could hardly believe the deal they were getting. Where calling home was prohibitively expensive, a Reliance calling card offered them rates in the pennies. It became a phenomenon, $1.95 per minute, so homesick youngsters could talk freely with their loved ones.

There was one key difference in the two companies' offerings. Tata calls had to terminate on another Tata number, so the recipient in India needed a Tata phone for the call to work. For the company, this meant that the call never left Tata's network. Reliance callers could call any number in India but needed, therefore, to be routed over the domestic BSNL long haul and terminated on the network that owned the recipient's number.

Overseas callers would call a local number and enter a calling pin over a voice-based Reliance system that would then over the internet route a voice-over-IP or Internet call to India. It would then land at a Reliance centre in India, which would route a traditional call to the Indian phone.

The story goes that RIL's team, including Manoj Modi, Akhil Gupta, Pankaj Pawar, B.D. Khurana and Ashish Khurana and a couple of others sat in a joint meeting after the Flag Telecom takeover, with a mere $10 million budget to create an international calling card business. Several methods were devised, distribution channels were discussed and then it came up that the best way to minimize cost would be to bypass the termination charge. The technology was easy enough. The landing international call on the Reliance port would proceed further over another Indian number. The recipient of the call would see an Indian number on its caller ID.

While domestic call termination had dropped to 30 p per minute by 2004, an international call still incurred a charge of Rs 4.50 payable to the state-run telecom companies. In this case, the calling number on the domestic network appeared to be local, so the government companies levied local rates.

They caught on a couple of months later, but who would bell the cat? Was the matter too petty to make a move against Reliance Industries?

A case was raised requiring RIL to pay a small sum. The amount was is pegged at a little under Rs 85 crore in a TDSAT submission. RIL requested the amount be settled by encashing a bank guarantee already held by the department. The TDSAT rejected it, and the issue was generally see-sawing.

Then, a little less than a year after the service was launched, the Ambani brothers fought over the company, and there was an opportunity for the administration to take action. The instigation of the move is a matter of urban legend. Some say it was done by the incumbents that were reeling from the price shock Reliance had dealt the market. Others suggest it was a poison pill started by none other than Anil Ambani to weaken the hold of Mukesh's lieutenants on the company. Yet another theory says it was one of Mukesh's loyalists who wanted to punish Anil.

Amid Anil's quitting the IPCL board and his representations of governance issues with Anand Jain, a close associate of Mukesh Ambani, came a Rs 200 crore demand notice from MTNL on Reliance Infotel. An even larger amount was levied by BSNL, and the TRAI imposed a further fine on the telecom operator. If this was not enough, the Central Bureau of Investigation opened a case, summoning the members of the RIL team meeting to ascertain culpability. It all transpired in March 2005, the month that Anand Jain, Manoj Modi, and Bharat Goenka all cleared their offices at the Dhirubhai Ambani Knowledge City, where the telecom business was headquartered. The fines totalled around Rs 560 crore, of which Reliance paid Rs 180 crore and was in court battle for the rest until it was settled.

It seemed like the buck was stopping at the company's chief executive, Akhil Gupta, until the daily newspaper *Times of India* published an email sent by Gupta to Mukesh Ambani. 'I suggest that we hand over the sponsorship (or management) . . . Of the NRI scheme to MM/BDK (Manoj Modi/B D Khurana). I have three to four weeks before we go on vacation. I would assist the new sponsors during this time,' the *Times of India* quoted the mail.

'I have heard from several sources now that MM's office is spreading rumours that (I) (Akhil Gupta) was responsible for deciding to modify the caller line identification and not pay ADC.

'As you can see from my previous email, I had opposed it and put my warning in writing.

'I do not know what the motivations might be in the current environment.

'Would you please help in stopping this unethical nonsense from spreading and set the record straight?

It is very painful to see us paying huge penalties, spoiling our name and the person responsible gets to blame on someone else. What a shame.'[1]

This may have given some reprieve to Gupta but was also an indication that among the hierarchy of friends and family that surrounded Mukesh Ambani, Gupta was the most expendable. It is also rumoured that as Gupta distanced himself from RIL, Mukesh played a part in Gupta's induction at private equity firm Blackstone, where he headed the India operations as managing director for eight years.

The CBI concluded its enquiry, and fines were paid almost synchronously with Anil Ambani taking over the telecom business as part of a split in the Reliance empire between the brothers.

26

CDMA Gets Wings

The National Telecom Policy (NTP) of 1999 paved the way for two major changes in the competitive environment for mobile operators.

It first allowed MTNL and BSNL to offer mobile services, making the state-run companies a third participant and then made room for a fourth operator slot to be auctioned. For incumbent mobile operators, this meant a rationing of spectrum or airwaves, but the capital cost for a fourth player and latecomer disadvantages were so high that operators were not too bothered.

The authority's management was also rejigged after the NTP'99, swapping Justice Sodhi's leadership with former State Bank of India chairperson M.S. Verma. Given the former judge's history, the state-run operator breathed a sigh of relief to find public sector-based technocrats at the helm of TRAI.

Verma did not distort the transparent process set by his predecessors. In the final recommendations, he incorporated inputs from public sessions held in January 2000 and one more in May 2000. However, the meetings were quickly turning into jamborees, with corporate affairs officers of telecom companies being overshadowed by representatives of politicians and fringe sector constituents such as Telecom Watchdog, a non-profit organization. It became difficult to separate the constructive from the obstructive comments.

In one outlandish suggestion, the TRAI received a recommendation that operators should share as much as 40 per cent of gross revenue as licence fees. Incumbent operators feared this was the new form of sabotage. The Cellular Operators Association of India (COAI) recommended a share of merely 3 per cent. It explained that the remaining profit was needed to expand the network and capital expenditure on infrastructure.

TRAI made its recommendation of rules to introduce a fourth player in June 2000. The industry regulator said that companies had a margin to share as much as 25 per cent and still make a 16 per cent return on investment. However, it acknowledged that all zones of India could not be deemed equal. In the case of Jammu and Kashmir for example, TRAI proposed a lower revenue share—10 per cent—while for other lucrative service areas, 17 per cent was better suited, said the recommendation.

Verma's recommendation to Shyamal Ghosh, the head of the DoT was to auction the fourth licence in service areas to the highest bidder and impose that entry fee on state-run companies. More importantly, TRAI said it would be better not to restrict the number of service areas a bidder could select. In the previous attempt in 1995, it was capped at three service areas. In the 2001 auction, for the first time, the Indian government allowed a single operator to bid across all service areas of India. To make matters simpler, TRAI recommended that the Department keep the earlier qualification criteria on financial and planning items such as net worth and rollout obligations as set out for existing operators.

However, before calling for bids for a fourth slot, TRAI asked the Department to double check it had airwaves to offer, given that India had allocated less bandwidth to mobile operators than other countries. The maximum allocated airwaves in the majority globally was a pair of 12.5MHz, while operators in India received under 7MHz in metro regions and under 5MHz in other regions.

Most of these recommendations were accepted by the Department. Spectrum for the fourth operator was made available in the 1800MHz band. It was Sunil Mittal who made the most enthusiastic play for it, and Bharti secured licences for Mumbai, Maharashtra, Gujarat, Haryana, Uttar Pradesh (West), Madhya Pradesh, Kerala and Tamil Nadu, completing its footprint across much of India. Farm equipment major, Escotel bagged licences in Uttar Pradesh (East), Rajasthan and Himachal Pradesh. As expected, most of the bids came from players who had already tested the market, such as Chandrasekhar's BPL, Ambani-led Reliance, Sivasankaran's company Sterling Cellular and Birla and AT&T. Based on the final bids for each circle, the Department arrived at an all-India licence figure of Rs 1650 crore, which would be MTNL and BSNL's cost.

Operators were content with this outcome; it did not put them at a significant disadvantage to new entrants. However, the recommendations of June 2000 did clarify the regulator's stance on fixed service providers and airwaves for CDMA. The storm was brewing, the industry knew it as players canvased under a serene surface at a furious pace.

NTP'99 included the permission to grant airwaves to fixed line providers for CDMA service. Reliance and Tata had already begun toying with the idea of using this platform to launch services. So, when it reached out to the Department this time, MTNL partnered with ABTO—Association of Basic Telecom Operators—to present its case opposite the COAI. ABTO was an industry body parallel to the COAI of operators with an interest in CDMA mobile technology. With India's two largest business houses backing the bid, it was nearly a forgone conclusion that Wireless in Local Loop (WLL) would find its way to the market.

On 9 October 2000, the DoT still led by IAS officer Shyamal Ghosh, asked for TRAI's recommendation on what operators should pay to receive the spectrum and how revenue share with the government should work.

Cellular operators hoped they would get yet another fair hearing from the regulator on the open house. This was not fair, said Bharti and the other GSM operators. The landline operators were not charged a carriage fee for long distances, they did not incur high call termination costs. A call made from a CDMA mobile instrument, which would feel like a GSM call at a fraction of the cost. A CDMA operator could thus offer calls at half the price of a GSM carrier if it passed the price benefit to customers. This would amount to a 'back door entry', they pressed on the expression and the media lapped it up. The regulator was less moved.

Giving such mobile service rights to the competition would violate the licence terms under which Bharti and its seven peers started business in metro cities, said the operators.

When it seemed like it was not working, the opposition changed tact. Available airwaves for CDMA were limited and the pricing of the service, low. This would cause a glut of customers and inadequate supply. The country would be back to where it started, with long queues and dissatisfied customers, that's why GSM operators said WLL should not become mobile technology.

TRAI sided with this counterargument. It said that as long as GSM customers are allowed to roam freely across the service area and CDMA is restricted to a shorter roaming radius, the former will be able to command a premium. The threat of price erosion for mobile service operators came more from the entry of

BSNL and a fourth competitor, concluded the regulator. A case
in point, it said, was the Tamil Nadu circle, where competition
among mobile operators had driven call rates to a similar level
as fixed-line companies without changing other cost structures.
The high cost of handsets and the likelihood that companies
would need to sponsor the instrument for customers created a
cost barrier for CDMA operators, which would keep demand
in check and make GSM services more competitive.

The regulator rejected the incumbents' argument that a
CDMA approval would contradict licence conditions because,
according to the TRAI, those original terms lapsed with the
migration to a revenue share regime under NTP 1999.

TRAI's recommendation came on a cold January day in New
Delhi. The agency said that CDMA and GSM technologies
could not be treated at par, because of their fundamental
differences and to that end, restricting mobile services within
a short-distance charging area (SDCA) or a single locality
was the way to achieve a level playing field. That said the
authority was in favour of allowing compact or mobile handsets
on CDMA technology rather than only allowing larger fixed
wireless instruments. The players had argued that this was
an older, bulkier technology with an individual device cost of
Rs 15,000 a piece compared with the mobile handset which was
Rs 6000. In the case of CDMA, telcos fronted the cost of the
instrument, but it was ultimately borne by the customer as part
of their monthly charge. 'Therefore permitting mobile handsets
on cost considerations seems in the interest of the operator and
customer,' said the TRAI note dated 8 January 2001.

The authority proposed no further entry fee for fixed
service licence holders to become eligible to receive airwaves.
It recommended that the price of spectrum be matched with
that of GSM operators. Then, to further level competition, the
TRAI proposed to reduce the revenue share charge on cellular

operators to 12 per cent, the same as CDMA players in the metro cities.

The fixed-line players had touted the low cost and spectrum efficiency of CDMA as a technology. There were at least three big claimants for the airwaves—MTNL, Tata and Reliance, so the authority recommended that only 5MHz be allocated to each player, making room for four given the available spectrum.

The mobile service operators had already objected to the TRAI recommendations and awaited a final decision on the department's acceptance of them. Thus, the news of Telecom Minister Ram Vilas Paswan's press conference on 25 January was received with a mix of scepticism and backlash.

The air was thick in the thirteenth-floor room of Sanchar Bhavan as media specialists poured in. Printouts of what was to be later circulated were still moving from one room to the next between the cabins below for approval and corrections. The minister entered the room and the announcement began, skipping the pleasantries that sometimes preceded such meetings in Delhi.

The announcement was thrilling for Reliance and Tata but not so much for Bharti and its GSM peers. It said that India would entertain an unlimited number of fixed-line players. Entry fees set for fixed line operators came to a mere Rs 497 crore across India. Contrary to TRAI's recommendation, there was no spectrum charge to receive WLL airwaves. The government also allowed CDMA operators to issue mobile handsets. The only restriction imposed on CDMA players was that there could be no handover between one SDCA and another. A spectrum usage charge was set at 2 per cent for CDMA operators with 5MHz pairs and 3.5 per cent for GSM companies that were using 6.6MHz or more.

This was great news for BSNL and MTNL. In addition to an earlier announcement that mobile operators were free to use the technology they chose and were no longer bound to GSM, the new mandate meant the company could use all its airwaves and offer complete mobility on CDMA technology.

Paswan's administration offered GSM mobile operators a lower revenue share, in line with what was expected of WLL services. This meant operators would share 12 per cent of adjusted gross revenue in the prime service areas, 10 per cent in the mid-tier zones and 8 per cent in the least revenue-generating circles. The directive also allowed GSM players to offer fixed-line instruments on their service. It softened an earlier stance to block such attempts, for instance, when it disallowed Koshika's public calling booths.

It was their worst fear come true. The operators rushed to courts but could not get a stay order to prevent CDMA operators. The companies were issued licences and the airwaves would soon follow. The biggest private sector winners, Reliance and Tata Teleservices, each received all-India permits to launch WLL services.

It was once again time for dreams to fly. Sunil Mittal soon realized the cost of deployment in the 1800MHz band, airwaves the company got as the fourth operator, was far more than the 900MHz the company had used so far. Bharti remained undeterred in its resolve to conquer the Indian map and Mittal found friends at every corner. For now, however, it was to be greeted by fierce competitors.

Mukesh Ambani was ready to take on a new project of a magnitude that would make most others cower, and Tata saw a glimmer of hope in its telecom initiatives that it believed had begun to languish.

27

RIL's Big Hungama

When Marshal Towe moved from Ericsson to Qualcomm, it was because the latter was building a team that would sell infrastructure solutions. The company held the patent for CDMA technology but was hemmed in as vendors preferred to deploy GSM networks. Towe was to head the South Asia operations for Qualcomm, a region where the largest unpenetrated market awaiting large orders was India. When MTNL scoped the market in 1997, Towe was all over it. The company was happy to process an order at cost as long as there were loud public announcements. MTNL's deployment was an unprofitable step in the right direction. It served as proof of concept for other operators to follow suit.

From where Marshall stood, in this race between technologies, Reliance did not have a choice. The 900MHz band of airwaves needed for GSM were occupied. The technology had globally expanded to 1800MHz in competition with CDMA's 800MHz band and 1900MHz band. So, the Ambanis were destined to pay Qualcomm but not without breaking a sweat among its vendors.

The negotiations started with an easy waltz. A warm welcome over dinner in a family setting at the Ambani's palatial residence near Mumbai's seafront. From white-gloved waiters to royal silverware, every detail was curated carefully. Amid this, Towe and the Qualcomm co-founder and chairman, Dr Irwin M. Jacobs, discussed Reliance's telecom vision.

Over a period, Mukesh Ambani developed a deeper tech bond with Dr Jacobs, but at the turn of the millennium, the unveiling over dinner was simply of a grandiose vision. The licence was yet to be won, and the permission, as per current regulations, would be restricted to local loops, but over dinner, Dr Jacobs and the Ambanis, led by Anil in this conversation, discussed a full-scale wireless solution. They didn't seem too concerned about how it would be achieved, or what the technology was, it was just a wish list of all the aspects the network should deliver. Towe found comfort in the accord between the industrialists and Dr Jacobs. It was a sort of safety net in case negotiations went south and Reliance considered placing an order with a competitor.

The next phase was nothing like this one. It was the negotiation. Led by Mukesh's classmate and colleague Manoj Modi, the bidding process was nothing short of a military exercise. Fortunately for Towe, Qualcomm sold the infrastructure division to Ericsson in mid-1999 so it didn't matter whose service Reliance bought. A ten-member team from Qualcomm was appointed to design and plan Reliance's network. Then, Towe oversaw the bids as equipment vendors, Lucent, Motorola and Ericsson battled it out. It was less intimidating to be a consultant technology partner than a maker and implementation partner.

The vendor representatives were ushered into separate rooms on the same floor. They were invited to begin negotiations in the evening hours, around seven-ish and the meeting began fashionably late—by an hour or so. Then, as if by round robin, Modi entered the rooms one at a time, pressing for better technology specifications, wider coverage, larger capacities, and discounted pricing.

At the volume of business he was offering, it would make sense to manufacture locally, argued Modi. The raw material cost of a microchip was nothing, he exclaimed, a few grams of metal and a bunch of sand! So why the premium pricing, he wanted a deeper discount. It was 'brutal', recalls Towe.[1] These meetings ran into the wee hours of the morning—2 a.m., 3 a.m., the executives watched the hours go by as they were pitted against each others' proposals.

Finally, Reliance struck a balance between a larger order to Lucent and a portion to Ericsson. Meanwhile, RIL received approval to launch Wireless in-Local Loop services.

Mukesh Ambani's team, led by Manoj Modi, spearheaded the backend. RIL furiously began laying optic fibre cables across the country. When competitors abandoned landline projects because the cost of laying cable to homes seemed unviable and senseless, given wireless could achieve that end, Reliance Industries went to work on laying 6,00,000 kilometres of optic fibre cables around India. The group was able to lobby and secure more permissions than its peers, possibly at a lower cost than its competitors. That had more to do with Reliance's traditional persuasion capability with authorities. Mukesh Ambani planned to lay over 1,16,000 kilometres of optic fibre cables.

'Which is the best operating centre in the world?' Mukesh Ambani quizzed an executive at Tel Labs.[2] Tel Labs was a $3 billion spinoff from US-based Bell Labs, known for its advanced development of communication technology. The company had deployed one for AT&T in New Jersey, which was state of the art and up to date, replied the executive. Ambani pulled out a pocket diary and made a quick note.

Then, Mukesh promptly had another question. 'Can you arrange a visit there?' To the vendor's techie ears, this was music. When he visited the location, Mukesh had yet another surprising question: 'What will it take to build this for us?' Once he saw the value, Mukesh's decision was immediate. Work began.[3]

Sanjay Mashruwala had accompanied Mukesh Ambani to the control network operating centre in the US and was now tasked to build a parallel. Technology specialist Arun Sur stood in an open field with a big tree, explaining his idea of a curved screen in a round monitoring room, but he was incredulous that such a feat could be achieved in the timeframe of a service launch. Mashruwala's great gusto proved otherwise. Within a year, Sur was relocated from his Kolkata GSM headquarters to Mumbai, at the heart of a sparkling new CDMA network.

This was a true combined effort of the entire Ambani family. While Mashruwala took on the offices, Nita Ambani, Mukesh's wife, became involved with designing the township surrounding the telecom operator's headquarters—Dhirubhai Ambani Knowledge City (DAKC). Armed with the confidence of her father-in-law, Nita Ambani had won acclaim for her skills when she planned a township in Jamnagar, Gujarat. This was a complementary township to Reliance Industry's oil refinery. Her role started with adding a filial perspective when developing the township. She demonstrated dedication and attention to detail, standing long hours in the sun with builders and landscapers to get it right.

The Jamnagar township, meant to accommodate over 2000 families, contained a school, hospital, playgrounds, and landscaping features. Like Jamnagar, Mukesh envisaged that the telecom venture would require a dedicated task force. A township around it that could attract the best talent was the need of the hour.

The building of DAKC also fit nicely into Reliance's plan for a special economic zone in Mumbai's twin city called Navi Mumbai. This huge land parcel is situated close to the newly proposed second international airport in Mumbai. Landscaping started with a small temple and flowing gardens. Then came an artificial lake, followed by residential buildings. All designs were run past Nita Ambani, who reviewed them and approved construction.

Later, Nita Ambani was also involved in the company's branding decisions, and in public meetings, she expressed her opinions softly but definitively. Her presence in the boardroom came with some resistance, but over time, the tension eased. As the launch date neared, correspondence between Nita Ambani and Kaushik Roy, an established marketing and brand executive at RIL, increased, while the project in charge and the head of marketing strategy quit Reliance.

Nita emphasised on a campaign that captured the ethos from all corners of the country and portrayed an undivided nation.

The initial plan proposed by the Reliance team was to get celebrity endorsement, like the other telecom brands. In the midst of this frenzy of activity, Dhirubhai Ambani, the patriarch of the family and father of Mukesh and Anil Ambani suffered a fatal stroke before he could see the culmination of this effort to offer a phone call at the price of a postcard.

The face of Reliance's telecom venture came to be Dhirubhai with both Mukesh and Nita's backing. The slogan reflected that the telecom venture was Dhirubhai's dream for everyone in India. Nita had sanctioned a Samsung silver-grey flip phone to be launched in the market.

The service was launched with a call between Prime Minister Atal Bihari Vajpayee and Telecom Minister Pramod Mahajan on 28 December 2002, Dhirubhai Ambani's birth anniversary. The date found prominence over the years as a landmark when

the RIL Group readied its new announcements and initiatives.
Over the next decade, this date between Christmas and the New
Year when much of the world goes on vacation, the atmosphere
in Mumbai would be dizzy with anticipation of what Reliance
would do next.

The initial response to the mobile service offering seemed
tepid compared to the Ambanis' ambitions. Despite persistent
pressure from Manoj Modi, this handset still felt a little pricy
for the average Indian customer. Then, Mukesh Ambani came
up with a masterstroke: 'Monsoon Hungama'.

This programme offered customers a handset and two
months of free calling for a downpayment of merely Rs 501. As
the posters of 'Monsoon Hungama' went up, they netted in a
new class of users, India's massive middle class. It set the market
on fire. The programme opened on 1 July 2003 appropriately
amid Mumbai's torrential rains and overnight built serpentine
queues outside Reliance stores. The company was adding
around 40,000 customers each day!

The launch coincided with another regulatory
announcement that made mobile phones quite the rage—free
incoming or calling party pays. For the first time in India, the
TRAI mandated that the recipient of a call must not pay any
charges, along with a plan to taper the rates paid to an operator
for accepting and routing a call to a network number that
originated elsewhere.

The impact of the Reliance Phone was scathing on other
operators. Call rates had been on the decline, but they were
still hovering around Rs 3 per outgoing call and Rs 2 for
incoming calls. Suddenly, the market rate dropped below
Rs 2 for an outgoing call and collections on incoming calls fell
to merely breakeven on the termination charge of around 30
paise. Investors were concerned that Reliance would cannibalize
the entire market. Bharti's perception was the worst hit.

28

Universal Licence

Rajeev Chandrasekhar's blood was boiling. It didn't matter that he was the youngest member of Prime Minister Vajpayee's Council for Trade and Industry or that he had a special place in the heart of this government. The decision to allow WLL was wrong, and he would challenge the Union of India!

At the start of January 2001, soon after a recommendation from the TRAI appeared to endorse CDMA mobile phones, Chandrasekhar, as president of the COAI, filed a complaint with the TDSAT, the quasi-judicial tribunal that was technically equipped to deal with challenges to TRAI's decisions.

The COAI compiled a document of over 5000 pages detailing all the problems with the premise on which Reliance and Tata were being allowed to operate services.

Apart from the fact that the fixed service operators' licence was never designed for mobile offerings, there were some inherent disadvantages that the move posed for the GSM mobile operators. A CDMA mobile phone earned termination charges of a fixed line, which came at a premium because of the original BSNL agreement and paid none to mobile operators. They also did not pay termination to MTNL and BSNL. As a result, the call rates they offered were naturally lower and incoming calls could become free. There was even a case to be made to offer connections to throngs of people who would not make outgoing calls, as long as there was someone to call them. The GSM players felt not only shortchanged of exclusivity but also thrust into unfair erosive competition.

If a backdoor entry has to be allowed, at least create a level playing field, screamed the COAI application. The group had accepted higher competition when accepting the third and fourth operators in the fray, but that was on common grounds, the COAI argued.

The TDSAT's recently appointed chairman was a little moved by such submissions. Even as approvals and permissions flew in favour of the CDMA lobby, a year went by, and Tata and Reliance became ready to launch operational services. The anticipated boom in subscriptions brought the international spotlight on Indian mobility. The political power dynamic between the two lobbies polarized even further, trapping in its tug-of-war the Department and the TRAI. In this war, everything was fair game. Then on a Monday in March 2002, Justice S.C. Sen passed a succinct order that it was not the place of courts to interfere with the government's right to issue a policy.

Perhaps it was a way to extricate himself from the highly charged environment between the two lobbies, that the judgment seemed not to delve at all into any of the issues raised. It gave a green signal to launch services to the CDMA operators, and overnight queues spawned to lap up Reliance's monsoon offer.

The 'three-line order, written over a weekend', baffled and angered Chandrasekhar. He immediately rushed to the Supreme Court, only to find slim pickings among lawyers to represent him. 'We went and all the lawyers senior counsels had been hired by the ABTO guys,' said Chandrasekhar.

He found C.S. Vaidyanathan and Goolam Vahanvati, who formed the legal army of the COAI. They were facing Kirti

Raval, A.M. Singhvi and Harish Salve, who was the attorney general at the time. They argued before the Chief Justice of India G.B. Pattanaik and two peers, H.K. Sema and S.B. Sinha. The hearings were expedited. In the end, the bench came to the conclusion that the TDSAT was wrong to end the case abruptly. The apex court tossed the issue back to the TDSAT and demanded that the issue be reopened and its elements be examined.

The head judge said that the issue needed a relook with special attention to whether the government's decisions enabled a level playing field for all the constituents. Justice Sinha, while agreeing with the opinion to reexamine evidence, added that the scope of the case needed to be expanded to examine some fundamental policy changes. 'The learned TDSAT, therefore, has posed absolutely a wrong question and thus its impugned decision suffers from a misdirection in law,' wrote Sinha.

With a strongly worded direction from the Supreme Court, the COAI returned to the TDSAT. Two years had passed since the licences for wireless in the local loop were awarded. The CDMA service was operational and its experiential and technical specifications were more apparent than two years earlier. Justice Sen had retired from the bench and in his place returned Justice Wadhwa, who had once before been a dispassionate viewer in the telecom wars and was instrumental in creating the TRAI.

Arguments began with panache again as the judge listened to the telling of a strange set of coincidences that had led to the dynamic devolution of the mobile market that Chandrasekhar and his seven chief COAI members were promised in 1994.

Abhishek Singhvi labelled the GSM lobby's pleas as 'crocodile tears'. The opposition called attention to the timelines of events.

Vaidyanathan questioned the Department's 'hush hush' actions in which it passed half-accepted recommendations of the TRAI. Given the nature of changes to TRAI recommendations with respect to fees on CDMA operators, the lawyer said the Department needed a revised opinion from TRAI before implementation.

Vahanvati raised concerns that the government had flouted contract law, and that it was still bound to GSM operators by the original licence agreement, which assured controlled entry of competitors.

M Sundaram, who represented Sunil Mittal's Bharti, explained the perspective of the operator that had toyed with both mobility technologies. There is nothing like 'limited mobility', he said emphatically, arguing further that the government acknowledged that. When Bharti sought airwaves for its fixed-line operations, it was allocated codes only after it reassured the Department that it would not issue mobile instruments and use cumbersome ones instead. This appears to have been reiterated in the case of several other operators too—such as Tata Teleservices and Shyam Telelink, in the run-up to 2000.

Adding to that, advocate Gopal Jain said that the premise of allowing fixed line operators WLL services was that the cost per call on CDMA technology would come to Rs 1.20 for 180 seconds. In sharp contrast, the current metrics showed a cost of Rs 3.60 and by offering call rates at lower than their cost, Tata and Reliance were flouting anti-competitive rules. The anti-trust authorities must be summoned, he urged Justice Wadhwa.

Jain also shared rollout statistics of the Tata and Reliance networks, which not only fell below 30 per cent of what was expected but were also focussed in urban areas. Non-profit organization Kalyan jumped into the fray, raising the alarm that if the Department's intention in introducing CDMA was rural infrastructure expansion, the companies had squarely fallen short. They alleged that both companies were chasing lucrative city markets, where 85 per cent of customers were not required to roam outside a small footprint.

Kalyan was rebutted by a similar organization that claimed to foster technology in the country called Telecom Watchdog. It argued that at the time India selected GSM as a mobile technology, the alternate was still upcoming, but now both technologies were at par. As such the lines between the quality of service of one compared with the other were blurring. Besides, the geographical location that a WLL operator was restricted to under the rule of limiting movement to an SDCA was equivalent to a small district or 'taluk' which could hardly be considered roaming.

'Consumer is King', and they chose CDMA, thumped Abhishek Singhvi in court defending ABTO. Moreover, the telecom policy only contained a specific restriction on laying copper cables, wireless was never precluded as a right to fixed line operators. It is not the fault of Tata and Reliance that technology has progressed to fit all the phone features of a large device into a mobile instrument. Singhvi accused GSM operators of recommending a legal curb on technology at the expense of consumers.

The government lawyer, Kirti Rawal, made a much simpler argument. TRAI recommended accepting smaller instruments, which the DoT accepted. Since it is a policy matter, that is where it ends, he said.

As if the court battle were inadequate, at a conference of telecom operators, Union Telecom Minister Pramod Mahajan urged companies to be as innovative as Reliance. Rumour has it that AT&T's souring India adventure took a definitive turn toward an exit at this meeting. Battered from all quarters, the GSM lobby looked to Justice Wadhwa as arguments in the TDSAT closed.

Wadhwa was concerned with the presented coincidences and unusual changes in the government's stance running up to the WLL approval.

At the outset, Wadhwa's order said that the TRAI asked the wrong questions and got the wrong answers. The first question the body should have addressed was the legality of WLL, which appeared to be a falsely foregone conclusion. WLL Wadhwa said it was not built into the licence, even though Singhvi argued to that effect. Precluding copper cables was not synonymous with including all other technologies, the judge said. The service could not be treated as a value-added service for mobile operators and failed to distinguish itself at the end of the mobile customer.

By 2003, when a customer bought a Reliance CDMA phone and asked to roam, the sales agent allocated four numbers in different cities. These were usually pasted on a slip at the back of the phone. A call coming to any of those numbers would then be routed to the instrument on the number that was active at that time.

Wadhwa continued that the timing of approvals seemed odd. As soon as TRAI made the recommendation, it was followed up with a letter from Vinai Kapur, the then chairperson of CII, an industry body that rallied to convey business agenda to the government. The letter raised further doubts about the motivation for the government to change its opinion to allow mobile instruments.

The letter was a follow-up to a conversation between Kapur and the Department secretary on 25 August 2000. 'During our discussion regarding FSP's (Fixed Service Providers) being allowed to issue Handsets (in lieu of the Fixed phone) with limited mobility using WLL technology, you had opined that this should be in order,' said Kapur's letter that arrived six days after the call. His line of questioning was also endorsed by ASSOCHAM another large business lobbying body that was aligned to ABTO. Kapur pressed the secretary on an official notification to that extent. 'We would request you to please clarify the current situation so that we may advise our FSP members accordingly,' read the letter. The secretary forwarded the mail to a subordinate responsible for basic services, marking on it 'Pl Speak' indicative of a verbal instruction.

A news report filed by the *Hindustan Times* had already accurately predicted the approval process for WLL in September 2000. The facts played out exactly as per the report that quoted unnamed officials. The judge concluded that the paperwork process was undertaken after the decision rather than before it. The Department was in the process of making guidelines to approve WLL on the first day of 2001 while the TRAI recommendation only came eight days later, Wadhwa said. 'Going to TRAI was only a ritual which was in contravention of 5th proviso to Section 11 of TRAI Act,' in the final order.

Even more odd was a sudden change in the Department's acceptance of mobile instruments in WLL services. It had only been a month since the last time that the Department had actively sought reassurance from Essar, an aspiring WLL player, that it would not offer mobile devices to customers. Barely a month later, without Parliamentary approval, the licence agreement was changed.

In an order on 27 August 2003, Wadhwa said, 'In our view the note which was processed by DDG (BS) dated 3.9.2000 was motivated and did not represent the facts correctly and was recorded only after the receipt of the representations of CII and ABTO.'

The TRAI's initial recommendations concerned the fourth operator and then fixed-line operators, but neither mentioned WLL. The department followed up with a letter seeking approval. Thereafter, an opinion on WLL was sought, with a note pressing the TRAI chairperson to respond within a month.

Wadhwa's interpretation of the apologetic response from the TRAI chairperson for a delay was that he was pressure to release the note quickly. Moreover, the judge felt that there was little transparency and partial information sharing between the bodies.

Finally, the question arose of whether an SDCA (Short Distance Charging Area) was small enough to limit mobility. Wadhwa concluded that the SDCA was limiting in rural areas, but it did not apply in urban areas. All of Delhi came under a single SDCA, and Mumbai was divided into two but treated as one.

The judge concurred with Kalyan that the launch of WLL to foster service in rural areas had fallen short. Deployments demonstrated that the operators were focussing on metro areas. The operators were expected to provide over 42,000 village public telephones but had provided merely twelve. Moreover, the cost advantage was non-existent. 'Today's scenario shows that affordability is a myth and speedy roll out in rural areas is a bogey,' said the order from Wadhwa. The order revoked changes made to the fixed operators' licence agreement to include WLL services.

Wadhwa's reprimand had little effect on the final outcome. While Wadhwa headed this panel, the two other members voted in favour of keeping CDMA mobile phones as long as the cost of spectrum was identical between the two technologies. So, Reliance and Tata Teleservices were allowed to continue but would need to pay a licence fee retrospectively after TRAI ascertained the fee amount.

The bureaucracy was paralysed. From a civil servant's perspective, there were two vested (CDMA and GSM) pulling in opposite directions, both litigious and trigger-happy to raise corruption alerts, legitimate or otherwise. Any real direction would have to come from the political establishment.

At the turn of 2003 to 2004, Pramod Mahajan was moved from the telecom ministry and in his place came Arun Shourie. The journalist turned politician, Shourie had an ear to the ground and a practical approach to problem solving. The TRAI also had a new head, Pradeep Baijal. Under Shourie and Baijal, the TRAI mooted the idea of a Universal License, rather than segregation between mobile and fixed-line operators. Shourie feared the dispute between the players was detrimental to consumer interest. Migrating all operators to a common licence was the easiest workaround.

The TRAI was ready with a Universal License recommendation by 27 October 2003. Shourie preferred a simpler, one-size-fits-all approach but given the need for speed and the complexity of the situation, the newly proposed licence was called the Unified Access Service License (UASL). It had nuances that left room for interpretation.

When licenses restrict services that technology can provide, 'there is generally an attempt to breach the licensing regime', which in turn leads to higher policing and more sophisticated workarounds, explained the TRAI recommendation. The note pointed to the rerouting or call forwarding that WLL players were using. 'We are of the view that the licensing restrictions should not come in the way of technological developments as the artificial restrictions would encourage service providers to find loopholes in licensing regime and they will use technology or loopholes in networks/regulation to by-pass such restrictions,' said TRAI.

The next disruption may be caused by voice over internet protocol (VoIP), forecast the regulatory body, adding that unless it is included in the licence, this too posed litigation risk among operators. Therefore, licences need to be all-encompassing and modified to include VoIP.

The COAI objected. It called out the move as a means to legitimize Tata and Reliance's operation to a full-scale mobile operation. The TRAI however, said the restriction on the number of operators in the market was a function of how much spectrum was available and no longer a contractual agreement with mobile operators, so this objection was invalid.

TRAI opined that the market was large enough for all operators to coexist. It compared its growth curve with China and found that India was quickly headed to reach 100 million mobile users. The investment required to create the capacity would top Rs 50,000 crore and that needed all the deep pockets willing to chip in, said the regulator.

To create a level playing field TRAI said that it would equalize the entry fee for each of the operators under the Unified Access License. The regulator whetted three options. The first was to launch a fresh bidding process. It rejected this because, apart from being time-consuming, this would involve inducting a new player for which the government did not have airwaves. The second was to levy the difference between fees paid by fixed-line operators and mobile operators in 1995. The revenue-based migration in 1999 made the original licence fee calculations obsolete. That left TRAI with the third option, which was to use the amount bid by the fourth mobile operator in 2001 as the common benchmark for all. An all-India licence was valued at Rs 1650 crore.

The TRAI also flagged that Reliance had been advertising and offering mobile services using call forwarding, although it did not have a licence to do so. 'Reliance Infocomm is liable to pay the penal interest w.e.f. the date of signing its license agreement till the date of migrating to the Unified Access License Regime in addition to the entry fee paid by 4th cellular operators in respective circles,' said the official recommendation. Other similar operators, chiefly Tata, had not flouted the limitations of WLL and were allowed to migrate to the new regime without any punitive charges.[1]

Part Five

29

Bharti's India Conquest

In the trees outside Bharti's Mehrauli office nested chirping and industrious weaver birds. As Sunil Mittal and his team observed them, they likened their journey to that of this magnificent creature. 'Subliminally, perhaps, they have inspired all of us to build Bharti's network, step by step, one thread at a time, as a cohesive team, into something that is wonderful, efficient and user-friendly,' they said.[1]

Each move of Bharti's had been industrious and measured. The National Telecom Policy of 1999 had separated the men from the boys and Sunil Mittal was no longer the underdog. His ambition to launch an all-India service persisted since the very first round of selection when Bharti was awarded permission to launch in all four metro cities. Armed with strategic investors and funds, the time to move on was now.

The only other licence Bharti won was a small state, north of Delhi, Himachal Pradesh. Although its capital, Shimla, is associated with the romance of a hill station and tourist activity, its local spending capacity was lower than in many other states. Bharti made a fair go at it, launched services and won the hearts of local politicians. The company learnt how to operate outside the capital in the bargain.

In the recast auction of 1997, it then won a fixed-line licence in Madhya Pradesh. Then, there was a long gap. Political and financial turmoil disrupted progress in the sector.

For Sunil Mittal, who had spent the last two years consolidating, this was the time to move on with his ambitions. As if an invisible hand was guiding Bharti to its destination, the owners of JT Mobile checked if Airtel would be interested in buying the company. Clauses in the New Telecom Policy gave reprieve to acquirers in case their predecessors had raked up unplayable debt.

Sunil Mittal was ready to jump at the opportunity, but with what money? Mittal and private equity company Warburg Pincus collided by a stroke of fate. US-based Warburg Pincus saw the burgeoning sector and mid-sized firm Bharti, which stood out in its survival against deep-pocketed players. Charles R.(Chip) Kaye was leading Warburg's move into Asia's emerging markets that promised to deliver higher returns than Western economies. 'I distinctly remember hiring a set of consultants who told us not to do it,' recalls Kaye.[2]

Team members at the telecom company also seem to recall that consultants were unkind to Bharti in general. For the executives at Bharti, this was fodder for feeling the fire to prove their pessimism wrong.

Bharti's pitch was so convincing that it walked away with a $30 million cheque from Warburg in 1999. This was enough to start an acquisition spree beginning with JT Mobile. The private equity attracted other investors as well, such as International Finance Corporation, Asian Infrastructure Fund Group and New York Life Insurance. Warburg invested $290 million further in Bharti over the next two years. The private equity's commensurate stake rose to 19 per cent in Bharti Tele-ventures, which it encashed for $1.8 billion in 2004. Bharti executive Deepak Gulati remembers Pulak Prasad of Warburg

Pincus, who served on the company's board, saying that the investor had bought into the quality of the promoter and its management. Warburg's faith remained undeterred even when Bharti made moves in variance to the laid-out plans.

JT Mobile was held by a consortium of partners. The largest was Telia from Sweden with 26 per cent. Jasmine of Thailand owned 13 per cent. The two were foreign partners and, therefore, a little removed from the day-to-day operations of the company. Shipping and chemical group Sanmar held 20 per cent and was mostly a silent partner. Operationally, the company was led by Rajamohan Rao of United Telecom, which held 11 per cent and the Parasrampuria family acted on behalf of a UK-based investor, the RK Associates, through its company Parasrampuria Credit and Investments which held the rest of the equity.

The company had licences in Andhra Pradesh, Karnataka and Punjab. While it began deployment in the first two, it ran out of funds before starting Punjab. The uncertainty in regulation made foreign partners wary of investing any further. Moreover, the south India-based promoters understood the Andhra and Karnataka regions, but they feared Punjab would be a very different experience.

A disagreement emerged between the partners. The Ruia family-owned Essar Group was keen to acquire the Punjab licence when JT Mobile was coming close to its one year deadline which required a minimum scale of deployment as part of the licence agreement. The partners agreed to hand this over to Essar, except for PCIL. Versions on PCIL motives to block the sale vary. Some say it was because they wanted JT Mobile to make a go of deploying in Punjab, but the more popular story is that PCIL wanted to cash out from the sale disproportionately. This led to an uncomfortable exchange of letters and then litigation between the parties from 1996 onwards.

The Punjab licence was transferred to a subsidiary and farmed out to a company called Evergrowth, owned by Essar. However, a suit filed by the Parasrampuria Group cast a shadow that would haunt the company for long. The group wrote to the DoT, which led to the suspension of the licence. A clarification from Essar then ensued that its investment was not for equity but for management rights of the network in Punjab.

This tiff between domestic partners spooked the foreign investors, who wanted out. The company was bleeding cash, and there were no funds to expand or meet the licence commitments. JT Mobile first approached Rajeev Chandrasekhar's BPL Mobile for a potential buyout. BPL, as a group, had interests in Bangalore and was closer to south India than any of the other operators. Then, as if to test the market, JT Mobile's partners requested Bharti for an acquisition proposal.

Sunil Mittal and Akhil Gupta exchanged notes, crunched some numbers and moved on it fast. 'It was practically closed over a single conversation,' recalls one executive. In barely two months, after a few promoter conversations and a short diligence process, the deal was sealed. The diligence was scant because Bharti was investing in the licence. The remaining assets it knew were limited. The payout to the owners was not significant either, but all the future financial liabilities would fall on Bharti.

In December 1999, a month after the new telecommunications policy was announced, Bharti invested Rs 400 crore in JT Mobile for management control and 18 per cent equity. Clearing all dues of PCIL, over the next two years, Sunil Mittal also bought out Jasmine and Telia. Dealing with the disputed Punjab licence was not as easy.

Ironically, as the Mittals' home state, the Punjab launch was the only one in which the team recalls seeing emotion and impatience from Sunil Mittal. 'For every other investment, the foundation of the investment was cold, hard numbers,' recalls one of the team members.

Bharti took charge of the two functioning circles and focussed on their turnaround parking the issues of the Punjab licence to be sorted later. A member of the core team was deployed to take the reins. Deepak Gulati was the chosen one. Appointed as JT Mobile's chief operating officer, Gulati opened his score in April 2000 with an announcement of Rs 150 crore more investment into Bharti Mobile, as JT Mobile was renamed.[3]

All said and done, the experience of acquiring JT Mobile was a good one. While Akhil Gupta continued to battle the court and the regulator over the issue of the Punjab licence with frequent mail exchanges, dealing with the promoters was successful. More importantly, the inorganic growth catapulted Bharti into reckoning with its Mumbai-based competitors. Sunil Mittal was hungry for more!

Others were watching this transaction and beginning to develop an interest in Mittal. Next in line was a consortium led by Crompton Greaves. The service provider was Sky Cell. It was losing to competition from the RPG Group, which had captured the bulk of the Chennai market.

Sky Cell was ailing and most of its partners wanted out for different reasons. The two partners from the US, Millicom International and BellSouth, were facing troubled times in their home markets. With auctions and other capital expenditure requirements back home, the companies wanted to ditch what seemed like an unpredictable investment in favour of cash. The fourth partner in the group was DSS Enterprises, which was undergoing a succession struggle between the sons of the founders, Ajit and Satwant Singh. As a result, the company was also being pulled in multiple directions.

The most obvious buyer for the company once again was BPL Mobile, which already had service in the state of Tamil Nadu. Chennai is Tamil Nadu's capital, but since it is one of India's four metro cities, its licence was auctioned before the rest of the state. A later ruling by the Department of Telecom merged the Chennai and Tamil Nadu licences, as a result, the anticipated interest in Tamil Nadu was due to be higher than in other parts of India.

Once again, taking small incremental steps Bharti pipped BPL Mobile in acquiring the company. Chandrasekhar was distracted because he set his sight elsewhere. This acquisition was not quite as smooth as that of JT Mobile for Sunil Mittal. The company was locked in a messy court case and power struggle for several years between the Singh brothers, who wanted different things from their shares. The issue resulted in operational difficulties, such as the appointment of the chief executive, mutiny within the ranks and even delays in court filings because the staff in key positions was aligned with DSS.

Despite the setback on the last acquisition, Sunil Mittal continued his consolidation journey. His last buy was Kolkata's Spice Cell. It was perhaps the fastest deal of them all.

Modi Telstra had secured licences in Karnataka and Punjab in the second round of licence allocations. At around five years after the operator made India's first mobile phone call, Australia's Telstra wanted an exit and the team at the company believed that Kolkata's revenue opportunity was pale, compared with the investment requirement.

'Mr Modi was looking for a suitor. Sunil Mittal was up and coming. We met him jointly and hit it off well in the meeting. The deal was done in seven days,' said Umang Das, the CEO of Modi Telstra.[4] It was a straightforward 100 per cent buyout deal. Anil Nayyar took the keys from Das.

As Bharti closed this transaction, a new wave of regulations was on the way. The government was paving the way for a fourth operator, and Bharti was a top contender for any slots it was eligible to secure. The company applied for them all and received eight new licences for an equal number of service areas, including Mumbai. In these circles, it received bandwidth in the 1800MHz frequency band instead of the 900MHz band in the first round of licences. When it received the permit, Bharti had not realized the magnitude of difference between the airwaves.

30

Let's Make an Institution

'Profit and money are secondary, I need your help to build a world-class company,' said Sunil Mittal.[1] The year was 2000 and he was surrounded by the Himalayas at a plush resort near Kathmandu, Nepal.

Bharti's dream of becoming an all-India player looked imminently achievable. The Mittal brothers took top executives to an off-site meeting in Kathmandu, Nepal. This was the second such gathering in the company's history. In addition to the Mittals, Akhil Gupta, all the presidents, and circle chief executives were present.

The brothers spoke of the management as pillars of realizing the explosive expansion across India and potentially outside the country as well. They offered the management autonomy and trust. The professionals revelled in this articulation. Here was a shareholder giving a free run to executives to learn and implement best practices. Many of them remember receiving open offers to join Reliance. The salary offer started at 1.5 times what Bharti or Vodafone was offering and could go up to 2.2 times depending on how further negotiations went. 'They were also playing on our ego by offering senior designations. I remember being offered a President's role and a year later Reliance had nearly 100 presidents,' said one executive.

Some did leave, such as B.D. Khurana and Ashwini Windlass. Success at RIL tended to be hit-and-miss.

Mittal encashed goodwill at once, as he asked each one of the members present there to expand their work burden. Every member at the meeting was given one added responsibility which they took on happily. Under the restructuring of the company's management, Anil Nayyar was made president of the company's mobility services and Badri Agarwal took charge of landline services restricted to MP for the moment. The pride and excitement for those who stayed at Bharti was such that 'you were willing to do double, triple work without feeling tired', said Viresh Dayal, a team member who had worked with Sunil since the push-button venture with Siemens.

Sanjay Kapoor at BCL was made in charge of the west zone and relocated to Mumbai. The region had many recently acquired licenses such as Maharashtra, Gujarat, and Madhya Pradesh.

Veteran N. Arjun took charge of laying a national long-distance network. The teams below them too underwent some overhaul, putting those who had experienced the start-up of Delhi in key positions, each empowered to take spot decisions. Bharti was also adding management capacity as it grew. A newly inducted team member from BPL Mobile, P. Swaminathan, was handed the south zone.

With power comes responsibility and at this stage. Each head was accountable for the smallest details. 'Circle chiefs would analyse and file exact geographical coordinates each time a site was to be added along with projections of subscribers it would cater to and return on investment,' said one such executive.

Akhil Gupta's role was also expanded to spearhead acquisitions, new licence applications, and maintaining relationships with partners, including foreign investors and banks. He was designated as the company's joint managing director, alongside Rajan Mittal.

Bharti's weed-like growth needed re-channeling. As it grew
some of the personal touch began to inevitably fade. At the off-
site, the company's executives discussed the future of human
resources and corporate governance at Bharti. Mittal decided
this needed a deeper look. Upon their return, consulting firm
McKinsey was commissioned to review both the internal and
external environment for Bharti and recommend actions to best
navigate them.

An unexpected fund infusion from an Asia Pacific investor
put the jet fuel in Bharti's rocket ship.

Singtel, Singapore's sovereign telecom operator, was
looking to build an international portfolio. The company held a
near monopoly in its home market. It priced its plans high and
enjoyed a superlative operating profit margin, but the population
and, therefore, the growth potential for Singtel at home was
capped. The company explored Indonesia, the Philippines and
Australia with little success. As it quietly scouted the Indian
landscape, the company held meetings with all telecom service
providers and sought one with Bharti towards the end of
its search.

On the day Sunil Mittal was away for work and given
Singtel's intent was ambiguous, he deputed Viresh Dayal to
make the presentation. Armed with a PowerPoint file curated
by Director of Marketing Hemant Sachdev, Dayal scuttled into
a meeting room with the Singtel honchos. Dayal recollects that
Singtel's interest in the company barely took an hour and a half
to become palpable. The team leader, whom Dayal remembers
as being called Mr Sin, said he was keen to proceed without
delay. The next step would be to meet Sunil Mittal.

Singtel was already considering a potential investment in BPL
Mobile, which was led by Rajiv Chandrasekhar and apparently
outdoing its competition in capturing India's highest revenue-
generating service area. BPL Mobile had ambitious goals. It was

keenly pursuing a three-way merger deal with the Tata and Birla groups. The merger would set the entity far ahead of any other operator in India. As a result, the company was keeping its cards close to its chest. Singtel, unaware of Chandrasekhar's plans, was cautious of the secrecy.

Dayal left the Singtel team waiting in the meeting room and walked over to check if Sunil had returned from his prior engagement. He found Sunil in his office, walked in and explained the situation, requesting Mittal's appearance. Mittal went over to greet the Singtel team.

It was thus Post that the Singapore sovereign telecom operator launched a diligence exercise on Bharti. This diligence, however, was not restricted to air-conditioned offices and troves of paper records of the company. Singtel sent investigators to talk to dealers on the ground and distribution partners at the backend and test the network and signal emission sites across Andhra Pradesh and Punjab. After it came on board Singtel was 'culturally less arrogant' investor than others, said an executive.

It bought out Telecom Italia and triggered the exit also of British Telecom and New York Life Insurance.

Impressed with the transparency of the organization and its founders, the ties with Singtel deepened to include undersea cables bridging continents and landing ports from data traffic from other parts of the globe.

Singtel's follow-up investment strengthened Bharti's financial armoury, but more importantly, acted as a pre-IPO placement from a globally recognized strategic partner.

Bharti was now in a run-up to its initial public offer, a corporate fundraising method that Reliance Group's founder Dhirubhai Ambani had tapped in the late 1970s and counted as a pinnacle of business achievement. Many companies had done the same, but Bharti was the first one in the Indian telecom sector.

'Sunil was not welcomed in the Bombay club,' recalls a colleague. Many others felt the same way, including Rajeev Chandrasekhar. Misconstrued mining of Bharti's prospectus for Additional Depository Receipts (ADRs), a way for Indian companies to list stock on US exchanges, used in derogatory news reports.

The company's financial results were looking up. The brand was doing well, and the media had taken a shine to Sunil Mittal's underdog story. Yet, from the time it readied plans to launch an IPO, headlines about Bharti appeared to evoke ghosts of the past.

The prospectus for public listing in 2002 disclosed pending litigation and government action, including the CBI case against the group's former generator business. The document spanned 360 pages, but to the Delhi headquarters of Bharti, it appeared that journalists splashed only the salacious fine print.

Bankers told Bharti of Mumbai-based investor meetings in which competitors put the company down quite convincingly. There appeared to be one-on-one communication with vendor partners Siemens, Ericsson and Nokia. No one explicitly said anything to Bharti, but their payment cycles became more rigid. 'We saw a little bit of hardening, which lasted for around a year before it relaxed,' Dayal said.

News reports also emphasized the looming threat from the launch of Reliance's telecom service that could annihilate Bharti. Hemant Sachdev's team that handled brand perception was put in overdrive. A decisive approach to tap India's three main religions—worship, cricket and Bollywood—was set in motion. The company tried to secure endorsements from celebrities it saw in its likeness. Stars that had risen on the back of talent.

The most prominent of them are upcoming musical maestro A.R. Rahman and cricket sensation Sachin Tendulkar.

Both initially turned Bharti down. Rahman was producing an on-stage musical, *Bombay Dreams*, with Andrew Lloyd Webber. With much persistence, Rahman conceded to meeting the Bharti team. Sachdev was warned that Rahman had kept at bay offers from the likes of Coke, Pepsi and even big cinematic productions with directors and producers like Karan Johar and Yash Chopra. Sachdev met Rahman at his London-based studio, which was equipped with three pianos and a skylight.

In a shy manner, Rahman said that he failed to see his appeal in Bharti's advertisement given that he did not have a visual brand recall. The mobile operator was trying to transition the purpose of a mobile phone from a communication device to an entertainment platform. Rahman's music would build that bridge, which Sachdev pressed on.

When Rahman was finally convinced and proposed his fee, it exceeded Airtel's budget. Eventually, the two met midway. The artist was acutely focused on the creative product and the innovation music brought to Airtel. A shoot took place for Airtel's first television commercial in London. At Rs 5.5 crore, Airtel ran a campaign with Rahman's music composition that came to be associated with the brand Airtel for over a decade. Its signature tone became so popular that it was modified for all platforms and could even be heard in the reverse gear alert of the small family car Maruti 800.

As the company ironed out brand perceptions, the thrust of Bharti's public listing was going to rest on institutional investors rather than the retail segment. It was a first for team Bharti. To cover major destinations and investors they split into two teams. They were powered by the leading investment bankers of the time, Nimish Kampani and Hemendra Kothari.

Akhil Gupta and Anil Nayyar left for the US, while Sunil Mittal and Sanjay Kapoor took on European investors. It was a busy fortnight. Sometimes, they visited cities without checking into hotels or doing laundry. On at least one occasion, they bought shirts for the lack of clean clothes in the overnighter they carried on the frenzied trip.

The price for the listing was fixed at Rs 45 a share. The issue was fully subscribed to in five days. A banker recalls a rival saying they would bring the price down to twenty-five within the year and 4.5 shortly thereafter. The share took an unfortunate turn even sooner than that given the bang with which Reliance launched its 'Monsoon Hungama'.

'The share went down to Rs 19 from Rs 45, what we listed at—and then around Rs 11.50. That was one of my most difficult periods. We didn't have the resources at that time, we just had the raw horsepower. That's all,' recalls Sunil Mittal.[2]

When the Reliance Group entered the sector, it chafed call tariffs down to Re 1 per minute from Rs 2.49, eroding Airtel's revenue because the company was forced to match pricing.

31

Necessity Is the Mother of Invention

In 2002, RIL spearheaded a raging war against Airtel. Reliance's telecom venture set call rates at half of Airtel's, and Anil Ambani-led investor interactions were driving the Airtel stock to the ground.

The Bharti's did not end in a big celebration or party. The only ostensible rewards from the issue were Akhil Gupta's Mercedes and bonuses for some old-timers like Sachdev and Dayal.[1]

It was time for another company offsite. This time, the team was fifty-strong! They arrived in Agra with uncertainty over a fight or flight reaction to the war that had been unleashed.

Some who were in the meeting remember Sunil Mittal giving the analogy 'the tree that bends survives the storm'. The implication was that Bharti should duck the harshest wave and ready itself for re-emergence. With that came two key decisions, that revved up the audience, but only temporarily. The first was to follow the disrupter rather than challenge it. As such, the focus was to go low-key and minimize marketing expenses that had included offers to dealers and sops to new customers. The second was to double down on in-house expertise and pare the rest.

Kohli recollects that the plan was to focus on strengths and disrupt the deep-pocket telecom game. The company decided to adopt an outsourcing plan. 'What we knew was people, brand, government, and the market.'[2] The rest would be farmed away to specialists

That came with some pain but panned out rather well for the organization. Bharti decided to outsource its network, technology and call centres.

As Mittal put it, managed services were a compulsion. 'When we had two to three million customers, me and Akhil aimed for twenty-five million. There was no way we could pick up so many engineers and IT professionals. We are not their first port of call. We needed thousands of engineers.

'So, we started outsourcing some key functions. We told Ericsson, "Since you are putting up the network, you manage it yourself." We transferred 1100 of our engineers to them. We did the same with IT with IBM.'[3]

The ride was not easy. In the first two months, it did not seem like an experiment that would succeed. Ericsson's team took time to figure out what had already been deployed. Partly also because a lot of the backhaul or long-distance connectivity of calls was over wireless in India compared with wired copper or optic fibre networks elsewhere in the world. The time Ericsson spent navigating the network was time Bharti did not have because it caused network disruption, and each glitch meant a dissatisfied customer in a dog-eat-dog fight for revenue. The quickest resolution was for Ericsson to onboard the people who had deployed and managed the network thus far.

Bharti's entire teams, barring the chief technology officer of each service area, were transferred to Ericsson. They knew the nuts and bolts of the network. In an age when people were realizing the power of the Internet, and communication still tended to be analogue, the lags in feedback from on-ground executives made Airtel's circle heads feel they were losing control. There was confusion about accountability and the network suffered.

It was a turbulent time even at Ericsson where wheels were in motion for a chief executive change from Hellström to successor Carl-Henric Svanberg. As Akhil Gupta and Svanberg thrashed out reams of the outsourcing contract, they agreed to measure billing on a dollar per erlang an hourly unit of measuring traffic on a telecom network. Hereafter the upkeep of the network was left in the hands of Manoj Kohli and Bharti's chief technology officer Don Price. Transitioning to a new model was the most challenging part, communication between teams was key. It took six months for both sides to find a mutual rhythm. Kohli equated it to a tandem between jugglers, keeping all the balls in the air. 'The journey was fun,' he said.[4]

Just like Ericsson, Nokia too was Airtel's partner from its acquisitions in regions like Kolkata and West Bengal. A similar outsourcing contract was drawn up with Nokia under the leadership of Jorma Ollila. Eventually, north and south zones were given to Nokia while east and west zones were Ericsson's purview.

This was also the time when mobile consumption exploded in India. Subscriber addition was hitting millions, equivalent to the entire cellular market of a small European nation. Airtel suddenly found itself grappling with its information technology equipment and infrastructure. Having tested the outsourcing model with the network, technology came next.

The contract, however, was more involved this time. It needed a component of hardware, software and engineers—all of which would require upgrades at short intervals. Drafts of this over a thousand-page document went back and forth for six months before it was finalized. In all this while, the execution of the contract was already on its way; a bit like tying shoelaces while running!

The details on the contract document ran deep. They included aspects such as planning and governance mechanisms that set the tone for accountability. Since the companies were collecting data as they negotiated, some of the information collected on the go was turned into clauses that helped institutionalize change, rather than leaving subjective decision-making for each contemporary crop of engineers. The move began with Ashish Chowdhary, who held the first meeting with IBM. He had a short stint with Bharti in its high growth years, then went on to head technology for India at Nokia until iPhone maker Apple appointed him as its chief executive for the country.

The last in the string of outsourcing, so successfully tapped by Bharti, was the call centres or BPOs (Business Process Outsourcing). While the world was leveraging India's English-speaking youth, willing to work night shifts to support different time zones, Bharti decided to leverage it for regional language call centres. In this case, unlike networks and IT, the company decided to adopt multiple vendors who would deliver customer service. At the outset, the company hired around 50,000 agents across four vendors. The move included transferring Airtel's existing call centre operations to the outsourcing partners in the region.

Bharti pioneered outsourcing for a telecom company, reducing the expense burden on the operator. A model that the company hoped to replicate in other, similar geographies in the years to come. It definitely pleased Singtel which once again increased its equity in the company.

Apart from the advantages of reducing capital expenditure and people management, outsourcing these functions also deleveraged Bharti's profit and loss statement significantly. In the January to March quarter of 2003, the company turned its first profit. It was a small one of Rs 256 million (25.6 crore), but a big jump from the Rs 71 million (7.1 crore) loss just three months before that. A press release read: Mr Akhil Gupta, joint managing director, of Bharti Tele-Ventures said, 'We have achieved positive PAT (profit after tax), much earlier than the market expectations.'

'This has been possible despite significant pricing adjustments including the mobile-to-mobile incoming free, introduction of schemes which incorporate incoming calls free for new customers, reduction in national long-distance rates and introducing discounts on international long-distance calls,' said the release.[5]

The celebration in the finance team was heard most prominently. For the better part of the preceding year, postpaid services, which accounted for nearly 80 per cent of revenue, had been suffering. The repayment cycle for users extended as long as ninety days without interrupting services and customers ran even bigger bills in the long-time window. The bad debt needed to be stymied. Saravjit Dhillon took charge of this one. For starters, this meant a rejigging of the billing system. It was a massive overhaul, that culminated in further outsourcing. The move came before British Telecom (BT) made a complete exit from Bharti and Dhillon, who had initially come from the UK operator could reach out to it for expertise. The billing system was upgraded to chase repayment with automated reminders.[6]

Then Dhillon proposed something that raised eyebrows around the organization. He was going to reduce the collection cycle to just ten days. The good news was that being in debt in India was culturally frowned upon. The persistent chase after bills became pending was working. The hard part, which turned out great in the end, was to get buy-in from regional offices on the massive change.

Kohli recalls that the cross-functional interaction among technology, network and finance teams found new meaning as part of this initiative. They all worked together to collate data and then act on it to ensure a smoother cash flow for Bharti.

The operating profit so soon after the initial public offer marked a big event for the company.

32

BPL 'Batata'

The turn of regulation with the national telecom policy triggered swift moves by Bharti and the seismic shift in the business environment was not lost on its better-placed competitors.

Rajeev Chandrasekhar's BPL Mobile sat at the apex of telecom jewels after making the most successful run at capturing the creamy market in Mumbai. BPL Mobile had suitors lining up, but he had an audacious dream to sit at the Mumbai industrialists' elite table.

The Tata Group was keenly watching the fast-paced consolidation in the sector. It had already explored two means to foray into an all-India market. However, the group was cautious of new players, not all of whom Tata's brass believed had played fairly in securing licences and cutting the Tata Group out. The trend did not seem to change in the new environment. On more than one occasion, executives from the Tata Group opened discussions with a potential partner or seller only to find that the target company had used Tata's offer to wield a higher price elsewhere.

There was only one other player with similar pedigree and values in Tata's eye—Birla. It made sense then for the two companies to join operations in Gujarat, Maharashtra and Andhra Pradesh. Tata's foreign partner, BCE Canada, was exiting, and Tata had the means to provide that. AT&T was an old friend of the Tata Group and was happy to form an equal three-way partnership. When they announced the merger between Birla AT&T and Tata, the press lovingly called the new entity 'Batata'—meaning 'potato' in Marathi.

The Tata Group was already focused on its fixed-line rollout under Tata Teleservices, so while the group intended to maintain oversight, Tata was happy to let Birla lead the management at Batata. That said, the executives from both sides trod on eggshells to keep up good appearances and as a result, there was often confusion about final decisions.

Even then, the conglomerates agreed that consolidation was the way forward. The two Mumbai-based groups found like-minded Harsh Goenka's RPG as a willing seller. Common to similar social circles in Mumbai, Goenka was looking to pare the Madhya Pradesh licence, which was proving too capital-intensive. The operation supported around 25,000 subscribers, but with deep-pocketed player Reliance Industries making a play for the region, it seemed prudent to hand it over to a competitor of a similar size.

The sale was meant to free capital for RPG to expand penetration in Chennai, where the group had become a market leader. Tata Group officials handled the buyout transaction with RPG. After a brief discussion, the two parties agreed that Tata would acquire RPG's service licence for around Rs 400 crore. RPG's foreign partner was Vodafone, gradually retreated from the Indian market—the deal, which was to be done in two stages also offered Vodafone an exit.

One story goes that even as the papers were being drawn up, Rajeev Chandrasekhar made a counteroffer to RPG and unsuccessfully upped the price Batata was offering. The other version is that BPL Mobile reached out to RPG over a similar period but was keen to buy Madhya Pradesh and Chennai circles. The metro city was synergistic with BPL's wider Tamil Nadu state presence. Chandrasekhar said the cumulative ask was too high.[1]

Given the dynamic of cellular telephony at the time, it wouldn't have been surprising for RPG to accept the better offer. Goenka however, chose to stick to the word he had given the Tata Group over the additional cash. In exchange, of course, RPG received a quick clean transaction and gratitude from the Tata chairman, Ratan Tata.

After the transaction, Batata could now offer services in the bulk of Indian midlands with the gaping absence of Mumbai, where BPL Mobile had consolidated its lead. The company also ran operations in Maharashtra, Kerala and Tamil Nadu under BPL Cellular, from licences it won in 1996. Having struggled with demanding foreign partners, whom Chandrasekhar believed ascribed the highest value in their ability to 'manage' the Indian promoter, the BPL Mobile chief saw reason in finding deep-pocketed local partners. AT&T had, after all, largely remained a silent partner with the Birla Group.

So, he took a merger proposal to Batata. The combined entity would have formed India's largest mobile company by subscribers, geographic footprint, and value. On its merits, joining hands made sense. All three groups concurred. The negotiation was stiff, and in the end, BPL was remunerated for its creamy customers. In the final merged entity, 49.32 per cent would belong to the BPL consortium (including France Telecom) and 50.62 per cent to the Birla Tata AT&T combine. 'We are indeed delighted that our original investment has today evolved into the largest cellular force in the country. This merger accords the benefits of scale to take consumer service to a new high,' said Kumar Mangalam Birla, chairman of Aditya Birla Group, at the official merger announcement on 28 June 2001.[2]

'AT&T Wireless is committed to working with our partners to build and operate quality wireless networks in India,' came a statement from Jordan Roderick, head of International Operations for AT&T Wireless Services, endorsing the merger.[3]

Yet, this was an ill-fated union. Even as integration began and the BPL team started running technology decisions past their Batata counterparts, Motorola filed a court case against BPL holding up any transaction in the company. In the wake of the imminent merger, Motorola expected to lose its business on BPL to Ericsson and Lucent. Both Birla and Tata had deployed networks with the latter two companies.

Motorola wished to recover any advances towards BPL's network rollout. The amount was a hefty $23 million, which Motorola asked BPL to pay or wind the company up in its court filing. Piling on were foreign financiers of the BPL, who feared being shortchanged if Motorola had its way.

As talks progressed, Chandrasekhar believed his dominance over the combined entity made the Birla Group uncomfortable. Tata, Birla and AT&T acted as one block and therefore held majority over BPL, but Chandrasekhar would be the single largest equity holder in this private company. Concerned over the governance practices of management under Chandrasekhar, the Birla Group pushed to appoint leaders from its ranks to head the company. That did not pass muster.

BPL Mobile had been Chandrasekhar's baby. The company had outlived the hardest of times and was the largest telecom greenfield operation till the turn of the century. Chandrasekhar preferred to remain in charge. As a result, the agreement timeframe lapsed and quietly fizzled from the biggest deal in the sector to nothing. The lost time and opportunity cost both companies heavily, but BPL hurt more immediately.

Expansion halted since the vendors pulled back. The Mumbai business was frolicking, but it needed to grow, and these court cases had clipped BPL's wings. Company executives suggest that management attention on BPL's business also waned as its leaders were distracted with litigation and the ambition to grow inorganically.

By early 2004, fissures between Chandrasekhar and his father-in-law, T.P.G. Nambiar, became public. Nambiar filed a mismanagement suit with the Company Law Board against Chandrasekhar, accusing him of incorrectly showing the shareholding pattern. Chandrasekhar may have been attempting to use some company equity to escape its financial troubles, but Nambiar implied it was something else. In any case, none of this was ever confirmed. The case was eventually settled out of court after the Essar Group acquired both BPL Mobile and BPL Cellular.

33

Siva's Tricky Moves

RPG's Harsh Goenka was struggling with a tricky situation. When he bid for a telecom licence, he did so with an American company called AirTouch. The investment by AirTouch was headed by an Indian–American engineer from IIT, India's premier technology institute, Arun Sarin. Sarin was a zealous participant on RPG Chennai's board and believed in the country's potential for mobile telephony.

By the time the sector emerged from its licence burden, AirTouch had unrecognizably transformed. In June 1999, Vodafone bought the US-based company, turning it into a subsidiary and its Indian investment philosophy out of the door. Goenka was trapped between a foreign partner wanting an exit, a growing retail business hungry for capital, and peers at Reliance and Essar urging him to sell the standalone Chennai operation. The telecom business needed funds in anticipation of Reliance's launch and plummeting call rates. So, when Vodafone asked to be bought out of the company, RPG did not immediately have spare funds.

Goenka may have offered to find a buyer for Vodafone, but before he could do so, there was an unexpected claimant to a board seat: Sivasankaran.

Siva's initial winning bid for Delhi had been marred by controversy, but he knew how to land on his feet. He sold his licence to Essar's patriarch, Shashi Ruia for a sum of $105 million, and with the newfound cash made a splash in global headlines by buying musician MC Hammer's house in California. Yet, for the restless Siva, telecom was still on his mind.

With cash available, he could buy into one. Turned out, it was not that simple. He accumulated minority equity in Bharti Airtel in 1997, possibly due to the JT Mobile, Punjab circle transaction with Essar and by accumulating small stakes from foreign players. When he had around 10 per cent he asked for a seat on the board. Sunil Mittal was not about to fold that easily. He refused. Pressure from within the ministry would not work on Mittal. Siva astutely picked that up. Eventually, the two struck an agreement for Mittal to buy Siva out for Rs 90 per share. This was perhaps Siva's only loss-making deal in the sector, but it was a learning experience.

When the government approved the fourth cellular licence in 1999, Siva jumped at the opportunity to secure one for his home state, Tamil Nadu, in a service branded Aircel.

RPG's Chennai operation tied right into Siva's plans for Aircel. Vodafone's interest in exiting the business in 2003 was Siva's opportunity to act. Perhaps he already knew that other shareholders would have objected if he tried an overt move to acquire the company. Instead, he closed an offshore deal with Vodafone to buy the UK-based company's share in a Mauritius entity that held 21 per cent in RPG Cellular.

Initially, when Vodafone informed RPG of a buyer for its equity in Mauritius, Goenka was keen to explore. After a bit of diligence, however, he realized this buyer was Siva. RPG rushed to the Company Law Board to block the transaction, but Siva's deal was a fait accompli. Goenka would need a board resolution to roll back the purchase. Alternatively, RPG had the option to partner with Siva, who wanted control of the company to combine it with his Tamil Nadu operation. Goenka preferred to exit than fight, and Siva bought him out to take complete control of the business.

During this time, Siva had also found a new friend in the Tata Group. It is unclear how Siva came in contact with the Tata Group head, Ratan Tata, but it was almost certainly in the context of telecommunications. Given his computer business, Siva was an early believer in the internet among Indians. On this, Ratan Tata concurred. The savvy Siva showed Ratan Tata the different applications the internet unleashed. Siva even helped Ratan Tata open a Yahoo Mail account, a service and search platform that was shrinking distances across the world at breakneck speed.

Ratan Tata saw value in association with Siva. Little did he know that this alliance would deal an irreparable blow to Tata Group's telecom aspirations.

The Tata Group and its executives were too gentlemanly to press vendors on telecom equipment and service deals. Ratan Tata once complained to a vendor. The same equipment was being sold to competitors at a lower price, and with better service solely because they were better taskmasters; the country head for the vendor remembers Tata's disappointment. Siva was known for his plain speak and brusque manner that could yield better outcomes for the Tata Group, which was pivoting to CDMA and needed fresh equipment.

The Tata Group appointed Sivasankaran as its contracted vendor to source equipment, giving Siva a definitive foothold in India's cellular market. Siva spent much of those two years nursing the Tamil Nadu operation, deepening political roots, and wrangling with equipment makers.

His internet cafe business, Dishnet, which he started in 1998, began to shine as the Indian middle-class turned adopters.

Popularizing his coffee in Delhi had started with servicing the Essar office headed by T.V. Ramachandran. It was part of the sale deal. Unfortunately, coffee no longer held Siva's interest. His heart hankered for a mobile company. So, he sold Dishnet in 2004 to none other than the Tata Group for Rs 270 crore. Siva said the sale was to focus on Aircel's telecom operation. That did not prevent him from milking the cafe segment for greater profit. He later bought out Tata's 35 per cent in the cafe chain branded Barista for which he already held the rest of the equity. He then sold it to Italy's Lavazza for an estimated tenfold profit. The exact size of the deal was never disclosed.

His special status with the Tata Group was lucrative for Siva in many other ways. He acquired an 8 per cent stake in Tata Teleservices, the group's CDMA foray, for around Rs 1000–1200 crore. The Tata Group loaned Siva the money to buy these shares. He set up office at Tata Group's luxurious hotels at partner rentals.

Siva applied for and received service licences in eight other service areas for Aircel in 2004. This is when he saw an opportunity with Batata, which would fit well with Aircel's licences and footprint. Armed with information on what had transpired with Chandrasekhar's BPL Mobile deal, Siva decided an offshore deal and quiet approach would yield him better results. Insurance firm AIG wanted to exit its small stake, below 2 per cent in Batata. It appears neither the Tata Group executives nor Birla knew about Siva and AIG's transaction until it became a thorn in Batata's stride.

Aircel's progress had also stalled. Siva alleged that the politicians had turned against him. Tamil Nadu's Dayanidhi Maran, who became union minister for Telecom, decided to frustrate the operator into selling, Siva told the Central Bureau of Investigation as he moved the investigator against Maran.[1] Publicly, Siva said that he was victimized because of the rough edges between Maran and the Tata Group.

Nonetheless, there was competitive bidding for Aircel at that time. T. Ananda Krishnan's Malaysian Maxis Group and Hutch Max were interested in the company. Sunil Sood, who later rose to the position of CEO of the company that Hutch morphed into, sat in the head office of Aircel, and Hutch paid an advance of Rs 100 crore in anticipation of a purchase. The money was returned after it was pipped by Maxis.

Siva received a handsome $800 million in 2005 to sell Aircel. Shortly after the equity transfer, the permissions holding up Aircel came through, and Maxis began building an even bigger company. The acquirer submitted a request to get an all-India licence and airwaves.

34

Two Hearts Part

In 2001, Batata applied for and won licences in additional markets as the fourth operator. As it embarked on greenfield operations, the operator needed to shed the 'potato' image. An 'Idea' was born—this was the new brand under which the company now sold its mobile connections. Even as work on the rejuvenated brand began, in the near term, its business languished.

Tata's energies had already been redirected to Tata Teleservices and Birla felt responsible and in charge of Batata. Tata Group came to own two Unified Access Service Licences (UASLs) across India since the migration to the new regime allowing CDMA operators to offer mobility—one in Batata and the other in Tata Teleservices. As per regulations a promoter could own only one.

The Tatas were accorded a one-time exemption to hold two licences until they could sell one. To the Birla Group, this meant that eventually Tata would sell its stake in Cellular.

Two years passed in the wait for the Tata Group to start the process to sell Idea's shares. Operations chugged along. Birla thought Tatas were dragging their feet out of inertia. Besides, the process of shoring up operations was somewhat on track.

It took almost a year for Idea to complete the acquisition of tractor-maker Escorts' telecom operations. The first round of talks failed—ostensibly because of regulatory hurdles. In reality, the dealmakers sensed a hustle from the seller. Idea upped the offer towards the end of 2003 to around Rs 300 crore. In January 2004, Escorts was bleeding because of the debt pile on its telecom venture and Idea was eager to add service areas. The deal was clinched.

Now, Idea had three more functioning networks—in Kerala, Haryana and Uttar Pradesh West—and licences for another three—in Rajasthan, Himachal Pradesh and Uttar Pradesh (East). Despite this, Idea trailed at the fifth spot as Bhati Airtel and Hutch blazed ahead.

Later that year, the government once again called for applications from existing operators who wanted to expand into new territories. Idea had its sights on Mumbai. To make the application, the operator needed to submit shareholder details. These included Tata's details. The Tata Group's response to the application was still sluggish. Once again, the Birla team thought it was emanating from a lack of interest. The group therefore filed an application with incomplete details. It was promptly followed up with a government notice to share shareholder details.

When it still did not receive Tata's response, the Birla team began to investigate. The first thing they found was that Tata's licence in Madhya Pradesh conflicted with Idea's licence. Tata Teleservices had a six-month window to apply for licences in areas where Idea was already present. It had apparently missed the window and received a licence at a later date. Submitting the details on the most current application could therefore cause trouble for both Tata Teleservices and Idea.

There was ostensible strain between partners because of this. Idea's growth compared with peers was mediocre. Thoughts of exiting the venture had crossed Birla. It changed when AT&T asked out of the venture given India's regulatory waffling and pressure on revenue in the US. Kumar Mangalam Birla assumed he would be acquiring the stake since Tata was mandated to dilute its shares in Idea. It came as a surprise when the Tata Group insisted on picking up half of the equity AT&T was selling. Deal magnate Sivasankaran put together a consortium led by Singapore Technologies Telemedia to make a bid for Idea in mid-2004.

The Birla team wondered if this had been done at the behest of the Tata Group. Was Idea being set up for a hostile takeover? As these questions circled, Birla found out about Siva's 1.7 per cent in the company he had bought from AIG. So, when Tata dangled the shareholder agreement asking for half of AT&T's equity, Birla agreed only as long as it would retain at least 50 per cent in Idea.

Fair and square? Tata did not think so. Tata wanted half excluding Siva's shares. Birla would have none of that, Tata's shares combined with Siva's could form a majority 51 per cent.

Battle lines were drawn. Officials at Birla still recall the reluctance with which the decision to battle Tata was taken. 'We were pushed into a corner, and we could either cow down and disappear or fight,' recalls a senior. Birla took the battle to the DoT. They filed a complaint of misdemeanour and lack of governance on the part of the Tata Group.

Tata, in turn, sued Birla for breaching the shareholder agreement. Idea Cellular, which continued to lose ground as competitors raced ahead, was also affected.

Siva sparked the rivalry between Ratan Tata and Kumar Mangalam, but in its closure, he had little interference.

Each group with its baggage took giant steps towards the snapping of bonds. Birla's complaint, Tata's lawsuit and the tense negotiations cost Tata and Birla much more than money. Mukund Rajan, who was Ratan Tata's executive assistant when this was unfolding, wrote in his book that this became a point of no return for relations between Ratan Tata and Kumar Mangalam Birla.[1] Ties broke not only in the mobile business but also in other sectors, like Tata Steel, which Tata Sons bought back from the Birla Group. Ratan Tata who was once a mentor to Kumar Mangalam Birla was now just another competitor.

It took several years for the issues to be resolved. In the end, the Tata Group was left with Tata Teleservices and by 2006, Idea under Birla applied for airwaves in more service areas and readied itself for a grand public listing.

35

Yin and Yang

Where Ratan Tata and Kumar Mangalam were shedding their mentor and mentee skins, Reliance Infocomm too was caught in the middle of sparring brothers.

In June 2002, even as Reliance Infocomm was in the process of getting ready, the founder of the group Dhirubhai had a fatal stroke. He did not leave a will. The death of Mukesh and Anil's father was the of undoing their unity. They even disagreed on the nature of their parent's involvement in their lives.

Mukesh recalled his father giving him an education beyond books. 'We were not micro-managed . . . However busy he may have been, whatever the pressure, Sunday was for his wife and kids. I try to do the same with my family. And it has to be non-academic. It is easy to be with your kids and say let's do homework together. But we try to do things, beyond doing lunches and dinners. I learnt that from my father.'

Anil's take on his father's approach was different. 'My mother really supported my father through those tough times. I don't think I recall—during my entire school or college career—my father spending time with me, sitting with my homework or my tuitions or anything of this sort. It was left to my mother, who was just a high-school graduate, to be on our case.'

The divergence in their perspectives was always apparent, but few imagined what was to transpire.

In telecom, Anil preferred to participate in industry consolidation by buying ailing mobile operators, but the company took a different approach under Mukesh Ambani.

Anil wanted to launch services quickly and tap financial markets that saw high value in the telecom business. Mukesh preferred to spend longer perfecting the technology, but now that the patriarch was gone, investors got restless about the group's future.

So Infocomm launched a campaign that revolved around the recently deceased Reliance founder. Internal systems of the telecom operations were still a work in progress For example the billing system had several issues. If power to the mobile instrument was pulled midway through a call, it was never recorded as a call. It became a popularly published hack: yank the battery out of the device midway through a call to avoid any billing at all.

A fraud with devices also affected Reliance's performance. The police recorded uncountable FIRs (First Incident Reports) of lost phones. Insiders at Reliance suspected that this was a well-oiled machinery that hit the company in a short period before Reliance caught on. Instead of repaying for the device over two years, users were reporting the phone lost and stopped paying instalments. Anecdotally, telecom executives say that these phones were wiped and shipped off to be sold in Africa. The unpaid liability fell on Reliance Infocomm.

The migration to the Unified Access Service License and imposed penalties had also stripped Reliance of the intrinsic advantage of higher termination fees from other service providers. In 2005, amid ownership disputes between sparring brothers, the company took a Rs 450-crore write-off and forcibly disconnected eleven million subscribers.

In late 2004, the struggle over the Reliance business empire became public. The battle between brothers who were once complementary was emotionally charged and high decibel. Throngs of journalists crowded outside Maker Chamber IV at Nariman Point in Mumbai, the famed headquarters of Reliance. Every time the brothers left the building they were accosted with a thousand questions. Some were salacious, others genuine, but all were irksome for the Ambani duo. Anil displayed greater emotion to the point of getting aggressive with journalists on one occasion.

When the war began affecting family life, their mother, Kokilaben, brokered peace. The two brothers agreed to adhere to recommendations by a three-member panel headed by K.V. Kamath, ICICI Bank chairperson, and a senior business figure whom both Anil and Mukesh respected. Kamath suggested that Mukesh was running the petrochemical business well and should continue while the infrastructure business could go to Anil Ambani.

Reliance's telecom venture still hung in the balance. Anil insisted it was his. For Mukesh, this was his baby; Nita's involvement with it only made it more so. For Reliance, this was the first, highly visible direct-to-customer business that had the potential to revamp the group's image. Perhaps a way would have been to separate the GSM and CDMA operations of the company. But that was not meant to be. After acrimonious exchanges, the entire telecom business went to Anil Ambani, along with surplus cash to keep it going.

The legend goes that on an emotionally charged evening, Kokilaben had stepped in between the brothers and asked Mukesh to give the venture to Anil. With a wink and a nod Mukesh agreed. He had possibly hoped that Anil would see sense in partnering with him or sell the business. Mukesh Ambani's business therefore retained a first right of refusal in case the venture was put on the block for sale.

As part of the division senior executives were given a choice to pick which of the two split entities they preferred to stay with. Key telecom executives including Manoj Modi and Sanjay Mashruwala chose to stay with Mukesh.

Anil Ambani had his reservations about Mukesh's intentions. The brothers, therefore, signed a non-compete agreement within their verticals. Anil Ambani was in the hot seat set to work towards a restructuring of the business. He initiated a lobbying effort to permit dual technology operations so that CDMA operators could also offer GSM services and vice versa. He further simplified the company's holding structure and renamed the company Reliance Communications or RCom.

For Mukesh, the dream to deliver mobile communications was halted. Even as he watched the ecosystem and ached to get back in, this was not the time. His first task at hand was to appease the worried stakeholders of Reliance Industries and consolidate the businesses he now controlled fully.

36

Bharti, Hutch Emerge Victorious

The sudden mobile calling and instrument price drop had unleashed floodgates for consumers, particularly in urban India. From the fiscal year 2002 to March 2006 the country went from having seven million mobile subscribers to nearly 100 million. The growth was exponential and urban teledensity hit 53 per cent by December 2006, up from around 14 per cent just four years earlier.[1]

Growth was led by private players as the subscriber additions of state-run companies dwindled to less than an eighth of private companies. In 2006, for instance, public sector companies added 5.3 million users compared with 42.4 million among the private players. Mobile services dominated fixed-line services and accounted for nearly 80 per cent of the market.

India became one of the world's fastest-growing telecom markets trailing only China in the region. Foreign fund inflows reflected the upbeat market and were bolstered by the government's decision to increase the direct holding limit in telecom companies to 74 per cent from 49 per cent earlier. A government estimate of direct foreign investment in the sector until December 2006 pegged the figure at Rs 11,809 crore with a sharp spike in 2001 that took the amount from a stagnant Rs 4000 crore to Rs 8500 crore.

The deep-pocketed players were embroiled in corporate politics which gave Hutch Essar and Bharti Airtel a good opportunity for a clear run. Hutch had launched an internal marketing programme to tap the 'ABCD market', or sell to ayahs (nannies), bearers, cooks and drivers. These were typically migrant workers in urban India best suited to using wireless services as affordability increased.

Over the past half-decade, Hutch Essar was rebranded to Orange when Hutchison bought a stake in the French telecom major. It was then churned out to Hutch Pink when the parent company's link with Orange was broken. This company refrained from celebrity endorsement but evolved a local, event-based promotion programme. Its subscriber base certainly suggested its campaigns worked.

The average monthly revenue per user had eroded for all the companies from Rs 1000 in March 2000 to around Rs 450 by March 2004, a level at which it has settled ever since. The numbers, however, more than made good on economies of scale. Company valuations reflected this as valuers were no longer looking at cash burn or absolute profits, they tended to ascribe worth based on a multiple of the product of subscriber base and average revenue. It sent telecom companies' share prices soaring.

Bharti, which had once dropped to Rs 19, hit a high of Rs 429 a piece by March 2006.

BSNL and MTNL had all but succumbed to competition. The state-run operator justified its loss in the market as a late entrant. Rural phone penetration was still under 2 per cent and the company was focused on serving that market.

In the consumer market Reliance and Tata were both losing out. The CDMA instrument was locked with a phone number and a carrier, while GSM offered the flexibility of a SIM card that could be inserted into any device. As a result, in urban pockets, multiple families owned SIM cards but shared a mobile instrument.

The CDMA handsets were also more expensive than their immediately comparable GSM equivalents. The two majors failed to convert high-paying customers given the scepticism surrounding the mobility and low prestige of a CDMA phone. The offering became most prevalent in the corporate market. With deeper cabled locations and more stable wireless technology for internet traffic, their networks were ideal for corporate transformation as organizations connected their field force.

The move in the corporate sector to data-based services put a new technology on both the operators' and government's horizon—3G. Its implementation was unfolding in Europe. The technology used GSM networks to deliver CDMA experience of higher capacity of both calling and Internet services.

Part Six

37

BSNL, MTNL Merger

The burden of licence fees, which were imposed on the companies as part of allocating airwaves for mobile services was shown as income on the state operators Bharat Sanchar Nigam Limited and Mahanagar Telephone Nigam Limited's accounts. To capture commensurate revenue, they heeded the advice of implementation partners. Where private companies were stagnating because of their limited footprint, the state-run companies were capturing market share in rural India.

In 2002 BSNL and MTNL held a promise to compete effectively with private players.

Its captive landline business, existing infrastructure, and deleveraged account books allowed it to generally lower product prices. The companies were able to attract customers at breakneck speed in rural and semi-urban markets. Then Minister Pramod Mahajan mooted the idea of a merger between the two state-run companies. Given the functional overlap, this made competitive sense.

Unfortunately, the merger was complex and proved impossible due to the hurdles that lay ahead. MTNL was publicly listed on stock exchanges, while BSNL was not. The companies' pay scales were not aligned. The infrastructure requirements for MTNL's metro cities were quite different from the expansive coverage needed for BSNL. The most significant hurdle, however, was political.

Mahajan was reassigned from the ministry shortly after mooting the idea. In his place came Shourie, who was focused more on resolving the high-decibel drama between the CDMA and GSM lobbies. The merger proposal did come up for review under Shourie in 2003 when the minister was in the thick of planning the Unified Access Service Licence. It was set aside.

The merger remained a floundering idea, until early 2005, when the new minister, Dayanidhi Maran, set the wheels in motion again. This time, ICICI Securities was appointed, under the watchful eye of K.V. Kamath, to create a detailed report on merger options between the two firms. Alas, that drew battle lines between the ranks of the two companies. Suspended in a state of uncertainty, this appears to be the collapse of BSNL and MTNL in the competitive market.

A pay cut for MTNL executives would be rejected, but to bring pay parity for BSNL staff, the government would need to fork out Rs 1200 crore.

Then came the matter of seniority. Folks at MTNL considered themselves more experienced at the same rank because the volume of customers and revenue from corporate ran in multiple folds of the BSNL portfolios, but the network expanse and retail consumer experience of BSNL trumped MTNL.

At the front of the battle lines were R.S.P. Sinha, chairman and managing director of MTNL and A.K. Sinha, chairman and managing director of BSNL. The latter publicly remained neutral but fought to amalgamate MTNL as a subsidiary. The MTNL chief, on the other hand, vetoed this as a move that would not result in any savings for the consolidated company.

Then the two companies began sending notices to each other to settle accounts which so far had operated on trust. BSNL sought 1840 crore from MTNL for using its backhaul infrastructure. These claims were fought over.

BSNL staff agitated to ensure officers from the metro cities were treated at par with them.

Figures from March 2005 showed that MTNL gained steam to secure the highest number of new subscribers, even though its total subscribers lagged incumbent players. Unfortunately, this marked the peak for the state-run operator.

Many of the leaders at the various levels of BSNL and MTNL were deployed or originally inducted at the Department of Telecommunications and deputed to the firms. One of the suggestions was to allow time-based promotions for BSNL folks while pausing those for MTNL. This led to rancour among the ranks of MTNL. With rife opportunities in the private sector, there was an exodus of staff. Those left were frustrated and unmotivated.

The state-run company that once ruled the market was left behind. The upgrade of mobile technology, which began to offer internet services such as email and fleet management rendered MTNL's DSL offering redundant. DSL was a dial-up-based Internet service. MTNL came to be associated with poor quality and apathetic customer service at a time when private companies were bending over backwards to lure clients.

Lower revenue did not mirror the company's debt situation that mounted in the face of the newly allocated spectrum, each time it was awarded to others. Ultimately, BSNL and MTNL needed multiple rescue investments from the Government of India, but the merger of the two companies continues to remain elusive.

38

What an Idea, Sirjee!

While the state-owned company languished, Birla and Anil Ambani were ready to make a fresh run at their businesses.

The separation from the Tata Group may have come with some angst, but the ball was now in Kumar Mangalam Birla's court. He had to reinvent Idea Cellular from a fringe player it was now seen as to a mainstream competitor.

The Escorts acquisition added three established businesses and three permits without any operations. Kumar Birla aspired to turn this company into an all-India operator.

At the end of 2005, Idea Cellular had an incumbent advantage in seven circles or service areas. This meant that in these seven markets, the company had airwaves in the 900MHz band rather than in the capital cost-intensive 1800MHz band which was assigned in 2001. Category A circles of Andhra Pradesh, Gujarat and Maharashtra and the category B circles of Haryana, Kerala, Madhya Pradesh and Uttar Pradesh (West) were holding Idea's ship steady while it rocked the boat expanding coverage to new regions.

The company had licences for thirteen service areas, the last of which was Mumbai. It received them after the shareholding issue was resolved between the Aditya Birla Group and the Tata Group.

If the company was going to fire all cylinders it needed funds. The sector was in season, and Birla elected to take the company public, launching a grand initial public offering. It started as most others at the time did with a pre-IPO placement to set price expectations.

'Since November 2005 . . . we have invested over Rs 25 billion in expanding and rolling-out our network,' wrote the company in its filings for potential shareholders. The company's subscribers were growing sharply from just over seven million at the end of March 2006 to nearly 12.5 million by December 2006. By this time, 'Our network covered 1,627 Census Towns and 1,980 other population centers.'

The statement was a reflection of the semi-urban strategy the company was adopting.[1]

The strategy was working as awareness and adoption penetrated India like wildfire. Amid this excitement investors were keeping a keen eye, and private equity player Providence took notice of Idea's journey.

The equity financier was already searching for an opportunity in the Indian telephony market and was rumoured to be in conversation with south Indian operator Aircel. In October 2006, as enthusiastic investment banks ran the Idea Cellular mandate, Providence became the largest of four to invest in Idea Cellular.

Birla diluted Idea to offload around 25 per cent of its stake, out of which around 15 per cent was bought by Providence Equity Partners. The others were ChrysCapital, Citigroup and TA Associates. The exact price of each of the transactions remained undisclosed. The estimated corpus raised by Idea Cellular was pegged at $550 million. Analyst reports later estimated this amount to be equivalent to a 30–35 per cent discount on the listing price of the share.

In Providence, the Aditya Birla Group had found a long-lasting partnership that was extended as Idea needed more funds. Meanwhile, the company readied for its public offering due in the first half of 2007.

Idea found a comfortable position in the marketplace. It was not competing for the prime markets that leaders Bharti Airtel and Hutch focussed on but expanded rural appetite to make its proposition an attractive one. As a result, it became a synergistic partner to the leaders who began to count Idea Cellular as the third dominant voice in the clutch of incumbents after Bharti Airtel and Hutchison.

It was no surprise then that investment banks were lining up for what was, at the time, the largest IPO in the country. Four investment bankers ran the issue and another two associated with it: lead managers JM Morgan Stanley and DSP Merrill Lynch and senior lead Citigroup and UBS. Kotak Mahindra Bank and JM Financial were also involved.

On 5 February 2007, the group held a lavish and widely attended press conference at the Taj Mahal Hotel in Mumbai. Media cameras lined up at the back, their numerous cables forming a bulge, sandwiched between the tape and the grey-blue carpet as they ran to the speaker's table at the head of the room.

Journalists bickered over slots for exclusive interviews with the executives after the main event, as Dr Pragnya Ram, chief communications officer, prioritized channels for the chairman or diverted journalists to other executives. The group was lavish in spreading the word, so between bankers, executives and management peppered across the room, there was a spokesperson for anyone with a mic or notepad and pen.

Their commentary was no different than what was being said across the board, but still, every word was reported on this announcement of the Rs 2125 crore IPO that hit the market barely a week later. The issue was priced between Rs 65 and

Rs 75 a share. At the upper end of the spectrum, Idea Cellular was valued at around $4.5 billion.

The purpose of the fundraise was to build, strengthen and expand the network and related services in the new circles including the Mumbai circle, pay fees and capital expenditure for national long-distance operations, and redeem preference shares the company had issued. The IPO proceeds were also allocated to cash out some existing shareholders to the tune of approximately Rs 315 crore, and a component was allotted for employee stock options. The offer opened on 12 February 2007 and continued until 15 February.

Such was the enthusiasm towards this public offering that when it closed it was fifty-seven times subscribed, meaning applications to buy shares were fifty-seven times the number the company was willing to sell.

It naturally meant that Idea could command a price at the highest end of the IPO range. It also meant that the company received the cash reserves it needed immediately. When it was listed on 9 March, the stock price went even higher to close on the first day at Rs 85 a piece.

The success inspired Idea to make a bid for B.K. Modi's Spice Communications. Spice was the first operator in Punjab and Karnataka with 4.4 million subscribers. It had claims to several firsts on the Indian mobility scene but had now run out of funds. The group needed to exit if its other businesses were to survive. For the buyer, the deal came with a foreign partner committed to the long haul and cognizant of the Asian culture—Telekom Malaysia, later renamed Axiata.

In June 2008, word got out that a deal had been in negotiations for at least a couple of months. As its contours shaped, it was a sweet and cash-positive one for Idea Cellular. It was broken into four parts. First Idea would acquire all of the nearly 41 per cent stake held by the Modi group for Rs 2176 crore. This represented a share price of Rs 77.30 per share of Spice compared with the Rs 50 level it was trading at.[2] Thrown along with this was a Rs 544 crore non-compete fee, so that the Spice Group would stay out of the sector and stop pursuing licences.

Spice would then be merged with Idea Cellular by way of a share swap in the ratio of forty-nine shares in the merged entity for 100 in Spice Communications.

The Aditya Birla Group company, along with Telekom Malaysia, which owed 39 per cent of Spice, would then jointly make the mandatory open offer to Spice shareholders to buy to 20 per cent more of the company.

Finally, Idea would sell 14.99 per cent, just short of 15 per cent, of the combined mobile phone operator to Telekom Malaysia for an investment of approximately Rs 7300 crore through preference shares priced at Rs 157 per share of Idea Cellular.

The acquisition was announced with great fanfare, but it also brought its share of regulatory troubles that were revealed over time. Around the completion of the transaction in August 2008, Idea approached the DoT regarding its licence and spectrum in the service areas that it had received in 2008, along with other new operators.

After the acquisition, the company would have two licences in Punjab and Karnataka—a situation which was not permissible under the government regulations. Idea offered to surrender the licence and airwaves it had received before the proposed Spice transaction. At the time, Idea was advised to apply for a merger of licences because neither the new licence nor the airwaves had been put to use. Idea Cellular was under the impression that following this, its licence agreement would be amended to suit the lay of the land. Given that Spice already had 4.4 million subscribers. Idea expected this to grow further, and the company would become eligible to receive more spectrum. The newly allocated airwaves would fill that void.

This solution left the company with spare airwaves until its subscriber base ramped up. The DoT realized this when planning to auction 3G airwaves in 2010. So, when Idea applied to merge licences at the high court, the DoT resisted and eventually got an ex-parte order to prevent the Idea merger with Spice.

Two years and significant related investments after the fact, the company fought back to retain its assets. 'Apparently, to cover for its inefficiencies, the (telecoms ministry) is now indulging in duplicity and muscle flexing. Idea will resist and not be bullied,' said the company in a strongly worded press release as it tried to stem the damage to its share price arising out of the government's move.[3]

Idea Cellular prevailed and the transaction was completed in March 2010 in the run-up to the 3G airwave auction.

Although Idea Cellular was the youngest venture of the Aditya Birla Group, it quickly became a household name. In the group's Mumbai head office, the joke was that the Birla Group would be known for Idea Cellular rather than the Rising Sun logo that it advertised.

39

A Towering Idea

In 2001, Sunil and Rajan Mittal proposed the idea of a common infrastructure company with Hutchison. It was summarily shot down because Airtel wished to control it under the leadership of Rajan. The idea was to partner with the rival operator to host a base station on a shared telecom tower. At the time, when the number of towers per service area ran in the hundreds, location advantage made for a competitive difference between one company to the next.

The companies once again mulled this over bilateral talks in the second half of 2005 in an inconclusive negotiation.

Then, in 2006, as authorities examined allowing Reliance to enter all-India GSM services in addition to its CDMA offering, the TRAI launched a consultation process on infrastructure sharing. 'The need of the hour is to roll out telecom services at a faster pace and at an affordable price to ensure higher penetration of telecom services in rural areas,' the TRAI said in a paper dated 29 November 2006 in which it raised several questions for operators.[1]

The regulator pointed out that nearly 60 per cent of the network cost rests in passive infrastructure, so curbing that would make economic sense as long as operators' antennae can point in different directions. This would not only prevent the deterioration of network performance in dense areas like Mumbai and dark spots in expanses of Delhi but also stem the damage to the skyline as towers mushroom.

'We propose that all infrastructure set up beyond a cut-off date specified by the Authority should be mandated for sharing for at least three service providers,' RCom responded to the TRAI consultation.[2] The other to concur on mandating telecom tower sharing was a lesser-known company called GTL Infrastructure.

Bharti Airtel maintained for most of its answers that market forces should be allowed to determine the best course of action for companies, but did 'strongly recommend that the back haul sharing should be permitted through suitable modification in licensing conditions'.[3]

TRAI had asked one more question on whether there was any situation under the sharing of infrastructure that would be detrimental to subscribers. 'We do not foresee any adverse impact on the consumers. On the contrary, the consumers would be benefited by better service due to increased competition,' was the unanimous response.[4]

The TRAI paper was relevant only for active infrastructure sharing. The UASL had a clause that allowed telecom towers and other passive infrastructure sharing. So, among operators, this was more of a wake-up call. Most importantly, Reliance's stance on mandating sharing got the leading operators thinking.

The situation, too, had turned since the first time the idea was mooted. With eight operators in the market and diverse portfolios, sharing towers seemed eminently feasible. More importantly, the ecosystem had evolved, from the lessor of land to the maintenance of equipment. Local authorities wanted their pound of flesh raising the prices of the right of way to lay cables while civil activism questioning the health impact of towers was on the rise.

In addition to that were nuisance issues telecom companies faced, such as petrol and power theft and technical monitoring of equipment. In one instance in Uttar Pradesh, while trying to pilfer electricity from the diesel generator on a tower, a person was electrocuted. The court issued a warrant against the chief executive of the company for negligence. In a higher court, it was later clarified that the thief had broken into the tower compound and there was an out-of-court settlement with the family concerned.

These were time and resources service operators, growing at breakneck speed, could ill-afford. Managing towers was becoming a time-consuming and specialized task.

Hutchison was in the throes of a potential sell-off at the cusp of 2006–07; at a meeting between Asim Ghosh, Arun Sarin, and the Ruia brothers the operator saw merit in the argument for sharing towers. They decided that the end game would be to make a passive infrastructure company with Bharti Airtel.

The two moved quickly on a trend that seemed imminent. They entered into a tower-sharing negotiation. This time Akhil Gupta, Bharti's finance wizard, and popularly known as the fourth Mittal brother after Rakesh, Sunil and Rajan Mittal, led the discussions.

With vested interests on the line between sales and marketing teams, the negotiation was a tough one. Neither of the companies was willing to fold in all the towers. Bharti had more towers than Hutch, but such a scenario was not new to Asim Ghosh. The two began drafting shareholder plans. There were seven service areas where the tower portfolios of Hutch and Bharti were too divergent, so these were parked aside.

As conversations progressed, the two market leaders found another keen participant in their conversation—Idea Cellular.

The towers that the Birla company had in rural India were complementary to both portfolios, but their number and value were inferior to that of the incumbents. Sanjiv Aga, the recently returned CEO, represented Idea.

Bharti Airtel and Hutch had negotiated they would be equal partners in the venture, but the stake to be given to Idea was still under negotiation. Idea sought 18 per cent in the final venture, while Bharti and Hutch offered it 14 per cent.

Due diligence began. Time was of the essence, given the imminent entry of more players and the need for capital at the incumbents. Fortunately, Akhil Gupta was up with the numbers. Each tower was valued independently, and a sort of tower exchange was undertaken. In some cases, the value of the tower or the number of slots available on a tower, was less than a counterpart, but its location offsets the difference. There were some towers with such a high rental that revenue from it did not match its cost. On Express Towers, for example, the revenue from traffic on it merely covered 30 per cent of its cost. The consideration in some of these, however, was complete coverage. Without coverage over Nariman Point, operators would lose high-value South Mumbai customers.

At the end of negotiations, the final verdict was that ownership of Indus Towers, as it was named, would be equal between Vodafone and Bharti at 42 per cent each and the remaining 16 per cent would go to Idea Cellular. Bharti and Vodafone folded into 29,400 towers and Idea 11,200 towers spread over sixteen service areas.[5] The three operators had a preference to lease a slot on any of Indus Towers' infrastructure which would thereafter be available at commercial terms to any of the new telecom operators.

Vodafone nominated the CEO and CFO, Airtel the chief operating officer and supply chain head and Idea deputed the human resources head and chief technology officer. There was a debate on where to set up the office. Was it better to remain close to the towers or the clients—Bharti, Vodafone and Idea? Eventually, it elected to stay near the client in Gurgaum, earlier known was Gurgaon, not far from Airtel's head office. One of the early Indus Tower executives nominated by Hutch recalls Akhil Gupta telling him that 'the objective of this company was not to boost service operators', it was important to retain the value in this company.

The first reconciliation of accounts turned out to be a mammoth task. After the towers were transferred, the team found that records often proved unreliable. On one occasion, on paper, the tower was functional including operational expenses, but on the ground, there was no tower at all. Accounting of the assets—electronics, power, cooling—needed to be checked and corrected. Operational requirements needed to be tweaked to reflect a correct state. It took a year and a half for the first audit to be conducted.

Hereafter, Indus Tower brought on board an independent CEO, B.S. Shantharaju. 'As a joint venture, this was a leap of faith for all three players,' said Shantharaju. Along with him came an entirely new team for Indus Towers that ran the business competitively, sourcing tenancies from not only the incumbents but also new players in the market. 'The JV parents trusted us to streamline the business by introducing technology and processes without questioning biases.'

Airtel took the opportunity to carve out the company's remaining towers that were not part of the deal into a separate company, Bharti Infratel. This company was left with around 22,000 telecom towers over the service areas that Indus Towers did not cover. The hive-off was effective from 31 January 2008, Sunil Mittal said in the investor call on 25 April 2008.[6]

The model was financially suited to the service operators. Telecom towers accounted for the bulk of the capital expense of the telecom companies. It was financed with borrowings.

That, in turn, raised the debt-to-profit ratio of the operators, putting pressure on the balance sheet and the ability to borrow further for expansion. Hiving off the towers changed a capex-intensive business to an operational expense that cash flows from telecom subscribers could address.

The additional cash from leasing out towers to new operators was useful too. Since any new lease spanned around fifteen years with a minimum commitment and inflation escalation, the contract was bankable. Therefore, the tower company could borrow more money backed by an operator's commitment to pay. At the outset, Indus Towers received a loan of around Rs 12,500 crore.

The money would be used to set up more towers and expand the tower portfolio. For Indus Tower, the location of the towers would be governed by the needs of its anchor tenants—Bharti, Vodafone and Idea. The combine competed now with the world's largest telecom companies by portfolio size and sat at a comfortable tenancy ratio with the assurance that it would only rise. Such was its success that the company wrote a Harvard University Case Study on its formation and business model.

40

Anil Takes Charge

Much like Kumar Mangalam Birla, Anil Ambani, too, was ready to shake things up.

Once Mukesh and Anil Ambani agreed on the contours of the separation, Reliance Industries embarked on separating its businesses. The first step was to identify the companies, which was easy. The next was to secure board approval, which came quickly, and finally, passing a shareholder resolution.

Mukesh Ambani, who was the chairman of the company after his father's passing, spoke to the public shareholders at the company's annual general meeting in August 2005. He promised that the demerger of these businesses, for which each shareholder would now receive shares separately, would ultimately unlock value and increase management focus in each area.

'It (the demerger) seeks to take RIL forward into a trajectory of exponential growth. The Board has approved, in principle, a reorganization of RIL's businesses,' Mukesh Ambani said in his speech. 'The Board has now proposed to de-merge from RIL the power, financial services and telecommunication services businesses.

'As far as the Infocomm business is concerned, RIL held convertible preference shares in Reliance Infocomm worth

Rs. 8,100 crore (US$ 1,840 million). RIL decided to exercise the option of converting preference shares of Reliance Infocomm Limited to equity shares of face value of Re 1 each at a price of Rs 32 per share. RIL thus effectively holds 66 per cent of Reliance Infocomm Limited. This represents a significant value for RIL shareholders.

'I am happy to say that my younger brother, Anil, has taken the mantle of leadership of these de-merged business undertakings. All of us admire his drive and energy. This will be a source of great strength for the businesses under his leadership. I wish him and his talented team every success in realizing the enormous growth opportunities in these sectors. Both of us will have the opportunity of serving all shareholders with enthusiasm and dedication.'[1]

The resolution was passed, and both Ambanis began sorting out their businesses' affairs. In February 2006, Reliance Infocomm wrote off Rs 4500 crore. The company said it was the cost of bad debt or irrecoverable sums of money. The two biggest contributors to the write-off were bills that customers refused to pay and handsets that Infocomm had invested in but had no takers and were becoming obsolete.

The recast of the previous year's financials was done in the interest of shareholders, the company said. To observers, however, it was clearly in the run-up to Anil Ambani inheriting a balance sheet he backed.

Reliance Communication Ventures was listed on stock exchanges on 6 March 2006, officially marking the control of the Anil Dhirubhai Ambani Group (ADAG) over the company that owned a controlling stake in Reliance Infocomm, Reliance Telecom and Reliance Communication Infrastructure. Anil Ambani denounced the cross-holding pattern of these companies as opaque in his very first investor meeting, held in the same month he took control. To address and simplify the structure, as Ambani explained, the company's board had approved a restructuring on 12 March 2006. As per the new structure, Reliance Infocomm was merged into its holding company, Reliance Communications, which was turned into an operating entity. The other companies were converted to 100 per cent subsidiaries of RCom.

Surrendering cross holdings between companies, and direct holdings in the subsidiaries of ADAG gave the promoters of Reliance Communications a 63 per cent stake in the company from an earlier direct holding of 38.27 per cent. It also diluted the stake of the public shareholders from 61.73 per cent to 37 per cent. He also bought and folded the large landmass of Dhirubhai Ambani Knowledge City into Reliance Communications. Apart from the network operating centre, this land included constructed and planned housing and other facilities that Nita Ambani is widely considered to have conceived.

While he pitched the infrastructure depth of the venture, Anil Ambani was convinced that GSM services were the way forward for the venture.

As the cost of mobile calls dropped from 2004 onwards, a SIM card became affordable to the lower economic echelons. The price of a mobile instrument, however, had not fallen sufficiently for the lower middle class to afford one each. Migrant workers in urban areas often shared an instrument to call home using their own SIM cards. The CDMA phone could not do this because the SIM card was built into the phone instrument. In contrast, a SIM in a GSM phone could simply be unplugged and replaced with another. In key pockets of Mumbai and Delhi, there are as many as four or five phone numbers being used on one instrument, making high-value calls to remote locations in rural India.

As a result, CDMA depended on postpaid businesses with long cash cycles; GSM services had a high cash flow since a lot of the business was prepaid and the overall all-call rate on a prepaid plan was higher than the average.

The younger Ambani had started laying its foundation to make a technology shift as early as 2005 when the separation of RIL businesses between the brothers was already on its way.

As owner of a part GSM network already, he believed it would not be difficult for Reliance to further that agenda. The easiest means would have been to buy an existing operator. What could be better than Hutch, which trailed only Bharti Airtel and Reliance in its size?

41

Vodafone's India Adventure

Anil Ambani embarked on the journey to acquire Hutchison Essar.

Li Ka-shing had had a good run in the Indian market. Over the last half-decade, three major events shaped his view on India.

The first was the regularization of WLL, or CDMA operations, to a mobile service. The second was Essar's manoeuvres that brought Hutch an all-India footprint and led to an arbitration case against its partner.

Essar helped resolve the tiff between Rajeev Chandrasekharan and the BPL family that had brought the mobile operator to its knees. Essar's Delhi operation had been merged with Hutch's Mumbai when Essar embarked on mopping up BPL because it held licences for many of the lucrative Indian service areas apart from the leading presence in Mumbai.

Hutch's understanding was that Essar would round up the equity in BPL Mobile, operating Mumbai and other areas, from the Nambiar family and fold that into the entity that operated in Mumbai and Delhi. For this, Hutch put up the acquiring capital and agreed to pay Essar a substantial sum at the end of the transaction. Essar complied and transferred most of BPL into the joint venture with Hutchison and collected its reward for completing the transaction. A merger with the most valuable Mumbai circle was still pending and after all had been said and done with Hutch, it appeared that Essar would not give up BPL's Mumbai operation.

An oddly timed government objection said the merger was anti-competitive, pausing the combination of Mumbai's two leading operators, BPL Mobile and Hutch. The dispute landed Hutchison and Essar in the Bombay High Court. The Essar Group de facto ran BPL Mobile, which was later rebranded as Loop and remained a fierce competitor in the market.

The rule was that no promoter could own more than 10 per cent of competing network operators. As a substantial owner (33 per cent) of Hutchison Essar, the Ruia family-owned group could not hold equity in BPL Mobile. Essar on paper held 9.9 per cent in BPL Mobile, and its equity changed hands in multiple transactions in Mauritius. It later became known that the majority stakeholders in the Mumbai operator were I.P. Khaitan and Kiran Khaitan, brother-in-law and sister of Essar's promoter Shashi Ruia. On the ground, all the operations of BPL's Mumbai service provider were managed by the Essar Group, including investor and media meetings that sometimes took place at the Essar headquarters opposite Mumbai's Mahalaxmi racecourse.

The Bombay High Court referred Hutch's challenge to arbitration. The Hong Kong-based group sought compensation for the value it had ascribed to the Mumbai operations of BPL Mobile. However, both parties knew that the arbitration would be a long-drawn affair and by the time a verdict was reached, the market and the businesses would have moved on.

The issue became even more troublesome when BPL Mobile, under Essar's care, applied for an all-India service licence in 2007. To capitalize the company for such payments, another equity transaction, again in Mauritius, was allegedly

undertaken in contradiction to a status quo order that the Court
had issued pending arbitration.

The third event that shaped Li Ka-shing's India outlook
was dealing with local regulators. The foreign direct holding
regulations required 49 per cent Indian shareholding. It was
lowered in November 2005 to 26 per cent. Hutch required an
Indian partner to hold equity in the operating entity in India.
Theoretically, Essar was this partner, but two-thirds of Essar's
equity in Hutchison Essar was held overseas. Uday Kotak,
who had earlier helped with this predicament, wanted to cash
out. Hutch mulled options.

For a while, the company considered employee stock
options. When the group explored a public listing, the
task appeared daunting. To then park its stake, Hutchison
assigned options to its own trusted lieutenant, Asim Ghosh.
The chief executive of the Indian operator was issued a loan
backed by Rabobank Hong Kong to purchase Hutch's equity.
Analjit Singh bought Kotak's shares in 2006 for a little
over Rs 1000 crore. Between them, the two executives held
15 per cent but their voting rights were vested with Hutch.
They held the right to nominate themselves on the board of
the company.

During the course of expanding across India, Hutch
had accumulated smaller outfits. In some cases, the
promoters retained equity, leaving them with minority
stakes. The most notable of them was 5 per cent held
by the Hinduja family. When the threshold for foreign
investment was increased to 74 per cent, Hutch undertook
an equity restructuring under which IDFC bought out
the Hindujas. After this structuring, for the Indian
authority, as per the local accounting standards, Hutch held
51.96 per cent in the telecom operator, but under US SEC
reporting standards, it held voting rights for 61.88 per cent.

Hutch decided to test the market for buyers. Any sale was contingent on the Essar Group's approval as it held a first right to refusal.

The Indian telecom industry was booming, and there were many interested in buying this large market leader. Many domestic bidders joined the fray as industry figures shot past any projections. Bidding began in the second half of 2006. Hutch opened its books for diligence to many including the Hindujas, Essar Group and Anil Ambani's Reliance Communications.

Interest also came from international investors ranging from private equity to strategic players. Among them was Arun Sarin.

Several years before the Hutch opportunity, Sarin was at AirTouch Communications in San Francisco when Vodafone bought his company.

He was no stranger to Indian shores. Apart from his native ties, in more recent years, he had partnered with RPG to launch services in Chennai after the first round of licences. In 1997 he was nominated AirTouch's president and chief operating officer at the time. Two years later AirTouch was acquired by Vodafone, the RPG partnership was also transferred to Vodafone. At Vodafone Sarin was cast in a low-key role, but he remained on the board of RPG's mobile business, quietly keeping a tab on its evolving shape. The sale of RPG to Siva's Sterling was a natural tapering of Sarin's involvement with Indian telephony.

Three years hence, Sarin was nominated to head Vodafone Plc in London. By this time, Sarin had been involved in adequate mergers and acquisitions to become a devout believer in growth led by consolidation. Sarin's first step thus as Vodafone's chief was to embark on acquiring US telecom operator AT&T. Vodafone already had control of Verizon, and the combination with AT&T would have put the company in pole position in the US. That was not to be. His attempt was scuttled when Vodafone's board shot down the acquisition proposal.

The subsequent two years turned out to be a cooling period for the world's largest mobile service provider and presented an opportunity for Sarin to relook at its strategy. Operators had overpaid for 3G licences in Europe. Growth in these markets had saturated. They accounted for 70 per cent of Vodafone's revenue. So naturally shareholders would soon come asking Sarin about future growth and returns. He spearheaded a new strategy to explore emerging markets. Two hit the mark— Africa and India.

For Sarin, India was homecoming. His desire to join the Indian Air Force in his father's footsteps was a distant dream from decades ago. His purpose had since been realigned to telephony. He received a hero's welcome back to Indian shores. Of course, he brought with him the promise of multinational corporation money . . . a lot of it. The stars were well aligned. A meaningful deal in India would re-establish his winning streak.

In October 2005, he decided to move Vodafone to buy 10 per cent of Bharti Airtel, which, under Sunil Mittal's guidance, had emerged as the Indian bellwether. The British company forked out around $1.5 billion for the transaction, which was broken up into two parts. Vodafone International, based in the Netherlands bought 5.6 per cent and the group's Mauritius entity bought 4.4 per cent. The deal capitalized Bharti into its next round of growth. Yet, there seemed little room for Vodafone to further expand its interest or control over Bharti. So, when the next best opening came up with Hutchison, it was too good to pass up for Sarin. Thankfully, Vodafone got Bharti's blessings on its bid easily enough.

Vodafone also appeared to be the preferred choice of Hutch's management team. Vodafone was not only bidding a slightly higher valuation than others, it also agreed to take on Hutchison's liabilities and retain the shareholding structure through Analjit

Singh and Asim Ghosh as 15 per cent equity partners without voting rights.

Asim Ghosh, CEO of Hutchison Essar, held a meeting with the top brass of the Indian team on the ground and asked a question: Who would you like to see as the acquirer of the company? A vote among twenty or so executives present in the room ended in favour of Vodafone. The general consensus was that a transition to Vodafone would be easier as cultural change would be less going from one multi-national to another compared with a transition to a promoter-driven Indian company.

Vodafone made a whopping $11 billion offer to buy out Hutch in December 2006, which the latter gladly accepted.

However, the Ruias who had stayed out of the Hutchison boardroom so far were not going to be taken so lightly. Essar's relations with Hutch had been tense at best for some time. The group now resisted a deal with Vodafone.

Vodafone was advised to find another Indian partner. But with a 33 per cent stake in the company, the Ruias had veto powers. Essar was ready to flex how much more power it had. On 6 March 2007, after the deal was announced and the key regulatory permissions were in place, Essar filed an objection with the Foreign Investment and Promotions Board of India to bar the transaction because Vodafone held 10 per cent in competing Bharti Airtel.

Sarin, along with some members from the Vodafone team, visited the Ruias' sea-front bungalow at Walkeshwar, Mumbai. An option was for Vodafone to buy out Essar and find another Indian partner. Could Anil Ambani have been that partner? Before that could be explored to a deeper measure, it became clear that the Ruias were not ready to exit. They did, nonetheless, want the option to exit in three years, at a price higher than the one Vodafone was paying Hutch.

Moreover, even though they were not selling, they bargained for payday on a change of hands between strategic investors of Hutchison Essar. To Sarin and his team, who were hosted and reassured of support from the Ruia family, partnering with the Ruias seemed like the best and perhaps only option because Essar could always scuttle a deal with its refusal rights.

An agreement was hashed out over the course of the week and on 14 March, Essar withdrew its objections. A day later the group was paid $415 million to accept Vodafone as a buyer, remove any claim of the group from management of the company, scrap the right to refuse Vodafone selling its shares and withdraw its objections to the FIPB.

Essar negotiated to sweeten its deal by securing the right to sell in three years as well as a tag-along ride in case Vodafone decided to divest. Essar received a 'put option' that would mature in 2009 and last till 2011, under which Vodafone would need to buy or arrange a buyer for Essar to exit.

While Essar withdrew its complaint, the move had highlighted the transaction for the regulator. It caught on to the discrepancy between India and US shareholding disclosed by Hutchison. It also sought clarification on the nature and rights of Asim Ghosh and Analjit Singh's shares. It did not impede the transaction but uneasy correspondence with the regulator delayed it.

On 15 March, Essar signed a term sheet with Vodafone International through its Indian entity Essar Teleholdings, which held 11 per cent of the Indian operator, and Mauritius-based Essar Communications which held Essar's remaining 22 per cent equity.

Vodafone's Netherlands subsidiary agreed to buy Hutchison's 52 per cent in the Indian operator by purchasing a company in the Cayman Islands that held the shares for $11 billion. The enterprise valuation of the operator as a corollary was around

$19 billion. The transaction was to be completed in Mauritius. Once it had agreed to buy Hutchison Essar, Vodafone divested its stake in Bharti Airtel by the 5.6 per cent directly held in the Netherlands entity that bought Hutchison's stake.

The final announcement was made with much fanfare, especially internally. It included a budget of nearly $50 million for rebranding, as Hutch's signature orange colour was swapped for Vodafone's red.

Vodafone elected to retain Hutch's successful pug tailing a boy campaign, which struck a chord with users. Having established continuity, Vodafone launched several other attractive advertisement campaigns over the next few years. In an environment where competitors relied on celebrities to promote networks, one of Vodafone's contrarian and most successful campaigns was with ZooZoo, launched in tandem with a cricket tournament (IPL). This was an egg-like creature caught in comical situations that reflected the society the advertisement was targeting.

The group also quickly rolled out the network across India, because although Hutch had accumulated pan-India licences, several of the service areas still had minimal deployment. Sarin retired in 2008 handing charge of the global operator to Vittorio Colao. Shortly thereafter, in February 2009, Vodafone deputed Marten Pieters to succeed Asim Ghosh as chief executive of its Indian arm. 'In those still relatively early days of mobile (making a success of Vodafone-Essar) meant new customers and revenue market share. It also meant that we were not satisfied with the number three position we had at that moment,' said Pieters. Vodafone trailed Bharti Airtel and Reliance Communications in terms of subscriber base, which was the most tracked metric of the time.

Vodafone soon realized that operating in India was like operating in twenty-three separate markets that were socially,

economically and culturally unlike each other. Pieters recalls
the dilemma of investing in Bihar, which on paper had a huge
population and therefore, revenue potential, but the capital
expenditure to cover the state was higher than other regions.
Bharti's experience in Bihar demonstrated a great aptitude for
technology among users but lower than average per-subscriber
spending on the network.

Cost optimization warranted the sharing of some capital-
intensive infrastructure for which the stage was already set.

42

The Taxman Taps Vodafone

On the ground, Vodafone was off to a running start, but on the regulatory front, the acquisition experience was onerous. Soon after it paid Hutchison, the Indian taxman questioned the transaction and sought $2 billion from Vodafone. The exchequer said under prevailing laws, this should have been withheld by the acquirer and sent to the government. Vodafone sought to redirect the queries to Hutchison, which had already encashed, but to that, the regulator's response was that it had no control over Hutchison as the company had already exited India, unlike Vodafone. 'It was the talking point in every meeting with media, with investors, and even on private parties,' said Pieters, although the shareholders' issue had no operational bearing on Vodafone Essar.

Vodafone appealed this levy. It went to the Bombay High Court, then the Supreme Court. At the outset, it appeared to be a pressure tactic from the tax regulator, but soon, it took the form of payday in politics. From there, it seemed like there was no way to retract, even if there was institutional will to do so. The ballooning interest costs put the levy on Vodafone at $3.4 billion in 2012 as the company fought against it. There was political involvement as well, with members of the UK parliament raising the Vodafone matter in diplomatic meetings with the Indian finance ministry.

Vodafone argued that its transaction with Hutchison had taken place outside the country. Money had been exchanged between a Netherland-based Vodafone entity to a Hong Kong-based Hutchison Telecom through the Cayman Islands. Between tax exemptions for the islands and the international nature of the transaction, Vodafone argued the Indian government was treating the operator as an agent for tax collection from Hutchison. The Indian government should prosecute Hutch overseas rather than Vodafone, it said. On the other hand, the 15 per cent equity that is continued to park with Asim Ghosh and Analjit Singh Vodafone conceded would be subject to taxation.

The tax authority disagreed. The entire asset being exchanged was based in India. The value creation was an outcome of the Indian consumer. The tax department must get a share in valuation spike, it said.

The India Supreme Court ruled in favour of Vodafone. In January 2012, it said that the current provisions absolved Vodafone of the liability because the tax notification to levy withholding tax on transactions completed overseas for an Indian asset was issued after the date of the Hutch–Vodafone deal. A settlement with the Government of India seemed imminent. Then, at his budget speech, barely a month after the SC judgment, Finance Minister Pranab Mukherjee announced a retrospective amendment to the law that allowed the exchequer to tax transactions retrospectively.

This caused upheaval because it affected Vodafone and nearly a dozen other transactions. General Electric sold its business process outsourcing unit Genpact to US-based private equity players, Japan's Mitsui sold 51 per cent of its stake in miner

Sesa Goa to the UK-based Vedanta Group, and AT&T sold its 16.5 per cent stake in Idea Cellular to the Tata Group.

Rumour has it that after the SC judgment, Vodafone rebuffed attempts of the ruling Congress Party to solicit funds from the telecom operator which led to a change in the administration's will to resolve this. However, Vodafone was quick to serve arbitration notice to the government on behalf of its Netherlands entity.

The notice was sent to Indian Prime Minister Manmohan Singh, with copies marked to Finance Minister Pranab Mukherjee, Telecom Minister Kapil Sibal and Law Minister Salman Khurshid. Shortly thereafter, Vittorio Colao, chief executive of Vodafone Plc and non-executive chairman of Vodafone India, Analjit Singh, headed to meet Mukerjee who invited the revenue secretary and international taxation chief into the room. In this meeting on 1 May 2012, not much was resolved.

Arbitration proceedings were commenced. Both sides dragged their weight. Under the proceedings, a panel of three arbitrators was to be set up. In 2014, a change in the Indian political topography raised Vodafone's hopes for a speedy recovery. The Narendra Modi-led Bhartiya Janta Party came to power. It had made resolving the previous government's 'tax terrorism' one of its election agendas. Newly appointed Law Minister Ravi Shankar Prasad vocalized that retrospective modification of the law was less than ideal in any circumstance.

To its disappointment, Vodafone found no change in stance from the new administrators. The company was still hopeful that the new ruling party would resolve matters in arbitration quickly and to its satisfaction. However, when it came down to the brass tax, a $2 billion payday was something that even the new government was willing to fight for.

To proceed with arbitration the sides had to agree on a panel. Both could nominate one panelist and the third had to be appointed by mutual agreement. The government nominated former chief justice of India R.C. Lahoti and Vodafone's choice was Canadian trial lawyer Yves Fortier. It took eight months and at least three tries before the two agreed on Abdulqawi Ahmed Yusuf, vice president, International Court of Justice, as the third arbitrator. The arbitration proceedings took another five years, and the case remained unresolved till 2024.

43

Vodafone Takes Control

In 2011, Vodafone was in the middle of a storm. Not only was it furiously battling a $2 billion tax demand, but the company also needed capitalization to deploy 3G service, as it combated unprecedented price wars.

Essar's option to sell was maturing, and the group was intent on making the most out of it. In January 2011, Essar decided to fold its telecom business into a listed entity along with the contract that said Vodafone would buy the Indian operators' shares.

Under the option, Essar had a put, or sell, option to tender its 22 per cent which it held overseas. If the Indian conglomerate exercised this, Vodafone had a call, or buy option, that allowed it to buy the remaining 11 per cent held in India. Essar's move to place this option in a listed company was designed to reverse list its shares in Vodafone. The listing would have set a floor price of $5 billion for Vodafone to match.

This was the latest attempt to wrangle more out of the UK-based operator was the latest in an already strained relationship between the partners. 'It is clear that the DNA of Essar and Vodafone was not very compatible. I believe that the Ruias for a long term have hoped that they could still wrestle the control over the Company from the majority shareholder(s). As long as that had not happened they were acting very opportunistic and clearly always first looking at their own interest (and not so much the best interest of the Company),' said Pieters.[1]

Heightened competitiveness in the industry, burgeoning debt costs and the struggle with regulators were eroding Vodafone India's company value. Shareholders in the UK were asking questions about poor returns from India's investment. The looming re-entry of a second Reliance Group into the market made matters worse.

Vodafone was unwilling to relent on Essar's latest move. The group lodged its protest with the Securities and Exchange Board of India, the capital markets regulator, and the Bombay Stock Exchange in an attempt to prevent irrational pricing for its shares. The Essar entity had a 5 per cent market float of shares, which was scarce enough to be artificially managed to reflect an undue 'fair value' for the shares Essar was trying to sell to Vodafone.

The Essar Group had used the Vodafone put option as collateral to raise funds for other businesses and an assertive UK partner could shake investor sentiment. The Indian group tried an alternate route. It referred to an RBI circular issued barely a year ago to peg the valuation of its 11 per cent shares held in India higher than the remaining 22 per cent that were overseas. The Essar Group demanded $600–700 more than the agreed price. Vodafone was determined not to flinch. By the end of March 2011, the two parties agreed to proceed with the $5 billion deal while exercising both the put and call options.

Now, Vodafone needed to find an Indian partner who would take on the Essar stake so that the company could remain within the foreign shareholding guidelines mandated by India. Fortunately for Vodafone, Ajay Piramal, chairman of Piramal Enterprises, had cash on hand from the sale of his pharmaceutical unit to Abott and did not have an immediate plan to deploy it. Piramal promised to be a non-interfering partner, as long as he was guaranteed a 17 per cent return and an exit in two years.

Even as the transaction was closing Essar secured an additional $460 million from Vodafone, much of which was put in an escrow account in case this transaction too became subject to withholding tax.

In 2013, the Indian government allowed foreign telecom companies to hold 100 per cent of their Indian arms. Vodafone was finally able to acquire all the equity in its Indian unit from safekeepers Piramal, Analjit Singh and Asim Ghosh.

The operational entity, however, by this time, was under severe stress. Two rounds of rather expensive spectrum buying had tipped its debt-to-equity ratio into an uncomfortable zone. Pieters was holding on in the hope that he would be able to publicly list the company in India before taking retirement. Unfortunately, that was not to be. When he passed on the baton to the next chief, homegrown Sunil Sood, in 2015 the equity markets in India were soft across sectors and even more so for telecom which had seen too much turmoil from the 2012 licence cancellations.

The year 2015 was good for incumbent operators as customers returned after shopping forever retreating offers from competing networks. The looming launch of the new Reliance hung over their heads, but it was delayed by half a decade and for now, the team felt secure. In Vodafone's year under Sunil Sood, the company clawed back its market share and consolidated ties with high-paying customers in key markets.

44

One Bride, Two Suitors

As Vodafone cemented its entry into India around 2008, Bharti felt ready to look overseas. Their common thread was competitor, Anil Ambani.

The India success story was well established. Airtel was the undoubted winner of the decade. The transition from a daily frenzy in 1999 to a comfortable cruise in 2009 did not make Sunil Mittal any less ambitious. A little less than a decade ago, Mittal was convincing investors to take note of Airtel, now, with cash in hand, he was in a position to be an investor.

The company had toyed with small opportunities in Seychelles, Sri Lanka and even Bhutan. In April 2008, while detailing the company's annual results, Sunil Mittal fielded several questions on Bharti's merger and acquisition strategy. It was a pointer to what investors, including Singtel, Bharti's largest overseas shareholder, were seeking.

During the course of the annual investor call, Mittal and his team set the stage for what was going to come next. 'I think the company as is now ready to go farther ahead and look at some opportunities around the globe,' said Mittal. He added that from the past signature of making small buys, Bharti was ready to look at targets that were 'medium to meaningful' in size.

Akhil Gupta, Bharti's numbers man, added, 'On the acquisition status, we are interested in 50,000–60,000 population countries, we are doing some of those separately . . . In any international acquisition the only consideration we would have is that it should be value accretive, it should be good for our company and the shareholders and it should add value.'[1]

These statements were not made out of context. Sunil Mittal received unprecedented attention at the World Mobile Congress held in Barcelona and organized by the global GSM Association, or GSMA. At a key meeting in this forum, Manoj Kohli, chief executive of Bharti Airtel, was seated next to Phuthuma Nhleko. He was the group president and chief executive of a South Africa-based telecom operator MTN. The two got talking and thus began a series of interactions between the companies that landed Sunil Mittal an invitation from the MTN board to discuss a merger with Bharti Airtel.

MTN had explored sale options earlier, although nothing had fructified. It was listed on the Johannesburg Stock Exchange. As of 31 December 2007, it had an annual revenue of R102.5 billion[2] (around $14.8 billion on contemporary conversion rate) and an operating profit of R43.2 billion ($6.2 billion). This was on the back of a subscriber base of around twenty-four million.

The group had a footprint in twenty-one countries across Africa and the Middle East. All the operating companies were held through arms in Mauritius and Dubai.

The companies revealed on 5 May 2008 that talks between the two groups were 'exploratory', but the headlines next morning read as though Bharti had made an acquisition offer. Reports estimated that a full purchase of MTN would cost Bharti over $35 billion. Neither company had validated any such figure. They had to announce talks due to stock exchange regulations, otherwise, at the time it was made public, the negotiation was barely a back-of-the-envelope calculation.

'Bharti would like to clarify that it has not made any offer to acquire the whole or part of MTN. Therefore, the speculation around a bid by Bharti in a section of the media is incorrect and misleading,' the company issued a brief press release the day after it had announced merger talks.[3]

Then, again, a week later Bharti issued a press clarification, Bharti would like to reiterate that these discussions are still exploratory in nature and may or may not lead to any transactions.[4] The principal uniting factor for the two companies was that their markets were emerging and therefore some of the business models could be transposed. The amount of money involved, however, was a hindrance and as a workaround, the groups were toying with share transfer and management control options.

The news of Bharti's aspirations received global attention and in less than a week, the Indian operator had a competing bidder from UAE—Emirates Telecommunications Corp.

Bharti charged on with negotiations that culminated in a term sheet for the merger on 16 May. However, when the MTN board considered it, armed with a counter bidder, it believed it had more leverage to flex. Instead of signing off on this sheet, it changed the contours of its offer. The version sent back to Bharti involved the family and Singtel trading majority equity in Bharti for a minority stake in the combined MTN.

This irked Bharti, which pulled out of further discussions. Then the company issued a detailed explanation of its decision. 'Bharti's vision of transforming itself from a home-grown Indian company to a true Indian multinational telecom giant, symbolizing the pride of India, would have been severely compromised and this was completely unacceptable to Bharti,' the operator said.[5]

The South African operator also sought to reprice the transaction with Bharti given that MTN shares had risen significantly in the two weeks after it became the cynosure of competitors. 'Bharti will not engage in a bidding war at any stage. Bharti would also like to thank over a dozen Internationally reputed bankers from the US and Europe who have given confident letters of funding of over USD 60 billion,' Bharti said in its statement calling off the transaction.

It was not until a day later that it became apparent that another competitor scuttling Bharti's deal was none other than homegrown Reliance Communications. As soon as Bharti disengaged, Anil Ambani's company entered into exclusive negotiations for forty-five days to arrive at a merger deal. 'We are delighted to be engaged in exclusive negotiations with MTN Group to achieve a partnership, which would provide investors, customers and the people of both companies a unique and global platform for exponential growth, creating substantial long-term shareholder value.'[6]

What was unconscionable to Bharti was not a concern to Anil Ambani. For nearly three weeks, the groups engaged in negotiations, thrashing out details and valuations. The combination of RCom and MTN would have put the company among the world's top ten with a subscriber base comparable to AT&T's.

Meanwhile, RCom was forging ahead with its expansion plans even as it negotiated with MTN. The company closed another acquisition with UK-based mobile virtual network operator Vanco. The deals were RCom's way to success, repeated company executives.

Anil Ambani agreed to swap his 66 per cent in RCom to become the largest shareholder in the MTN combine. Discussions were still ongoing over who would manage the final entity when Mukesh Ambani got a whiff of plans. In his separation agreement with Anil Ambani the elder Ambani had agreed to stay out of the telecom business, but also made a 'good

faith' pact that his firm would have first right of refusal in case
Anil ever puts up RCom for sale.

The transfer of RCom shares to MTN was classified as
a sale. To that end, Mukesh was within his rights to invoke
the refusal right to buy RCom. RIL wasted no time in sending
notice to Anil, RCom and most importantly the MTN Board,
that should the merger under consideration meet muster, equity
in RCom would first need to go through Mukesh. The South
African firm now found itself inserted in a family struggle,
that it had no intention of juggling. Anil Ambani maintained
a brave face even as he called his brother's move a 'mala fide
effort to disrupt the talks' and MTN made a statement to say
it was staying the course with the younger Ambani. 'Reliance
Industries' claim is legally and factually untenable, baseless, and
misconceived,' stated a statement issued by RCom.[7]

Anil Ambani attributed this move to jealousy. 'RIL's claim
is born out of mounting despair and frustration at Reliance
ADA Group's continuing successes,' said the RCom press note.
The return of Mukesh into Anil's affairs raked up memories of
the bitter separation barely two years ago, and Anil did not pull
his punches. 'RIL's actions are anti-consumer, anti-investor and
anti-globalization, and against the vision, beliefs and principles
of the founder of the Reliance Group, late Shri Dhirubhai
Ambani. Reliance Communications dismisses RIL's claim with
the contempt it deserves.'[8]

Such was Anil Ambani's conviction that when RCom and
MTN could not close a transaction by 9 July, both extended
the period of the exclusive negotiations to 21 July, despite RIL's
claim. The confidence was misplaced.

Even as he tried to find a legal workaround, Mukesh
Ambani initiated arbitration proceedings to purchase RCom
stock and prevent the merger with MTN. At least for some
time, senior executives at RCom believed that sources from

Bharti had convinced Mukesh and his team that MTN intended to buy an Indian asset, not merge with it. RIL, under Mukesh's instructions, acted the only way it knew how to stop the transaction.

After the filing of the arbitration suit, there was no way around it, so both RCom and MTN called off the conversation. It was an unusually short press release for RCom that read, 'Owing to certain legal and regulatory issues, the parties are presently unable to conclude a transaction. Accordingly, it has been mutually decided to allow the Exclusivity Agreement to lapse.'[9]

A rather telling quote from MTN later echoed the South African operator's intention. 'We continue to seek value-accretive expansion opportunities in emerging markets, and we believe that we have the potential to act as a consolidator in the currently depressed global economy,' said Nhleko in MTN's 2008 annual report.[10]

On second thoughts, Bharti Airtel was still the emerging market player that made a good fit. So, MTN came back to India for a second dance in May 2009. Wiser from the last experience and more aware of each other's expectations, this time, moves during negotiations were more transparent and reported daily to the press.

On that note, the very first press release clearly established the broad equity contours of the deal. 'Bharti would acquire a 49 per cent shareholding in MTN and, in turn, MTN and its shareholders would acquire an approximate 36 per cent economic interest in Bharti, of which 25 per cent would be held by MTN with the remainder held directly by MTN shareholders. Bharti and MTN have agreed to discuss the potential transaction exclusively with one another until 31 July 2009.'[11] The deal was pegged at $23 billion in cash and share swap.

Sunil Mittal had also brought SingTel on board such that the investor would remain a stakeholder in the combine after the merger. With the major contours in place, the main hurdle to cross was bringing on board MTN's shareholders and arranging financing for Bharti Airtel.

While the money was easy to source, D Street[*] worried about the impact on Bharti from diluting its stock to raise funds. On the day of the announcement, Bharti's shares fell. Hopes for MTN on the other hand rose, this might be the final deal.

Just two days after the deal was announced, four of MTN's top shareholders declared they would vote against the deal in its present form. Bharti was sure it was not cowing down on the terms they sought, so Mittal and his team canvassed once again as they had done in the past. They were able to get an affirmative public statement from MTN's second-largest shareholder, Mikati's of Lebanon to endorse the deal. Then, the company's largest shareholder, Public Investment Corp, endorsed the transaction if Bharti increased the price consideration for MTN.

It was a step in the right direction, but still far from the destination. A month later Sunil Mittal remarked to the press that for the moment, with other aspects still in the air, Bharti was not looking to increase its acquisition offer for MTN but may consider a raise of between five and ten per cent closer to deal signing.

Bharti worked continuously to close loose ends. It arranged financing, and Sunil Mittal had to resign from the board of Standard Chartered Bank (SCB) to avoid a conflict of interest. SCB was an advisor on the deal. Bharti then applied and received approval from the Indian stock exchange regulator to allow a 36 per cent stake in Bharti to change hands without triggering the mandatory open offer.

The apparent point of failure emerged when the South African government reserved its right to block the sale of this

---

[*] (Dalal Street: location of the stock exchange in Mumbai)

fifteen-year-old company, which has been a success story since the country's liberation in 1994. The companies extended the sunset of exclusive talks twice in the hope of convincing regulators.

Given the magnitude of the deal the finance ministries on both sides got involved. Eventually, the South African government blocked the deal because it wanted to preserve the local talent and sought a dual listing for the combined Bharti Airtel, which was against Indian regulations. The listing could have occurred using secondary instruments such as Global Depositary Receipts, but that was not amenable to the South African government.

It was an unhappy parting of ways for willing partners. 'We hope the South African government will review its position in the future and allow both companies an opportunity to re-engage,' said Bharti.[12] MTN said the deal failed because the two companies failed to unite the regulatory, economic and legal framework. The South African Rand took a pummelling against the dollar and stocks of both companies were muted.

The management of MTN revisited India a couple of times over the next two years. Bharti did not engage in any further conversations, but Anil Ambani entertained this confusing company that had swung from being a seller to becoming an acquirer. In June 2010, talks once again gained steam. This time, ministers on either side assured that politics would not take a seat in negotiations. Anil Ambani was scheduled to fly to South Africa, potentially to firm up a deal, but talks fizzled out with even less fanfare than before. On subsequent MTN trips news leaked of a potential revival of talks with RCom, but nothing concrete emerged from it.

Sunil Mittal had decisively moved on. On 30 September 2009, Bharti suffered a mid-week setback, but the eternal optimists spearheading the company awaited a new dawn.

45

Airtel Takes Africa

Sunil Mittal was sure of one thing after the MTN setback: It was time to look out. And that he did. Barely five months later, on 15 February 2009, Airtel announced it was in exclusive talks with Zain.

Four days earlier, 11 February was a tense day at Bharti. In the wee hours of the morning Sunil Mittal, Akhil Gupta and Manoj Kohli waited at the airport to board the company plane. They had an invitation from Kuwait to discuss the takeover of Zain Group's Africa telecom arm. The three were aware of MTN and Vivendi's interest in the asset, and that could play hooky with Bharti's general philosophy to stay away from a bidding war. The wounds from MTN were fresh so the optimism was subdued with a hint of nervousness. Sunil Mittal knew his mind and Bharti's ever-so-slightly flexible proposal.

Badr Al-Kharafi, Nasser Al-Kharafi's eldest son, was on the tarmac in Kuwait to welcome the team. The welcome came as some relief to the nerves and stoked a feeling of positivity among Bharti executives. They checked into the Sheraton to freshen up and swiftly headed to the Al Kharafi headquarters to reach by 9.30 a.m. Kharafi and Sunil greeted each other and glanced downwards. As the saying goes, 'You can tell a lot about a person from their shoes.' The two were wearing the same limited edition Moreschi's. They both noticed it, hugged and a deal was in the making.

Before meetings began, Sunil Mittal asked to have the room with Nasser Al-Kharafi to thrash out the essentials.

What seemed to have been established behind closed doors was that both of them wanted this equally and that set the tone for the rest of the day. Tough negotiations took place amid warm hospitality. Nothing being discussed would be a deal breaker. Akhil Gupta pushed for a written agreement that would at least lock both companies into exclusive talks for a period. It was meant to set aside the noise from the discussion rooms over the next few weeks.

The three had learned from the MTN experience that the broad contours must be on paper, so they negotiated. In a few hours, they had a price, basic terms, and acceptable words for a Memorandum of Understanding. As they headed out of the room, Mittal and Al-Karafi showed their colleagues the matching shoes that had brought them luck.

With that, the trio headed back to the Bharti jet that was primed and ready for the last six hours. Victorious, the three honchos headed home to Delhi at 6 p.m. local time with a thrill in the heart that mimicked the whirring sound of the jet's engines on takeoff.

The next step was to get a sign-off from the company boards. It came the very next day for Bharti. For Zain, it took a couple more days, but Al-Kharafi lost no time in touching base with Sunil Mittal, who was on the plane en route to the Mobile World Congress in Barcelona when he took the call. By 15 February, the two were ready to announce the talks public.

It was time to send out the due diligence teams. Kuwait, Bahrain, Dubai, Nigeria, Tanzania, and Kenya were all centres of research and negotiations. There was a point when the teams hit a snag. On 2 March, Mittal, Al-Kharafi and key team members were supposed to meet in Beirut. Mittal brought Chua Sock Koong, chief executive of SingTel along. The estimated value of some assets needed to be modified. The legal liabilities and assurances arising from the transfer of ownership were also under contention. The meeting ended on a grim note. The lucky shoes were missing. Al-Kharafi was wearing them, but Mittal's pair was elsewhere.

The two then met again to negotiate in Kuwait later that month, but this time Al-Kharafi had the wrong pair on. The strain on the negotiations was showing. The team observed it. Thankfully, there was no breakdown of talks. The two continued to explore options that would fit mutually.

Then came the final date of signing a legally binding agreement on 26 March, in London. Mittal's team surely reminded him of the lucky shoes and so must have been the case with Al-Karafi. Mittal's pair was lying in New Delhi, although he was already in the UK. Mittal called Jet Airways chief Naresh Goyal to ship them to London, only now the signing date and location had moved to 30 March in Amsterdam. When he alighted from the plane Manoj Kohli asked Mittal if he had remembered to carry the lucky pair. He had.

Al-Kharafi, on the other hand, was travelling into Stockholm without them. He had them couriered so that when they met in Amsterdam, that was the first thing they tapped, and a synchronous dance neared its conclusion. Al-Kharafi adjusted the final sale price by a few hundred million which had been grounds for friction.

Bharti Airtel became the new owner of operations in fifteen African markets. Ten of them were top-ranked. The group had a subscriber base of forty-two million and it was beginning to unveil value-added services like banking the unbanked in many of these regions. The acquisition cost Bharti $10.7 billion, funded mostly through debt.

The major stakeholders had agreed, but Bharti's path still had obstacles. The biggest one came from Nigeria, Zain's most profitable market, where a minority shareholder Broad Communications Group raised a dispute, and another tried to overturn Zain's original acquisition in 2006. It took almost a year for Bharti to close the transaction and complete the acquisition. In June 2010, when the deal was closed Bharti readied its man for the job. It then came as a happy surprise that Manoj Kohli offered himself for the job including a move to Nairobi, Kenya. It was an unexpected offer from an executive who had enjoyed the top position in India and was seen as a family man. Just like that, Kohli was designated chief of Airtel International including Africa, Bangladesh, Sri Lanka and the Channel Islands.

Kohli had led Bharti India to become a full-scale operator, transitioned the company through the outsourcing phase and had the promoters' complete trust. He was also confident of a sharp turnaround of the loss-making Zain assets. In his first appearance as chief of Africa Kohli promised more than doubling subscribers in Africa in just two or three years.

However, within the first three weeks of the acquisition administrations imposed higher Know Your Customer or KYC norms that led to a churn in subscribers. Bharti also discovered that like in urban India, Africa had a high incidence of dual SIM or one person owning two mobile phone numbers. In its first quarterly report, just twenty-three days after completing the acquisition Kohli said that the real subscriber number had fallen to thirty-six million from the originally stated forty-two million. The on-ground mobile penetration was just 20 per cent compared with earlier estimates of 30 per cent. The statistic made Kohli hopeful that the scope for growth was high.

Having toured and studied the countries Bharti had 'clear insight that each country is unique, each market is unique, customer behavior, customer expectations are unique, and hence we need to customize our strategy, customize our solution for each country. At the same time, the good news is that governments are fully aligned with Bharti's agenda, Bharti's plan and all governments have given us a very positive welcome and encouragement to deploy our brand all over Africa', Kohli told investors.[1]

A quarter later the enthusiasm was subdued as Kohli said, 'Elasticity definitely exists in Africa, how much is difficult to say, I think it will take us another two quarters of experience whether it is the same as India.'[2] The company had reduced and simplified telecom tariffs and in the process captured 3.7 million new subscribers, a high for Zain Africa which had been languishing on both the revenue and operating profit front for over a year. Kohli explained this was the outcome of low investment. Kohli said a number of things that raised investor hopes sky-high. He spoke of an IT outsourcing contract with IBM and hoped to complete this soon. For BPO services Bharti had signed on IBM, Tech Mahindra and Spanco. The companies were expected to start call centres closer to the service locations.

The average revenue per user of Zain Africa was much higher than India's at over seven dollars per month and the premise on which Mittal, Gupta and Kohli were operating was that once they applied Bharti's offshore model the profitability of the company would surge. So, tinkering with price points was also worth a shot. 'I truly believe that there is major elasticity in each of our 16 markets. During the last few weeks, we have done some tariff intervention and already manifested some of these elasticity,' said Kohli.[3]

That worried the investors. Would Bharti trigger the scathing tariff erosion in the African market that was playing out in India? 'We are not here for a price war, we are here for stable prices but competitive prices,' Kohli reassured onlookers.

For Airtel Africa, the devil lay in its higher cost per employee which stood at $4000 per month on a blended basis.

This was expected to remain static but the outsourcing model was scheduled to reduce the number of employees on the company's books creating a net effect of a lower overall cost.

The initial success and anticipation from the acquisition were so resounding that by the end of the year, investors became impatient when the debt began to bleed the cash off Bharti's books and a turnaround on several of the operations remained sluggish. Akhil Gupta first spoke of expense in Africa in May 2011, 'Africa is a very high-cost continent for the telecom industry and that reflects in the tariffs and everything and we felt as we went in that there were certain structural changes which we needed to bring.'⁴ Among other things, there was already a plan to spin off a telecom tower company.

The biggest issue the company faced was one of local protectionism. When Bharti tried to offshore functions like technology or call centres to IBM or to its own Indian arms, local governments protested and blocked the moves to retain local jobs. Dealing with local laws took time and the turnaround of the company took longer than anticipated.

Kohli had suggested that Airtel would touch 100 million subscribers by 2013, and the operating margins too would be shining. Yet, at the end of the financial year to March 2012, Kohli found himself saying, 'The elasticity of voice is far lower in Africa vis-à-vis what we saw in India. And that is why elasticity/moderate elasticity and high seasonality affected our voice revenues this quarter.'⁵

In the quarter ending 31 March 2013, Africa's revenue was $1.2 billion with an operating profit margin of just 25 per cent. The revenue fell slightly from the previous quarter and rose merely 5 per cent from the same quarter a year ago. Subscriber growth remained sluggish. After three years, the company still had under sixty-three million subscribers. The capital expenditure for 3G services compounded operating expenses that could not be contained and high interest rates on a huge debt dragged Airtel Africa into losses.

The investor community became restless. It did not help that Airtel was fighting a scathing price erosion and ballooning capital expenditure in India because of the 3G spectrum and new competitors through 2010 and 2011. Sanjay Kapoor believed in a decentralized approach to management. He appointed regional directors, to control circle chiefs, to remain nimble in a hyper competitive environment. Kapoor's way of management had divided the company into his loyalists and others. Human Resource teams had long tales to tell about the attrition in Airtel India, which was on an unprecedented high. It got flagged in some of the investor reports at the time and came with an explanation that Airtel was now a much bigger outfit and part of this attrition was an outcome of a slimming exercise for the organization. Kapoor remembers two programs called 'Agile 1' and 'Agile 2' in which Airtel was enlarging individual roles while reducing the overall staff size.

Investors also asked why Kapoor emphasized marketing more than the network. The reason was Airtel's debt that was weighing on its profit. To alleviate the pressure, Kapoor was pacing network investments. The move contradicted Airtel's earlier philosophy. The network had always trumped marketing, and the operator preferred to stay at the cutting edge of technology.

The company had bought 4G airwaves and Mukesh Ambani's company was threatening to launch a competing service. However, Airtel did not launch a 4G pilot in Pune until 2012. The 3G expansion, too, was slower than investors would have liked.

Meanwhile, special projects head Gopal Vittal was being recognized for his thorough approach and creative solutions to expand the use of data services in an effort to increase average revenue per user. It was what the company and possibly the industry needed desperately at the time. Ensuing his success, Vittal was nominated as joint managing director and chief executive of India at Airtel in February 2013.

Internally, that did not sit well, because Airtel had over the two years polarized into Kapoor supporters, who stood by him as he had done for many of them as he rose through Airtel's ranks. Kapoor's departure in March 2013 triggered an exodus of many among the top management. An *Economic Times* report said the number was eight of the top thirteen executives quit because they did not want to report to Vittal or felt sidelined in the management rejig.[6] Airtel recognized this. Consequently, for the first couple of years, various functions under Vittal as CEO still had dotted reporting lines to Manoj Kohli, who had returned to Delhi and was designated managing director, Akhil Gupta, or Sunil Mittal, who once again became an executive chairman of Airtel, after having relinquished the role in the previous restructuring. The new CEO of Airtel was not attention-seeking. He stayed on the course even as outsiders questioned his grip on the company's people. Mittal and Gupta gradually slipped increasing amounts of control to Vittal who by 2014 became the accepted head of the organization and was promoted to the position of managing director. Kohli assumed a group-level position in businesses other than telecom. He moved from Bharti to Softbank in mid-2015.

The Reliance Industries' launch had not yet taken place, although the company's participation in multiple rounds of spectrum auctions suggested it was planning something big.

Part Seven

46

Anil Ambani, A. Raja Align

As he set about soliciting permissions to acquire Hutch, Anil Ambani found he may have yet another option.

The strength of Reliance had always been to build assets from the ground up, and Anil Ambani decided to take a leaf from his father's playbook. A familiar face in the corridors of Sanchar Bhavan, Anil Ambani knocked at the door of Dayanidhi Maran, minister of telecommunications and information technology, to get a dual technology permit and offer both GSM and CDMA services. This was not the first time the idea was mooted in the ministry.

In May 2005, Maran had already asked for the TRAI's opinion on allocating spectrum to new players, which the authority had shot down.[1] It had been in cold storage, until a new prospect of spectrum for 3G, or third-generation GSM, services was initiated. The defence vacated some airwaves in the 2100MHz band, much higher than the 800 and 900 operators were using for mobile phone services. That opened up an opportunity for another technology change for the incumbents.

In September 2006, TRAI under Nripendra Mishra revised its view. A recommendation published for opening the sector to 3G services said that the earlier recommendation falsely linked 2G and 3G as interdependent technologies. The authority now believed that '3G cannot be perceived as an automatic extension of 2G and would need to be viewed as a kind of standalone service for specialized needs and its allocation criteria has to be specific separately.'[2] A corollary to this was the potential opening up of the market for an additional two or three players. The regulator also advised spectrum in use by government departments like space and defence should be reframed to vacate spots for commercial use.

Maran initiated a request from the DoT to the TRAI to recommend a limit on the number of telecom operators allowed to offer service in the Indian market. Political unrest unseated Maran from the Ministry of Communication before he could act. In May 2007, after the closure of the Vodafone–Hutch deal, he was replaced by his DMK political party mate and relative Andimuthu Raja, popularly known as A. Raja.

This minister promised that 'during my tenure, my efforts and endeavour would be to provide the communication facilities to the people at the lowest ebb of the social order'.[3] Under him the ministry's focus was on rural networks and lowering the price of a phone call to below Re 1 per minute.

He lived up to that promise, as state-run operators BSNL and MTNL launched an IndiaOne Plan in September 2007. This offering obliterated the distance-based billing that had so far prevailed and brought the calling rate per minute to Re 1. Still, Raja's bigger project started with Anil Ambani's journey to fix his group's former choices.

Ambani's request for airwaves to start a nationwide GSM operation raised two questions. The first was how to free the spectrum frequencies that any new operator would require? Raja listened keenly to Ambani's pitch on the inefficient use of spectrum by existing GSM telecom operators. Perhaps some could be taken away from players already in the market?

The second was whether it was permissible for an operator with a CDMA operation to simultaneously be given permission to offer GSM services. The backlash from existing players was bound to be loud and vociferous. The ideal situation was to broadbase the approval for the market in general. Rumour has it Raja casually tested the market for the appetite for new licences with folks from the business world he knew. The response was resounding. So, he followed up on the status of the recommendations.

His general inclination to allow more players into the fray was not missed on TRAI who offered an opinion on 28 August 2007 in response to Maran's original query. 'The Authority is not in favour of suggesting a cap on the number of access service providers in any service area. It is not advisable to exogenously fix the number of access service providers in a market which is in a dynamic setting,' said TRAI.[4]

In addition to this, the regulator on its accord recommended starting a process to improve efficiency in spectrum utilization. 'There is a need to tighten the subscriber criteria for all the service areas so as to make it more efficient from the usage and pricing point of view,' the TRAI recommendation read. TRAI further said that for the same number of subscribers in less dense areas, the spectrum allocated per subscriber could be lower because the footprint is geographically spread wider.

Technologically it was explained by coverage area and the ability to reuse a frequency at an adequate physical gap so that the airwaves do not clash. Still, TRAI believed more spectrum should be given to existing GSM operators based on a new subscriber-linked allocation calculation: 'Authority further recommends that the GSM operators and CDMA operators should be given additional spectrum beyond 2X4.4MHz in GSM and 2x2.5MHz in CDMA after the operators achieve the mended subscriber base and also submit compliance of rollout obligation.'5

TRAI argued for a market-discovered price for spectrum in the 3G and other bands, but for the frequencies being used by existing operators, it hedged with multiple options. Its recommendation explained that legacy issues of price discovery for the licence and spectrum in 2001 for the fourth operator would play truant in creating a level playing field in the existing frequency bands: 'Authority is not recommending the standard options pricing of spectrum, however, it has elsewhere in the recommendation made a strong case for adopting auction procedure in the allocation of all other spectrum bands except 800, 900 and 1800MHz.'

The Department had already set an administrative fee at which existing operators could buy additional airwave frequencies in these bands after reaching the 6.2MHz threshold for GSM players and 5MHz for CDMA players. Auctioning them to others at a different price would create a market imbalance.

In this opinion, the authority also recommended a one-time spectrum payment for any operator using more than 10MHz of spectrum. Its price recommendation escalated from category 'C' circles to metro cities. This had the potential to hurt incumbent players that were already using a wider spectrum than 10MHz.

The TRAI suggested companies should be allowed to retain or forced to return spectrum depending on subscribers after mergers and acquisitions. The regulator also said that a merger between a CDMA and GSM operator should be allowed as long as the final entity reported the two businesses separately for government fees. This paved the way to enable a single company to offer service on both platforms or 'dual technology license'.

The Department of Telecom under Maran had already asked the authority to comment on whether dual technology would be permissible.

TRAI's answer to this question was 'yes'.

'The Authority recommends that in case a licensee wishes to deploy any other advanced and efficient technology for providing mobile service, then the DoT should allocate spectrum subject to its availability,' said TRAI, adding that this may be needed for technologies other than GSM and CDMA such as WiMax or Wi-Fi, which did not exist when the earlier policies were conceived.[6]

For Reliance this was not sufficient. RCom did not choose to turn off its CDMA operation and substitute it with a GSM one, it wanted to build a parallel network. It was not enough for the government to allow companies to pick the technology on their network. RCom needed additional spectrum allocation. The TRAI policy obliged on that account too, stating the following.

'Authority recommends that a licensee using one technology may be permitted on request, usage of alternative technology and thus allocation of dual spectrum. However, such a licensee must pay the same amount of fee which has been paid by existing licensees using the alternative technology or which would be paid by a new licensee going to use that technology . . .

'On payment of the specified fee for the Service area for which the LICENSEE wishes to provide plurality of technologies, the licensee may be given additional spectrum equal to the initial spectrum allowed in the license for that technology.'[7]

Armed with this opinion Raja and the DoT needed to have spectrum vacated to allocate to aspirants.

In August 2007, the communications ministry told the Rajya Sabha (Upper House of Parliament) that the defence services had already been requested to vacate and release some of these airwaves by moving partially to cabled solutions.[8] The government could also recover some airwaves from existing operators if it enforced higher efficiency in spectrum usage.

Since licensing mobile services, the government has had a subscriber-linked allocation plan in place. At the start of a licence, a 4.4MHz pair was allocated, and as the subscriber base grew, this was expanded to 6.2MHz and then, in stages, up to 15MHz. The TRAI, in its recommendation, said that technological advancements made it possible for operators to be more efficient in using their airwaves, and therefore, the government was within its rights to 'tighten the subscriber-linked criteria'.

TRAI recommended setting up a technical committee to review matters. Raja suddenly saw an opportunity to secure airwaves for more licences than merely dual technology spectrum for the CDMA players. Interest was palpable. The DoT said it would welcome new operator applications until 10 October. But on 24 September, the ministry under Raja issued a press statement accelerating the deadline to 1 October. The appetite for these was higher than Raja had anticipated. The papers poured in, and before the deadline was up, the DoT was looking at 575 applications.

On 19 October 2007, the DoT accepted all of TRAI's recommendations. It removed the cap on the number of telecom operators and allowed dual technology. Anil Ambani promptly offered Rs 1651 crore to secure GSM airwaves across the country, and that was a done deal. The incumbents thought this to be a severe miscarriage of justice. They filed a lawsuit that led to the rise and fall of Anil Ambani's flagship—RCom.

For Raja, after addressing Reliance's spectrum requirement, lay a challenge to identify other winners of new licences.

The events that followed on this account attracted suspicion of corruption that put Raja behind bars, at least for a period of time.

First, the ministry sought an opinion from the Law Ministry on whether it could eliminate some applicants by accepting only those applications submitted within a day of the invite. Raja overruled an unfavourable outcome from the government's legal arm and considered only those companies that had applied by 25 September.

Then a rather ludicrous situation developed at the DoT on 10 January 2008. In the morning, it was rumoured that the telecom ministry would issue LoIs, or Letters of Intent, to accepted applicants. At around 1.45 p.m., the ministry announced that only 121 applicants who had filed requests by 25 September were eligible to proceed. Then at 2.45 p.m. the DoT issued a press statement that it would issue LoIs to the final winners who completed the forms and made payments on a first cum first serve basis—the payment that amounted to Rs 1651 crore if applying nationwide.

Sanchar Bhavan turned into a set from Ninja Warriors for the rest of the day. The Department officials were asked to set up counters to issue eligibility notices and requisite LoI forms within an hour. Another counter one level up was placed to check completed documents and validate them and a third to accept demand drafts from applicants.

From the time the gates opened, it was survival of the fittest and the older executives were pushed around. Security was called into the room and among other actions it escorted, Mahendra Nahata, CEO of Himachal Futuristic, off the premises. Meanwhile, the Idea Cellular representative who had sat at the ministry for three subsequent days in anticipation of such a moment was overrun by bulkier counterparts from other companies and all semblance of a queue vanished.

Groups of people from each of the applying companies formed relay teams, grabbing LoI letters from the officials' hands, filling out forms and rushing payments to the counter before others could. Some were frustrated by the speed of one official compared to the adjacent one who approved applications faster.

At 5.30 p.m., the DoT shut its counters, and several of the regulars in Sanchar Bhavan's halls were left baffled at what had just transpired. The ministry, however, lost no time in announcing the final winners: T. Anandakishnan's Aircel, Anil Ambani's Reliance Communications, Ratan Tata's Tata Teleservices, Shahid Blawa's Swan Telecom, Venugopal Dhoot's Datacom, Sanjay and Ajay Chandra's Unitech, C. Sivasankaran's S Tel, and Rajiv Malhotra's Shyam Telelink.

47

Mobile Number Portability

The play for 2G licences, assigned at a prescribed price, was one of valuations. Thus, it was not surprising that most of the winners found a deep-pocketed strategic partner rather quickly, even though there was an overhang from a global economic slowdown in 2008.

It happened in quick succession and each of the spectrum winners raised multifold of what they had paid into the telecom ventures. Like the application submission and licence award, Swan Telecom was first off the mark, selling 45 per cent to Etisalat for $900 million. The deal was announced on 23 September 2008.

Less than a week later, Norway's leading telecom operator Telenor bought a controlling stake of 60 per cent from Unitech Wireless for $1.07 billion. On 13 November 2008, Tata Teleservices partnered with NTT Docomo, which bought 26 per cent of Tata Teleservices for $2.7 billion. In January 2009, Siva partnered with a consortium headed by Bahrain Telecommunications Co, or Batelco, to sell a 49 per cent stake in S Tel for $225 million.

Left among the new players was only the Videocon Industries-owned telecom operator. Telenor had held negotiations with Videocon summarily before striking its deal with Unitech. Rumour had it Venugopal Dhoot, chairman of Videocon Industries, was waiting for Mukesh Ambani to re-enter the segment. Reliance Industries always preferred to build and keep control. As Dhoot turned down suitors the word on the street grew louder, but Mukesh Ambani had signed a non-compete with Anil Ambani which barred him from entering the telecom business. Dhoot too vehemently denied any such rumours, adding that Videocon was an emerging conglomerate looking to diversify. The group had invested in other related fields including music store chain Planet M and assembly of mobile handsets. Service operations were synergistic to these businesses, Dhoot maintained.

Amid such high-decibel deal-making, Reliance Communications' silence was conspicuous. Yet, it did not surprise spectators. The Hutch bid seemed like an aberration and to the staff, Ambani always indicated that the GSM operation would be complementary to the CDMA one. Given deep-pocketed competitors were making forays in the marketplace, eyes were turned on Anil Ambani's next move.

Ambani's RCom needed a quick rollout and a means to challenge the incumbents, who enjoyed not only a lion's share of subscriber additions but also an average monthly revenue per use of around three times that of the CDMA service. The most pronounced reason for this was the handset lock-in.

Reliance Communications needed to shake customers away from competitors. In 2006, when Anil Ambani took control of the mobile operator, Reliance Communications boasted of being the second-largest firm in terms of subscribers. By 2008, when the company got its GSM airwaves it had slipped to third and in some areas to the fourth position.

Ambani used another page out of the family playbook to attract customers. In October 2008, he slashed prices to half of the prevailing call rates. It was in tow of Tata DoCoMo's per-second billing plan, which pegged a second of calling at 1 p, but RCom's pricing was even lower. With CDMA customers already on discounted prices and GSM yet to begin, the move promised not to hurt RCom as much as it hurt established players. The tactic, however, felt incongruous with the intent. Ambani was not gunning for the rural masses, he was looking to convert the high-paying urban customers who were less likely to be lured by low call rates.

Ambani recognized that the cream customers were agnostic to price and fixated on retaining their phone numbers. As a proponent of number portability, he had been batting on the front foot to catch these customers since 2005. During his many visits to the telecom regulatory offices, TRAI heard him, which set the wheels in motion on 22 July 2005.

Under TRAI chief Pradip Baijal, the authority initiated the conversation on portability with a consultation paper collecting inputs from other major players. The authority said this was in anticipation of an explosive boom in the Indian telephony user base. The country's phone penetration was just under 10 per cent and the TRAI consultation opened the field for comments from the players. As usual, meetings were held at four major centres to solicit views.

It took until March 2006 for TRAI's final recommendations, a couple of weeks before Baijal's retirement. The regulator said in the interest of time and the growing pool of mobile service customers, the country should adopt Mobile Number Portability (MNP) rather than Fixed Number Portability. Its implementation should be done within each service area before making it an all-India phenomenon, or full number portability. The implementation, said the recommendation of 8 March, should be in a phased manner starting with the metro cities. In this recommendation,[1] TRAI listed the steps, such as nominating a service provider with ports to bridge all the networks, the sharing of costs between operators, and a tentative launch date of 1 April 2007.

The incumbents were naturally reluctant. The debate and dissent, paired with a change of guard within the administration left room for further deliberations. As a result, not only was there no movement on this subject, but even after the implementation date had passed, the recommendation did not feature on the Department of Telecommunications' agenda. It took a nudge from the anti-trust regulator in October 2007 to bring MNP back to the fore. When it did, mayhem was breaking loose over new licence applications, dual technology spectrum allocation, and additional spectrum for incumbents. It was not until December 2007, when Raja's jugglery with the law ministry was coming to an end that the DoT accepted TRAI's recommendation for mobile number portability. New entrants celebrated this move.

Yet acceptance and implementation are often a chasm apart. The process of setting up an exchange required a specialist exchange that all the operators plug into and finance. While the selection of the service provider was initiated on April 10, 2008, the actual set-up of the exchange took several years more. A licence to provide portability was issued in March 2009. The regulations for the service were issued on 23 September 2009. As with everything else, the rules went through amendments and the final service was deployed between November 2010 and January 2011. Mobile number portability was available nationwide on 20 January 2011. The COAI maintained that the service was issued merely to benefit Reliance. Naturally then, the other industry bodies supported the move.

In 2008, however, the delay was a boon for Airtel, Vodafone and Idea Cellular because five new operators stood armed to pinch market share, apart from Reliance and Tata, which were entering with their GSM services.

By the time MNP was started, the dust on operator launches had settled. While the influx of new operators had more than halved call rates, subscribers purchased SIM cards to shop for offers rather than as a permanent shift to a new operator. As a result, many in urban areas carried two SIM cards—one to receive calls and the other to make them. The incumbents lost the outgoing call but not the customer.

When MNP finally arrived, Mukesh Ambani's re-entry into the sector was imminent. Nevertheless, in 2011, that still appeared distant enough for operators to focus on their 3G service offerings as a differentiator to retain cream customers.

48

Tata Finds Tower Partner

The expenditure on running two networks at a time when competition wiped out operating margins was debilitating for both RCom and Tata. They decided to emulate the incumbents and raise funds against their passive infrastructure.

Anil Ambani hoped to partner with some of the new operators to increase the tenancy on RCom's 48,000 telecom towers.

It is rumoured that Anil Ambani and Shahid Balwa, who received a licence for Swan Telecom, had been in talks earlier. Swan Telecom could have been a potential target for Ambani in case his application failed. The two denied any such connection. Then, Balwa signed Etisalat as its equity partner and when the company was ready to set up a network, it became a telecom tower customer for RCom.

Indus Tower was perceived as a captive company of the incumbent players, and new players were wary of renting in large numbers on its network. Their concern was legitimate. On Indus Tower service operators could have been at the mercy of established competitors.

The Tata and RCom towers were mostly singly occupied but still presented a similar problem for new operators looking to expand quickly with less upfront investment.

In view of the opportunity, Ambani spun off the tower and passive infrastructure company. It was named Reliance Infratel and was put up for a public listing in the hope of a hefty payday for Anil Ambani's telecom operator. RCom also set up a subsidiary with Alcatel Lucent, which would manage the RCom GSM network and potentially take on other clients.

The new operators were lining up to strike telecom tower deals with long lock-in periods and contracts that could be leveraged. The business model quickly became one that mimicked the real-estate industry rather than a service sector. It attracted non-telecom players to jump in and offer towers on lease. Their unique selling point was that they would never be competitors' service operators.

Essar and SREI, Hemant and Sunil Kanoria's infrastructure and finance group, took the most visible plunge into the telecom tower sector. Both already had small, localized portfolios of towers already. Essar had it owing to its history as a telecom operator. The SREI group had financed, acquired and managed towers from B.K. Modi's Spice Telecom. As a result, the finance company held roughly 5000 towers around Kolkata, West Bengal and a few in Karnataka. These were parked in a company called Quippo Telecom.

Multinational corporations were also betting on the enormity of the Indian telecom tower market. American Tower Corp, or ATC, which had spent the last half-decade consolidating and rationalizing operations globally decided to open an office in New Delhi in 2007. The global tower company brought on board Amit Sharma as its India chief. Sharma had been associated with the mobile telecom sector since its inception. He had worked with Motorola and shared a rapport with key players and executives in the sector.

ATC's approach was to accrue towers by acquisition. It initiated discussions with SREI's Quippo Telecom.

The Kanorias negotiated with ATC but quickly decided to set their sights elsewhere. They engaged in talks with the Tata Group which was trying to sell its telecom towers to free cash for its GSM launch with NTT DoCoMo.

ATC moved on and in March 2009 consolidated the market in bite-sized deals starting with the purchase of Xcel Telecom. The tower company was the brainchild of former BPL Mobile head Sandip Basu, incubated by private-equity Horse-Shoe Capital's affiliate Q Investment based in Mauritius. It had around 1660 telecom towers peppered across fifteen service areas. ATC paid Rs 700–800 crore for the deal which put its tower portfolio in India over the 2000 mark. It was but the tip of the ocean. India's predicted requirement over the next couple of years exceeded 3,00,000 towers with three times those many tenants. This deal became the benchmark of telecom tower valuations for the series of transactions that followed.

SREI meanwhile doubled down on Tata's Towers. Tata Teleservices was divided into two companies, the publicly listed Tata Teleservices Maharashtra Ltd (TTML), which operated in the Mumbai and Maharashtra service area and Tata Teleservices Ltd which functioned in the rest of the country. The separation of the tower companies mimicked this. Tata hived off Wireless-TT Info Services from Tata Teleservices and 21st Century Infra Tel from TTML. Separating the latter took longer to complete because of the regulatory hurdles it needed to cross as a listed entity.

The Kanorias proposed a plan that appealed to the widely diversified Tata Group. They proposed to buy 49 per cent of Tata's tower company and to run it as an independent tower operator. With financing against the tower portfolio, SREI proposed to more than double the tower portfolio in fewer than five years and thereafter expand to new territories such as Bangladesh. Thus, SREI became a sizeable tower operator instead of cashing out of Quippo.

In August 2009, a consortium of financiers that included IDFC, funded SREI's 30 per cent stock purchase in Wireless TT Info Services, which was priced at approximately Rs 2400 crore. The valuation pegged each tower at roughly Rs 72 lakh per tower. It came at a discount to other contemporary transactions, but analysts explained this as an outcome of falling costs and the valuation of towers.

SREI then acquired another 19 per cent in Wireless TT Info Services in exchange for its 5000 towers as Quippo was folded into the combined entity. After the transaction, the Tata Group held 51 per cent of the company which was rebranded to Viom Networks.

Under the agreed terms, Tata nominated five board members including the chairman as a majority holder, but the deal factored in a management premium for SREI. At the time the transaction was closed, Viom had around 18,000 telecom towers. Tata Group appointed Subodh Bhargav as the chairman of the tower company. Bhargav was an old hand in the Tata Group's senior management.

The deal worked well. Tata Teleservices acted as an anchor tenant for the existing towers as well as the ones planned ahead. Complementing them was a bulk tenancy contract with Uninor, the joint venture between Unitech and Norway's Telenor. In a short while, Uninor accounted for over 20 per cent of Viom's revenue and the company had a higher tenancy ratio than its peers.

Under a year later, in March 2010, 21st Century Infra Tele was also transferred into Viom. This time the valuation had fallen steeply again to just Rs 52 lakh per tower even though they were in the Mumbai service area. Yet, Tata was pressed to close the deal at any cost.

It had launched per-second billing on its GSM platform Tata DoCoMo at nearly half the prevailing market rate. The mobile service operator was bleeding cash. It needed to replenish its coffers in anticipation of the upcoming 3G auction.

49

Anil in China

After parting with the Kolkata service area, B.K. Modi's Spice Telecom was now left with the Punjab and Karnataka service areas. Even as other players were consolidated, Modi's Spice, still led by Umang Das continued to hold ground in its service areas. As its immediate competitors grew larger, Spice Telecom found itself cash-strapped due to rapid network capacity increases, and it needed a cost-effective way to keep pace.

China's ZTE offered the operator a way out of its predicament in 2006. ZTE was a telecom equipment company trying to shed the tag of low-cost, technologically poor Chinese manufacturing that the country's electronics had come to be associated with. To prove itself in the marketplace it needed live customers and working exhibits.

Das was looking for a partner willing to finance a low setup cost to be returned as income from customers trickled in. ZTE was willing. It provided equipment and setup services along with export credit so Spice Telecom could increase its network presence without forking out any cash. This in turn allowed the company to apply for an all-India licence when Raja opened bids. Spice was not one of the winners.

The induction of ZTE into its network, which had once been the Nokia's vestige, gave the Chinese company a foothold in the Indian market. Following ZTE came Huawei, which took its telecom equipment even more seriously, offering future-proof technologies and switches that could later be adjusted to provide 3G and 4G services. Spice Telecom's adoption of equipment from these companies set a precedent for others, especially those that found themselves in a similar bind.

At the outset, no one considered Anil Ambani's RCom as one such company. As a finance specialist, the younger Ambani was eager to experiment with various market instruments. The first was Foreign Currency Convertible Bonds (FCCBs) raised in March 2006 and February 2007 each with a five-year expiry. The company raised $500 million in the first round and a billion dollars in the second. The second bond, which had a zero coupon or interest rate, was priced to be converted at Rs 661 per share, a humble 30 per cent gain in share price at a time when telecom stocks were shooting because of the sharp growth in subscribers in India.

The cash, however, had immediate use with lower forthcoming returns. In July 2007, Ambani acquired a US cable network and internet-based services company called Yipes for around $300 million. It was to be folded into Flag Telecom which was still an unprofitable international business for RCom. There were licence fees to pay and the Rs 4500 crore write-off that was still on the company's books. A lot of the CDMA business was postpaid and as a result, in the case of any disputes and there were always too many, the company was left holding the baby. Cash was always wanting.

By 2008, Anil Ambani had discovered that his ambition for RCom and the availability of cash to see them through were not in sync.

An acquisition of Hutchison Essar that would have included credit financing may have alleviated the situation, but as a new owner of freshly issued spectrum, RCom had to deploy a greenfield network.

Cash-strapped RCom needed a solution to deploy its GSM services network. The Chinese companies had satisfactorily demonstrated they could run reliable networks. RCom had started with a minor $200 million contract for base stations as a pilot project with Huawei in mid-2007.

Favourable payment terms that reduced the cash burden on the company made Chinese equipment vendors an obvious choice for Anil Ambani, who authorized another order estimated between $500–750 million with Huawei. It was not for a lack of trying from Ericsson which had historically been the deployment partner for RCom. The European company simply could not meet the discount and more importantly the financing structure that the Chinese one was offering. Ambani could have the equipment and execute deployment with nearly no cash outflow because the equipment came with a loan facility with a Chinese bank.

Ambani's relations with the Chinese only grew more profound as the operator's cash crisis deepened.

On 15 December 2010, Ambani announced from New Delhi that his group had secured a facility of nearly $2 billion from the China Development Bank. Around $1.3 billion of this was assigned to cover the cost of 3G airwaves that RCom had bought. The rest was allocated towards telecom equipment and services that RCom would avail of as it built up its network. There was a key condition: RCom's network service additions had to be sourced from Huawei and ZTE, the Chinese telecom equipment vendors. The order inevitably came at the cost of Ericsson and Nokia as they were sidelined. The company could not use this loan facility to pay off existing outstanding amounts to the European vendors.

In 2012, the FCCBs matured. Anil Ambani was backed into a corner because the company share price was at a heavy discount to the conversion price. Shares of RCom closed at Rs 94.40 on 29 February 2012, when the first FCCB redemption fell due. In the past, ICICI Bank had helped Reliance resolve such a situation by mopping a similar bond from the market at a discount and settling with the company. However, on this occasion, the bank declined, and Anil Ambani needed cash to pay lenders.

Once again, Chinese lenders came to the company's rescue, lending $1.8 billion between three—Industrial Commerce China Bank, the China Development Bank and the Export-Import Bank of China. The ties were deepened even further and the window to perform shrunk. The banks agreed when Ambani pointed to the rising value of RCom's land bank in the heart of Navi Mumbai or New Mumbai sitting at the outskirts of India's financial capital and an emerging hub in its own right.

Little did Anil Ambani know that leaning into the new equipment manufacturer and the Chinese partners would return to haunt him and the company.

50

A New Tower Plan for Ambani

Anil Ambani tried to boost equity valuations by proposing divestments. The two most prominent were Reliance Infratel, the passive infrastructure arm that housed the telecom towers and optic fibre cable network being used by Reliance Communications, and Reliance Technologies, a company specializing in IT deployments for enterprises, particularly focused on consumer businesses that needed billing and customer relations management systems.

The valuation of telecom tower companies was soaring, and RCom's portfolio was considered prized. The company had secured the best spots on ideal terms.

Anil Ambani wanted to divest this to an equity investor, but the premium he sought was not readily available. Non-operational investors preferred to park money in Indus Towers because it had assured tenancy and rentals compared with a single-operator-owned outfit like Reliance Infratel.

Ambani needed to set a benchmark price for his company. He thus offloaded a small five per cent equity, much like a pre-IPO placement, for a lofty Rs 1400 crore valuing the entire portfolio at $6.75 billion on 8 August 2007. The investors buying the 5 per cent were revered names in the financial circles—Fortress Capital, HSBC Principal Investments,

Galleon Group, New Silk Route, GLG Partners, Quantum Fund (George Soros) and DA Capital. Strategic investors, however, saw through the move. Each investor had picked under 1 per cent and correspondingly risked too little capital to be serious. While the share price of RCom rose from the news, it did not reflect this massive valuation.

Rumours spread that the five per cent placement was a quid pro quo for Ambani companies or personal funds investing in the schemes of the outfits that purchased equity in Reliance Infratel. RCom's credibility suffered in several investor forums.

The group was already hurting from a 2009 audit report which said that RCom had underreported its revenue in the previous two financial years by nearly Rs 3000 crore in an effort to save government licence and spectrum fees. Anil Ambani said, 'A vicious and mala fide campaign of falsehoods and disinformation has been conducted against the Reliance Anil Dhirubhai Ambani Group,' in a press statement after the auditor's report.[1]

The move was intended to 'hammer' RCom shares was the claim. Ambani accused the media of falling prey to campaigns run by competition to compromise the IPO of its tower company. Information was being passed via e-mails from false IDs and the distribution of papers in unsigned and unmarked envelopes was designed to 'unleash a campaign of calumny and disinformation,' Ambani said.

Was there a parallel between current events and those preceding Bharti Airtel's IPO? The current situation vexed Ambani.

'I must straightaway point out that whatever alleged remarks the special auditor has arrived at are completely unilateral, biased and prejudiced, because, contrary to basic standards of professional conduct, and against all auditing norms and practices, the alleged report/findings have not even been discussed by the special auditors with RCOM till date—

even though they have been conducting the audit for the past more than 6 months.

'In addition, the special auditors, apparently at the instance of our corporate rivals have far exceeded their terms of reference and recorded unwarranted and completely incorrect findings on matters beyond the scope of their audit, thereby again demonstrating their bias and prejudice,' Anil Ambani said in a public statement.[2]

The audit was originally launched on other COAI telecom operators and was later extended to include Bharti Airtel and Reliance Communications. It was an independent audit by a chartered accounting firm Parekh & Co. Ambani questioned the firm's standing in the face of KPMG which had audited the company's financial results and filings. In anticipation of the IPO, RCom books had also undergone a SEBI-appointed peer review group audit in May 2009.

Notwithstanding Ambani's protests, the bad press and the lukewarm stock market response put a spanner in the works for the proposed Reliance Infratel's public offering. RCom had filed regulatory papers, the DRHP or draft red herring prospectus, with the Securities and Exchange Board of India.

Despite vociferous attempts, and half a dozen serious conversations, Ambani was still searching for a financial investor who could swoop in to buy company shares at the price he wanted. The wait left Ambani where he began, or perhaps he was even worse off.

He explored equity-linked fund-raising options including, parking shares as collateral but none offered RCom the valuation the chairman felt the company deserved. RCom continually toyed with value-unlocking options, including large-scale mergers and acquisitions. A scuffle over MTN led the junior Ambani to shed his non-compete agreement with his elder brother, Mukesh Ambani. The two signed a pact allowing Mukesh to pursue telecom in May 2010.

By 2010, the company was pinned down. Competitors were looking to launch 3G services, which would cement loyalty from their cream customers. RCom had borrowed and spent lavishly on accumulating 3G spectrum, but the repayment was aspirating all of its free cash. At the end of 31 March 2010, RCom's annual results showed that finance costs, or the amount the company was paying as interest on its loans, had trebled from around Rs 400 crore in 2008 to approximately Rs 1200 crore in 2010.

The GSM network still needed large-scale investment, and the cash was simply missing. The pressure to turn the finances around and capture revenue market share was immense. The market was beginning to discount Anil Ambani's flagship company as lost when a confident Ambani made a press statement of a rebirth with Chinese funding.

The telecom tower market demand was still robust and sufficient for GTL Infrastructure to forge its path in tandem with Indus, Viom and Reliance Infratel. The company was hived off from GTL Ltd. which had been in the news for the wrong reasons. Having sold off its business process outsourcing business to Orange, Manoj Tirodkar, founder and chairman of GTL turned the company's attention to managing and servicing telecom towers for companies in Europe, including Ericsson. From that emerged the opportunity to complete the outsourcing chain by owning the tower as well.

After sampling the business overseas, Tirodkar saw great potential for the business in India. The country did not have a third-party, non-telco tower operator. Apart from mobile telephony, businesses like radio also needed telecom towers to transmit signals. So, GTL Infrastructure became the main focus of the group as it began to build a tower network. Business was roaring because the appetite for slots on a serviced tower was high. GTL had been raked into an equities fraud controversy and Tirodkar saw the telecom tower business as an opportunity to get out of that mire and into the big league.

If consolidation was the way to go, GTL Infrastructure was going to be a consolidator, planned Tirodkar. He approached Essar Telecom to buy its around 4500 telecom towers. The first round went well. Then SREI swooped with a purchase offer from Viom. More competition was to follow as a third bidder entered the fray—ATC. Essar eventually sold to ATC.

Tirodkar meanwhile found a keen negotiator in Aircel, the last operator looking to divest its telecom towers. Aircel had received all-India licences but had a reluctant promoter, T. Ananda Krishnan. He was dragged into a political controversy after Siva alleged he was forced. The Central Bureau of Investigations opened a file on Anandakrishnan who no longer travelled to India for fear of being detained.

Siva accused politician Dayanidhi Maran of delaying approvals for Aircel and forcing him to sell the business to Anandakrishnan's Maxis in exchange for a Rs 550 crore investment in Sun TV which was owned by the Maran family.

On the ground, Aircel needed capital but could not raise equity or debt. The sale of the towers seemed like the middle ground. GTL Infrastructure was keen to bag the asset. It was an extensive portfolio with an anchor tenant that was looking to expand its footprint. It appeared to be a match made in heaven. In January 2010, after a month of negotiations, GTL collated all its resources and offered a cash deal of Rs 8400 crore to Aircel, on which the operator jumped. The Maxis chief executive officer at the time was Sandip Das, who took a special interest in Aircel. He had once been on Analjit Singh's team to build Hutchison-Max. Das was based in Malaysia, and the company's day-to-day operations fell in the purview of Gurdeep Singh who was designated as Aircel's chief operating officer.

Singh emphatically told reporters at a joint press conference with GTL Infra that the new cash-rich Aircel would expand its footprint across Indian territories. The company expected to double the number of base stations it had. As a result, along with the deal to sell its 17,500 towers, Aircel sold GTL Infra the right of first refusal for the following 20,000 site rentals it would require. This meant that every time the operator needed to add a wireless signalling base station it would first request GTL Infra to provide a suitable location. If GTL refused Aircel could approach other tower operators.

Tirodkar, too, reassured media and investors that there was such a high value to be earned from the deal. The company on its combined portfolio of 32,500 towers had a tenancy ratio of a little over one. This meant that there was only one tenant on most towers. When this would hit 2.4, the company would begin to accrue cash over the interest charges it was paying to finance the loans it had taken to purchase Aircel's towers. The interest rate on the loan issued by a consortium led by the State Bank of India was over 8 per cent.

Tirodkar explained that the valuation and stretching of GTL's resources made sense because of the potential for rental from five new entrants in the 2G market, thirteen service operators vying for 3G technology, and new FM radio channels soon to be launched. Companies were forking out millions for government approvals and they would naturally accelerate rollouts too.

After the merger with Aircel, GTL Infra caught Anil Ambani's eye. RCom saw a potential solution to its cash problems. Anil Ambani's team decided to meet with the tower company's smaller rival, GTL Infrastructure, in June 2010. The two started to tango around a potential takeover of Reliance

Infrastructure. They called it a 'merger' rather than an acquisition catering to sensibilities and pride.

Where RCom needed cash, Tirodkar sought operator neutrality for the tower portfolio. By mid-June, the two groups had curated a charter that might work for both sides. The value of RCom's towers was estimated at Rs 30,000 crore and that of GTL Infra, after the Aircel merger, at Rs 15,000 crore. To acquire the tower assets, GTL Infra would offer Rs 15,000 crore in cash to RCom for a complete exit.

Then shareholders of RCom, including Anil Ambani, would receive equity in the new combined entity. As a result, the final shareholding of the new company would be: Tirodkar and GTL 30 per cent, Anil Ambani 26 per cent, RCom shareholders 24 per cent and GTL Infra shareholders the rest. The transaction was split into multiple steps, such as transferring RCom towers into a special purpose vehicle to detach them from other company assets. Meanwhile, GTL Infra needed to raise debt and prepare the stock exchange filings. Finally, upon approval, the equity transfer would take place.

A deal with GTL was a little infra dig for Anil Ambani who had promised investors that he would bring on a world-class financial or strategic investor. Until negotiations had advanced into a concrete term sheet, Reliance maintained an incredulous denial of even considering a deal with GTL. This contradictory posturing of the larger group made Tirodkar's potential lenders even more nervous than he felt. Eventually, he insisted on a joint statement in the interest of public shareholders. RCom maintained it denied the news because it needed to secure board approval and issue stock exchange notices before publicly acknowledging the proposal. RCom, in typical style, decided to break the news on a Sunday.

It preferred to tap the news cycle on the weekend because stock market traders responded most sharply to Monday morning headlines. The Ambani tag carried adequate weight for all media outlets to turn up even on a Sunday. Business news over the weekend tends to be lean and RCom was sure to get disproportionate attention from reporters and editors.

GTL Infra and RCom made a public statement on Sunday, 27 June 2010.

'GTL Infra and RCom agree on over Rs 50,000 crore transaction to create the world's largest independent telecom tower company,' read the public announcement. Contours of the remaining deal had already leaked into the press. RCom said the deal would result in a debt reduction of Rs 18,000 crore because, in addition to the cash infusion from GTL Infra, it would also transfer some of the telecom towers' debt to the new entity. The deal was a complicated one. The companies said it would take a month from the announcement for it to conclude. The sunset for the original document was set at 31 July.

Due diligence began on a per-tower basis. GTL Infra rationalized that RCom's towers were complementary to the Aircel portfolio. Both companies could use the other's tower sites to complete their networks. The current proposed combination would result in a company with around 80,000 towers and 1,25,000 tenancy slots. As they delved into details, both sides began to develop disagreements.

Reliance expected a valuation equal to, or higher than the private equity placement made in Reliance Infratel. As they tussled over financial terms the agreed time for closure lapsed. They extend talks for another month. A frequent question asked in key strategic meetings in the Ballard Estate RCom headquarters was, 'If GTL can make the asset profitable then why can't we,' recalls an executive present in the room. It was an impossible question to answer.

RCom, it seemed, shopped for other offers on the back of the one with GTL—although nothing was ever made public or fructified. Before long, another month had passed and this time the companies did not renew its end date. The deal agreement along with the deal lapsed and the statements made by the companies were telling. GTL told stock exchanges, 'Despite efforts, both parties have neither extended the Term Sheet nor entered into any definitive transaction agreements as envisaged. Consequently, the process of merger as originally contemplated would not take place.'

RCom said, 'Reliance Communications Ltd. is now engaged in discussions with certain other strategic and financial investors to pursue a similar transaction aimed at a significant reduction in the Company's debt and unlocking of value for RCOM shareholders from the passive infrastructure and related assets in its 95 per cent owned subsidiary, Reliance Infratel Ltd.'

On the day of the deal failure, the impact was felt deepest on GTL Infra's stock, but it was RCom's image that hurt in the long run. Many industry experts thought of this as a sweet deal for RCom, which gave Ambani a reputation as a more difficult negotiator and partner than before.

51

Pandora's Box—Auction 1.0

While the old-school licences and spectrum for 2G services were under contention, the world had moved on to a newer technology.

A. Raja came under fire for the confusion caused by administering licences and spectrum for mobile services when he opened the market to new players. Various court cases had been filed, and a political storm was brewing over the granted licences. Yielding to the pressure from existing players' lobby and in line with TRAI recommendations, he opted for a public auction for 3G service airwaves in the 2100MHz band.

The DoT issued a guideline for it on 1 August 2008. Hot on the heels of licence allocation to new players, this would have been a masterstroke, only Raja once again found that he did not have the requisite spectrum to allocate for this auction.

He approached the Indian defence services to vacate airwaves in the 2100MHz band so he could sell it to telecom companies. Only this time, the forces were not as amenable. Originally, the defence held 100 per cent of airwaves, of which some were released between 1994 and 1999, then again in 2004. At the end, the defence held around 65 per cent in the key 1800MHz band and 900 MHz band. In other frequencies, the forces continued to hold all the airwaves till agreed otherwise.

Some airwaves had also been left vacant in anticipation of the growth needs of incumbent operators. As per their service conditions operators were entitled to more airwaves as their subscriber base grew to preassigned numbers.

In December 2006, when Raja planned to award more 2G licences, the Defence was reluctant to vacate more airwaves for the Ministry of Telecom. After contentious standoffs between the telecommunications and defence ministries, the prime minister's office formed a group of ministers to resolve the spectrum dispute. Telecom was a high-yield sector for the government plugging holes in the fiscal deficit. The ministerial group concluded the forces would vacate spectrum for mobile operators in exchange for an optic fibre cable network to be laid by the Department of Telecom. The release of the spectrum would then occur in a phased manner.

Since Raja elected to prioritize the 1800 MHz band, the airforce released those airwaves first. Then, between December 2007 and March 2008, the DoT was scheduled to lay the cable network. Thereafter, the defence would vacate airwaves in the 2100MHz and Raja's auction could proceed as planned. The Ministry of Defence resisted compliance with the ministerial group's decision until the government threatened to charge defence services for the airwaves at commercial pricing.

The telecom department did not deliver the cable network. A year later, the optic fibre project was still mismanaged and unfinished. The Defence forces refused to release further airwaves. Raja created more 2G slots using the airforce spectrum and by reclaiming airwaves that were reserved for incumbent operators. The award of 2G licences had filled the market with thirteen telecom operators. For 3G, however, the DoT could not proceed with an auction in August 2008 because it had no airwaves in the 2100MHz band.

Eventually, in 2009, the prime minister had to intervene again seeking airwaves for 3G services from the Ministry of Defence. The government needed the auction desperately to raise funds in the wake of an election that year. The DoT had scraped together unused adequate airwaves in the 2100MHz band for one operator. After the nudge from the political establishment, the Defence sector vacated some more. The ministry could then accommodate three or four players throughout most of India. The telecom CEOs called this an 'artificial scarcity' that would result in competitive bidding.

For the incumbents, subscriber-linked criteria for additional spectrum had been revised. They saw 3G airwaves as a means to lighten the load on 2G networks that were brimming. For the new players, it was the data-oriented services that would rake in the profits since calling rates were commoditized. In the short term, this was good news for the government. It had upped the reserve price for 3G spectrum nearly fourfold and still had enthusiastic takers. India is divided into twenty-two service areas, or circles, each with a separate licence and spectrum price to be purchased individually.

The auction was designed by investment bank N.M. Rothschild and UK-based DotEcon. It served as a model for all future spectrum auctions by the government. The auction was crafted to stop only when the highest bids for all service areas were detected simultaneously. Companies could not bypass rounds to increase the price faster than the scheduled uptick.

To make bids, companies paid earnest money and were assigned eligibility points. To bid for all twenty-two service areas of India, a company needed 350 eligibility points. Most companies bought adequate points. The rules of the auction allowed companies to use these points as they wished. They did not need to lock onto their preferred service areas at the time of buying eligibility points. They had the option to buy less than

350 points and bid only for some service areas or even change their choice of regions as bidding proceeded. If a company bought points for Mumbai and Delhi but later found the prices of these circles were too high, it could bid for a larger number of less valued service areas as long as it had eligibility points to cover those circles.

The bidding occurred in clock rounds for all service areas before returning to the first. For each circle, an operator ticked 'Yes' or 'No', which would govern the pricing for the circle in the next round. This continued until the number of buyers exactly matched the slots on sale across all regions.

As the auction progressed, to remain eligible bidders needed to maintain a minimum activity level by deploying eligibility points. Initially, companies had to use up 80 per cent of their points. Companies needed to place bids to keep their points active. If they did not, the surplus points were annulled for future rounds. They could then only bid for circles adding up to the lesser number of points. The required activity level increased to 90 per cent midway and 100 per cent towards the end of the auction. Thus, towards the end of the auction, the bidding ferocity increased, unlike a typical auction where bids taper off as prices rise. It also meant that in initial rounds, no one could wait and watch. In some cases, it made sense for companies to place bids in service areas they did not intend to buy, for the sake of retaining their eligibility points.

Price escalation in each round was predetermined. If there was less demand than the number of slots the increase was zero. If bidders matched the slots available or that number was just one more, the price increase in the next round was 1 per cent. If there were two additional bidders, the price rise was 5 per cent and if there were three or more, the price increased by 10 per cent.

At the end of every round, there was a provisional winner for every service area. Since everyone was bidding for the same price, this winner was based on seniority, which was decided by the overall amount a company was spending in the auction. If that was on par, a winner was selected at random.

There was one exception in the rule on retaining eligibility points: a provisional winner for a service area could decline a bid in the following round and still retain eligibility points for the next round. This became important in companies' strategy to park their points in a low-cost circle and become winners. They retained those points to skip the next round and move to the target service area in the third round. For the government, this meant a price escalation even for those service areas that had few takers.

The ability for a provisional winner to withhold bidding in a round without losing points gave birth to a problem or opportunity, as companies chose to see it. The bidding teams created a strategy that was in one bidding room called 'drop kick'. It involved dropping bids in alternate rounds to control the price uptick over the next round. Theoretically, for three slots there could have been five bidders but only three bidding in each round to limit each escalation. For example, if operators A, R and V were gunning for the same circle and placed bids in round one. A became the provisional winner and did not bid in round two. Operators R and V continue to bid in the second round. Without A's bid, the demand appeared to be less than the three slots, so escalation is zero. Instead, if A chose to bid in the next round the increase would be 1 per cent. This move was opaque to operators other than the provisional winner.

Near the end of the auction, this caused a different set of problems. The auction was programmed to end when the number of bidders matched the number of slots available. However, if a provisional bidder held back in the hope of winning based on the previous round, or in an attempt to slow price escalation, the auction could suddenly end without giving them a chance to make a final bid. As a result, near the perceived end of the auction, all the participants were bidding out of uncertainty. In the 3G auction, it happened to a bidder in more than one service area that after the battle seemed to prolong endlessly they pulled back in one round and that turned out to be the last.

Bharti Airtel, Vodafone, Reliance Communications, Idea Cellular, Aircel, Tata Teleservices, Etilsata, STel, and Videocon competed for the airwaves.

The auction began on 9 April 2010. The portal was available for bidding from 9 a.m. to 7:30 p.m. The war rooms, often set up on the executive floor of the operators' headquarters near the chief executive's office, were accompanied by dedicated smoking rooms adjacent so that none of the members had to leave for too long. The executives inside were not allowed to communicate with anyone outside the room. They sat long hours on computer terminals, consulting chief financial officers, who on occasion placed calls to lenders to ensure they would be able to quickly raise funds.

As a last-minute move to optimize bidding, the government allowed operators to raise short-term rupee debt to pay for spectrum and later refinance it with global, low-cost debt. The provision helped operators with on-the-spot flexibility and the government with quicker payments ahead of upcoming general elections.

The enthusiastic new operators bid aggressively, and incumbents replied in kind. The auction lasted 183 rounds over thirty-four days. There was the occasional news leak. By the end of the first two weeks key leaders complained that the bidding was 'irrational' but they still bid in an effort to defend their turf.

Bharti, Vodafone and RCom were the most aggressive bidders. Idea Cellular was the next rung of applicants taking calculated steps to optimize population coverage on a smaller budget. Surprisingly lively participation came from Aircel, which not only bid aggressively, it also stayed the course till quite a late stage.

Etisalat, Videocon and STel had different bidding strategies. They bought fewer eligibility points. Etisalat made a deposit for 311 points while STel purchased eighteen and Videocon just twelve. Videocon made only two bids very early in the auction for Kerela and Uttar Pradesh West. Thereafter it was as if the company withdrew in favour of some other plans. The positioning fuelled the rumour that the company was merely holding onto a licence to be taken over or plugged into another outfit. The proximity between Venugopal Dhoot and Mukesh Ambani continued to be closely watched by the media.

STel was focussed on Bihar, Himachal Pradesh and Orissa. It bid initially and stopped when the intensity got out of hand. Etisalat bid for thirteen service areas including Mumbai and Delhi but only held on until about halfway through the auction. Thereafter, it withdrew.

At the end of the auction, there was just one clear winner: the government. The collections from the auction totalled Rs 67,719 crore ($15 billion), nearly double the target of the finance ministry. Even the first downpayment payment was adequate to fill the coffers and bolster pre-election spending on subsidy programs and advertising. The roaring success of the auction, which by Raja's admission surpassed the wildest dreams only sharpened the contrast of the price of 2G airwaves for new operators. There was enough clamour already that spectrum had been awarded for a song to the detriment of serious players.

For the operators, the 3G auction outcome was less ideal. None of the private operators was able to secure an all-India presence. The tussle between the defence services and DoT continued even after the auction when the ministry sought more airwaves to accommodate more players. 'An MoU was signed between the Ministry of Defence and Ministry of

Communication & Information Technology (MoC&IT) on May 22, 2009, for the release of 2G and 3G spectrum. Further release of spectrum during the year as per MoU is contingent on fulfilment of timelines/triggers in the MoU,' Defence Minister A.K. Antony wrote to the upper house of Parliament in July 2010.[1]

BSNL and MTNL were first off the mark because the state-run operators received spectrum in December 2009. This was a slot in addition to the auctioned airwaves, which was mandatorily awarded as part of the licence conditions since 2000. The companies got all India airwaves but were saddled with the winner's curse. In the quarter after the auction, BSNL recorded its first quarterly loss. It then went on to ask the government to return the money it had forked for the spectrum so that it could invest in infrastructure, but money once spent seldom returns.

Among the private players, Bharti and RCom bagged thirteen service areas each, the highest any operator secured. They paid Rs 13,000 crore and Rs 8500 crore respectively. While both of them won Mumbai and Delhi, the most expensive service areas with the highest premium to the base price, the key difference was Reliance's focus on the less sought after areas in west India where it had a stronghold since the start of mobile services in the 1990s. Bharti on the other hand went for more pricey service areas consolidating its legacy networks like Andhra Pradesh, Karnataka, and Tamil Nadu.

'We are working to make 3G really a pan-India proposition,' said Manik Jhangiani, group CFO Bharti Airtel in November 2010. Sanjay Kapoor, chief executive added, 'Our belief is that spectrum being a technology-agnostic asset would drive demand in three ways, firstly by addressing opportunities traditionally attributed to 3G, secondly by decongesting the 2G space, and finally by driving a mass market opportunity of hand-held based internet connectivity,' on a call with investors.[2]

Idea Cellular won airwaves in eleven service areas while Tata Teleservices and Vodafone each won nine. Analysts were relieved that companies had not bid beyond their coffers, but the organizations had stretched themselves the furthest they could. The experience in Europe had demonstrated that such high prices could be folly. In Europe in the early 2000s companies had paid too much for 3G airwaves and struggled to justify this cost against revenue that built over time because of low market appetite.

India would be different, promised the local CEOs. India was a virgin market, unlike the West that relied on cabled internet. There were sceptics who believed the Indian consumer would not understand or use the internet. Companies like Bharti Airtel knew better. They had experienced technology adoption in least likely areas with low education levels. Geographically sparse and highly populated Bihar was a case in point. Manoj Kohli remembered how the company started with only internet based mobile recharge packages and customers in Bihar intuitively adopted them.

Moreover, Idea's Sanjiv Aga assured investors that part of the price paid for 3G airwaves would be justified by the levy the company would be able to charge other operators trying to roam on the local network. The agreements in question were called Intra Circle Roaming, or ICR, agreements. This entailed a company, like Aircel, that had lost in the auctions renting capacity on an Idea network to offer 3G to its customers. As a result, for each area, it did not matter how many operators there were, the three or four 3G airwave winners would service the entire local population either directly or indirectly.

They would soon find a problem with that. The DoT said this was not permissible.

52

Yet Another Auction

A couple of days after the 3G auction, the government also put up airwaves in a higher frequency, 2300MHz. These airwaves were to power a Wi-Fi technology called WiMax. Its standards were established in the 2500MHz band. BSNL and MTNL were even allotted slots in the 2500MHz band in anticipation of the auction, but the defence services once again refused to vacate those airwaves. As a consolation, a lower and readily available frequency was put on auction.

Disappointed with the frequency band, some key WiMax players chose to stay away from the auction. To incentivize buyers, the DoT offered a 10MHz pair of spectrum per block compared with just 5MHz for 3G. Those that remained interested mulled using the airwaves on offer for a still evolving and non-standardized technology called 4G LTE. It was designed to transfer large data packets in a short period.

Fourth-generation mobile technology was an upgrade on 3G. Just like CDMA and GSM in the 2G wave, there were two separate standards in 4G technology. One that ran on Time Division Duplex, or TDD, and the other on Frequency Division Duplex, or FDD. While TDD used a single frequency to uplink and downlink signals FDD did so over two separate frequencies. As a result, on a TDD connection traffic could move either from the subscriber to the tower or from the tower to the subscribe. In FDD, however, both could happen simultaneously. The key enabler for FDD was more spectrum because one frequency or channel was used to send information, another to receive it and a third, buffer frequency, to create a gap between the two, so that information does not get mixed up. The 4G LTE service for high-speed data transfer over FDD was tested and had deployments, but the over-TDD, it was still being explored. Primarily one company, Qualcomm was working on the next phase for that technology.

The global mobile communications chip maker was betting on the scale of Indian and Chinese companies, which seemed like they would simultaneously adopt 4G services and create a mass market. At such a time, the choice made by Indian regulators appeared to be stacked in favour of companies gunning for 4G.

Still, established operators had elected for 3G spectrum. The issue was user access to 4G. India's market remained extremely price sensitive, and mobile handsets that included frequency range and features of 4G were nearly four times the cost of the average instrument used in India. Operators preferred to spend on a technology that could be immediately used. They were in part also looking to move voice customers on to the new airwaves.

Hence the competition in the auction—called the Broadband Wireless Access (BWA) spectrum auction—was likely to remain less fierce.

There was more good news for BWA spectrum aspirants. The spectrum usage charge, which was set at as much as 4 per cent of revenue for 2G, and by corollary 3G, services, was merely 1 per cent for the 2300MHz band.

This created interest among more bidders and stemmed a potential auction failure. Some mainstream operators had been lured back to the BWA band because 3G prices had soared and they hoped this frequency could partially compensate for a miss in the 2100MHz band. This was especially true for Bharti Airtel.

Airtel executives informally checked Aircel's rationale in bidding higher for BWA airwaves. Driven from the top, Maxis, Aircel's Malaysian parent and its team believed in the consumer attraction for high-speed mobile internet. So Aircel was keen to pick up the spectrum even though it appeared to be competing in a different category.

Idea Cellular bid for a long while and then stopped bidding in the last several rounds. Vodafone, RCom and Tata Teleservices quit the race at an early stage, and did not think the spectrum merited the attention it was being given.

In addition to the operators, internet service providers were interested. Among them was also Qualcomm. The company had no intention of launching a private service, but given the expected damp enthusiasm, Qualcomm thought it would build and transfer a functioning business to a buyer once technology was proven.

It appeared that aspiring wireless internet service providers were livening the auction up. Operators believed the confidence and enthusiasm these companies were showing for wireless internet was ill-founded. Among them was Tikona Digital founded by a former Reliance Communications head of data centre and corporate connections, Prakash Bajpai. Another was Augere which was a consortium led by Sanjiv Ahuja, a former chief executive of French telco Orange. A third, and one that seemed to bid most keenly, was the little-known Infotel Broadband Services.

Infotel's insistence on buying the airwaves raised alerts among the sector's leaders towards the end of the auction. As they looked through all the filings of the company, they found that it was held by Anant Nahata, Mahendra Nahata's son and part of the Himachal Futuristic Group. The stated objective of this two-year-old company was to offer WiMax solutions to corporate customers.

History suggested that this might be Nahata's newest stunt in the sector. One competing operator joked about the company's ability to pay the amount Infotel had bid. Mahendra Nahata had dabbled with ancillary businesses to the telecom sector since the debacle of his basic service licence bid in 1996. Among other things, the Himachal Futuristic Group had set up cable networks and even offered internet services in some northern parts of India. In Punjab, the group offered telecom and leased line services on a terrestrial network.

The BWA auction lasted a total of 117 rounds spread over eighteen days. Nahata's company was the only one that bid consistently through the entire auction, with utmost clarity that it would bag an all-India footprint. When the auction closed, Infotel Broadband was the only company across both airwave sales to have secured an all-India footprint in the same band. The cost for this was Rs 12,847 crore.

Since there were only two slots of 10MHz paired, or 20MHz in total, it was only possible to have one other winner in each service area. Qualcomm fought till the last round to secure Mumbai and Delhi and secured them. For it, those were the most critical, although its bidding pattern was spread out over service areas where literacy was high. The company earlier placed bids in Gujarat, Andhra Pradesh, Karnataka, Tamil Nadu, Kerala and Haryana.

Aircel started with an apparent focus on the Southern states, such as Tamil Nadu, Kerala, Karnataka and Andhra Pradesh along with metro regions Mumbai, Delhi, and Kolkata. The company had a strong position in 2G services on the eastern banks, especially Assam and West Bengal, so it was synergistic to pursue airwaves in these circles. At about the halfway mark of the auction, watching the escalation of BWA spectrum prices and jaded from the recent 3G experience, Aircel backed away from the expensive metro cities, and doubled down on home turf in Tamil Nadu and West Bengal. The outcome of this one was more successful than the just-ended 3G auction. It secured airwaves in all its major service areas and was the last bidder fighting for Assam, holding up the closing of the auction. In the end, it secured Andhra, Tamil Nadu, West Bengal, Bihar, Orissa, Assam, North-east and Jammu and Kashmir.

RCom started strong in strategic service areas but dropped off midway not to return. The same was true for the Tata Group, which spread itself across a larger number of service areas but decided not to pursue it further beyond the half mark.

Tikona attacked the auction based on population density and corporate hubs. Since securing the two obvious metro cities was impossible, it pursued the second-best option. In the end, it bought airwaves in Gujarat, Uttar Pradesh East and West, Rajasthan, and Himachal Pradesh.

Augere was interested in five service areas, but in the end only secured Madhya Pradesh. With just one service area, this company, which was formed by a consortium of financial investors under Ahuja, appeared to be marginalized and an acquisition target if the airwaves amounted to something useful among evolving technologies.

Sunil Mittal's Bharti Airtel was bidding to plug the gaps in areas where it had not secured a 3G slot. At the outset the company bid for spectrum in twelve service areas. It defended home turf Delhi and financial capital Mumbai till a fairly late stage in the auction, but in the end bagged only four service areas: Maharashtra, Karnataka, Kolkata, and Punjab. Not that the company was putting this spectrum to work immediately. 'On BWA, at least two competing technologies are available—

WiMax and LTETDD and we want to be sure that we make the right choice,' Sanjay Kapoor explained to investors a few months after the auction.[1]

What few realised until the penultimate day of the BWA spectrum auction, was that Nahata was not repeating a mistake. The bidding was done at the behest of Mukesh Ambani, who had over the years struck up a relationship with Nahata. It seems as though Nahata was at some point closer to Anil Ambani and appeared together in several political events of the Samajwadi Party in Uttar Pradesh. The party's affairs were led by general secretary and politician Amar Singh who helped nominate Anil Ambani to the Rajya Sabha, or Upper House of Parliament, in 2004. Anecdotes from friends suggest that Nahata was instrumental in deepening those ties. This could not be independently verified.

People close to the events suggest that Mukesh Ambani at the time was less keen on Anil's decision to enter politics. However, Nahata helped at a time before the Reliance Group split, and some accounts suggest that he switched sides at the time of its division. In March 2006 Anil Ambani resigned from his post as MP, primarily because his business and political interests seemed at cross purposes. Nahata continued to remain close to the political establishment in Uttar Pradesh.

In any case, on 10 June 2010, when the *Economic Times* reported that RIL would use this route to re-enter the telecom business, competitors were visibly riled at their dismissal of the BWA bandwidth and its constituent bidders. A day later, RIL's board approved its re-entry into the telecom space and made an offer to buy 95 per cent of Infotel Broadband for Rs 4800 crore to be paid to the company as fresh equity issuance and take on the nearly Rs 13,000 crore liability it had from the spectrum auction.

A precedent of fresh equity infusion to buy a significant stake in telecom companies had already been set during the 2G allocations. Mukesh Ambani's move could not be challenged. The elder Ambani later said that he returned to telecom because his daughter was disappointed with the speed of internet at their home when she came home to visit from university. The truth is, most of the team that had created the original Reliance Communications network was alert and readied for this project. Those like Arun Sur, who had stayed with the telecom company under Anil Ambani, because their skillset was suited best for telecom, were invited back to Mukesh's fold. Reliance's stated objective in the board approval was to create an only 4G-based mobile service provider. This was not a data or internet streaming play; Reliance was coming for the voice customers that accounted for well over 90 per cent of the industry's revenue.

'India has not kept pace with the world in terms of more advanced communication technologies,' Mukesh Ambani told investors at the company's annual general meeting just days after the purchase. 'Broadband wireless technologies is at the heart of our search for competitive advantage and economic prosperity,' he said. As he spoke of India pole-vaulting a generation of mobile tech, he said, 'Reliance can now offer fourth generation wireless Infocomm services across the nation.' Adding to that a glimpse of a portfolio of businesses that plug into the broadband play such as health, education, and e-banking, Mukesh Ambani emphasized, 'The possibilities are limitless.'[2]

To the incumbent telecom operators, this was reminiscent of Reliance's first CDMA 'back door' entry as they called it. There did not seem to be a legal way around it, so they would need to brace for impact. That would be difficult given they had all just paid a pretty penny for airwaves and barely had adequate funds to deploy 3G services let alone accelerate to 4G. Fortunately, they had time. They were confident that RIL would take at least eighteen months to set up a network and launch a service.

53

The 2G Scam

Manipulation of the new 2G service licence-allocation process reeked of foul play. It was then logical that aggrieved parties complained. In 2009, a series of complaints went to various enforcement agencies. A non-profit organization Telecom Watchdog complained to the Central Vigilance Commission (CVC).

Siva Sankaran's S-Tel filed and won a case in Delhi High Court regarding the changed cut-off dates when Raja eliminated applicants. The Delhi High Court ruled that the change in selection date was illegal, resulting in a later date in airwaves for S-Tel. Meanwhile, the CVC tossed complaints over to the Central Bureau of Investigations for a deep dive.

The CBI then registered a complaint against unnamed Department of Telecom officials and began its search for a culprit. The Comptroller and Auditor General, an industry body that acts as the accountant to the government, compounded the controversy. In its annual report published at the end of March 2010 the CAG flagged that there had been 'irregularities' in the 2G allocation of airwaves because opinions of the Finance and Law Ministries were disregarded.

During this period, the Income Tax department tapped the phone lines of lobbyist Nikita Radia who ran a public relations company, called Vaishnavi. Radia's company had the unique distinction of representing rival and savvy groups—Tata and Mukesh Ambani's Reliance. The tapes were leaked publicly in May 2010. They contained quid pro quo conversations that led authorities to believe there was a power-broking and gratification nexus between Raja and other industrialists that led to 2G spectrum allocations.

On 8 November 2010 came the real blow that escalated the entire matter into a nationwide crisis that was termed the 2G Scam. The government may have lost Rs 1,76,645 crore on the spectrum allocated for 2G said CAG which was under the leadership of bureaucrat Vinod Rai. The astronomical figure made headlines all over the country and brought a blinding spotlight on Raja, diffusing onto the ruling party.

'The implementation process [of 2G spectrum allocation] does not withstand the test of scrutiny.' The report said that given the price at which 3G spectrum was sold, the amount collected for the 2G airwaves reflected revenue loss for the government. 'That there has been loss to the national exchequer in the allocation of 2G spectrum cannot be denied. However, the amount of loss could be debated. To ensure that such lapses do not occur in any Ministry or Department of the governmemt, there is an imperative need to fix responsibility and enforce accountability for the lapses.'[1]

Minister A. Raja was forced to resign on 10 November 2008. To diffuse the situation, Congress appointed Kapil Sibal as telecom minister. Sibal promised a 100-day program to clean up any issues in the ministry. Subsequently, he pronounced that the government had lost nothing, and the CAG figure was flawed. Other than that, the ministry continued business as usual.

When a shadow was cast on Prime Minister Manmohan Singh's role in the affair, the ruling Congress Party was caught off guard. Singh eventually talked to the media about the dilemma his office faced. 'I would like to say that in projecting these events an impression has gone round that we are a scam-driven country and that nothing good is happening in our country,' Singh told electronic media on 16 February 2011. 'Some people may say that we are a lame duck government that I am a lame duck prime minister, we take our job very seriously, we are here to govern and to govern effectively.'[2]

In question was the PM's letter exchange with Raja in November 2007 which seemed to show that the Congress government had turned a blind eye to Raja's manipulation. The PM maintained that his office had relied on assurances of transparency by Raja. Singh said that complaints his office received after spectrum allocation were from companies that were aggrieved which made him trust the ministry's actions over external objections. 'I was not in a position to make up my mind that anything seriously was wrong with Mr. Raja's doing at that time,' he explained.

The Central Bureau of Investigation (CBI) doubled down on a fact-finding mission that was as humiliating for most executives as it was headline-grabbing for the press.

The CBI called all top executives from all major telecom companies. It turned the heat on the new players. Unitech promoters The largest number of stories of bullying from the authorities seemed to pertain to Sanjay and Ajay Chandra who had sold equity in their telecom arm to Norway's Telenor and Shahid Balwa, who sold equity in Swan Telecom to Etisalat. There were others also caught in the ire of the CBI as it turned on the heat on established groups such as Anil Ambani's RCom and Ruia-owned Essar—both had received airwaves. Gautam Doshi fielded questioning on behalf of RCom. Vikas Saraf who was considered Essar's leading finance and negotiations man was repeatedly named in the CBI enquiries.

Raja, DMK leader M. Karunanidhi's daughter, and telecom department officers were all implicated, interviewed and some jailed. Raja was arrested in February of 2011 and remained in prison for roughly a year.

Supreme Court judge O.P. Saini heard the matter. After a year of hearings, logically foul play in spectrum allocation seemed apparent, but when the CBI submitted its charge sheet, evidence to assign blame on any individual was lacking.

Ahead of his retirement, Justice Saini decided to roll back all new 2G licences granted under Raja in a landmark order on 2 February 2012. In total, 122 licences were cancelled. Airwaves given to dual technology players RCom and Tata remained untouched.

It was the foreign investors that were left holding the baby. Overnight, Telenor and Etisalat, which had already invested in substantial sums to launch services had entirely lost their business in India. There was an appeal to the order both in local and international fora. However, not much changed on ground.

Telenor still hoped it could retain a foothold in the market. Its launch was arguably the biggest among new players and its deployment most advanced. The company had quickly secured telecom towers. Spearheading India's strategy was Sigve Brekke, Telenor's head of Asia Pacific who some years later was elevated to hear the Norwegian company globally. Brekke made frequent visits to the country to fine-tune its regional strategies. The Indian consumer was acutely price-sensitive. In the Mumbai circle, the company had introduced dynamic discounts. This was a smart billing system that prompted a user to make more calls for a smaller per minute fee if the traffic on the network was low. In contrast, when the network was congested, the calls would become full price. As a result, usage on its network was spread over both geography and timeframe, leading to less congestion and better caller experience. None of the other operators were using a comparable discounting system at the time. From a customer uptake perspective, the company was doing well.

Telenor wished to remain in the market despite the cancelations. The company applied for fresh licences and bought spectrum in subsequent auctions. Its presence, however, was restricted to seven service areas and never grew to a meaningful size.

Etisalat preferred to back away from its deployment. The authorities seemed partial in chasing its partner Shahid Balwa-owned DB Realty. Etisalat's exit left Punjab National Bank and Standard Chartered Bank with staggering loan defaults, that were raised against the equipment that was being installed.

After the 2012 order, Saini retired from the Supreme Court. A special bench was created under his supervision to prosecute the case further. The CBI submitted reams, trying to explain a nexus between Balwa's companies and Unitech's Chandras and A. Raja.

Over the next year as hearings continued, the buzz around the 2G scam fizzled. In 2014, the administration changed, and a new BJP government led by Narendra Modi came into power. Matters could have gained steam, but that did not happen.

In 2017, the special bench acquitted all accused in the case and all challenges to this outcome were unsuccessful till 2024.

54

3G Becomes a Winner's Curse

The companies thought they could justify the high cost of 3G spectrum by netting other operators' customers via roaming agreements. The government did not agree. Incumbent operators, Idea, Vodafone and Airtel were quick off the block to sign intra-circle roaming, or ICR, agreements. Opposers were quick to question the legality of the move and take it up with bureaucrats as a flouting of licence conditions. In the December 2011 Parliament session, Minister of State Communication Milind Deora told the Lower House that '3G ICR is in violation of licence condition'.[1]

The bureaucracy was wary and conservative after the arrest of A. Raja and the subsequent jamboree of investigations. Unwilling to take a decision on the matter without a court order, the government blocked it and penalized operators. The regulator worked through the legal requirements and slapped Bharti, Vodafone and Idea Cellular with notices on Friday, 23 December 2011. It gave the service providers just one day to suspend services arising from these agreements. Operators had no recourse in the window they were given. The courts were shut the next day because of the weekend and were commencing their winter vacation in the week that ensued. The operators appealed to the emergency court judge for relief. They were heard, and a judge stipulated a stay on the DoT notice until a hearing at the TDSAT (Telecom Disputes Settlement and Appellate Tribunal).

The two-judge bench of the TDSAT heard both sides of the argument. Operators said they were entitled to enter into intra-circle roaming agreements because the UASL had liberalized spectrum use. The licence also allowed companies to enter into long distance carrying agreements intra-circle, which meant that they could use each other's cabled network for faster signal transmission.

The government said that the licence condition limited operators' roaming agreements to offer only services they were permitted to provide. Data service under 3G was not something an operator's native network could offer unless it had bought airwaves. This formed clause 2.2 of the licence agreement, which said, 'except those services listed in para 2.2 (b)(i) licensee cannot provide any service which require a separate licence'.[2] While 3G was not a listed service, internet and data connectivity were.

The government argued that roaming between operators is a 'facility' not a service in itself. Through 3G ICR agreements operators were trying to offer a service that they could not otherwise offer. Providing 3G services via an intra-circle roaming agreement would be equivalent to becoming a mobile virtual network operator (MVNO), which was barred.

An MVNO internationally is a company that either has no network or has a cabled network but no airwaves. It buys minutes in bulk from a mobile operator and repackages them for its customers. In 2008 the government had barred MVNOs in the Indian market. Discussions to approve it in the late 2010s were underway but had not reached a culmination.

The TRAI also echoed the DoT's stance in an advisory issued on 20 October 2011. The body had raised concerns over allowing intra-circle roaming agreements in August 2008. This was prior to the 3G debate. TRAI's stance was that new operators would form these agreements and launch services using the airwaves allocated for one operator to service customers worth two. Meanwhile, the newly allocated spectrum would lie idle, degrading the quality of service to the consumer.

That raked up controversy on Tata's agreement with Richard Branson's Virgin, that flamboyantly launched service in Mumbai on 2 March 2008. At the time, in addition to the regulator, competing operators had questioned the validity of the agreement to power what the challengers termed an MVNO. At the launch event in which Branson unveiled the Virgin Mobile brand logo as he rappelled down the facade of the Hilton Towers at the waterfront of the Indian Ocean at Nariman Point, the UK-based businessman made a special note that this was not an MVNO agreement, but simply a brand extension for Tata's services.

The judges were divided on the 3G ICR matter. The member on the panel agreed with the government and opined that the operators must stop all ICR services. The chairman favoured telecom operators, because by forcing them to discontinue service within a day, without giving service providers a hearing, the DoT had flouted 'natural justice'. The notice from the DoT was set aside in the order of 3 July 2012 with guidance that the Department should give operators a chance to voice concerns and then decide on the matter more objectively.

The DoT, in its wisdom, reissued notice to Bharti Airtel on 28 September 2012. The notice came with a Rs 350 crore fine. By this point, the TDSAT became dysfunctional because its judges retired without replacements. Bharti appealed to the Delhi High Court.

The Delhi High Court stayed the action from the regulator and redirected the case to adjudication on 3 October 2012.

In the meantime, the high court told the company to collate a list of customers and revenue arising from 3G ICR agreements. The DoT was unfazed. Hot on the heels of issuing Bharti a notice, similar letters also went to Idea and Vodafone. They, too, challenged them in separate cases.

Reliance Communications decided to take the government's side against Bharti. It challenged the order of 3 October for tacitly allowing Bharti to use ICR agreements in the wait for an outcome. The Delhi High Court heard the matter again and came to the same conclusion as before—the matter was too technical and best resolved in adjudication. In its order dated 20 December 2012, the high court set a timeframe of four weeks to complete the process.

On the same day, the same court also dealt with a public interest litigation from the government, that had earlier sought to bar private operators from using roaming agreements. When this was first filed, the TDSAT was still in session and seemingly close to a verdict, so the Delhi High Court forwarded it to the tribunal. Now that the tribunal was no longer functioning and its last verdict left companies in limbo, the DoT revived its plea in the Delhi High Court.

The judge ordered to club Bharti's case with Idea and Vodafone. Soon, the government issued letters to the other two operators to cease all ICR agreement-related activity and then added them to the adjudication process. Next, the High Court appointed a committee that would hear the companies and make a ruling on the matter. The first hearing was held on 4 January 2013. Bharti submitted written responses to questions raised in the hearing on 16 January.

Unfortunately for the operators, the adjudication outcome was not significantly different from the earlier government-led processes. Bharti's claim was rejected, and the government imposed its Rs 350 crore penalty. Bharti again challenged the decision on 15 March 2013, and a single judge approved a stay on the levy as well as action recommended by the committee.

The penalty letters for Vodafone and Idea came without clear guidance on whether the companies had a right to be heard. Only Bharti was able to present its case. By the time a clarification reached the companies, the battle had already moved to the Supreme Court. Vodafone and Idea Cellular still appealed the penalty orders in the Delhi High Court on August 5.

Meanwhile, the functioning of the TDSAT was restored in July 2013 after the appointment of two new judges. The Supreme Court also said that this matter was too technical for a general court and therefore tossed the matter to the newly instated bench of the TDSAT to issue a final order. The High Court did the same for Vodafone and Idea's cases. Once again, all three incumbents landed before the tribunal, fighting to keep the roaming pacts that allowed them to offer an all-India service.

The judges this time around agreed with operators to allow intra-circle roaming services. The final order said that the licence conditions themselves do not bar operators from striking these agreements. The final TDSAT decision relied on the auction invitation and the subsequent exchanges between the operators and the government. The judges said that participation in the 3G auction did not mandate a new telecom licence, and the existing one was adequate. Therefore, a company with a 2G licence was entitled to offer 3G services. 'The prohibition of intra-circle 3G roaming would have the direct result of under-utilisation of 3G spectrums which is plainly not in national interest,' said the final judgment. Quashing all the earlier orders the judges allowed intra-circle roaming and pointed out that this would be an option even for MTNL, BSNL and Reliance Communications that were appearing against the incumbents.

On the ground, the TDSAT's decision made no difference. The telecom industry had moved on to 4G technology as Mukesh Ambani's Reliance Industries was nipping at everyone's heels to accelerate upgrades. Most of all, the government had already conducted another spectrum auction, a third that failed and still had one more in the pipeline. Telecom Minister Kapil Sibal urged his successor to challenge the validity of 3G ICR agreements in a higher court, but the relevance of the pact itself diminished sufficiently for the fight to dissipate.

55

The Failed Spectrum Auction

The cancellation of licences awarded by Raja in 2008 freed up spectrum for the DoT. Those who had lost it clamoured for a means to regain it. There was enough spectrum in the 1800MHz band to accommodate three new players in all service areas except Mumbai and Delhi where availability was slightly over two slots.

The Supreme Court's directive in 2012 was that another auction would set the new benchmark for cost of airwaves revised from the 2001 figure that Raja had used in allocating licences in 2008. The DoT decided to auction its spectrum in the 1800MHz and 800MHz bands. This was a way to discover the market-determined price for the airwaves. DoT now had to decide on the floor price for the airwaves.

The Department had never expected the 3G auction to be as successful as it turned out. Using it as a benchmark to set the next auction floor price seemed incorrect. The 3G airwaves were not strictly comparable with the essential underlying spectrum in the 900MHz and 1800MHz for GSM players and 800MHz for CDMA. However, the officials were afraid to lower the starting price for fear they would be accused of corruption in the wake of the 2G scam. The entire establishment was treading on eggshells in the aftermath of Raja's arrest and CBI enquiries.

None of the regulatory bodies were going to stick their necks out to reduce the base price.

After much deliberation, the government set a floor price of Rs 14,000 crore for a 5MHz slot across India in the 1800MHz band. Technical consultation suggested that airwaves in the 800MHz band were more valuable than a higher band because of their natural long-distance coverage and better quality of transmission. The government pegged the starting price for it at 1.3 times that of the higher band. Companies would, therefore, start bidding for 5MHz of airwaves across India in the 800MHz band at Rs 15,000 crore.

Officials were aware that not all those who had lost licences were looking to return to this turbulent market. Auction failure was a possibility. As a hedge, the DoT reduced the block size of airwaves to 1.25MHz, hoping to attract incumbents and genuine players. Any of the incumbent operators looking to top up spectrum would prefer to buy in bite-sized pieces.

As expected, the interest by the time of the 14 November 2012 auction had petered out. It ended in a swift fourteen rounds spanning barely two days. None of the new licensed entrants bought an all-India presence. The absolute auction value for the government was little changed. It raised a mere Rs 9408 crore. Spectrum in the 800 MHz band remained untouched and over 50 per cent of the airwaves offered in 1800MHz were unsold. Bihar was the only region where airwaves in the 1800MHz band were sold out. Delhi and Mumbai had no bidders.

Uninor, the joint venture between Norway's Telenor and real estate major Unitech, was one of the few biddings actively to offer telecom services, but it was cautious and bought just enough to keep a toehold in the market. The company bought 5MHz of airwaves in the 1800MHz band in six service areas for Rs 4018 crore.

Videocon bought airwaves in seven service areas, albeit the more inexpensive ones. It paid the government Rs 2221 crore. None of the other companies that lost airwaves took part in the auction.

All of them filed arbitration suits against the Indian government in the hope that international economic pressure would force the government to modify the Supreme Court's punishment. The foreign investors argued that they were punished for the corruption of their local partners.

In a way, auction participation was illustrative of the nature of investments made. A bulk of the expenditure that Swan Etisalat had made for instance came from borrowings from Punjab National Bank. Shahid Balwa and Swan were tangled deep in the 2G scam investigation, so Etisalat's priority appeared to be to cut its losses.

For Telenor, acceptance of the high price and a stripped operation was a sharp comedown from threatening the government of its exit from the country if auction pricing remained high. Telenor's investors were wary of India. A society general note, quoted by *Bloomberg*, said that Telenor's shares could get a 15–20 per cent boost if only the uncertainty and overhang of its India investment were to be removed. 'It is not a threat, it is a reality,' Executive Vice President and Asia Head Sigve Brekke said at the time. This was after urging the government to put a rush on the auction so that it could resume the network it had already put in place.

Government officials dismissed this public squabble the company had picked. Telenor had gained the reputation of routinely fighting with the establishment. It was at the time also fighting the administration in Bangladesh over tax. Telenor slapped a claim of $14 billion on the Indian government when it filed its arbitration case in March 2012. The bureaucrats feared a corruption enquiry more than they desired to attract Telenor's foreign investment.

After all the harsh words and the stern indication that it would take its global funds to other shores, Telenor had elected to stay. The company had been scoping the Indian market since 2001 and never quite agreed on the valuation to enter on. Having missed a major appreciation, it chanced it in 2009. Exiting from India in 2012 would have set the company back on its overall goals by nearly three years. India's explosive subscriber growth was supposed to plug in with Europe's stagnant one since the economic bust of 2008.

Telenor had some other synergistic markets like Bangladesh, where it held a pole position. India's population advantage was not one it could ignore.

'In my book, there are two types of people in business. The first looks for excuses to opt out of challenges and looks for scapegoats for crises like the one we faced back in 2012. But the second type sees our past struggles and current situation as positive challenges, as a tension that keeps our people motivated and on-their-toes. This is what our Indian operations have become,' Sigve Brekke, head of Asia Pacific at Telenor wrote in an authored newspaper article in 2015.[1]

At one point in 2014, Telenor was adding only marginally less customers in six service areas than Vodafone was doing across the country. Brekke said the stripping of its all-India licence had made Telenor realize that the country operated more like a continent in circle-wise silos. Yet, it faced an uphill task trying to provide internet connectivity over a 2G network, when leading players were offering 3G.

What dragged further were Uninor's hostile equity partners that had to remain invested because of foreign direct holding laws. The taint and financial drain on the company owing to jailed promoters of Unitech Sanjay and Ajay Chandra limited the company. Debt for telecom operators had dried up since licence cancellations and the Chandra brothers were blocking equity infusion. So, Telenor's Indian operations skimped on expenses that could tip customers in its favour.

As soon as the government liberated foreign ownership in a mobile operator, Telenor mopped up Unitech's shares. The company declared an operating profit before the three-year mark since inception, but its net profitability remained elusive. Norway's telecom leader was hoping to fix that soon.

Little did this company know the onslaught Mukesh Ambani was about to wreck on its ilk.

56

Surprise Spectrum Fees

Although the 2012 auction failed, it set a benchmark for the price of spectrum that existing operators were using. The second part of O.P. Saini's 2G judgment asked the government to level all administered spectrum to the cost of auctioned airwaves.

The TRAI and the DoT interpreted this to mean a retrospective levy on all companies with more than the basic subscriber-linked spectrum on or before 2012. A note to retrospectively charge operators was placed before the cabinet and approved on 8 November 2012.

Published a little before the 1800MHz spectrum auction, the contours of the dues to be paid by operators were such: no additional charge if the operator had 4.4MHz or less of airwaves; if it was using up to 6.2MHz, then from 1 January 2013, it would pay a charge for the extra block as per the discovered price in the auction; if it did not wish to pay, it could surrender the airwaves. Any company that had more than 6.2MHz for GSM or more than 5MHz for CDMA prior to 2013 would incur a retrospective charge for the additional airwaves from 2008 till end-2012.

The charged amounts varied for each company, and of course affected only the incumbent operators, most of all Bharti Airtel and Vodafone. They held as much as 12MHz of spectrum in key service areas because under the 2001 and 2003 policies of the government, operators received extra spectrum every time they met a subscriber criterion. The additional airwaves came with a higher 'spectrum usage charge' or the revenue share that the government claimed from companies.

The retrospective levy was called the One-Time Spectrum Charge (OTSC). Based on the auction floor price, the cumulative amount across operators was estimated at around Rs 31,000 crore.

In the auction that followed a week after the OTSC directive, the government did not sell all the airwaves, but the ones that were sold exceeded the reserve price. In the few service areas where no spectrum was sold, the benchmark for the one-time spectrum charge OTSC was determined by future spectrum auctions.

The calculation was fairly complex. At the end of the 2012 auction, Bharti's charge was roughly Rs 3947 crore and Vodafone's was pegged at Rs 3599 crore. The rough total for all the companies was around Rs 27,000 crore.

Another court battle spanning over a decade ensued, but this time the incumbents were not fighting together. Aircel filed a suit in the Madras High Court, Bharti Airtel in the Delhi High Court, and Vodafone's case was in the Mumbai High Court. In Mumbai, the DoT's enforcement of this penalty was stayed almost immediately on 28 January 2013. The court ordered the government not to take any 'coercive' action and tossed the matter to the TDSAT. Loop Mobile filed much later but was eventually also heard by the TDSAT.

Tata Teleservices surrendered spectrum in areas other than Delhi and Mumbai under protest. The incumbents that had networks calibrated to the airwaves could not do so, but some other small tranches were deflected back to the exchequer.

It took until 4 July 2019 for the TDSAT to relieve operators of the penalty's fate. The TDSAT made three distinctions in levies the government could charge operators. It said that spectrum till 6.2MHz is not to be charged at all. If more spectrum than that was allocated before 1 July 2008 (the record date for new licensing under A. Raja) the operators would be liable to pay additional spectrum charge prospectively from 2013. For spectrum allocated after July 2008, operators would have to pay the additional charge from the date of allocation.

Like they did in so many other matters before, the operators appealed the decision in the Supreme Court. Atypically, their first application to appeal was rejected. Then, with some modifications and a little more cajoling, the court accepted the challenge which was still being heard in 2024. The outstanding amount per operator post interest on the time lapsed between the levy and court decision-making rose higher than Rs 15,000 crore. The liability arising from the penalty weighed on the operator's books diluting their financial standing with investors, at a time when an aggressive challenger, Reliance Industries, stood at the doorstep. Analysts asked frequent questions about this levy and what this meant for capital expenditure.

Companies needed more on-ground infrastructure to compensate for fewer airwave frequencies. The financial costs of borrowing for 3G spectrum and network deployments were denting profitability, without much apparent revenue upside. A reduced number of players in the market had put pricing power back in the hands of incumbent operators, but there still loomed questions over the future of profits and return on equity in India. This was reflected in their gradually upward-mobile share prices.

57

Rethink for Policy and Jio

The 3G ICR debate raised other questions for the Indian regulators. If the company paid the auction price for spectrum, was it restricted to using it only for government-specified purposes? With administered spectrum that had been the case. GSM spectrum was only for those services, CDMA operators could not shift technology, even though by 2010, both technologies could use either frequency.

In 2011 this raised a debate about spectrum liberalization. At the heart of it was the competition Reliance Industries was expected to give other companies. Mukesh Ambani's company had secured airwaves in the 2300MHz band at a fraction of the cost of mainstream spectrum and was to pay only a per cent as revenue share to the government. The government had auctioned this spectrum thinking of alternative technologies, but RIL planned to use it for mainstream mobile services. Having auctioned it with one set of rules should the government go back to make amendments?

The only ray of hope mobile companies clung to was failed early tests by Reliance. Mobile coverage using the 2300MHz band was patchy at best. Evolving standards in 4G technology had by 2011 veered towards using the 1800MHz band, or 2G spectrum in India. By 2012, there were base stations in the market that could use 1800MHz frequency to offer 2G and 4G simultaneously and dynamically. This meant that an operator could allocate an entire cell site to the 2G network and could automatically offer 4G services from it as a 4G-enabled phone logged on. Similarly, technology was evolving for operators to use the 900MHz frequency to offer 2G and 3G services.

The telecom department's suggestion that some spectrum was liberalized but not all impeded this multi-technology use by operators. The TRAI and the DoT said that auction-bought 1800MHz spectrum was liberalized but not administered spectrum. Vodafone India CEO Marten Pieters had over the 2G scam period emerged as the leader who called it as it was without cowering from retaliatory action from the regulators. He was vocal on the liberalization issue. The spectrum was always liberalized, he emphasized. Sanjiv Aga CEO of Idea Cellular chimed in saying those were the terms of the licence ever since the fourth operator licences were auctioned in 2001. The licence agreement that operators held said that once they had received the airwaves, they could offer any service within the ambit of mobile telephony. Reliance on its CDMA network for instance was offering EVDO service, which was a technology that enabled fast relaying of data and therefore content such as videos on the mobile phone. Then what was this new debate?

The TRAI acknowledged the prominence of the use of 1800MHz for 4G LTE services globally. Shortly after the 2G licence reversal of 2012, the TRAI issued a consultation paper to equalize administered and auction-bought spectrum. 'The spectrum assigned for 2G services is for a specific technology; it cannot be used for any other technology, until its use is liberalised,' said a TRAI note dated April 23, 2012.[1] TRAI proposed liberalizing spectrum by auctioning airwaves across the spectrum to establish a benchmark price and imposing it on the administered spectrum. Operators could then trade spectrum and re-farm all the airwaves as they came up for licence renewal in a couple of years.

This brought the regulator to the concept of refarming and harmonizing the spectrum. Since the spectrum had been allocated ad hoc over the years, companies had tranches spread across the band. From a network and spectrum utilization perspective, sequential frequencies are better.

In its recommendation, TRAI included operators' opposing views and overruled them.

Vodafone preempted a regulation and challenged the proposal in the TDSAT, only to be tossed back to the TRAI until the consultation process was complete. The TDSAT reassured Vodafone that it could return to court should the outcome of the TRAI's exploration be unsatisfactory.

After the November 2012 auction, pricing for most of the 1800MHz band was established. The TRAI had issued a pricing benchmark for the 800MHz and 900MHz bands, but the DoT was still struggling to determine the market price of airwaves in the 800MHz band and in 1800MHz where there were no bidders.

Mainstream operators were beyond concerned. The regulator was suggesting a spectrum cleanup by auctioning the airwaves they were using to operate. Their twenty-year spectrum allocation window for airwaves in the 900MHz band was coming to an end in 2014. The licence included an option to request an extension of ten more years, but the administration appeared diffident to grant it. A fair amount of back and forth between the companies and the regulator happened but there was no respite.

The bureaucrats were worried they would be accused of corruption if they allowed an extension on the lease of airwaves. They openly agreed that it made sense to renew licences, but on paper, they had maintained that the spectrum would need to be auctioned.

The incumbents faced grave risk of losing their core ingredient to a higher bidder. The backend work to rejig operations to new frequencies would be enormous, not to mention the loss of customers owing to potential downtime on the network. Replacing the 900MHz with 1800MHz would mean a need to at least double infrastructure. So, these operators were not only protesting against spectrum auctions, they were refraining from participating out of self-preservation—a failed auction would mean lower starting prices for the next one.

That did not prevent the government from auctioning some available frequencies in the 900MHz band in March 2013. In this auction the government offered 95MHz in the 800MHz band across most India service areas, 42.5MHz in the 900MHz band offered only in large cities Mumbai, Delhi and Kolkata, and 57.50MHz in the 1800MHz block in service areas where there had been no bidding in the previous auction.

The TRAI's logic the argued for a change in floor price. It linked the spectrum band with its efficacy. The 800MHz and 900MHz airwaves have a longer reach with lesser distortion because the size of the wave is larger. For telecom deployment, this means reception points, or towers, can be wider apart, and the signal is received better indoors without boosting it. These bands had equal value set at two times the 1800MHz band, recommended the TRAI.

Since the 800MHz block had already been offered to no avail, the government decided it needed to be repriced. The amount the government lowered the reserve price surprised market players. The starting price of the spectrum was halved from the previous auction. The same logic, however, was not extended to the 900MHz band. There was a paucity of available 900MHz spectrum and the rest of it was in use. The government ascribed it a higher value at two times that of the 1800MHz band.

The incumbent operators protested. The nature and function of both 800MHz and 900MHz were similar. Increasingly mobile handsets were equipped to toggle between either band. So why this differentiation? They abstained from the auction.

The response to it was worse than tepid. Only one operator signed up to participate in it—Sistema Shyam who operated the MTS brand. This was a company looking to launch CDMA-based services, so it only wanted a pair of 2.5MHz in the 800MHz band. The auction started and finished on 11 March 2013 at the end of three auction rounds. Its resounding failure was a smack that only made officials more resolute about auctioning airwaves operators were already using.

A government auctioning airwaves in use by the country's leading telecom operators was highly unusual around the world, but in 2014, the Indian Department of Telecommunications did it. In informal conversations officials at the ministry admitted to the folly in this. The TRAI members agreed that this was a strange process being undertaken in the name of a level playing field. They even admitted that it risked setting back India's telecom progress that seemed poised to pole-vault a generation and head straight to 4G. On record, none of them could roll back the decision. This led to the spectrum auctions in 2014, 2015 and 2016.

Following representation from existing telecom operators and the debacle of the 2013 auction, TRAI revisited its opinion on auction pricing. The 2G scam witch hunt was tapering off. The aberration of the 3G spectrum auction and therefore, the absurdity of the Rs 1,76,000 crore loss figure of the CAG was established. Elections were once again around the corner. The anti-incumbency sentiment was high, and a change in government was likely. A new regime promised greater stability at the center than the volatile ongoing term of the Congress Party-led UPA government. The telecom administration was a little more relaxed when deviating from earlier decisions.

The TRAI published a new recommendation on spectrum auction and pricing in September 2013. 'Conditions in the sector and in the overall economy have changed considerably between the time of the auction of 3G spectrum in the 2100 MHz band and the present,' said the TRAI. In its recommendation, the regulator took divergent views on valuing different bands in the spectrum rather than linking them all to each other. It also said that linking prices to the 3G bidding would be wrong, and that the auction reserve price should be lower than its estimated value to attract more bidders. It recommended that the base spectrum price should discount its value by 20 per cent.

In the 2014 auctions, the country offered 1800MHz band airwaves starting at 45 per cent of the price of previous auctions for Mumbai and Delhi. It also put up slots in Mumbai, Delhi and Kolkata in the 900MHz band in use by incumbent operators. The TRAI dropped the reserve price in this band to 30 per cent of the earlier one.

The auction started on 3 February 2014. Participation was for survival rather than growth. The incumbents needed to retain their airwaves to limit disruption to their network. Reliance Industries that had so far maintained it would only use 2300MHz frequency for its network became a surprise bidder in this auction. Both Tata and Reliance made a few early bids in the 900MHz band. However, both backed away after the first ten rounds. The network in Delhi was most fought over between Vodafone and Bharti Airtel. In Mumbai, Bharti's network was on the 1800MHz spectrum, so the clash was less intense.

In the 1800MHz band, however, there was intense bidding from the Reliance Industries' company, which had been branded Jio. Its participation validated competitors' views that a network on 4G airwaves alone was impossible. After three years of trying various combinations, Jio was relenting and buying airwaves to complete an operator's portfolio. Now that pricing was tipped in its favour, Jio was mopping airwaves in the 1800MHz band. It bought airwaves in fourteen service areas covering the key four metro cities and high population density states. In Mumbai and a few other service areas, the operator opted straight away for 6.2MHz of spectrum.

The purchase of the spectrum established a clear intent, even if the timeline was unclear. In June Mukesh Ambani announced, 'The year 2015 will see the phased launch of Reliance Jio across India.'[2] Trials and pilot launch of services were already underway and Ambani had invested Rs 70,000 crore in the business. The company had grown from 700 people in 2011 to 10,000 in 2014. In addition to the local trusted lieutenants, Reliance Jio's sprawling campus in Navi Mumbai housed international executives, some of them were expatriates Jio's senior management had interacted with during idea exchanges with Deutsche Telekom.

For established players, this was terrible news. They were content with the thought that not only would Jio need to price its services based on the massive investment, but it would also continue to experiment and therefore find it hard to retain customers. Vodafone's Pieters had repeatedly maintained that Jio was not a threat until it actually launched service, when answering media and investor queries. Idea's Himanshu Kapania said that India's voice market was still underpenetrated, pole-vaulting to data would not affect the operator's 2G business.

The 2014 auction lasted till 13 February 2014. There was no participation from new operators other than Telenor, which just added spectrum in small increments in the existing service areas. Bharti, Vodafone and Idea Cellular added airwaves to supplement their 3G portfolio.

For the government, this was a successful auction. It lasted sixty-eight rounds; prices rose in each category even though some airwaves remained unsold. It also set the tone for the government's action for all the other licence renewals, as licences awards were phased out from 1994 to 2001. The government was then set for more auctions over the next two years.

By this auction, the process was established. Operator war rooms were ever ready, and the financial teams had more experience on auction strategies and parking eligibility points to avoid price rises in key areas. They entered the 2015 auction with more evolved game theories to attack airwave buying. This time incumbents were also prepared to take on Jio—the only meaningful competitor that had risen since the 2008 licence allocation.

Spectrum to be renewed in the 900MHz band for many service areas, 800MHz almost pan India, 1800MHz where it was left, and one slot of 5MHz in the 2100MHz band was on offer. The reserve price in the 1800MHz band was surprisingly higher than before. The change was in tandem with the action in the previous auction. Other airwaves remained discounted as their market value was still to be ascertained.

Players used provisional wins and bid only in alternate rounds. This kept prices in check for service areas they wanted. That inevitably meant escalation elsewhere. The March 2015 auction lasted 116 rounds. Its most distinguishing feature was the rebalancing of airwaves prices across regions and frequency bands.

Among the incumbents, there was an unspoken code to live and let live, which meant that they did not vie for each other's existing airwaves. This did not apply to Jio. Mukesh Ambani's company was aggressively buying airwaves in the 800MHz block, which would plug in perfectly with the 1800MHz and 2300MHz the company already had. With the 800MHz block, Jio would own the most comprehensive spectrum portfolio among competitors.

Bharti stayed out of the 800MHz band. Idea and Vodafone, however, took turns to bid in some circles. Jio responded in kind and bid in the 900MHz band in the first quarter of the auction. Thereafter it settled back in the 800MHz band. There was a showdown between Vodafone and Jio towards the end of the auction in North-east that irked Jio back into the 900MHz band in Rajasthan and Uttar Pradesh forcing Vodafone to retreat from the 800MHz band, after the price of its existing 900MHz spectrum shot up.

When the auction closed, Jio added nearly double that of its competitors in the 800MHz band. In the 1800MHz band, Jio bought big blocks once again, this time mostly plugging the circles it omitted in 2014. It doubled up on areas where indoor coverage was getting tricky. For instance, in Kolkata where building density is high and consumers sit in constructed locations, signalling indoors was difficult on the 2300MHz band without a low-frequency, high-range airwave.

Tata and RCom also picked up incremental spectrum in the 800MHz band. The incumbents successfully defended their spectrum holding in the 900MHz band, the most significant block of which went to Bharti Airtel. Nevertheless, Jio's accumulation of spectrum riled them.

Sooner or later, they expected RCom to fold into Jio. Spectrum was a competitive edge incumbents could not afford and Jio was using it as a building block. Nearly Rs 1,00,000 crore without a launch, this was a network paying lower spectrum usage and built ground up rather than in incremental patches over years of technological evolution.

Operators raised an alert on the limit of spectrum a single entity was allowed to hold. Overall, Jio was touching the 50 per cent mark on owning spectrum. The regulator saw no harm in this. It had set limits by frequency band, and on that front Jio was in the clear.

By the end of the 2015 auction, only seven serious players were left in the marketplace—Bharti, Vodafone, Idea, RCom,

Jio, Tata and Aircel. Awaiting them was yet another auction in 2016. That was not top of mind. The imminent launch of Jio threatened the existence of some and the profitability of others. Jio's spectrum investments alone were pegged at Rs 34,000 crore.

'Jio is now present in all of the 29 states of India, with a direct physical presence in nearly 18,000 cities and towns of our nation,' said Mukesh Ambani. The company was beginning to showcase its technology and engage with investors. It had built plug-in services such as JioMoney, a digital wallet, a cloud service, and was working on a content bank to power a video streaming service. Jio was also in talks with various state governments to distribute government subsidies over the Jio platform. 'Our roadmap is to have 100 per cent national coverage within the next 3 years.'[3]

Ambani said, 'I am glad to announce that the financial year 2016–17 will be the first full year of commercial operations for Jio,' and the operators waited on the edge of their seats to see what this tsunami would bring after six years and six times the original investment outlay.

58

Managing Anil's RCom

Anil Ambani's ADAG Group waffled between a cut-and-dry business approach and a softer more inclusive approach with its management. Anil Ambani had low patience and called things as he saw them. If a person was in his good books, then he greeted them with princely treatment. When an executive fell from grace, the wrath was scathing.

As a result, his immediate entourage remained reserved, and seldom voiced disagreement. Key group executives like Amitabh Jhunjhunwala arrived at public events little before Anil Ambani and checked on the arrangements for his boss. In other groups, this was left to public relations teams. During crunch years, this severely affected talent retention and therefore the management approach at the ADAG flagship company Reliance Communications.

After the failed attempt to merge with MTN, the divestment of Reliance Infratel looked dicey, and Reliance Communications, which had reduced call rates below those of other companies but was struggling to win, Anil Ambani believed it was time to refresh his top management.

The company's hiring began with a network specialist Naresh Gupta. S.P. Shukla, a senior team member of the original Reliance umbrella and head of RCom's CDMA business, was reassigned to special projects making room for a new mobile chief executive—Syed Safawi.

Safawi came from Airtel. He was heading the East and West service areas there along with a leadership position in the international business. His departure from Airtel coincided with Kapoor's nomination to become the next CEO of Airtel. Heading Reliance's newly launched GSM service and an existing CDMA business that needed repurposing was precisely the challenge Safawi thought he needed.

RCom was already gearing up for the 3G auction. The company needed to find an investor and lower its debt profile. Investors appreciated promoter-led companies that were headed by professional CEOs. Safawi was also offered autonomy to achieve a pole position in the market.

Unfortunately, RCom was caught in a catch-22 situation. It needed to plough money into the business to raise more of it. At the end of Safawi's first year, it seemed RCom was losing both in the customer and investor marketplaces. Safawi on the other hand believed there was too much micromanaging for him to exercise the autonomy he was promised. He reported to Satish Seth and within the organization, several of the other sub-businesses had created a direct reporting dotted lines to Seth, which was encouraged as a means to keep a check on the CEO. It was a difficult time for the sector and a turnaround in fortunes looked elusive.

Ambani ascribed financiers' unwillingness to fund the company to its slipping market position. There were a few tense exchanges between him and Safawi, as neither was willing to change their stance on what was causing the decline. Ambani found himself doing the leg work to raise funds from Chinese firms.

By mid-2011 the two agreed that this was the end of their journey together. RCom hired Shamik Das, the chief executive of S Tel, a joint venture between Sivasankaran and Bahrain's Batelco. Das was named chief operating officer and head of mobility business under Safawi. It is unclear whether Das was initially hired to increase Safawi's compliance but over time, Das's comings and goings to the ADAG headquarters increased and Safawi's decreased. Planning, execution, partnership and supply chain management were the strengths that backed Das' hiring, the company said in a press statement.[1]

Safawi's two-year contract was allowed to lapses in February 2012, ending his term at the company. Now, Das was on probation.

In 2012, coinciding with Shamik Das's appointment Bahrain's Batelco and RCom announced they were in a non-binding negotiation to partner. Nothing conclusive emerged from it.

The organization was restructured to a more regional model with eight heads covering India's twenty-two service areas. It extinguished the four—north, south, east, west—division leadership to create a 'leaner' and 'flatter' company. Das was expected to create a more uniform customer experience and consolidate sales and network management efforts to optimize the company's spending. Based on the communication, it was his fifteen years of experience at Airtel before MTS that RCom was counting on. Das was a chartered accountant by training and to that end, RCom had hoped he would be able to get more bang for the buck.

Between December 2011 and May 2012, RCom's leaders, Anil Ambani, Amitabh Jhunjhunwala and Satish Seth had a falling out with Das as well. Instead, they appointed Gurdeep Singh, the former chief operating officer of Aircel, who had been eased out of his role by Maxis, Aircel's Malaysian parent. Internally, Aircel had investigated related-party transactions on contracts the operator gave to technology and telecom tower service vendors.

Gurdeep Singh had the reputation of being well-versed in bureaucratic relations and having a temperament suited to adjusting to the toughest promoters. He was a good fit for RCom, which had its share of troubles with the administration. His experience in GSM services was a bonus.

The first thing Singh did, or undid was Das restructuring of the business. Six months into his term, RCom reverted to a centralized control. This time there were no granular control pockets, not even the four—east, west, north, south. The latest idea was to take collective decisions at the corporate level and then push them down regionally. In order to do that, each zone was asked to prepare detailed financial notes on a per telecom tower basis.

To stem the cash drain RCom was facing, Singh's next move was to shut unprofitable telecom towers. These fell into two categories—ones with rentals so high, that revenue was not commensurate and ones that were so remote that they serviced too few customers. Singh's argument was that these towers were guzzling cash. The move would immediately arrest the operating expenditure that was depleting the company's cash.

The move, however, triggered a vicious circle for the company. It alienated the genuine, high-paying customers because the network became patchy. Instead, it attracted the low-yield subscribers who were shopping for offers. In the investor community, RCom was now seen as a telecom company that was reversing its capital expenditure and readying itself for a predator. RCom, therefore, started getting clubbed with fringe or trailing players in the mobile market.

In January 2014, Singh initiated yet another restructuring. This time, the company was also split between CDMA and GSM technologies. The rationale was that the technologies addressed completely different markets, which should be reflected in their strategy. Singh brought in two more senior staffers: Nilanjan Mukherjee, an internal candidate to head the CDMA business, and Ramesh Menon, another Bharti alumus, to run the GSM operation.

The separation was also supposed to help secure investment. The CDMA business that once prided itself on being India's second-largest operator by subscribers had slipped to a distant fourth place. Too many potential investors seemed to discount CDMA and were unwilling to invest in the combine. Segregating the two businesses gave the company an option to sell shares in just the GSM arm. After the separation, RCom would have the flexibility to shut the CDMA business entirely if it chose not to renew its airwaves when the licence period ended in six years. Analysts had forecast the complete demise of CDMA technology in three or four years.

Yet, the bulk of RCom's profitable revenue came from the CDMA platform that corporate customers used for data services like fleet management. Once the two businesses were separated, a choice of one over the other was confusing for investors.

Running two separate networks was too expensive and the synergies Ambani had thought that could make them more efficient remained absent. So, even as the company orchestrated its third management restructuring in as many years, there were no easy answers to be found to alleviate its pain points.

The new structure was designed to free Singh to explore growth opportunities in the GSM business. For instance, he initiated a tie-up with Apple for iPhones and Android to build apps and internet features. However, the sales of the phones reflected the demographic the company was serving. For instance, the first 2500 iPhones sold out at breakneck speed, but thereafter the next 10,000 took months. Investors feared that inventory held by the company or even phones furnished to customers on instalment schemes would create a cash abyss as it had done in the first instance with CDMA phones and 'monsoon hungama'.

Since his appointment, Singh had successfully reversed the trend of falling revenue at RCom. Profits were an entirely different matter. A sale of equity or debt-free fund raise was still elusive. All the waffling and empowerment and then the stripping of power of executives lower down in the organization led to a loss of talented staff, not just in the sales outfit but also in the technical and network management teams of RCom.

It was not long before RCom's image proliferated as a network that would plug into Mukesh Ambani's bigger telecom play. When the company proudly announced that it had struck an optic fibre sharing deal with RIL which would fetch Anil Ambani's company some Rs 800 crore annually in 2013 it deepened the conviction that the company would fold into Jio.

59

Tata's Pesky Partners

Tata's partnerships in the telecom space were stressful. At least in part, they undermined the group's aspirations in the sector.

At the outset, their chief negotiator, Siva had triggered a falling out with the Birla Group. There were three more that followed—the Indian government as a shareholder in VSNL which was later named Tata Communications, Japan's NTT DoCoMo, which bought stake to launch Tata's GSM operations, and SREI on the telecom towers.

After Tata bought VSNL, the Government of India owned 26 per cent of it. The company ran the long-distance cabled backbone across India to carry call and data traffic. In 2002, it was a very strategic company because all operators, including state-run BSNL and MTNL, used its long-distance network for a per-call fee.

VSNL's acquisition came along with a plan to separate the land bank the company had as a government organization. Tata Group had agreed on a purchase valuation excluding the land. So, the group was not to be compensated for it, but other public shareholders needed to be remunerated based on the value of the land. Hence the land had to be valued, potentially a buyer had to be found, and then divested along with a per share payout.

The government said it would transfer the 773 acres of land held in prime locations in Delhi, Pune, Kolkata and Chennai, into a separate company. Equity in the new company would then be distributed according to the shareholding pattern of VSNL before Tata's purchase. The land's book value in the financial statements of VSNL was a mere Rs 1.6 million, but the forecast of current market value put the land worth at Rs 6000 crore and rising fast.

The government had considered undertaking this process prior to VSNL's sale but dropped the idea because of the potential impact on its NYSE-listed American Depository Receipts. The move could be viewed as government appropriation, which would have affected VSNL's sales.

When Tata bought VSNL it came with the condition that this land would be spun off and the acquirer could not buy the de-merged entity that would hold the land. When the land was transferred from VSNL, the company was asked to pay stamp duty and capital gains as is the norm for real estate transactions. The Tata Group objected to taking this from VSNL, or Tata Communications as it was renamed. It asked the government to incur the cost. Regulations allowed capital gains to be waived because the original asset belonged to the government, but there was no workaround stamp duty. The spin-off and its consequent monetization for the government was therefore delayed.

Tata's objection turned into a tit-for-tat situation. The government blocked Tata Communication's equity sale to raise funds for capital expansion until the demerger was completed. The company borrowed what it could using debt, but that resulted in a cash haemorrhage on account of interest. Since this was not a consumer-facing organization and dealt mainly with larger corporate buyers across the globe its billing cycles spanned longer, the pinch on cash felt more severe. Tata Communications continued to have a stronghold on the landline and dedicated broadband services to companies in Mumbai and Delhi, but the profitability slowly slipped away.

Meanwhile, the government deregulated the laying of national optic fiber. Tata Communications was not only systematically losing customers, but these customers were turning into its competitors. Bharti Airtel for instance went from being among the largest customers to a scathingly price warrior in a span of just two years, explained N. Srinath, chief executive of Tata Communications.[1] By 2006, most companies had built some form of backhaul infrastructure. Tata Communications needed to substitute this income with high-end corporate billings, for which it required investment in data centres, technology and segment upgrades to remain relevant.

The Tata Group considered merging its telecom assets—Tata Communications and Tata Teleservices—to offer customers a combined solution. The dongle-based wireless internet connectivity service was a fast-emerging winner in corporate fleet management, which was combined with corporate phone and leased line offerings. The Tata Group offered customers a single product which was then broken into back-to-back contracts for the two companies. The organizations could be made leaner by eliminating common functions between them. Shareholders came in the way. The government representative on the Tata Communications board made passing several resolutions difficult.

It took till 2019 to resolve the demerger of the surplus land. The government exited the company in 2021. Tata was free to take it in the direction of its choosing, but that was bittersweet. By this time, most of Tata's telecom businesses flirted with bankruptcy and were sold. The infrastructure is still in use and has adequate internal customers to keep it going.

* * *

Tata's partnership with Japan's NTT DoCoMo also hit the rocks. In 2008, after it received its dual technology licence, Tata Teleservices was later than its competitors in finding a strategic partner. Its signing came at a time when the world economy was unravelling from a global meltdown after the bankruptcy of Bear Stearns. Most investors were retreating. The NTT DoCoMo Group had some investments in the internet space in India, and discussions of a larger play in telecom were on the table. Yet, the Japanese company had been wary of Indian businesses. When it was approached by the Tata Group, the Japanese investor offered to partner via preference shares, a form of debt investment that can get converted into equity if certain conditions are met at the time of maturity.

Ratan Tata insisted Tata Teleservices needed fresh equity infusion and mounting its debt would not help. NTT DoCoMo was just short of pulling out when a gentleman's agreement between the newly appointed chief of NTT DoCoMo Ryuji Yamada and Ratan Tata, along with a promise from Tata to guarantee DoCoMo an exit, helped conclude the deal. NTT DoCoMo bought 26 per cent in Tata Teleservices for $2.7 billion on 12 November 2008.

Tata had hoped that the sector and the company would perform so well that the group would be able to sell more stake to NTT DoCoMo and nearly completely exit the company.

The NTT DoCoMo infusion was quickly spent on the GSM rollout. The brand Tata DoCoMo was launched using NTT DoCoMo's cutting-edge technology to offer per-second billing in June 2009 for 1 p per second. Until then, operators offered per-minute rates, and the average price was close to Re1 per minute. Tata DoCoMo's move triggered a sharp fall in call rates across the industry. During the first few months, as customers signed on, Tata DoCoMo seemed like a success. But it was short-lived.

Tata had promised to buy out NTT DoCoMo of Tata Teleservices in five years for half its original investment price if the partner requested. This was documented as a put option. The Japanese company could invoke this if equity value eroded and Tata could not find another buyer at fair market value.

In January 2012, NTT DoCoMo's network in Japan glitched, causing a network blackout in Tokyo. There was an explanation call, an upgrade planned on the network and a punitive pay cut for Yamada. In the next annual board meeting Yamada was replaced by Kaoru Kato, a new chief executive of NTT DoCoMo who saw the India investment with scepticism, more so because when he was appointed in June 2012, international protest against the Indian ecosystem had reached a crescendo after the Supreme Court revoked 2G licences.

At Tata's famed South Mumbai headquarters—Bombay House—Ratan Tata had announced his retirement and left things to the group's first independent chairman Cyrus Mistry after a one-year handover that started in 2011.

When NTT's option matured in 2013, the chemistry between the groups was lacking. The valuation of Tata's telecom company in India was diminishing disconcertingly. Tata had been unable to make a dent in the market despite two subsequent equity infusions, one with DoCoMo's participation and one without. The Japanese partner was keen on an exit, and it appeared that Tata was delaying the inevitable.

In April 2014, the Japanese partner elected to exit India, and intimated Tata and its shareholders that it was invoking its option to sell. Initially, the two groups were engaged in finding solutions. The Tata Group asked NTT DoCoMo to wait till it found another buyer. The Tata Group entered into rudimentary talks with Vodafone to sell Tata Teleservices. The company had too much debt and too little revenue with the burden to support two completely independent networks—CDMA and

GSM. Marten Pieters was still leading Vodafone and the UK-based operator was interested in deepening its corporate ties. It offered to explore a merger further if Tata threw in Tata Communications' assets. Tata was not amenable to that.

The Tata Group used Vodafone's interest in the company to stall DoCoMo's exit. News of the Vodafone Tata deal circled for much longer than it was actually on the table. Nine months later, DoCoMo got a whiff of this and rightfully felt deceived. It pursued the option to cash its shares for $1.3 billion.

This time, the Tata Group said it could not complete the transaction because it was bound by the law. It quoted a change in the foreign currency regulations set out by the Reserve Bank of India, which were a measure to prevent the flight of foreign capital. The central banker termed all pre-agreed equity pricing illegal—sale of Indian shares needed to be revalued to a fair market price at the time of sale.

In a valuation done by the Tata Group, the fair market value of the company was nearly nil, far below the option price. The regulator would disapprove, said Tata. At an in-person negotiation held in Singapore, Tata offered DoCoMo half of the half it was promised.[2] The Japanese partner walked out and started legal proceedings against the Tata Group in an international court of arbitration. The spat with its partner brought a fair degree of disrepute to the Indian conglomerate. The estranged partner called the central bank's rule a fig leaf the Indian conglomerate hid behind to avoid payment. Tata lost its arbitration, which mandated the Indian company to find a way to repay NTT DoCoMo. There was diplomatic engagement from both countries to arrive at a solution.

By this point, the RBI made a stand in Indian courts to shoot down Tata's request to make any such payment. Meanwhile, Tata Teleservices' business deteriorated so much that it was no longer able to service its debt. The banks were coming calling to collect. The Tata Group's apex company Tata Sons had to plug a shortfall of nearly Rs 4000 crore that accounted for Tata Teleservices' operating loss. Only then did its lenders roll over the company's debt. The loss of face was unpalatable for Ratan Tata, who was readying to take back control of the entire group.

Turmoil, in the leadership of the Tata Group, once again turned the fortunes with DoCoMo. In 2016, Cyrus Mistry was sacked as the chairman of Tata Sons in favour of Ratan Tata. Five months later, the two sides agreed on a joint submission to the Delhi High Court to honour the arbitration verdict. The RBI continued to object as the deal with DoCoMo would set a precedent for several others. The court overruled RBI's jurisdiction over an international order and NTT DoCoMo was paid $1.3 billion. DoCoMo released a statement that it continued to respect the Tata Group and would put this face-off behind to perhaps co-invest in another venture.

Even as the wager with NTT DoCoMo unfolded, the Tata Group was engaged in a battle in the telecom tower business.

In the interest of making an independent tower company the Tata Group had handed management control of Viom Networks to the SREI group even though Tata owned 52 per cent. Business at the company was roaring with new operators and 3G rollouts. However, all was not as it appeared, alleged the company secretary Arun Bansal. The complaint said the Kanorias, along with trusted aide Arun Kapur, were working hand in glove to siphon money from the company. The amount pegged in the complaint was Rs 300 crore, but there were veiled accusations of more in September 2011.[3]

It was relatively easy to start corrupt practices with telecom towers. Bribery through misreported use of diesel was almost routine across all companies, only the magnitude varied. Many of the telecom towers were in locations that did not receive round-the-clock grid power. The telecom tower sector hit a high of being the country's second-largest diesel user. As a result, all towers were fitted with diesel generators. Often, the owners or the staff guarding the tower would take some of the expensive fuel, and companies accepted it as the cost of doing business. A larger dent could be made by under reporting the rental on the tower and paying multiple parties for high use of fuel. Since fuel was a pass-through cost to the telecom operators renting the tower, over reporting fuel costs did not affect the profit of the tower company.

Another corrupt practice in the sector was gratification by assigning contracts and maintenance orders to related parties for kickbacks.

'Viom financials are materially untrue and reflect untrue state of affairs,' Bansal wrote to the company board.[4] The company was in discussions at the time to buy GTL Infrastructure.

The complaint did not detail how money was being taken from the company. It forced Tata to launch a forensic audit of the company by big four accounting firms KPMG. The report was hushed when the audit was completed and never made public. It did, however, follow a slew of changes at the top.

Arun Kapur, stated the SREI-appointed chief of the company, quit. The SREI group issued a statement saying it was an outcome of the audit. Viom noted that certain other 'non-performing' individuals in other functions had been fired. The KPMG report cleared the Kanorias of any wrongdoing. The SREI group maintained all along that the business itself was above board.[5]

Subodh Bhargav also quit as the chairman of Viom. Bhargav did not reveal why. His reputation was one of being completely upright and honest, and his tacit exit from the company was telling.

There were rumours later that a detrimental KPMG report of a majority-owned Tata company would tarnish the brand globally, and so the findings were reworded to soften the impact and implicate as few individuals as possible. Unverified accounts of people close to the firm said that the borrowings SREI was making to build telecom towers were being rerouted to other infrastructure projects within the group. That naturally came at the cost of the shareholders of Viom.

Even as this drama unfolded at Viom, licence cancellation after the 2G scam annihilated the tower sector's business. Viom lost its revenue from Uninor, which lost all its licences. It accounted for nearly 20–25 per cent of the tower compnay's turnover. There was another 10 per cent from other defunct operators.

Still headless and debt-laden, Viom appointed Syed Safawi, former chief executive of Reliance Communications to head the company in July 2012. He had experience working with Airtel and Coca-Cola and then dealing with RCom's high debt phase. It was a tainted office for executives to take up because of the corruption allegations within the company and the struggle between its promoters. Safawi elected to take the challenge because he had something to prove, if not to those who had questioned his abilities at RCom, then to himself. His mandate was to ready this company for sale to other strategic telecom tower players that were dwindling on the Indian horizon. Upcoming auctions, the imminent entry of RIL was all that kept the glimmer of hope alive.

At Tata's corporate level, however, dealing with all the drama, paired with the attrition at the top levels of Tata Teleservices distracted the group that was already in a weakened state against others in this cutthroat market.

Part Eight

60

Building Jio

Mukesh Ambani had watched his telecom ambitions falter since he had let RCom go. It was the group's future. While Mukesh put his heart into building the petrochemical business with his father, this had been an exciting project that met an untimely end.

The technology may have changed, but Mukesh and his team's philosophy had not. They set out to conduct in-depth research and look at the most advanced technologies available. The promise of new technology always seduced Mukesh Ambani, who suffered no fools, but listened most intently if he found something new. He then circled back to the team to ask about how this could be included in his company's network deployment. The heart of his new network resided in Reliance Corporate Park in Navi Mumbai, adjacent to DAKC and RCom's specially designed control centre.

Reliance Corporate Park is a 550-acre compound in Navi Mumbai and housed special projects for Reliance, for example Reliance Lifesciences prior to the telecom operations. A ready building here was dedicated to the start of telecom operations and three more were immediately commissioned to eventually accommodate around 20,000 employees. A single-storey structure with airy courtyards and enclosed rooms was created

to make the innovation centre, where researchers could try and
test various parts of the service. A helipad on one building top
was a travel essential to connect the Ambani home Antilia to
the campus.

Reliance cast the net far and wide and visited many
operators around the world. The team studied what the world
was using high-speed connectivity for. Continuity across
three screens—phone, computer and TV—remained the only
profitable way to capture a customer. RIL could deliver Internet
over three channels—4G for the mobile phone, SIM-enabled
Wi-Fi dongles and optic fibre to the home. In their search for
cellular excellence, the team examined operators around the
globe including AT&T and Deustche Telekom. The biggest
take away for Mukesh Ambani was automation, automation
and automation.

RIL was quick to appoint consulting firm Accenture and
equipment maker Alcatel Lucent for a feasibility study and
network plan to launch a 4G network on 2300MHz bandwidth.
When the consultants proposed a three-year launch plan, RIL
pushed back for a faster time to market.

RIL knew this spectrum did not lend itself to long-range
base stations. It also was not good enough to deploy access
points on the road, because 2300MHz cannot penetrate thin
walls, let alone the concrete ones that are used in most Indian
buildings.

The workaround in the first drafted plan was to lay optic
fibre cables down to the last mile and mount 'small cells'
connected over cable at short distances—for instance on all bus
stops, billboards, and of course, telecom towers. To connect the
indoors, the small cells would be mounted in building lobbies
and store fronts in malls. The small cell was an emerging
technology that worked like a mini base station without the

voluminous machinery, high power consumption and cooling requirements. It looked like a control unit of a traffic light, so it was discrete. A battery would be adequate to power the small cell when grid power was cut.

The number of points required for small cells was several times that of a conventional telecom network. RIL explored quick and cost-efficient means to telecom tower building. Among the solutions it explored setting up low-cost, light-weight but sturdy carbon fibre structures to mount small cells was one that found favour. Mukesh Ambani and Manoj Modi went to the US to buy a company in the carbon fibre business. It was selling under distress but negotiations in this case did not work out. Partly because of the sellers, but partly also because even as the talks were ongoing, RIL realized that small cells would not be sufficient for a full-scale deployment.

The catch was the optic fibre cable network. The team building Reliance Industries' telecom business was the same as the one that had once built RCom. Those like Arun Sur, who were still with RCom, moved back under Mukesh soon after RIL's plans became public. The optic fibre network was planned keeping the nearly 1,00,000 km of RCom's cable in mind. Much of RCom's cabling was long-distance, connecting major hubs of cities and villages. To achieve the service Reliance Industries was hoping for, it needed high speed last mile connectivity. Which meant it needed to lay cables in the middle of busy cities.

In some key areas, this proved more challenging and expensive than the company had envisaged. Over the last half a decade, Reliance Industries and key executives had built deep ties with the administration. Between Nikhil Meswani and Manoj Modi, RIL was sure to get cable laying rights where they wanted. The resistance they faced was thus surprising. Municipal authorities, city boards, local bodies were looking to be remunerated. They expected higher fees and took longer to approve right of way to dig roads and put down cables than the team initially factored.

There were some roads that proved practically impossible for RIL to lay cables. The widest-told urban legend is that of placing optic fibre on Pedder Road in Mumbai which houses the sprawling twenty-seven-storey Ambani home, Antilia. At first, it was Meswani cajoling authorities. When his efforts yielded no results, it was Manoj Modi's turn. After over a year of waiting, Mukesh Ambani himself decided to get involved, but could not secure permission to dig and place a cable on Pedder Road.

There was also some internal misreporting on the progress of cable laying. For instance, in Kolkata, the team reported that 100 per cent of the network rollout was done, but when the tech team arrived to set up, it found that only about a quarter was functional. In several areas, trenches had been dug out, but there were no cables.

The company was creative in trying alternatives, for example, reviving the defunct Bombay Gas Company network, which was established in the late 1800s to distrubute coal and gas for street lighting. This underground network ran for about 400 km across South Mumbai. Since the company had tunnels in areas where permissions were hard to get, it became an exciting resource for telecom companies. It ran optic fibre through these tunnels and marketed space on the cables to telecom companies.

As a result, Reliance Industries' plans suffered setbacks. The wireless network would almost certainly need to do some backhauling, which would choke bandwidth on the promised 4G network. The shakeout of players after licence cancellations in 2012 created an opportunity in the market. Investor impatience could have motivated RIL to launch a partial service, but that was unacceptable to Mukesh Ambani. At this telecom company, everything was to be automated with mathematical precision.

In 2003, the telecom company was launched under time pressure and faced hiccups with its billing system and other technical issues. RIL was not going to repeat old mistakes. Ambani wanted a 'NASA'-level network operating centre. The building may not have been tailor-made, but the facilities were no less impressive. Ambani insisted on implementing a network that would not only feed information into the control centre but could also be controlled centrally, for instance, changing the angle of a signal-receiving dish.

So that year (2012–13), Reliance added some management depth to its telecom ranks. It started with a plan to introduce Mukesh Ambani's children, Isha and Akash Ambani, to the business. Along with them, the company brought on board specialists from overseas as well as India. Its in-depth consultation with Deutsche Telekom had introduced folks that Ambani believed could help build processes.

There was also the impending need to find a name and brand for the company in anticipation of a grand launch. Mukesh Ambani and in tandem Manoj Modi's business philosophy arose from their experience with the polyester and oil businesses. From the accounts of Jio executives, there were three central tenets applied in the telecom business.

At the outset the product trumps the brand, so the relevance of a brand is secondary. Image building and artistry were left in Nita Ambani's care, who Mukesh Ambani trusted from experience.

Next, professional expertise can be captured in processes. Ambani was prepared to recruit the best in the industry at premium pay packages to keep them on board for short periods.

Lastly, when it came to employees, a flattened structure worked best to motivate juniors and pressurize seniors towards peak performance.

Parts of this philosophy did not sit well with Indian professionals and the cultural context but in the West, short-term contracts that lapse are not seen as a firing. It took a certain temperament among senior professionals who often found public meetings with Manoj Modi could get brusque. It was not uncommon for a senior's mistakes to be ridiculed in large public meetings, or for presentations considered to be under-researched to be shut down.

As a learning ground, Reliance was a two-way journey. The company offered adequate resources and opportunities for its people to get training and complete in-depth research. When other Indian companies were looking to pick products off the shelf, Reliance aircrafts were ferrying staff back and forth from China, as its researchers and network professionals worked to get the ball rolling on building 4G enabled devices and equipment. RIL created infrastructure for vendor companies to deploy teams on the Reliance Corporate Park campus to perfect the solutions they were offering the Indian conglomerate.

In keeping with the original Reliance management policy, in charge of this new venture were family or quasi-family members. Mukesh Ambani took a leaf from his father's book to keep ultimate decision-making in-house. At the top sat Manoj Modi and Sanjay Mashruwala. Hetal and Nikhil Meswani who are cousins to Mukesh Ambani also feature in the inner sanctum. In 2011, Arun Sur, who shared Mukesh Ambani's curiosity and knew how the company operates, was brought back into the fold. Returning to develop and build the network was Mathew Oomen, after having led the technology function at Sprint.

The executive floor for Infocomm had an open design where Akash and Isha sat with the company's top brass. They were at the beginning being mentored by Sandip Das on telecom, marketing and external expectation management.[1] Of course, there were other asks on the children's time. Isha Ambani was simultaneously getting involved with Nita Ambani's school, which over a decade had taken pole position among the nation's educational institutes. She was also destined to soon thereafter ship off to Stanford University and complete an academic degree, that at one time Mukesh Ambani had ditched midway to build Reliance.

Akash was beginning to get involved with Reliance's cricket team Mumbai Indians that plays in the Indian Premier League. Still, the lasting image employees at Reliance Corporate Park held of their leader was that of a young Akash hopping out of the helicopter with his father, rolling up the sleeves of his white shirt as he headed for town hall meetings. It was perhaps in late 2013 or early 2014 that investors recall Akash Ambani sitting in on events and corporate result announcements, sporadically answering questions. As is often the case with high-profile heirs, the first impressions were underwhelming, but over the next couple of years, as Akash gained confidence, the opinion of his observers course corrected.

There was much to learn from outside professionals. Reliance hired expatriates on two—or three-year contracts. For instance, Rainer Deutschmann was brought on as chief product and innovation officer, Caroline Seifert was chief of brand and design, and Tareq Amin led technology and automation.

On the network side, there was emphasis and rigour in creating processes. The numbers the operator disclosed prominently featured the young average age of this unemotional juggernaut that rewarded performs and suffered no fools. Mukesh Ambani thematically asked for everything 'in a box', so 'network in a box', 'sales in a box' which meant that after the complex deployment, the remaining interfaces should be compact and simple. To that end, by mid-2013, labour-intensive buildouts were on way along with creating detailed manuals for each process that was being put in place.

Mukesh Ambani studied and engaged extensively with the evolving technology platforms. Each time he discovered something better, he insisted on uprooting an earlier implementation, and a new process began.

For instance, the onboarding and billing systems. First Ambani asked for a single form to sign customers on. Then it was moved to a digital format. The online form with a box to scan documents was all eventually done through software. The digital team worked on populating and validating the onboarding form directly from the national identity card—Aadhaar. At one stage, when Aadhaar was envisioned to include biometric data, Jio mulled a biometric induction which would need no manual filling of any form. The automated populating of fields based on an Aadhaar card scan worked. However, giving such access of a national database to a private entity came riddled with issues for the government and flouted privacy regulations. The government therefore barred access and Jio's process once again required some manual input and express consent when subscribers signed on.

For the billing system, the team studied many models, including that of Netflix to see how traffic was monitored. What the Reliance team realized was that it could not pick an off-the-shelf product because consumption in India differed vastly from other places. Research was needed, and Mukesh Ambani had his own ideas on how the company would do that.

RIL consequently hired faster than it needed. Its executives were left with nothing to do, but it still hired others. In a way, this was a DNA test for its people. This was a high-tech company where only those who got busy survived; the others read newspapers and became redundant.

At the end of every quarter, Manoj Modi is said to have put around 10 per cent of the top-paid executives on ice. The way it played out for many of them was an increased engagement with an immediate subordinate, recast designations, or a new hire with very similar profiles. Seldom were they 'fired', but the message was clear.

For the seniors leaving RIL's telecom venture, options outside were limited. The overall havoc in the industry with new operators shutting down and ancillary businesses tapering off was ill-timed for such employees, who found it challenging to find a job, especially at the wage RIL was offering.

Navigating a launch was proving exorbitant for RIL. The bill was close to Rs 50,000 crore. While RIL financed a small portion of it, the bulk of it was debt. The philosophy that applied to the staff also applied to the external team of vendors. It started with a $500 million bond, and then, over the next three years, two more bonds of $1 billion each were raised from the international market.

When the company was scouting for bankers and vendors to help raise these funds, what was put before them was a slim report card of Infotel Broadband, the company that RIL had acquired, and a lot of material on the depth of RIL which would honour the bond. When one banker in its third round of raising funds asked for more details about Infotel and the nature of capital expenditure, he was rebuffed. The security was from RIL, there was nothing more to be discussed. If he found it difficult to proceed, RIL would take its business elsewhere. As such for the first few times, it was a different lead bank and a separate legal team each time. In each case, the fees were the lowest possible because firms used the brag value of working with RIL's latest venture.

When there isn't that much on paper, face time plays a special role in finance. In the face of investor clamour arose a new star among the ranks of the company. Handling investor queries was Anshuman Thakur, who, sell-side analysts said, was left alone to answer questions and make presentations. He had joined Reliance Jio from investment bank Morgan Stanley. Thakur was generically referred to as the investor relations head of the new company. Analysts felt at times he was deftly evading questions, because while the network was in flux, and it was for a long time, even he did not have answers to pointed questions they asked.

In 2013, the company hired Sandip Das as its president to head the telecom venture. Das was wooed while at his post as group chief executive of Maxis in Malaysia that oversaw the Indian telecom operator Aircel. Possibly, the attraction and fit were because Das saw the potential in the 4G network during the 2010 bidding process for Aircel. Or perhaps because he made a good fit when it came to showcasing the company to the world.

When Das' contract expired in 2015, Reliance put Thakur at the helm of the company, to the surprise of many observers. It was in the run-up to an imminent launch of service and most expected a high-profile appointment to get the ball rolling. Thakur, however, held his own, until Akash Ambani shaped up to take over.

61

The Brand

Over two years from 2010, Reliance's telecom arm became a large company that begged for a more encompassing and memorable brand than Infotel Broadband or just '4G' as it was internally referred to. Ambani steadfastly held his first tenet—product trumps branding. Yet, history had taught him that one size does not fit all, and branding and image had a role to play in uptake. If it needed to be done, consistent with the principles applied to technology, it had to be the best. The company sought out and hired specialists and experts both internally and as vendors.

Ambani turned to a 2003 team member, Kaushik Roy, who had left the group and was making a feature film. Ambani asked Roy to pause his movie to help him with 4G, and Roy obliged.

When branding expense proposals were submitted, Ambani and his team sought numbers—like return on investment. Brand executives were unable to offer satisfactory replies. Often, branding exercises yield notional results or ones that cannot be quantified. In the balance sheet, they are accounted for in the 'good will' column, that cannot be cashed. Eventually, instead of splitting hair over value, the expert branding team was redirected to take cues from Nita Ambani.

Having worked on the all-India branding of the telecom business's first avatar, Nita Ambani knew immediately that the new telecom brand needed to be linked to the existing Reliance logo, which is a flame in a circle.

Reliance consulted UK-based Venturethree that tinkered with the mother logo of the 4G brand, or the base on which the name would go. After proposing a few other shapes, it seemed the RIL circle was the way to go if the group's identities were to be linked. Meanwhile, back home, Nita Ambani, Roy, a few other members from marketing, and to some extent Isha Ambani weighed in to finalize the name of the company. They came up with several options. The one that stuck was 'Jio' which could be mirrored to 'oil'. Those were after all the roots of this Reliance empire. Nita Ambani insisted that any new brand of the company had to be steeped in Indian and Reliance's heritage.

Venturethree worked on potential logo designs with the name 'Jio'. Advertising agency Leo Burnett was also brought on board. From 2013 onwards, the company name for Reliance's 4G venture was established as Reliance Jio Infocomm, its brand identity was still elusive.

As the logo went through more changes, time passed. In 2015, Jio brought on board branding specialist Caroline Siefert to bring a global feel to the logo. Siefert brought with her other German team members. Globally, logos were moving from soft vignettes and multicolours to solid single colour panes, presented Siefert. The Apple and Google logos, among others, had seen these changes in this last wave of renewals, she said.

Nita Ambani took the feedback and called to drive consistency between the group's brands and entities. She was particular about picking the right shades of colours to appeal to a pedantic audience in a nation where matching centres can be found at nearly every street corner. Here within ten shades of blue, only one is actually referred to as blue, and Ambani wanted to be sure that her colour choice would match the terminology of its users. The colours she homed in on were consistent with earlier choices within the ambit of the Reliance Group. For example, the blue was chosen to match that of the Mumbai Indians cricket team logo and the yellow matched the one used for branding Dhirubhai Ambani International School.

No launch could be successful without a divine blessing. The family priest was consulted on the design to check it for any astrological or numeric lapses and then to pray for the final product. A few tweaks were introduced at this stage. For instance, the design that would encapsulate the text and the angling of the letters. Some experts were disappointed by the outcome at least in part because their suggestions were not taken on board. In the end, it was Nita Ambani's decision to make. Involved with her was Isha Ambani, who was imbibing the artistic touch to business.

A silent change occurred during this time. Isha Ambani moved in with her team to take charge of marketing and branding. Meanwhile, Akash Ambani was immersed in product development, building Reliance Jio from the eyes of the young and restless.

62

RIL Builds the Ecosystem

There lay another big challenge for Reliance Jio. In 2010, when it bought airwaves, the company was counting on a quick evolution of standards and end-user instruments. At least in India, that metamorphosis seemed slow, even as RIL's chairman Mukesh Ambani spoke of the changing device mix in shipments leaning towards 4G-enabled phones. Investors stirred by competitors raised questions about who would use 4G services. The Indian market and consumers would be satisfied with 3G services for email, astrology, cricket scores and Bollywood gossip. As long as the need is served, the consumer would not care whether it was done over 3G or 4G, argued competing companies.

The 'digital revolution' that RIL was talking about would need more than connectivity. Bharti Airtel was first off the mark to launch the 4G service in Pune in the second half of 2012. It was an anticipatory move ahead of Mukesh Ambani to test the market. Airtel's experience was that a 4G network was dependent on the backhaul network. When that was overloaded, the delivered speed would drop to 3G or even 2G speeds. RIL was trying to fix this problem by laying cables where possible.

Airtel also found that the key users of the service were either video gamers processing high-resolution images or a younger profile of consumers who would set video downloads such as movies overnight to watch on a small screen. The bulk of entertainment remained on the big screen. Consumption of streaming video and music still seemed a while away. Even video calling was still a distant use case because it needed a better network on both ends of the call.

Mukesh Ambani had thought of this. When he spoke of a digital ecosystem, he meant a plan and strategy that did not become obvious until a couple of years later.

In 2006, the company announced the launch of a retail initiative with an initial outlay of Rs 25,000 crore. Although launched, this venture was still floundering. In digital India, retail would find a new meaning—India would shop online. Unlike the global sourcing model that had made Amazon so successful, RIL believed that online shopping in India would need to display the same localization and flexibility that its corner shops offered. The telecom and retail teams soon began work with small-scale retail stores to digitize inventories.

Tying up closely with that was financial services. This was on Mukesh Ambani's mind since the termination of the non-compete clause with Anil Ambani. He had in fact begun discussions with investment and technology company D.E. Shaw in June 2010. The two inked a pact in 2011 with an objective to start mobile-based financial services for retail consumers, offering services that ranged from regular trade and money transactions to unconventional investment options such as carbon trading. The two created a 50:50 joint venture in the hope of applying for a banking licence which was about to be opened by the apex bank, the Reserve Bank of India. Not everything succeeds in the same way, and the D.E. Shaw partnership fizzled out, but Jio's ambition fructified in other ways.

The digital wallet was set to transform the Indian market. A newly launched company, Paytm, was slowly making a dent.

Led by founder Vijay Shekhar Sharma. It was backed by a conglomeration of investors, including Japan's Softbank, USA-based Berkshire Hathway and China's Ant Group, the owner of Alibaba. Paytm also applied for a banking licence, which it did not receive, but the company's mobile banking licence was more or less in the bag.

The Indian market was Reliance's for the taking. The innovation centre was put on the job to create an all-encompassing, truly Indian mobile wallet for the mass consumer. Even as it did so, Reliance decided to partner with the one firm that would undeniably get a mobile banking licence and could even help with immediate penetration—State Bank of India, or SBI. This is the country's largest public sector bank catering to the masses, with technology at the core designed to handle the unique nature of Indian banking service consumers. The stated objective of the Jio–SBI joint venture was to bank the unbanked. State Bank of India's 30 per cent shareholding in the venture made it a suitable company to distribute government cash subsidies under specialised schemes.

When national elections brought about a regime change in 2014, Prime Minister Narendra Modi took the helm. His push for a digital India and Reliance Jio's service portfolio matched perfectly. So much so that RIL used Modi's picture to advertise its services. Vijay Shekhar Sharma at Paytm also followed suit. The government later sent notices to both companies barring them from using the picture.

The demonetization of the 500- and 1000-rupee notes in November 2016 gave a real boost to the digital wallet business. In the public arena, Paytm seemed to have won. JioMoney, as Relaince's service was branded, quietly benefited, not least from the contract to pass on government subsidies. Linking mobile numbers to financial services brought loyal and revenue-generating customers to Jio's fold.

Financial services and shopping, however, were not going to be the bandwidth-guzzlers that would drive customers onto the Jio network. The primary data use, as repeated market studies showed, was for photos, videos and entertainment. RIL's buildup in that started with external content that subscribers could consume. Reliance's eventual answer lay in Jio TV or a digital box to offer cable TV that was developed at the Jio innovation centre.

The starting point was systematic cable access to households. In addition to reaching homes where the company was able to lay cables, Jio made local acquisitions such as Hathway Cable and Datacom which offered cable TV and high-speed internet services and Den Networks, another all-India cable TV provider. Jio was planning to discount access to content and anticipated a backlash from content producers when it pushed them to lower prices. Traditionally, Indian consumers have leaned into free content which makes money from advertising rather than subscription.

Jio thus embarked on a journey to create captive content as a differentiator for its platform. The company chose to syndicate projects in local languages with regional flavours rather than gunning for large mass-market options such as Bollywood. Over the years, the Ambani family has built rapport with Mumbai's film industry and was able to attract the best talent and scripts for its platform. The title list soon grew to mainstream content.

The portfolio was incomplete without news. For years, RIL held preference shares and was a white knight for Prannoy Roy's NDTV. Even as the market predicted a takeover in 2014, to the industry's surprise, Reliance announced the takeover of Network 18. This move made more sense than buying NDTV because not only did Network18 lead with its news channels, CNN-IBN, CNBC-TV18, and CNBC-Awaz, but it also led in the entertainment segment with channel Colours.

The most significant content generation across the world, however, is not industry but individual photography and edits. The boom in services like TikTok and YouTube convinced Ambani that capturing these thousands of terabytes was essential. Jio proposed to offer a cloud storage solution that mimicked Google's cloud and would automatically store phone backups, photos and other content for users who signed up. It took a while to perfect, and rumour had it that this was the service that held up the launch towards the end.

Jio also created Asha—an automated voice assistant for its phones, an equivalent of Apple's Siri or Amazon's Alexa, but designed to understand several Indian languages. Software teams were in overdrive to create a seamless user experience among this suite of services the company was offering.

Research on the devices RIL planned to offer along with its service ran parallely. Samsung and LG which had been left with losses at the end of the CDMA experience, were sceptical of entering similar mobile service plans which would leave a debt on their books. Fortunately, the personal finance sector had evolved over the last decade and Jio could create bundles for consumers that would have byte-sized monthly payments backed by Microfinance organizations. Unlike Monsoon Hungama this time the debt for the mobile phone would rest on the consumer rather than the telecom operator.

Reliance was planning to introduce entry-level devices. It initially preferred Samsung make and brand the low-cost phone, but that was a no-go. The Indian company thus began to research mobile devices. It instigated the rise of several Indian phone manufacturers such as Lava as it shared the outcome and asked these companies to assemble phones as per Jio's specifications.

Jio then launched a Reliance-branded phone under a new identity called Lyf, combining to make 'Jio Lyf', which translates to 'Live Life'. The phones came in four categories—Earth, Water, Wind and Flame. Each category had some key features, and each comprised phones ranging in price and technical specifications. In the run-up to the launch, Jio had phones from Rs 4000 to Rs 25,000 on offer. The devices were manufactured by Samsung, Micromax and Intex.

The bottom-end device looked like the early Nokia feature phones with a small screen and a numbered keypad. It did not have smart features, but including an AV output which could be plugged into a TV by HDMI cable or old-school banana plugs. It could operate as a dongle to stream video onto a bigger screen. The high-speed internet as Jio then imagined it would be used to cast content on a large screen. The rhetoric around how a small screen would not lend itself to an audio-video format was yet to play out. On this phone, anecdotal evidence suggests Jio lost some money because in the end, consumers were happy to watch content on a mobile phone screen.

Jio also launched dongles that could emit a Wi-Fi signal supporting up to six devices. These were targeted at small and medium-sized business users who could work from co-work areas. They became a popular solution in high-density residential areas, where multiple family members often shared connectivity at home. They also brought new subscribers into Jio's fold, who did not want to change phone numbers but were curious about its mobile Internet proposition.

63

Jio's Launch

The industry was bracing for scathing price erosion when Jio launched its service. Every passing year gave them a breather. After the 2012 licence cancellations the incumbents, Bharti Airtel, Vodafone, and Idea Cellular, had consolidated their market share while Aircel, Uninor, Tata Teleservices and RCom had come to be fringe players fighting it out in selective markets. Industry leaders now pegged Jio services to be launched between Rs 300–500 for customers, which would be lower than their offers, but manageable in their erosive impact on finances. These assumptions were based on placeholder submissions the company had made to TRAI on its tentative pricing plans for customers.

Each year around Dhirubhai Ambani's birth anniversary on December 28 the anticipation of a launch reached its crescendo and then died down by March. The calendar pages flipped as the years ticked from 2011 to 2015 and the competition felt it was more and more ready to take on the newest competitor. Then Reliance held Jio's mega launch on 28 December 2015. A soft launch, it was called, and the service was opened only to employees, friends and family. They alone accounted for 1,50,000 people on the network. They were handed free connections to trial the network, provide feedback, and test various services.

The Jio team meanwhile studied the backend—data usage, traffic handling, signal handovers and billing systems.

The launch platform was used to showcase the Ambani family's involvement and togetherness. It started with a prayer to Lord Ganesh by Nita Ambani. The ceremony also accorded time and visibility to Kokilaben, Mukesh Ambani's mother, Isha and Akash Ambani. It was concluded with a speech by Mukesh Ambani.[1] It also included performances by brand ambassador and actor Shah Rukh Khan and music composer A.R. Rahman.

The competition thought Jio had launched a service without a billing system in place, hence the employee launch of a service free of charge. Jio announced it will make voice calling free forever. That did not bother competitors. They assumed the fee for data services would cover the cost of calling, and in the end, would not make a difference on the total outflow for the consumer.

The in-house trial was to end before 1 April 2016, because to mark the first full year of operation. When no announcement around that date competitors felt even more secure. 'The billing system is faulty like before,' said one. 'They are trying to perfect technology which will never happen,' said another. 'The network is a live entity, which changes fluidly, it can't remain perfect across such a large operation for more than a moment,' said a chief of a network management company. Reliance was busy incorporating the feedback it had received from its current users.

They boasted of the actual internet speed they experienced. Competitors discounted this as the pleasure of a vacant network and that would hit a snag once the capacity fills up. Reliance was listening and furiously paddling under the surface of calm waters.

In mid-April, when Reliance Industries reported its quarterly results, a special segment was dedicated to Jio's status.

The company had spent about Rs 1,34,000 crore, in what it called a 'startup'. It was yet to generate its first rupee. Investors hung on to its every word. The statistics appeared lukewarm. The company said, on average its users had consumed 26GB of data a month. This included voice calls because the entire network operated on internet protocol or IP. Voice consumes so little data, that it is an insignificant part of the 26GB, explained Anshuman Thakur.

At a time when data was charged on a per GB basis if the cap of usage was 26GB a month, incumbent operators figured it would be affordable to compete by diluting their charges. After all, average calling on the Jio network was still lower than that on Airtel's network. Jio recorded an average of 355 minutes of voice calls per user per month, while Airtel was clocking around 415 at the time.

Lyf phones had been made commercially available across Reliance Retail outlets, and initial reports suggested they were doing well. This did not bother incumbents, because these were unlocked phones that could be used with any network. In a way, it was good for them because it helped build the 4G phone ecosystem which in turn helped operators alleviate more traffic from their overflowing 2G capacity.

So, in July, after the first quarter of financial year 2016–17 when incumbent officials spoke of Jio, it was with a sense of irreverence. Perhaps less so for Bharti Airtel, but Vodafone, Idea, and RCom all spoke of a comfortable coexistence. Little did they know the all-engulfing wave that was about to hit.

On 1 September 2016, Mukesh Ambani took the podium at Birla Matoshree Hall near Bombay Hospital in south Mumbai. It was the RIL AGM, and this one was even busier than usual. The welcome desk on a temporary bamboo-supported awning welcomed shareholders to register lifting them out of the rain-inflicted muck being dragged by slow-moving vehicles,

primarily black and yellow cabs, through the narrow access lane
to the hall. The maroon door to the dimly lit inside of the hall
lay slightly ajar, atop the granite stairs lined with RIL's investor
relations team. The canteen to the left of the door was abuzz
with the sound of cutting chai, waiters ferrying breakfast and a
humdrum of gossiping visitors.

Reliance had rightly anticipated that this year's AGM
attendance would overflow even though the hall had seating
for over a thousand. A tent had been pitched on the walkway
further left of the canteen with an open-air screen and seating
for those that could not be accommodated in the hall. Members
of the media peppered the outdoor seating. Mobile phone
signal reception inside the hall was particularly weak, and
everyone was expecting 'Breaking News'. At least a few were
aware of an analyst meeting scheduled with Manoj Modi and
possibly Mukesh Ambani just across the road immediately
after the AGM.

When Mukesh Ambani said, 'My Dear Shareholders,' the
room, the tent and the canteen fell silent as if someone had
cast a spell on the over 1000 people present. The speakers
amplified and the soft voice echoed. Ambani knew that on this
occasion the most sought-after announcement was that on Jio.
Perhaps that echoed his own excitement. He jumped right in.
'Jio is dedicated to realizing our Prime Minister's vision for 1.2
billion Indians,' he said referring to PM Modi's vision of digital
India—which encompassed smart cities, online governance, and
banking services among others. 'I believe, in the next twenty
years as human civilization, we will collectively achieve more
than what has been achieved in the last 300 years ... Today, India
is ranked 155th in the world for mobile broadband Internet
access, out of 230 countries. Jio is conceived to change this.[2]

'Data is the oxygen of Digital Life, and oxygen must never
be in short supply,' said Ambani. With that Ambani announced

a slew of free services. All voice for Jio Customers would be forever free. He then went on to detail tariff plans—Rs 50 per GB of data, special discounts for students, structured plans with devices—all the while saving the punchline for the end. Free, free, free—while customers could select these tariff plans, from 5 September 2016 they could enrol and use Jio services till 31 December 2016 for free. Apart from the telecom service, the remaining portfolio of services, including subscriptions to entertainment platform was free. That was a blow competitors were not ready for. It was called the 'Jio Welcome Offer'.

'Today, I set a target for team Jio to acquire 100 million customers on the Jio network in the shortest possible time, and create a new world record,' said Mukesh Ambani. The company spoke of 100 million in 100 days.

Then, he looked outside. Even as the traffic built up on the employee-launched network, existing operators had rediscovered a way to fight new competition. Choke interconnectivity. They had faced this against BSNL and could now use it against Jio—the interconnect. In the week prior, reports had picked up that data worked fine on the Jio network but not on voice calls. The hushed external narrative was that internet-based calling has always been a challenge. Mukesh Ambani dispelled this by saying, 'In the last week alone, Jio customers suffered over 5 crores call failures to other networks because of insufficient interconnect capacity provided by incumbents.'

Jio later went on to involve TRAI, alleging telecom operators were flouting quality of service rules. The other operators confirmed they had allocated the regulator-mandated capacity for the number of subscribers Jio disclosed. 'We are grateful to the TRAI for enabling a constructive dialogue today on the matter of providing PoIs to Reliance Jio and appreciating all the issues on the table,' wrote Airtel in a press statement on 9 September 2016.[3] The company raised the issue of the established pricing on interconnect usage charge, or IUC, in tandem with the points of interconnect to be offered. 'Following the commercial charging of services by Reliance Jio, which is expected by Jan 1, 2017, the traffic will inevitably get to a more balanced level and PoIs will be less of an issue,' said the telecom bellwether.[4]

There was some amount of trickery in this capacity. While the switches were in place they were at least on two networks programmed to accommodate a greater number of callouts from the home network to Jio's than the other way. This meant, that when a caller from the other network called a Jio number the call would go through but when a Jio caller dialled in, the call was routed through a thinner pipe causing congestion and call drops. When the regulator called for that explanation, operators said the allocation was proportionate to the subscriber base of either company. For instance, if Jio had one-fifth of the customers of another company, one-fifth the capacity was allocated to incoming calls and four-fifths to outgoing. It boiled down to a court case, a regulatory challenge and even a competition commission enquiry until companies increased capacity to provide for Jio callers on their network.

The 'Welcome Offer' was a roaring success marred only by supply shortage. Queues outside Reliance Digital and Xpress Mini stores ran in thousands. Overnight, there was also a black market for Reliance Jio SIM cards. However, after the first week of euphoria died down, subscribers still growing at a fast pace began to peter out.

To capture subscribers Jio had several hurdles to cross. For starters, the company needed to convince customers there was enough value in the service to upgrade mobile instruments at a least cost of Rs 3000. The killer app that would trigger this migration was still to be discovered, and while Jio was working to set up the ecosystem, the timeline for uptake was still unclear.

Unlike in 2002, when market penetration was low and natural elasticity was high, mobile penetration was touching 80 per cent in 2016, and there was an inertia to be shaken off. Jio also needed to target high-end customers who would use the phone as their primary service. The CDMA experience had taught the company that settling for the masses was inadequate.

Marten Pieter, head of Vodafone, believed that the delayed launch of Jio, which had eaten into a quarter of its twenty-year licence period and its mainstay of low pricing made the company vulnerable and less of a threat to competitors. He said globally, markets accommodate four players, although the fourth typically struggles. 'There are certain segments of customers in India that are not price sensitive at all (see the success of luxury brands). That brings us to branding.' This was the market Jio needed to capture, Pieters believed.[5]

Towards the end of the month, incumbent telecom companies had convinced the investor community that Jio would cannibalize the market share occupied by fringe players. This accounted for around 20 per cent of the market or around 120 million subscribers.

Those closely involved, however, suspected the worst. Idea's key investor from Malaysia, Axiata began to look for an exit by November 2016.

Jio extended its free offer by another three months in January. The offer was given another name because the anticompetitive regulator set a limit on promotional offers. The end result, however, was the same—free, free, free. Once again, optimism about the service increased. In February, Jio reported hitting a subscriber base of 100 million.

In April the free services were continued. When the clamour from fringe players increased, Reliance Jio launched a subscription plan that required a payment of Rs 99 a year to retain services. While new numbers were enabled after this deposit, old subscribers who did not make this payment remained active for at least six more months. RCom, Tata, Aircel and Uninor were now in trouble. As the Uttar Pradesh circle chief of one of these companies said, 'How do you compete with free?'

Fringe players had launched family engagement programmes, celebrity events, and promotions for vendor partners, but customers on their network were shopping for deals, such as half-price data service at night. Free outdid anything it could offer, and customers jumped ship.

Operators were not far behind. Telenor decided that there was no fighting in this market. It declared bankruptcy and sold to Airtel in September 2017 to make a swift exit. RCom cried foul against Jio's anticompetitive actions to no avail. It battled lenders who came to claim their dues despite plummeting revenue.

RCom eventually declared bankruptcy and was absorbed into Reliance Jio. Meanwhile, Tata Teleservices and Aircel sold out to Airtel incurring their debt but transferring future liabilities.

Once Jio had entirely captured the fringe player's market, the company attacked Idea's rural and semi-urban markets.

Part Nine

64

Vodafone Has an Idea

Vodafone's journey in India was plagued by the Indian withholding tax case, the struggle with the shareholders, and an oddly turbulent regulatory regime. The local management, starting with Marten Pieters, always maintained that this had not affected its UK-based parent's commitment to the country. Chief Executive Vittorio Colao fielded investor questions and shareholder ire over India's lack of performance. The global economic bust of 2008 led to hardship in European markets like Spain, Italy, and Portugal. India was supposed to alleviate some of that pain, but it was proving ineffective.

It was not for a lack of trying. The company had accelerated and launched services across the country. It was matching calling plan offers. A lot of Vodafone India's efforts were geared towards employee satisfaction including well-being guides, annual off-sites, and career planning at most levels. Marten Pieters had a core strategy group of twelve top executives who would meet regularly to take company-level decisions. To that extent, centralization at Vodafone, including control of regional promotion plans and small-scale events, was higher than Airtel. Yet, even among the twelve Pieters thought decision-making was lacking. He was brought in to streamline the Indian arm, and before he retired from the post, Pieters had hoped to list the company publicly.

Call rates crashed in the aftermath of new licences in 2009. Vodafone UK wrote off £2.3 billion of its asset value in India on the back of that. The impairment in the company's financials was reflected in its full-year results published in May 2010. Colao was sure that something substantial needed to change. At the end of the appraisal cycle of January 2012, Vodafone India undertook a management rejig to streamline top Indian functions with the way Vodafone UK operated.

A more apparent succession plan was created with Sunil Sood as chief operating officer and Sanjoy Mukherji as chief marketing officer. An internal memo suggested this was being done in anticipation of a public listing. Instead of just two regional heads, the roles were split to create North, South, East and West heads. It coincided with Essar's decision to sell shares in the company and 3G rollouts after an expensive spectrum purchase in 2010, all mounting impending expenses on Vodafone's Indian arm.

Possible relief seemed to come from the enterprise business market, which was booming with multinationals and could be lucrative for Vodafone India. It was better positioned to capture high-paying corporate clients as a global company. However, Vodafone was also cognizant that Jio's aggressive cabled network buildout could become a key differentiator in the business segment. The UK operator doubled down on landline and 3G connectivity for businesses, although it needed to use some of the 3G airwaves to diffuse traffic on the 2G network.

As it did so, it approached Tata Teleservices, which was looking to gracefully exit a partnership with Japan's NTT DoCoMo. It found two significant synergies—the first was the enterprise business, backed by the leased line network, the second was the 1800MHz licence for 2G and a network that lay fairly vacant. Vodafone knew that it was this band that would be crucial to 4G launches. Tata however had a massive debt as a result of its GSM rollout. Moreover, parts of its enterprise business were held in Tata Communications, formerly VSNL, which Tata was unwilling to fold into a potential merger. Vodafone abandoned a merger with Tata.

Vodafone India itself was reeling under massive debt given that it was not possible to raise equity money while shareholders battled it out. Then in March 2014, Vodafone UK acquired 100 per cent of the company giving Colao some legroom to take action. Over the next couple of years, as the looming buzz of Jio's launch haunted conversations, and equity markets faltered scuttling chances of a public listing, Vodafone tried other merger and acquisition options. It scoped out Aircel and the post-licence cancellation operation of Uninor. By 2015, Jio had still not launched. It appeared operators were regaining pricing power, raising hopes and expectations of all potential sellers.

Still, the company was sceptical about its Indian arm. 'India is the world's master at coming up with new regulation by the month, so, of course, there is always a degree of variability there,' Nick Read, the company's chief financial officer told investors on 19 May 2015.[1] His view was partly influenced by the undulations on the tax case and partly by the uncertainty following licence cancellations over the 2G scam. Surprise charges had stemmed as its outcome such as one-time spectrum usage charge or the additional expense to liberalize old airwaves.

In 2016, before Jio's launch, Vodafone decided to approach Idea Cellular to explore a merger. The two companies appeared to be in the same boat and could leverage efficiencies on combining. They would need to take the proposal to Kumar Mangalam Birla and Himanshu Kapania, Idea's CEO.

Himanshu Kapania was homegrown talent within Idea Cellular who assumed the ship's mantle after Sanjeev Aga retired in March 2011. He was considered an ear-to-the-ground chief, known for his no-nonsense focus on executing network growth. The politics that came with the post was more learnt than natural for Kapania. Given that the company had just acquired expensive, 3G spectrum, fast paced and effective execution was the company's need of the hour.

In the pre-Reliance Jio phase, Idea had an advantage. It was tapping the booming semi-urban markets. As such, its pricing power was a little lower than Vodafone and Airtel but growth occasionally outstripped the larger competitors. Idea became a household name and its success was heady. The company signed high-profile events, such as the Filmfare Awards, that made it very popular at Aditya Birla Center in Worli, Mumbai where the bulk of the group's cerebral muscle works.

On ground, too, work was high decibel albeit cash-consuming. In August 2016, when the Aditya Birla Group undertook a restructuring, less than half a year after inducting Standard Chartered investment banker Saurav Agarwal, the assumption meant to free capital for Idea Cellular. Agarwal, who a year later joined the Tata Group as its chief financial officer, was considered a specialist in the technology, media and telecom vertical. Analysts clamoured that the move was in anticipation of Reliance Jio's entry that could stymy Idea Cellular's meteoric rise. Clear and categorical denials from Kumar Mangalam Birla about the intent behind restructuring were taken with a pinch of salt; not the least, because word had gotten out that Vodafone was sniffing for a partner in Idea.

Their best synergy lay in the 1800 MHz airwaves that Idea held for 4G services. Vodafone had global expertise in the technology and given the right raw materials could move to a deployment fast. So, the India team, now under Sunil Sood, took a proposal to the Birla Group for a merger. In terms of value, Vodafone was larger. The UK-based parent was also readying itself to infuse capital to alleviate the Indian arm's debt burden that was kissing Rs 85,000 crore. [2] A fair combination would put Vodafone in charge with a controlling stake in the combined entity. Although the Birla Group did not have appetite to pour cash into the business, Kumar Mangalam Birla insisted on a combined entity that would be headed by the Birla Group. Discussions between the two were short-lived in early 2016.

Jio's onslaught that began in October of 2016 softened both Vodafone and Birla's stance. For Idea, the writing was on the wall, and something needed to change. Vodafone invested Rs 47,700 crore in the Indian company to reduce its debt ahead of a potential 4G deployment in September 2016, but barely two months later, found itself writing off yet another €5 billion (approximately Rs 37,500 crore) on the company. This time the Indian asset dragged quarterly profits of the group at a time when Colao and Read were trying to appease investor anger by demonstrating a turnaround in other regions.

Idea Cellular on the other hand recorded a drop in its sales and profitability. In the last quarter of 2016, the company's revenue fell by nearly 7 per cent from the immediately preceding quarter. This, despite the seasonal strength for mobile companies in the final quarter owing to major festivals like Diwali, Christmas and New Year. Idea also recorded a net loss in the quarter to December 2016 even though the calling minutes per user rose and there was a slight uptick in data used.[3] Company executives were perhaps more worried than analysts who were not buying the explanation that the drop was due to capital expenditure on 3G and 4G networks.

The rhetoric reverberated that Jio would target Idea's rural market before pressing Vodafone and Airtel's urban market. Sunil Mittal's words to his team and investors alike became famous. He said that to avoid getting caught by a tiger on the chase, you only have to run faster than the other prey. Idea and Vodafone were the prey; Jio was the tiger.

Both Idea and Vodafone understood the need to do something to arrest their losses. There was strength in unity. When they met again in January 2017, the question was no longer 'if' but 'how' a merger could work. Vodafone needed to isolate its Indian arm from its other businesses, while Idea was looking to save its customer base without cash burn.

Vodafone quickly appointed its battery of consultants: investment bankers Morgan Stanley, UBS, Robey Warshaw, Bank of America Merrill Lynch, Kotak Investment Bank, and Rothschild; legal advisors Slaughter and May and S&R Associates. Idea Cellular turned up with an in-house team. Saurabh Agarwal, a seasoned investment banker, led the charge for the Birla Group, and Ashish Adukia, head of mergers and acquisitions, both seasoned investment bankers, headed the group. Meetings took place in Mumbai, London, Abu Dhabi, and Dubai.

The deal was naturally complex and had many puzzling questions for negotiators. The combine would, on day one, become the country's largest telecom operator, but it would also be saddled with large amount of network duplication. This began at its basest level with telecom towers—and the stake in Indus Towers—that would affect Bharti Airtel. Would a merger of Vodafone and Idea also amount to combining Vodafone's 42 per cent in Indus with Idea's 16 per cent and place Bharti in a minority? Which technology platform would be retained? Which of the two tower rentals would stay? Which set of employees would be retained?

Often in deals of this scale, the devil lies in the details. The teams sat together for nearly two weeks. There was no scope for failure. Each demand was counter-foiled with another, and each concession was graced with reciprocation. Where Birla was afforded chairmanship, Vodafone was granted selection of the chief financial officer.

Both companies had overlapping value-added service arms for instance mobile wallet services, ring back tones, even corporate clients. A decision on which one to keep was necessary for each item. Time was of the essence; some of these questions were parked till later. The completion timeframe for the merger was set at a year and a half.

Vodafone's share in Indus Tower was parked outside the scope of this deal, while Idea's shares were included to bridge the valuation gap between the entities. Still, the difference between the two companies was nearly Rs 10,000 crore. Private equity investors were called to explore a share purchase in the combined entity to even out the shareholding between Vodafone and Birla. Investors like KKR and Canadian Pension Fund that might have been keen barely a year earlier, were hawkish in 2017. They preferred to wait and watch the sector's morphing after Jio.

Eventually, the two decided to call it a merger of equals when it was announced on 20 March 2017. The deal included an option for Birla to claw its way to equality in the merger. If that did not happen within four years, Vodafone would sell down its equity till they came at par. For the moment, Vodafone held 45 per cent shares, Birla 26 per cent and the public shareholders the rest. Vodafone relinquished some voting rights so that the two groups would have equal say in company affairs.

Together, the two formed a bigger company than Airtel. They estimated costs could be lowered by Rs 14,000 crore over a span of four years. The mega deal kept both Colao and Kumar Mangalam up for nearly three days as they thrashed out final senior-level appointments. Market reaction, however, was tepid at best. It could have been because of the two-month-long anticipation, or the grave task of realizing all that was promised. Vodafone Idea, or Vi was what the combine was rebranded.

The naysayers, in this case, turned out to be correct. With both partners only partially invested and a lack of capital, Vi's growth and expansion were slower than Jio and Airtel's, which quickly ate into Vi's precious, high-paying customer base. The parallel brands, networks, and staff ran on for too long confusing customers and raising the company's cost. Slapped with government fines over its spectrum and trade transfer, the company eventually reneged on statutory payments.

Worried that this would lead to a duopoly in the Indian telecom market, the government decided to offset penalties for equity. Vodafone Idea settled at a comfortable third place ahead only of the languishing state-run operator BSNL.

65

RCom, a Foundation for Jio

It was not uncommon for Anil Ambani to send instructions to his lieutenants about the business from his morning run. Weary-eyed executives received these messages, often linked to the financial or stock performance of the company, in the early hours of the morning and felt the urgency to make a move. Among the quickest ways to manage the market was news, which right or wrong trickled out of RCom's ranks to media houses, often offered as 'exclusive' or 'first' to expedite release. It was then circulated among the equity analysts to factor into their price projections for the company stock.

However, over time, this pattern became evident to stakeholders outside the company. The blip in stock price always corrected quickly. The trust equation in the company's ecosystem faltered, diluted the impact of even authentic narratives, and caused RCom's withering fortune and Ambani's authoritative handling of the establishment to diminish the group's political muscle. This, in turn, forced Reliance Communications to make some desperate decisions.

By 2012, RCom was being pegged as the underlying network that Reliance Jio would use. Analysts remained interested in the hope that this company would be amalgamated into Jio. RCom's communication reinforced this view. In repeated interactions,

Anil Ambani emphasized infrastructure deals with his elder brother's telco. Then, in April 2013, the company announced a deal that underwhelmed the market. It was worth a mere Rs 1200 crore spanning an unspecified number of years. It was to rent national long-distance optic fibre cables. They powered RCom's CDMA and GSM networks connecting most major cities across the country.

Even as RCom teams reassured all enquirers that this amount was being paid upfront, there was a trickle of information that appeared to emanate out of RIL that nearly half of it would be needed to restore and repair the infrastructure. The agreement details, which were never made public, supposedly had stringent performance criteria. RCom committed to vacate several fibre pairs for Jio. The problem was the cable network had fallen into disrepair over the years. In some cities, such as Chennai, the cable had been laid so close to the surface at the edge of the road, that poles of shanties or temporary street vendors during the rainy season had damaged the cables. In several places, the cable was not a complete cut but fibre pairs had been damaged to lower throughput. It was sufficient for RCom's call traffic, but data-heavy needs of RIL's 4G would be choked. The repair work was not as simple as fixing a break. The investigation to identify repair sites was the larger and more capital-intensive task. Joints in optic fibre can often create issues of light loss, which Jio was allegedly unwilling to tolerate.

It was however the need of the hour for RCom that had racked up a net debt of Rs 38,500 crore and cashflow could not service the loans. In June 2013, Anil Ambani's company signed yet another agreement with Jio. This time, the published amount was Rs 12,000 crore! It was a lease agreement for a slot on all of RCom's telecom towers.

Anil Ambani and his team were convinced this would impress investors and open new borrowing limits to tide the company over its cash crunch. Unfortunately, that was not the case. The fine print was not lost on specialists who within the hour deconstructed the deal to imply a discounted rental from the prevalent market pricing. At 45,000 towers over fifteen years, the rental came to Rs 15,000 per tower per month, said analysts. The prevailing market rental rate was closer to Rs 25,000 per tower per month.

Amitabh Jhunjhunwala, RCom's deal advisor, explained that the scale of the deal offset the discount. Yet, when the stock market reopened after the announcement, the company's shares tanked to a one-year low. There was no immediate cash inflow from it. The move had backfired. Thus, when RCom expanded its deal with Jio to intra-circle or city-wide optic fibre, the company did not make an official public statement. Executives indicatively told the press and analysts that there was a follow-on deal between Rs 3000 and 3500 crore.

It further fortified the feeling that RCom was ready to be a part of Jio. It coincided with Jio's bid for spectrum in the 800MHz band, which was completely synergistic with the airwaves RCom held. In August 2013, when RCom announced its corporate results, the press note came with several 'to be announced' developments. They included a follow-on deal with Jio, a sale of international assets that would fetch Rs 6000–7000 crore, and sale of the direct-to-home television business that would earn the company another Rs 2500 crore.

The company had partly repaid its $1 billion foreign currency convertible bond and an external commercial borrowing. It was a minuscule portion of the outstanding debt, most of which was falling due over the next five years.

A couple of years passed amid failed attempts to monetize assets. On the block was RCom's tower, direct to home, technology and overseas businesses. Investment bankers said nearly every deal negotiation ended with Anil Ambani getting cold feet, who feared he was underselling the companies. Meanwhile, RCom fell short of paying its spectrum dues from the auction of 2010. In January 2016, Reliance Jio stepped in to pay for the spectrum and liberalize RCom's original CDMA airwaves at roughly Rs 5600 crore.[1] This would allow RCom to trade airwaves, complementing Jio's spectrum holdings.

66

Not Too Big to Fail

The global economic meltdown 2008 had taught the business world a new meaning of 'too big to fail'. Governments had intervened to save private enterprises. Bankruptcy of these large outfits would have too significant a domino effect on the economy. Anil Ambani had hoped his organization could also reach that point. While the big-ticket acquisitions were failing, the string of pearls approach continued at RCom-acquired assets like cable company Digicable and other small enterprise-focussed companies such as ethernet provider Yipes internationally. By 2015, much like Ambani's RCom, several of the other fringe telecom players were ailing. Five years after the initial attempt to buy his way to supremacy failed, the strategy might still work to save bankruptcy. Bankers were as worried about RCom's credit default as Ambani was and were interested in finding a solution.

This time, the group attempted these in ascending order, starting with the smallest competitor: Sistema Shyam, which operated the MTS brand.

In November 2015, both companies issued a joint statement that RCom would acquire Sistema Shyam in a no-cash deal. The promoters of Sistema Shyam would pay off all of the company's debt and fold it into RCom in exchange for a 10 per

cent share in the combined entity for the Russian conglomerate
Sistema. The only liability for RCom would be a Rs 392 crore
annual spectrum due over the next ten years. Sistema did not
receive a board seat or veto rights with its equity.

The market remained disenchanted with RCom's moves.
MTS was an all-CDMA operator with 3.75 MHz of spectrum
in the 800 MHz band. 'This must be another play at the behest
of Mukesh Ambani,' clamoured speculating analysts who were
key in perception-building for the Anil Ambani company. They
pegged this acquisition as a means for accumulating spectrum
so RCom could continue its CDMA business after it traded
away its airwaves to Jio.

Then bankers, led by SBI Capital Markets, mooted the
idea of a merger between RCom, Tata Teleservices and Aircel.
It was motivated by desperation. Put together, the three had
debt exceeding Rs 1,00,000 crore, all on the brink of failure.
Perhaps the combination could yield a recast on debt and a
viable telecom operator. Cumulatively, the three companies still
accounted for around 20 per cent of the market in 2016.

Aircel's promoter, Maxis, had no interest in investing
further in the company, but its liabilities included looming fee
payments for 3G and 4G spectrum. Much like RCom, to cut
capital expenditure, Aircel shut down operations in five service
areas to focus on its more profitable south and north-east regions
of India. Then, it struck a deal with RCom for intra-circle
roaming, which meant that only one of the two companies was
running a network in overlapping areas and supporting each
other's customers.

For Aircel, this had meant a scuffle with GTL Infrastructure,
the company that had acquired Aircel's telecom towers and
was sitting on a future commitment to rent these towers to
the operator. GTL Infra demanded contractual penalties from
Aircel as it stripped operations. The service operator offered

to buy back the tower portfolio it had sold to GTL Infra at the current cost of the towers, but the premium GTL Infra paid on them was for network expansion. The tower operator threatened to shut tower equipment failing payment. For the lenders, this remained a dilemma. Both companies—Aircel and GTL Infrastructure—had debt to service.

Aircel had no choice, said a senior company official. It entered negotiations for a three-way deal between RCom, MTS and itself. The first part involved a merger between RCom and MTS, the second was a stock swap with Aircel. The final entity would tentatively be 40 per cent held by Aircel shareholders, 29 per cent by Anil Ambani and 10 per cent by Sistema. However, the pillars of the deal seemed compromised. The biggest one was retiring debt. Before the merger, both sides negotiated promoters would pay down existing debt to make the final entity viable. The amount was under contention.

Hope to reach a consensus dwindled between October and December 2015. The two companies made no headway in negotiations or expectations. Eventually, they decided to put a clock on a final deal by signing an agreement to exclusively engage in merger talks for ninety days. The stated objective of the deal was 'to mutually derive the expected substantial benefits of in-country consolidation, including opex and capex synergies and revenue enhancement', Reliance Communications said in its public statement.[1]

At the outset, both companies said they would transfer only Rs 10,000 crore of their debt into the merged entity and it was for the promoters to deal with the rest of it.

RCom had simultaneously signed exclusive negotiations with Tillman and TPG, private equity investors to sell the telecom tower portfolio. Ambani had hoped to retire around Rs 17,000 crore of RCom's debt via this sale. Then another Rs 3000 crore from the sale of optic fibre.

Jio's recurring rental commitments for the towers and fibre made the purchase for its buyers' cash neutral, explained executives at RCom. The company's total debt stood at around Rs 40,000 crore and was rising as its interest was capitalized to reduce the cash outflow. The sales of assets would merely halve RCom's debt. Analysts could not see any means for RCom to further pare its debt to Rs 10,000 crore for a merger with Aircel.

Aircel's situation was no different. It seemed unrealistic for it to reduce its debt to Rs 10,000 crore without a massive cash injection from Maxis.

Meanwhile, RCom's tower sale seemed to be on the back foot. The exclusive negotiation period was lapsing on 15 January 2016. The Tillman Group and TPG decided to extend the deadline but there was no explanation on what has held up the transaction. Company executives said that TPG was insisting on buying only the towers and not the optic fibre. Efforts were on to convince TPG otherwise. Selling the optic fibre separately to a third party would be next to impossible for RCom. The fifteen-day extension ended without any further outcome. The deal was off.

This, in turn, shook Aircel's confidence. The fact that RCom was headed by Gurdeep Singh, Aircel's former chief operating officer, did not help.

The two companies decided to increase the debt each one would contribute to a merged entity to Rs 15,000 crore. This in turn rattled the viability of the merged company. Investors feared that it might result in a paralysed operator with the same issues RCom and Aircel were facing now. Lenders were dismayed with the two needed to extend the sunset of their negotiations to 22 May 2016. Aircel sold its 4G airwaves bought in 2010 to Airtel for Rs 3500 crore in April 2016. Most of it was assigned to retiring parts of its Rs 18,000 crore debt. There was still much ground to cover, and no change in RCom's status.

With the apparent paralysis in closure, rating agencies finally bit the bullet and lowered RCom's investment rating. 'We changed the outlook on Reliance Communications Limited's (RCom) ratings to negative from stable on 7 April to reflect our expectation that a material improvement in the Indian telecommunications company's leverage, liquidity and refinancing pressure is unlikely over the next six to nine months, even if the company announces a binding tower sale transaction this quarter,' wrote Moody's.[2]

This usual one-page note captured stakeholders' frustration with the constant change of narrative at Anil Ambani's company referring to the many incomplete sales of assets. 'RCom continues to have a weak liquidity profile, and remains reliant on recurring covenant waivers from banks due to its high leverage,' it said.

It also highlighted the lack of control Anil Ambani had on the fate of his organization. 'RCom has to wait until Reliance Jio Infocomm Limited (R Jio, unrated) commercially launches its 4G services before RCom can start to offer its own 4G services to new customers on the networks and spectrum that it shares with R Jio.' That narrative was being prompted by executives at RCom, assuring debtors that the situation would be remedied when the company began billing 4G data customers.

Fitch downgraded RCom's debt to junk status a couple of months later.

Come 22 May 2016, a deal had still not been finalized between Aircel and RCom. They once more extended negotiations to 22 June. This time the press statement said there had been 'substantial' progress. Then, executives told the press off the record that the new agreement looked something as follows: Both RCom and Aircel promoters would hold a 50 per cent share in the final entity. They would each transfer Rs 14,000 crore of their debt into the final entity. The expected annual revenue of around Rs 25,000 crore from 120 million subscribers, with a market share of around 6 per cent and operating profit between Rs 5000–6000 crore.[3]

Unfortunately, for both companies, they missed yet another deadline. They extended the talks for another month. Had the deal materialized in January, this would have been around when the operational merger would reach a crescendo and close by September. Instead, the two companies were struggling to survive, vulnerable to Jio's market grab.

On this extension, company officials gave out further details, albeit all off-record. The plans had changed. RCom was now looking to transfer its wireless assets into a special purpose vehicle, or company, and put it up for a slump sale, which implied distress value. By doing this, it could hold on to the debt in what would be left of RCom—telecom towers and international operations. The special purpose vehicle would then be sold to Aircel, and the combine could continue to be headed by Aircel Chief Kaizad Heerjee. With all of that on the anvil, the deal seemed set to create the country's third-largest operator overtaking Idea Cellular at that spot.

Sistema would be given an additional 10 per cent in what would be left of RCom instead of the Aircel RCom combined. However, officials at RCom said that the Russian conglomerate could invest $500 million in the RCom Aircel wireless operator for shares. The Russian firm promptly denied this saying, it was in no way obliged to participate in the RCom–Aircel transaction.

When no announcement came by the end of the June deadline, there was no renewal announcement. Both companies reassured enquirers that a deal was still on course, but hope and interest outside was waning.

An official announcement on the deal on 15 September 2016 was a breath of fresh air. RCom and Aircel would have equal stakes and board representation in the final entity. The debt being transferred into the combine from either side remained at Rs 14,000 crore each, but how the rest of it was being pared remained unexplained.

RCom at its end had found another potential buyer for its telecom towers—Brookfield. This private equity firm specialized in infrastructure and saw value in the towers with Jio as an anchor tenant. Anil Ambani confidently announced that his firm would be left with no debt by the end of the year. That said, these deals were large and complex, not to be confused with thirty-minute pizza delivery, Ambani emphasized. By October, the merger with Aircel had received legal approvals, but there were hold-ups. Ambani reassured the media and analysts that administrative complexities such as identifying the correct team were all that was left.

Then, on 27 September 2016, Anil Ambani said his company was 'virtually merged' with Jio. That raised eyebrows. What he was trying to emphasize was that RCom was ready to leverage Jio's 4G network. Since agreements stated that Jio could not use 'Reliance' in its branding, Anil Ambani hoped that the prevailing perception would steer customers to his firm. The market, as well as his partners at Aircel, read it differently. To many, this was the inevitable end to RCom. But Anil Ambani was not ready to be counted out. It was a move designed to hold lenders off. It worked, but for too little time.

Jio's onslaught of free calling and services as it ran opening offers started to erode RCom and Aircel's market share. Fringe players pleaded with the DoT to alleviate their distress by lifting some licence and spectrum fees. Even a plea from the State Bank of India, the country's leading bank, that it was gaping at loan defaults, yielded no response from the DoT.

Bankers came claiming repayment at Anil Ambani's doorstep after failing fringe players. RCom and Aircel tried to quell fears by promising lenders a merger was on way. Outsiders were incredulous. Lenders worried that promoters would leave them holding the ball.

On 2 May 2017, the China Development Bank (CDB) decided to tighten its grip. It filed an objection in the country's companies' court NCLT against the merger between RCom and Aircel. That rocked an already unsteady boat. RCom's tower deal hinged on the operator's merger and survival in the market. CDB said the assets RCom was planning to transfer into the merged entity were collateral for its loans. RCom challenged CDB's stance. It had a shareholder agreement to complete its merger. CDB asserted that it also needed approval from 75 per cent of its lenders before it could proceed. The telecom operator had already filed to dispense with a lenders' meeting that CDB was now demanding.

CDB's filing was acrimonious to the point of accusing RCom and its management of cheating. It set off the chain of dominoes. Other bankers feared that if CDB was successful, it would be settled before them. So, Standard Chartered Bank and HSBC filed their objections staking a claim on their share.

Then came vendors who were owed money. Spearheading them was Ericsson, which had been spurned in the shift to Chinese equipment. Chennai Network Infrastructure, which was the Aircel company acquired by GTL Infrastructure, also filed a claim because most of its business was collateralized against the functioning of Aircel. It had a pending claim for service closure in five areas of Aircel and was waiting to cash in on the non-existent expansion plans.

For lack of any other alternative, Anil Ambani took his company to a joint lender forum (JLF), dominated by Indian bankers. The JLF was a scheme approved by the Reserve Bank of India to pause interest accrual and loan repayments, designed primarily for cash-strapped mid-sized organizations.

Lenders will incur 'zero' loss reassured Ambani asserting that this was not a typical JLF situation.

This dire situation was precipitated by Jio's free offering, Anil Ambani pointed the finger at his elder brother's predatory moves, souring what seemed like reconciliatory tones in the run-up to the announcement. In any case, the bankers had little choice, but for those covered under the JLF, this was an assurance of prioritized repayment. So they agreed to a nearly seven-month deferral on 2 June 2017.

In this period, RCom's nearly Rs 48,000 crore of debt would not incur interest, and the company would not need to repay anything. Immediately after a meeting with lenders, a vexed Anil Ambani addressed the media. As per the scheme, bankers could exercise foreclosure or bankruptcy after December. The leading lender at the forum was State Bank of India, followed by Punjab National Bank and then IDBI. Absent in the process were the company's foreign lenders which accounted for nearly 15 per cent of the telecom operator's borrowings. Ambani was confident it would not come to more severe measures.

He assured news followers that by September, the company would complete its tower sale and merger with Aircel, for which it had received three of five essential permissions. The new company would be named Aircom. Its management remained a point of debate, but that was secondary.

The group would use sale proceeds or leverage of remaining assets to complete debt repayment. The conversation with Brookfield remained alive, Ambani said. 'There is no unlimited deadline and no unlimited time. Provisions of various restructuring schemes as published by RBI naturally are open to be exercised after the standstill period.' This could include a Structured Debt Restructuring or conversion of debt to shares. 'In our case, the lenders clearly recognize that we are already on our way to do everything that they could have done.'[4]

The retail shareholders were reeling from the sharp stock price drop of the company which traded at 20 per cent of its price since rating agencies downgraded RCom. Ambani said, 'We are committed to work with rating agencies and engage with them and sort our credit ratings at the earliest possible.'

The first step was to get CDB to back its merger plans. Anil Ambani called the Chinese to the table. CDB is known worldwide as a strategic investor on behalf of its government. It typically finances real estate or infrastructure assets. The land and township Anil Ambani held adjacent to the iconic Dhirubhai Ambani Knowledge City, where RCom was headquartered, attracted CDB.

Ambani negotiated. Selling this land was a bit like parting with family jewels. CDB accepted it. On 2 August 2017, it withdrew its opposition to the merger between the two companies. Standard Chartered Bank and HSBC followed. They reserved the right to return to court if the resolution failed.

It was now Ericsson's turn to wrangle a settlement. It continued to block the merger. As court matters dragged on, the condition of both operators deteriorated. There were closed-door negotiations with Ericsson. They failed. Rumour among telecom honchos was that the Swedish company was making an example of RCom for the fate its defaulters would meet.

As the vendor continued a dogged pursuit, it added to the strain between RCom and Aircel. By the end of September 2017, they had reached the end of their patience, and merger plans between the mobile operators had collapsed.

Ericsson still held on; it filed for RCom's bankruptcy. It was followed by a host of lenders, then vendors including tower companies and office equipment makers. Ambani tried several attempts to ward the bidders off, negotiating away equity in the group's real estate in Navi Mumbai near the company's headquarters. Then, it made frantic asset and spectrum agreements with the only taker in the market, Reliance Jio. It was bailed out for cash payments to roll over debt, which only slowed down the sinking of its ship.

The matter remained in court for several years and eventually under the bankruptcy scheme was mostly sold to Reliance Jio at distressed values. As it did, it marked Anil Ambani's complete exit from the sector he had fought to keep back in 2005.

67

A Stable Market

RCom became the last of the fringe players to exit the market. The merger of Idea and Vodafone created the country's largest telecom company by market share, but its leadership was short-lived.

Vodafone's interest in the country's performance and, therefore, its desire to infuse further capital vanished. Looming government penalties and pending spectrum payments weighed so heavily on the company that capital investment incurred a setback. Just as the company missed the 4G technology wave, it was also delayed in its 5G endeavour.

The merger of people and teams took a little longer than the eighteen-month forecast. Cutting duplicate staff was key to reducing duplication in the merged entity. Vodafone staffers' pay scales were around 10 per cent higher than Idea's, which made executives in the international company nervous. Idea executives, too, were concerned they may be sidelined for the Vodafone staff. The selection process for the best fit created so much uncertainty that its best on-ground managers chose to jump ship.

Battered from all sides, Vodafone Idea approached the ministry for a solution for a workaround for its dues. Meanwhile, its market share dwindled, and the company again slipped to third place after Reliance Jio and Airtel. The government became increasingly concerned about this anti-competitive turn the Indian mobile telephony market had taken. It decided to offer a rescue package in 2021. Under this restructuring, companies could get a moratorium on interest fees for purchased spectrum for four years and settlement of other dues in exchange for equity. Vodafone Idea was quick to accept. As a result, the government became Vodafone Idea's largest shareholder at 33 per cent. The stake may rise from 2026 onwards when the company faces another Rs 2,00,000 crore repayment charges for its 5G spectrum.[1]

It took Jio well over a year to gradually phase in monthly billing. In mid-2019, Reliance Jio overtook Airtel in market share, but Sunil Mittal's company has consolidated its second spot and continues to enjoy patronage from premium customers in several key service areas.

The COVID-19 pandemic in 2020 provided the next big push to digitization in India, like the rest of the world. Jio's broadband and 4G services solidified its pole position as a provider of the internet needed for working from home.

There was a flurry of excitement in 2022 when a new entrant, the Adani Group registered interest to buy airwaves in an auction for 5G spectrum. The anticipation, however, was as short-lived as the auction itself. The one-week-long auction closed at the end of July. Adani bid for airwaves in regions strategic to its ports and infrastructure facilities. Low latency 5G services that operate in high-frequency bands have proven most effective for warehouse and logistics management.

As per TRAI figures, the country had 1.2 billion mobile subscribers at the end of June 2024. Subscriber numbers were little moved as urban tele density stood at 127 per cent, while penetration in rural areas still stood below 60 per cent. Private operators controlled 92.5 per cent of market share.

Both Airtel and Reliance Jio have captive customers and better pricing power as an outcome of lower competition. Since the beginning of 2024, both companies have been increasing call rates gradually but perceptibly while also focusing on value-added services. In the quarter to 30 June 2024, Airtel's average monthly revenue per user jumped eight per cent to Rs 209.

Even so, the price of mobile telephony and data services in India remains one of the lowest in the world without any state subsidy. The sector continues to be a success story in business as its two survivors stand poised to rake in profits while offering low-cost services to the masses.

Interview Thanks

I am grateful to the following people for their insights and for giving veritable depth to *Telecom Wars*.

Akhil Gupta (Reliance)
Akhil Gupta (Airtel)
Amit Sharma
Amitabh Jhunjhunwala
Analjit Singh
Anil Nayar
Anupama
Arun Sur
Ashok Ramachandran
B.K. Modi
Balaji
Balesh Sharma
C.S. Rao
Deepak Gulati
Hemant Sachdeva
Ishaat Hussain
Kaizad Heerji
Kaushik Roy
Kishore Chaukar
Kunal Bajaj
Mahendra Nahata
Manoj Kohli
Marshall Towe
Marten Pieters

Meet Malhotra
Parag Kar
Prakash Bajpai
Rainer Deustchman
Rajan Mathews
Rajat Mukherjee
Rajeev Chandrasekhar
Rakesh Thukral
Raza
Sandip Basu
Sandip Das
Sanjay Kapoor
Sanjeev Aga
Shantharaju
Subodh Bhargav
Sunil Ranka
Sunil Sood
Syed Safawi
TVR
Umang Das
Venkat
Vinay Rai

Endnotes

Chapter 1

1 Parliamentary session transcript, Rajya Sabha, 28 April 1982.
2 Interview with Rajan Mittal 8 July 2020.
3 A term used for senior bureaucrats or wealthy businessmen.
4 Shauvik Ghosh, 'Sunil Mittal | Ringing in the reforms', *Mint*, 16 February 2016, https://www.livemint.com/Companies/KUo6M-wkKWvSAjs1VcYX0QO/Sunil-Mittal--Ringing-in-the-reforms.html; Chhavi Tyagi, 'How Bharti Airtel's Sunil Mittal was once in financial crisis for the want of Rs 5000', *Economic Times*, 16 December 2017, https://economictimes.indiatimes.com/small-biz/startups/newsbuzz/how-bharti-airtels-sunil-mittal-was-once-in-financial-crisis-for-the-want-of-rs-5000/articleshow/62093302.cms?
5 Chhavi Tyagi, 'How Bharti Airtel's Sunil Mittal was once in financial crisis for the want of Rs 5000', *Economic Times*, 16 December 2017, https://economictimes.indiatimes.com/small-biz/startups/newsbuzz/how-bharti-airtels-sunil-mittal-was-once-in-financial-crisis-for-the-want-of-rs-5000/articleshow/62093302.cms?
6 Shauvik Ghosh, 'Sunil Mittal | Ringing in the reforms', *Mint*, 16 February 2016, https://www.livemint.com/Companies/KUo6M-wkKWvSAjs1VcYX0QO/Sunil-Mittal--Ringing-in-the-reforms.html

Chapter 3

1 Shauvik Ghosh, 'Sunil Mittal | Ringing in the reforms', *Mint*, 16 February 2016, https://www.livemint.com/Companies/KUo6MwkKWvSAjs1VcYX0QO/Sunil-Mittal--Ringing-in-the-reforms.html

Chapter 4

1 Société française du radiotéléphone
2 Shauvik Ghosh, 'Sunil Mittal | Ringing in the reforms', *Mint*, 16 February 2016, https://www.livemint.com/Companies/KUo6MwkKWvSAjs1VcYX0QO/Sunil-Mittal--Ringing-in-the-reforms.html

Chapter 6

1 The relationship of a son-in-law in Indian culture is treated as higher than others. Typically, on each visit, the son-in-law is showered with expensive presents and special treatment.
2 Off record interview with an executive in that room.

Chapter 7

1 As narrated by Rajeev Chandrasekhar in an interview.
2 This is from an on-record interview conducted with Rajeev Chandrasekharan for the purpose of this book on 22 June 2020.
3 This is from an on-record interview conducted with Rajeev Chandrasekharan for the purpose of this book on 22 June 2020.
4 Rahul Pathak, 'Legal action fails as Sterling Computers was forced to make public its contract', *India Today*, 15 July 1992, https://www.indiatoday.in/magazine/investigation/story/19920715-legal-action-fails-as-sterling-computers-was-forced-to-make-public-its-contract-766551-2013-01-03; 'C Sivasankaran: Once the country's most astute deal maker, now a bankrupt entrepreneur', Surajeet Das Gupta et al, Business Standard, 6 September 2014, https://www.business-standard.com/article/companies/c-sivasankaran-once-the-country-s-most-astute-deal-maker-now-a-bankrupt-entrepreneur-114090501264_1.html

Chapter 8

1 See case files of *India Telecomp Limited vs Union of India and Ors.*, 26 February 1993.
2 *India Telecom Limited vs Union of India and Ors.*, 26 February 1993 Delhi High Court Order.
3 This is from an on-record interview conducted with Harsh Goenka for this book on 5 May 2020.

Chapter 10

1   Shauvik Ghosh, 'Sunil Mittal | Ringing in the reforms', *Mint*,
    16 February 2016, https://www.livemint.com/Companies/
    KUo6MwkKWvSAjs1VcYX0QO/Sunil-Mittal--Ringing-in-the-
    reforms.html
2   This is from an on-record interview conducted with Umang Das on
    13 August 2022.

Chapter 11

1   Anil Nayar, business development head and later CEO of Airtel in
    an interview.

Chapter 13

1   'Passing the baton', Aditya Birla, 27 May 2005, https://web.archive.
    org/web/20071012131001/http://www.adityabirla.com/media/press_
    reports/passing_the_baton.htm. (Accessed 16 May 2020).

Chapter 14

1   Interview with Nahata.
2   'Rendezvous with Simi Garewal', 2002, https://www.youtube.
    com/watch?reload=9&v=u3TQ0HHXEQM   https://www.
    youtube.com/watch?v=9dxbjV0RfcU   https://www.youtube.com/
    watch?v=ypA71txfrJw (Accessed 11 June 2020). —, 'Nita and
    Mukesh', Face to Face Interview, 30 August 2003, https://www.
    youtube.com/watch?v=DT5FnnVTG7k (Accessed 11 June 2020).
3   'Rendezvous with Simi Garewal – Anil Ambani', 2002, https://
    www.youtube.com/watch?reload=9&v=u3TQ0HHXEQM;
    'Rendezvous with Simi Garewal – Mukesh Ambani', 2002, https://
    www.youtube.com/watch?v=9dxbjV0RfcU; 'Rendezvous with Simi
    Garewal Mukesh & Neeta Ambani Part -1', https://www.youtube.
    com/watch?v=ypA71txfrJw (Accessed 11 June 2020).

Chapter 16

1   Zafar Agha, Shefali Rekhi, 'Telecom Scandal: Opposition
    Determined Not to Let Go of Juicy Election Issue', *India Today*,
    31 December 1995, https://www.indiatoday.in/magazine/economy/

story/19951231-telecom-scandal-opposition-determined-not-to-let-go-of-juicy-election-issue-808108-1995-12-30.

2   Broadly reconstructed from the Rajya Sabha Minutes, 6 December 1995.
3   Rajya Sabha transcript, 2 September 1996 p. 230.

Chapter 17

1   Quotes based on best recollections of the executives interviewed.
2   Quotes based on best recollections of the executives interviewed.
3   Interview with executive on 18 May 2020.

Chapter 19

1   Delhi High Court, *Union of India vs Telecom Regulatory* on 16 July 1998.
2   'Qualcomm Announces Mahanagar Telephone Nigam Ltd.'s Commencement of First Commercial CDMA Wireless Local Loop Network in India', Qualcom, 26 June 1997, https://www.qualcomm. com/news/releases/1997/06/qualcomm-announces-mahangar-telephone-nigam-ltds-commencement

Chapter 20

1   Simi Garewal interview.
2   'Jyotindra Thacker of Reliance Jio in Conversation With Anant Goenka', *Indian Express*, published to YouTube, 25 August 2015, https://www.youtube.com/watch?v=7AXa3fS7oeI (Accessed 26 Jul 2020).

Chapter 22

1   Reconstructed from interviews several executives who attended these meetings.
2   Interview with Umang Das.

Chapter 24

1   Arun Shourie, 'Reservation Is Not Affirmative Action', Wharton, 30 November 2006, https://knowledge.wharton.upenn.edu/article/arun-shourie-reservation-is-not-affirmative-action/.

2   Ibid.
3   TNN, 'Shourie: VSNL Deal Fully Above Board', *Times of India*, June 4, 2002, https://timesofindia.indiatimes.com/business/india-business/shourie-vsnl-deal-fully-above-board/articleshow/12009200.cms?utm_source=content ofinterest&utm_medium=text&utm_campaign=cppst.

Chapter 25

1   Abheek Burman, 'Reliance "whistleblower" offered to quit', *Times of India*, 19 May 2005 http://timesofindia.indiatimes.com/article-show/1114978.cms?utm_source=contentofinterest&utm_medium=-text&utm_campaign=cppst.

Chapter 27

1   This is from an on-record interview conducted with Towe on 6 December 2022.
2   Reconstructed based on recollections of the executive concerned, interviewed for this book.
3   Ibid.

Chapter 28

1   Details for this chapter sourced from: Petition nos. 1, 2 and 3 of 2001, Telecom Disputes Settlement & Appellate Tribunal New Delhi dated this 8th day of August, 2003 petition no.1 of 2001.

Chapter 29

1   'Unsung Heroes', *Bharti Today*, 3 August 2002—in-house magazine of the Bharti Group.
2   Goldman Sachs, 'Talks@GS', Interview with Chip Kaye, Interviewer: Alison Mass, https://www.goldmansachs.com/pdfs/insights/goldman-sachs-talks/chip-kaye-f/transcript.pdf
3   'JT Mobile changes its name to Bharti Mobile', CIOL Bureau, 11 April 2000, https://www.ciol.com/jt-mobile-changes-bharti-mobile/.
4   On-record interview with Umang Das.

Chapter 30

1   This has been reconstructed based on the interviews of people present there.
2   Shauvik Ghosh, 'Sunil Mittal | Ringing in the reforms', *Mint*, 16 February 2016, https://www.livemint.com/Companies/KUo6MwkKWvSAjs1VcYX0QO/Sunil-Mittal--Ringing-in-the-reforms.html.

Chapter 31

1   This is based on an off-record interview with two individuals people in that circle.
2   On record Interview with Manoj Kohli on 15 July 2020 for this book.
3   Shauvik Ghosh, 'Sunil Mittal | Ringing in the reforms', *Mint*, 16 February 2016, https://www.livemint.com/Companies/KUo6MwkKWvSAjs1VcYX0QO/Sunil-Mittal--Ringing-in-the-reforms.html
4   On record Interview with Manoj Kohli on 15 July 2020 for this book.
5   Bharti Airtel Press Release dated 23 April 2003.
6   This is based on the accounts of two executives interviewed separately.

Chapter 32

1   Interview with Rajeev Chandrasekhar, June 22, 2020.
2   Press Release, 'Birla-Tata-AT&T and BPL team up to form India's premier mobile services Company', Aditya Birla, 28 June 2001, https://www.adityabirla.com/media/media-releases/bpl-team-up-to-form-india-premier-mobile-services-company (Accessed 30 April 2020).
3   Ibid.

Chapter 33

1   Surajeet Das Gupta, 'C Sivasankaran: A maverick prone to courting controversy and the CBI', *Business Standard*, 28 April 2018. https://www.business-standard.com/article/companies/c-sivasankaran-a-maverick-prone-to-courting-controversy-and-the-cbi-118042700853_1.html (Accessed 27 May 2020).

Chapter 34

1   *The Brand Custodian: My Years with the Tatas,* Mukund Rajan, Harper Business, 2019, p. 76.

Chapter 36

1   Source: TRAI.

Chapter 38

1   Draft Red Herring Prospectus filed with the Securities and Exchange Board of India.
2   ET Bureau, 'Idea Buys Spice for Rs 2,176 Crore', *Economic Times,* June 25, 2008, https://economictimes.indiatimes.com/industry/telecom/idea-buys-spice-for-rs-2176-crore/articleshow/3165723.cms?from=mdr.
3   Devidutta Tripathy, 'India ministry obtains stay order on Idea-Spice deal: sources', Reuters, 1 April 2011, https://www.reuters.com/article/idea-spice-idUSL3E7F12LB20110401/.

Chapter 39

1   'Consultation Paper on Infrastructure Sharing', 29 November 2006, https://www.trai.gov.in/sites/default/files/consultationpaper29nov06.pdf.
2   Ibid.
3   Ibid.
4   Ibid.
5   TNN, 'Bharti, Vodafone, Idea merge tower units in 16 circles', *Economic Times,* 9 December 2007, https://economictimes.indiatimes.com/industry/telecom/bharti-vodafone-idea-merge-tower-units-in-16-circles/articleshow/2607498.cms?from=mdr.
6   'Earnings Conference Call Transcript, Event: Bharti Airtel Limited Fourth Quarter and Full Year ended March 31, 2008, Earnings Conference Call, Event/Date/Time: Friday, 25 April 2008, 1430 hours', https://s3-ap-southeast-1.amazonaws.com/bsy/iportal/images/Transcript-Q4FY08_92AA5A4119B0892652526616CA69F4BA_1518432485553.pdf.

Chapter 40

1   'Chairman's Statement at RIL'S AGM on 3 August 2005', https://rilstaticasset.akamaized.net/sites/default/files/2023-01/Chairman%202005.pdf

Chapter 43

1   Email interview with the author on 16 February 2019.

Chapter 44

1   'Earnings Conference Call Transcript, Event: Bharti Airtel Limited Fourth Quarter and Full Year ended March 31, 2008, Earnings Conference Call', Event Date/Time: Friday 25th April 2008, 1430 hours', https://s3-ap-southeast-1.amazonaws.com/bsy/iportal/images/Transcript-Q4FY08_92AA5A4119B0892652526616CA69F4BA_1518432485553.pdf.
2   South African Rand.
3   'Media statement from Bharti Airtel Limited', 6 May 2008, https://www.bharti.com/press-release-2008-2009-more11.html.
4   'Media statement from Bharti Airtel Limited', 13 May 2008, https://www.bharti.com/press-release-2008-2009-more9.html.
5   Heather Timmons, 'South Africa-India telecom deal collapses', New York Times, 24 May 2008 https://www.nytimes.com/2008/05/24/business/worldbusiness/24iht-bharti.1.13178744.html#:~:text=%22More%20importantly%2C%22%20Bharti%20added,Group%20had%20no%20immediate%20comment.
6   'Reliance Communications and MTN GROUP to enter into exclusive negotiations', 26 May 2008, https://www.rcom.co.in/our-company/investor-relations/press-release-stock-exchange-disclosures/; https://www.rcom.co.in/download/2008-rcom-and-mtn-group-to-enter-into-exclusive-negotiations/
7   'RELIANCE MTN DISCUSSIONS', Reliance Communications, 13 June 2008, https://www.rcom.co.in/our-company/investor-relations/press-release-stock-exchange-disclosures/ https://www.rcom.co.in/download/2008-reliance-mtn-discussions/.
8   Ibid.
9   'RELIANCE COMMUNICATIONS AND MTN MUTUALLY DECIDE TO ALLOW EXCLUSIVITY AGREEMENT TO LAPSE', 18 July 2008, https://www.rcom.co.in/

download/2008-rcom-and-mtn-group-mutually-decide-to-al-low-exclusivity-agreement-to-lapse/.

10 MTN Group Ltd, 'Book 1 – MTN Group Overview', https://www. mtn.com/wp-content/uploads/2022/02/Book-1-MTN-group-overview.pdf.

11 'Bharti Enterprises: Privacy', n.d., https://www.bharti.com/press-release-2009-2010-media-statement-from-bharti-airtel-limited-new-delhi.html.

12 TNN, 'Bharti, MTN call off merger talks', *Times of India*, 1 October 2009, https://timesofindia.indiatimes.com/business/india-business/ bharti-mtn-call-off-merger-talks/articleshow/5073941.cms.

Chapter 45

1 'Earnings Conference Call Transcript, Event: Bharti Air-tel Limited First Quarter ended June 30, 2010, Earnings Con-ference Call, Event Date/Time: August 11, 2010 at 1430 hrs', https://s3-ap-southeast-1.amazonaws.com/bsy/iportal/ images/Transcript_Q1_10_260251C37A4F74ACDA86F 0C7A5EFEAE2_1518503370114.pdf.

2 Second quote from Sept 2010 transcript: Goldman Sachs.

3 'Earnings Conference Call Transcript, Event: Bharti Airtel Limited First Quarter ended June 30, 2010, Earnings Conference Call, Event Date/Time: August 11, 2010 at 1430 hrs', https://s3-ap-southeast-1.amazonaws.com/bsy/iportal/ images/Transcript_Q1_10_260251C37A4F74ACDA86 F0C7A5EFEAE2_1518503370114.pdf

4 Ibid.

5 Ibid.

6 Mankhotia, Anadita Singh and Chaitali Chakraborty, '8 out of 13 top executives leave Bharti after Gopal Vittal becomes CEO', *Economic Times*, December 30, 2013. https://economictimes.indiatimes. com/industry/telecom/8-out-of-13-top-executives-leave-bharti-after-gopal-vittal-becomes-ceo/articleshow/28116382.cms?utm_ source=contentofinterest&utm_medium=text&utm_campaign=cppst (Accessed 23 Apr, 2024)

Chapter 46

1 6 TRAI, Recommendations on Spectrum related issues, May 2005, paragraph (¶) 3.7.2

2   'Recommendations on Allocation and pricing of spectrum for 3G
    and broadband wireless access services', TRAI, 27 September 2006,
    https://www.trai.gov.in/sites/default/files/MNP.pdf (last accessed
    28 August 2024).
3   Government of India, Ministry of Communications, Press Release:
    16-May-2007 'Shri A Raja takes over as Minister of Communications
    & Information Technology'.
4   'Telecom Regulatory Authority of India Review of license terms
    and conditions and capping of number of access providers, New
    Delhi', TRAI, 28 August 2007, https://trai.gov.in/sites/default/files/
    recommen29aug07%5B1%5D_1.pdf.
5   Ibid.
6   Ibid.
7   Ibid.
8   https://archive.pib.gov.in/archive2/erelease.aspx

Chapter 47

1   'Recommendations on Mobile Number Portability', TRAI, 8 March
    2006   https://www.trai.gov.in/sites/default/files/recomm8mar06.
    pdf.

Chapter 50

1   'Media Statement by the Chairman on the Report submitted by
    Special Auditor to DoT', RCom, 15 October 2009, https://www.
    rcom.co.in/our-company/investor-relations/press-release-stock-
    exchange-disclosures/   https://www.rcom.co.in/download/2009-
    media-statement-by-chairman-on-the-report-submitted-by-special-
    auditor-to-dot/.
2   Ibid.

Chapter 51

1   Press Release, 'MoU With DoT to Release 3G & BWA Spectrum',
    Ministry of Defence, Government of India, 28 July 2010.
2   'Earnings Conference Call Transcript, Event: Bharti Airtel Lim-
    ited First Quarter ended June 30, 2010, Earnings Conference Call,
    Event Date/Time: August 11, 2010 at 1430 hrs', https://s3-ap-
    southeast-1.amazonaws.com/bsy/iportal/images/Transcript_Q1_10_
    260251C37A4F74ACDA86F0C7A5EFEAE2_1518503370114.pdf

Chapter 52

1 'Earnings Conference Call Transcript, Event: Bharti Airtel Limited First Quarter ended June 30, 2010, Earnings Conference Call, Event Date/Time: August 11, 2010 at 1430 hrs', https://s3-ap-south-east-1.amazonaws.com/bsy/iportal/images/Transcript_Q1_10_260251C37A4F74ACDA86F0C7A5EFEAE2_1518503370114.pdf.

2 'IGNITING TRANSFORMATIONAL INITIATIVES CHAIRMAN'S STATEMENT Thirty Sixth Annual General Meeting', Friday, 18 June 2010, https://rilstaticasset.akamaized.net/sites/default/files/2023-01/36th_rilagm2010.pdf.

Chapter 53

1 CAG Report for the year ended March 2010 has been prepared for submission to the President under Article 151 of the Constitution, p. 64, https://cag.gov.in/en/audit-report/details/2314.

2 'PM's Interaction with Electronic Media—Preliminary Transcript', PMO, 16 February 2011, https://archivepmo.nic.in/drmanmohansingh/press-details.php?nodeid=1196.

Chapter 54

1 Press Release, 'Violation of Licencing Norms', Ministry of Communications, Government of India, 14 December 2011.

2 'Telecom Disputes Settlement & Appellate Tribunal New Delhi', TDSAT, 3 July 2012, https://tdsat.gov.in/order_files/final/2012/July/070110004262011_939.pdf.

Chapter 55

1 Sigve Brekke, 'Lessons from the Road -- Fighting out of our class in India', Economic Times, 16 June 2015, https://telecom.economictimes.indiatimes.com/tele-talk/lessons-from-the-road-fighting-out-of-our-class-in-india/698.

Chapter 57

1 'Recommendations on Auction of Spectrum', TRAI, https://www.trai.gov.in/sites/default/files/TRAI%20Response%20on%20%20Auction%20of%20Spectrum.pdf.

2   *Reliance: An Enduring Growth Saga*, Chairman's Statement, Fortieth General Meeting, Reliance Industries, 18 June 2014, https://rilstaticasset.akamaized.net/sites/default/files/2023-01/40th_rilagm2014.pdf.

3   *Hyper Growth Platforms of Value Creation*, Chairman's Statement, Forty-first General Meeting, Reliance Industries, 12 June 2015, https://rilstaticasset.akamaized.net/sites/default/files/2023-11/Chairmans-Statement-RIL-41st-AGM.PDF.

Chapter 58

1   'RCom inducts Shamik Das as Jt President, COO', *Economic Times*, 14 November 2011, https://economictimes.indiatimes.com/markets/stocks/earnings/rcom-inducts-shamik-das-as-jt-president-coo/articleshow/10731885.cms?utm_source=contentofinterest&utm_medium=text&utm_campaign=cppst.

Chapter 59

1   The author was present at the media conference, and these are from her personal recollections.

2   Deepali Gupta and Arijit Barman, 'Tata vs DoCoMo: Two warring partners and one big mess', *Economic Times*, 18 August 2016, https://economictimes.indiatimes.com/news/company/corporate-trends/tata-vs-docomo-two-warring-partners-and-one-big-mess/articleshow/53748101.cms?utm_source=contentofinterest&utm_medium=text&utm_campaign=cppst

3   'Viom Networks denies reports of wrongdoing in company', *Economic Times*, 14 September 2011. https://economictimes.indiatimes.com/industry/telecom/viom-networks-denies-reports-of-wrongdoing-in-company/articleshow/9982503.cms?utm_source=contentofinterest&utm_medium=text&utm_campaign=cppst; ET Now, 'Viom Networks Chairman Subodh Bhargava quits', 6 February 2012, https://economictimes.indiatimes.com/viom-networks-chairman-subodh-bhargava-quits/articleshow/11780997.cms?utm_source=contentofinterest&utm_medium=text&utm_campaign=cppst (Accessed 7 May 2024).

4   'Viom Networks hires KPMG to probe an allegation into misappropriation of funds', 14 September 2011 https://www.domain-b.com/companies-organisations/firms-companies/viom-networks-hires-kpmg-to-probe-an-allegation-into-misappropriation-of-funds.

5   Arijit Barman and Surajeet Das Gupta, 'Viom chief quits as graft controversy snowballs', *Business Standard*, 21 January 2013, https://www.business-standard.com/article/technology/viom-chief-quits-as-graft-controversy-snowballs-112020700030_1.html.

Chapter 60

1   Chakravarty, Rajeev Jayaswal and Chaitali. 'Mukesh Ambani's Son Akash Joins Reliance Industries; Begins at Telecom Arm Reliance Jio', *Economic Times*, 17 February 2014, https://economictimes.indiatimes.com/news/company/corporate-trends/mukesh-amban-is-son-akash-joins-reliance-industries-begins-at-telecom-arm-reli-ance-jio/articleshow/30531661.cms?from=mdr.

Chapter 63

1   Nash David, 'Reliance Jio Soft Launches Its 4G Network With Employees Ahead of Commercial Launch of Jio Services', Firstpost, 28 December 2015, https://www.firstpost.com/tech/news-analysis/reliance-jio-soft-launches-its-4g-network-with-employees-ahead-of-commercial-launch-of-jio-services-3675015.html.

2   *Operationalising Hyper Growth Platforms of New Value Creation for A Prosperous and Inclusive India, Chairman's Statement*, 39th Annual General meeting, Post-IPO, 1 September 2016, https://ril-staticasset.akamaized.net/sites/default/files/2023-01/AGM%20SPEECH%20-%20Full%200109%20final.pdf

3   Danish Khan, 'Bharti Airtel says to increase interconnection points to Reliance Jio', *Economic Times*, 9 September 2016, https://telecom.economictimes.indiatimes.com/news/bharti airtel-says-to-increase-interconnection-points-to-reliance-jio/54250865

4   Ibid.

5   Marten Pieters, 'Reliance Jio launch good for consumers, tower companies, not so good for investors', *Economic Times*, 9 September 2016, https://telecom.economictimes.indiatimes.com/tele-talk/reliance-jio-launch-good-for-consumers-tower-companies-not-so-good-for-investors/1786.

Chapter 64

1   Vodafone Group plc Preliminary Results Analyst and Investor Conference Call, 19 May 2015.

2   Deepali Gupta, 'Vodafone infuses Rs 47,700 crore in India unit this
     fiscal', *Economic Times*, 22 September 2016, https://economictimes.
     indiatimes.com/news/company/corporate-trends/vodafone-infuses-
     rs-47700-crore-in-india-unit-this-fiscal/articleshow/54462920.cms?-
     from=mdr
3   *Idea Cellular Limited, Quarterly Report – Third Quarter Ended December
     31, 2016*, https://www.myvi.in/content/dam/microsite/pdfs/Results/
     Quarterly%20Report%20Q3.pdf

Chapter 65

1   ET Bureau, 'Pay Rs 5,600 crore for spectrum liberalisation:
     DoT to Reliance Communications', *Economic Times*, 13 January
     2016,   https://economictimes.indiatimes.com/industry/telecom/
     pay-rs-5600-crore-for-spectrum-liberalisation-dot-to-reliance-com-
     munications/articleshow/50547769.cms?from=mdr.

Chapter 66

1   Deepali Gupta, 'Reliance Communications, Aircel in talks to
     merge wireless business', *Economic Times*, 23 December 2015
     https://economictimes.indiatimes.com/industry/telecom/reliance-
     communications-aircel-in-talks-to-merge-wireless-business/
     articleshow/50280605.cms?from=mdr.
2   'Release: Moody's: RCom - Persistent Delays in Asset Sales and
     Strained Liquidity Drive Negative Outlook', 13 April 2016.
3   Deepali Gupta and Arijit Barman, 'Anil Ambani-led RCom and
     Aircel may complete $6-billion merger by July', *Economic Times*, 13
     June 2016, https://telecom.economictimes.indiatimes.com/news/
     anil-ambani-led-rcom-and-aircel-may-complete-6-billion-merger-
     by-july/52721638?em=ZGVlcGFsaS5ndXB0YUBnbWFpbC5jb20=
4   Press statements made at media conference on 2 June 2017.

Chapter 67

1   Yuthika Bhargava, 'How govt brought Vodafone Idea back from the
     brink & earned a neat profit in the process', ThePrint, 2 May 2024,
     https://theprint.in/economy/how-govt-brought-vodafone-idea-
     back-from-the-brink-earned-a-neat-profit-in-the-process/2066524/.

Glossary

ABTO: Association of Basic Telecom Operators

ADR: Additional Depository Receipts

ASSOCHAM: Associated Chambers of Commerce & Industry of India

AT&T: American Telephone & Telegraph

ATC: American Tower Corp

BSNL: Bharat Sanchar Nigam Limited

CAG: Comptroller and Auditor General of India

CBI: Central Bureau of Investigation

CCII: Cellular Communication International Inc

CDMA: Code Division Multiple Access

C-DOT: Centre for Development of Telematics

COAI: Cellular Operators Association of India

CPP: Calling Party Pays

DAKC: Dhirubhai Ambani Knowledge City

DoT: Department of Telecommunications

FCCB: Foreign Currency Convertible Bonds

FDD: Frequency Division Duplex

FSP: Fixed Service Providers

GSM: Global System for Mobile Communications

KYC: Know Your Customer

MTNL: Mahanagar Telephone Nigam Limited

NELCO: National Radio and Electronics Company Limited

NTP: National Telecom Policy

NTT: Nippon Telephone and Telegraph

OTSC: One-Time Spectrum Charge

PSTN: A Public Switched Telephone Network

RIL: Reliance Industries Limited

SDCA: Short-Distance Charging Area

SFR: Société française du radiotéléphone

TCIL: Telecommunications Consultants of India

TCS: Tata Consultancy Services

TDD: Time Division Duplex

TDSAT: Telecom Disputes Settlement and Appellate Tribunal

TGN: Tyco Global Network

TRAI: Telecom Regulatory Authority of India

VoIP: Voice Over Internet Protocol

VSNL: Videsh Sanchar Nigam Limited

WLL: Wireless in Local Loop

Bibliography

Reliance Story

Bhupta, Malini, 'Ambani Vs Ambani: When Brothers Broke Up', *India Today*, 27 December 2011, https://www.indiatoday.in/business/india/story/ambani-vs-ambani-when-brothers-broke-up-150083-2011-12-27 (Accessed 18 November 2019)

Bureau, 'Rate war intensifies; RCom unveils 50p/min plan', *Economic Times*, 6 October 2009, https://economic-times.indiatimes.com/industry/telecom/rate-war-intensi-fies-rcom-unveils-50p/min-plan/articleshow/5091753.cms?utm_source=contentofinterest&utm_medium=text&utm_campaign=cppst(Accessed9 May 2024)

Bureau, 'RCom appoints Safawi as CEO of mobility biz', 17 December 2009, https://economictimes.indiatimes.com/rcom-appoints-safawi-as-ceo-of-mobility-biz/articleshow/5347107.cms?utm_source=contentofinterest&utm_medium=text&utm_campaign=cppst (Accessed 9 May 2024)

PTI, 'Reliance Communication rejigs management; wireless business head Syed Safawi to leave', 1 February 2012, *Economic Times*, https://economictimes.indiatimes.com/industry/telecom/reliance-com-munication-rejigs-management-wireless-business-head-syed-safa-wi-to-leave/articleshow/11717679.cms?utm_source=contentofin-terest&utm_medium=text&utm_campaign=cppst (Accessed 9 May 2024)

PTI, 'RCom appoints Gurdeep Singh as CEO of wireless biz', *Times of India*, 30 May 2012, http://timesofindia.indiatimes.com/article-show/13672203.cms?utm_source=contentofinterest&utm_medi-um=text&utm_campaign=cppst (Accessed 9 May 2024)

Parbat, Kalyan, 'Arun Sur, Jagbir Singh quit Reliance Communications', 22 April 2011, https://economictimes.indiatimes.com/arun-sur-jagbir-singh-quit-reliance-communications/articleshow/8053420.cms?utm_source=contentofinterest&utm_medium=text&utm_campaign=cppst (Accessed 9 May 2024)

Bureau, 'RCom appoints Shamik Das to head wireless biz', *Times of India*, 14 November 2011, http://timesofindia.indiatimes.com/articleshow/10729352.cms?utm_source=contentofinterest&utm_medium=text&utm_campaign=cppst (Accessed 9 May 2024)

Philip, Joji, 'Idea may have to give up six overlapping licenses', *Economic Times*, 1 May 2010, https://economictimes.indiatimes.com/industry/telecom/idea-may-have-to-give-up-six-overlapping-licences/articleshow/5878708.cms (Accessed 15 January, 2020)

Bagchi, Pradipta, 'Dhirubhai Ambani passes away', *Times of India*, 7 July 2002, http://timesofindia.indiatimes.com/articleshow/15204217.cms?utm_source=contentofinterest&utm_medium=text&utm_campaign=cppst (Accessed 11 February, 2020)

—, 'Dhirubhai, R.I.P.', *Outlook India*, 7 July 2002, https://www.outlookindia.com/website/story/dhirubhai-rip/216337 (Accessed 11 February 2020)

ET Online, 'Mukesh Ambani: Asia's richest man keeps his friends close, has a fixed salary since 10 years, and is a favourite headline name', *Economic Times*, 19 April 2019, https://economictimes.indiatimes.com/magazines/panache/mukesh-ambani-asias-richest-man-keeps-his-friends-close-has-a-fixed-salary-since-10-years-and-is-a-favourite-headline-name/articleshow/68939829.cms?utm_source=contentofinterest&utm_medium=text&utm_campaign=cppst. (Accessed 11 February 2020)

Pandya, Haresh, 'Dhirajlal Ambani: Entrepreneur who transformed India's business establishment', *Guardian*, 30 July 2002, https://www.theguardian.com/news/2002/jul/30/guardianobituaries. (Accessed 11 February 2020)

Shastri, Padma, 'Reliance Monsoon Hungama draws in the crowds', *Times of India*, 9 July 2003, http://timesofindia.indiatimes.com/articleshow/66624.cms?utm_source=contentofinterest&utm_medium=text&utm_campaign=cppst (Accessed 11 February 2020)

—, 'Dhirubhais Infocomm Dream Finally Becomes a Reality', *Financial Express*, 27 December 2002, https://www.financialexpress.

com/archive/dhirubhais-infocomm-dream-finally-becomes-a-reality/69126/ (Accessed 14 February 2020)

Pandey, Piyush, 'Will Reliance Jio disrupt the market with 4G?', *The Hindu*, 27 June 2016, https://www.thehindu.com/business/Industry/Will-Reliance-Jio-disrupt-the-market-with-4G/article14404852.ece (Accessed 15 February 2020)

—, 'Nita and Mukesh', Face to Face Interview, 30 August 2003, https://www.youtube.com/watch?v=DT5FnnVTG7k (Accessed 11 June, 2020)

Singh, Andrew, 'The Ambani Family Tree: A Journey to the Life of Billionaires', Press Room, 8 August 2018, https://pressroom.today/2018/08/08/ambani-family-tree/ (Accessed 12 June 2020)

—, 'Rendezvous with Simi Garewal', 2002, https://www.youtube.com/watch?reload=9&v=u3TQ0HHXEQM
https://www.youtube.com/watch?v=9dxbjV0RfcU
https://www.youtube.com/watch?v=ypA71txfrJw
(Accessed 11 June 2020)

Times News Network, 'Rel Info writes off Rs 4,500 cr', *Times of India*, 20 February 2006, https://timesofindia.indiatimes.com/business/india-business/Rel-Info-writes-off-Rs-4500cr/articleshow/1421941.cms (Accessed 17 June 2020)

Kamal, Ananth, 'Spotted: Mukesh Ambani in New Jersey', Reddif, 5 July 2007, https://www.rediff.com/money/report/spotted/20070705.htm (Accessed 17 June 2020)

Dalal, Sucheta and Debashis Basu, 'Always invest in businesses of the future and in talent', Rediff, 19 January 2007, https://www.rediff.com/money/report/spotted/20070705.htm; https://www.rediff.com/money/2007/jan/18inter.htm; https://www.rediff.com/money/2007/jan/19inter.htm (Accessed 17 June 2020)

Sanghvi, Vir, 'Reliance didn't grow on permit raj: Anil Ambani', Rediff, 11 May 2002, https://www.rediff.com/money/2002/may/11ambani.htm (Accessed 17 June 2020)

Staff, 'Reliance Infocomm launches WLL services with three schemes', Exchange4Media, 8 August 2019, https://www.exchange4media.com/digital-news/reliance-infocomm-launches-wll-services-with-three-schemes-6757.html (Accessed 17 June 2020)

Roy, Saumya, 'The Nita Factor: Deciding the Future Course', *Outlook India*, 13 December 2004, https://www.outlookindia.com/

magazine/story/the-nita-factor-deciding-the-future-course/225935 (Accessed 17 June 2020)

—. 'Jyotindra Thacker of Reliance Jio in Conversation With Anant Goenka', https://www.youtube.com/watch?v=7AXa3fS7oeI (Accessed 26 July 2020).

PTI, 'Reliance announces new connection at Rs 501', *Economic Times*, 1 July 2003, https://economictimes.indiatimes.com/reliance-announces-new-connection-at-rs-501/articleshow/54282.cms?utm_source=contentofinterest&utm_medium=text&utm_campaign=cppst (Accessed 11 January 2023)

Bureau, 'Reliance Gateway to Acquire Flag Telecom For $207 Million', *Indian Express*, 17 October 2003, http://archive.indianexpress.com/news/reliance-gateway-to-acquire-flag-telecom-for--207-million/93269/#:~:text=In%20a%20press%20statement%2C%20Reliance,the%20extent%20of%2050%2C000%20kms (Accessed 28 Mar 2023)

PTI, 'Reliance, Tatas face CAG music', *Times of India*, 11 May 2005, https://timesofindia.indiatimes.com/india/reliance-tatas-face-cag-music/articleshow/1106707.cms (Accessed 14 June 2023)

PTI, 'Change of guard on the cards at Infocomm', *Times of India*, 1 May 2005, http://timesofindia.indiatimes.com/articleshow/1094425.cms?utm_source=contentofinterest&utm_medium=text&utm_campaign=cppst (Accessed 14 June 2023)

PTI, 'Mukesh takes Reliance spat to PM's court', *Times of India*, 4 May 2005, http://timesofindia.indiatimes.com/articleshow/1098692.cms?utm_source=contentofinterest&utm_medium=text&utm_campaign=cppst (Accessed 14 June 2023)

Kalesh, Baiju, 'Reliance Info to pull plug on 9.3L users', *Times of India*, 7 April 2005, http://timesofindia.indiatimes.com/articleshow/1070832.cms?utm_source=contentofinterest&utm_medium=text&utm_campaign=cppst (Accessed 14 June 2023)

Bazelon, Coleman, 'The Indian 3G and BWA Auctions', *Times of India*, 1 October 2010

Times News Network, 'Reliance Info pays Rs 150 cr fine to DoT', 7 March 2005, http://timesofindia.indiatimes.com/articleshow/1043998.cms?utm_source=contentofinterest&utm_medium=text&utm_campaign=cppst (Accessed 14 June 2023)

Tripathi, Devidatta, 'Rel Comm: MTN talks progressing despite Rel Ind claim', Reuters, 13 June 2008, https://www.reuters.com/article/idUSBOM135447/ (Accessed 23 April 2024)

Kalesh, Baiju, 'Split may give Infocomm to Anil', *Times of India,* 24 March 2005, http://timesofindia.indiatimes.com/articleshow/1060668.cms?utm_source=contentofinterest&utm_medium=text&utm_campaign=cppst (Accessed 15 June 2023)

PTI, 'Reliance Info denies links with Mahajan', *Times of India,* 14 February 2005, http://timesofindia.indiatimes.com/articleshow/1020990.cms?utm_source=contentofinterest&utm_medium=text&utm_campaign=cppst (Accessed 29 June 2023)

Times News Network, 'SC no to Infocomm plea for bank guarantee to BSNL', *Times of India,* 3 January 2005, http://timesofindia.indiatimes.com/articleshow/979567.cms?utm_source=contentofinterest&utm_medium=text&utm_campaign=cppst (Accessed 30 June 2023)

PTI, 'Reliance to acquire Flag Telecom for $207 mn', *Economic Times,* 16 October 2003, https://economictimes.indiatimes.com/wealthmakers-the-ambanis/anil-dhirubhai-ambani-enterprises/reliance-infocomm/reliance-to-acquire-flag-telecom-for-207-mn/articleshow/934046.cms?utm_source=contentofinterest&utm_medium=text&utm_campaign=cppst (Accessed 22 November 2023)

Bureau, 'Reliance buys Flag for Rs 950 crore', *Business Standard,* 13 January 2004, https://www.business-standard.com/article/companies/reliance-buys-flag-for-rs-950-crore-104011301014_1.html (Accessed 22 November 2023)

PTI, 'RCom places $500 mn equipment order with Chinese Huawei', *Economic Times,* 21 January 2024, https://economictimes.indiatimes.com/industry/telecom/rcom-places-500-mn-equipment-order-with-chinese-huawei/articleshow/2719140.cms?utm_source=contentofinterest&utm_medium=text&utm_campaign=cppst (Accessed 13 April 2024)

Parbat, Kalya, 'Reliance Communications may soon seal $1.5 billion outsourcing deal with ZTE, Huawei and Ericsson', *Economic Times,* 12 August 2011, https://economictimes.indiatimes.com/jobs/reliance-communications-may-soon-seal-1-5-billion-outsourcing-deal-with-zte-huawei-and-ericsson/articleshow/9571585.

cms?utm_source=contentofinterest&utm_medium=text&utm_campaign=cppst (Accessed 13 April 2024)

Parkin, Benjamin, 'Anil Ambani vs Chinese banks: court case exposes stunning decline', *Financial Times*, 17 March 2020, https://www.ft.com/content/af6efd52-645f-11ea-a6cd-df28cc3c6a68 (Accessed 13 April 2024)

Srivastava, Bhuma and R Jai Krishna, 'RCom to invest $3 bn for November launch of GSM services', *Mint*, 16 September 2008, https://www.livemint.com/Companies/NBIPyeDaQBYTJScWWadw8M/RCom-to-invest-3-bn-for-November-launch-of-GSM-services.html?facet=amp (Accessed 13 April 2024)

—, 'Reliance Awards $200M Contract to Huawei', *Forbes*, July 13, 2007, https://www.forbes.com/2007/07/13/reliance-huawei-contract-markets-equity-cx_rd_0713markets3.html (Accessed 13 April 2024)

PTI, 'RCom, MTN in exclusive talks over merger', *Economic Times*, 26 May 2008, https://economictimes.indiatimes.com/industry/telecom/rcom-mtn-in-exclusive-talks-over-merger/articleshow/3072477.cms?utm_source=contentofinterest&utm_medium=text&utm_campaign=cppst (Accessed 23 April 2024)

ET Online, 'Reliance Communications, MTN end talks', *Times of India*, 18 July 2008, http://timesofindia.indiatimes.com/articleshow/3251644.cms?utm_source=contentofinterest&utm_medium=text&utm_campaign=cppst (Accessed 23 April 2024)

Gupta, Deepali, 'Rel Infratel may combine its tower assets with GTL', *Economic Times*, 16 June 2010, https://economictimes.indiatimes.com/rel-infratel-may-combine-its-tower-assets-with-gtl/articleshow/6059183.cms?utm_source=contentofinterest&utm_medium=text&utm_campaign=cppst (Accessed 23 April 2024)

Bureau, 'RCom merges tower biz with GTL Infra', *Economic Times*, 28 June 2010, https://economictimes.indiatimes.com/industry/telecom/rcom-merges-tower-biz-with-gtl-infra/articleshow/6099463.cms?utm_source=contentofinterest&utm_medium=text&utm_campaign=cppst (Accessed 23 April 2024)

TNN, 'RCom, GTL call off tower deal', *Times of India*, 7 September 2010, http://timesofindia.indiatimes.com/articleshow/6509209.cms?utm_source=contentofinterest&utm_medium=text&utm_campaign=cppst (Accessed 23 April 2024)

Reuters, 'India's Reliance and GTL Infra to merge tower operations', Reuters, 27 June 2010, https://www.reuters.com/article/idUSTRE65Q0TM/ (Accessed 23 April 2024)

PTI, 'RIL, SBI sign shareholder agreement for payments bank JV', *Economic Times*, 1 July 2016, https://economictimes.indiatimes.com/industry/banking/finance/banking/ril-sbi-sign-shareholder-agreement-for-payments-bank-jv/articleshow/53009074.cms?utm_source=contentofinterest&utm_medium=text&utm_campaign=cppst (Accessed 19 May 2024)

Sen, Sunny, 'Mukesh Ambani's army of expats at Jio', *Mint*, 30 January 2018, https://www.livemint.com/Industry/lHFD4WXCoWs4B-PdiYgdFKJ/Mukesh-Ambanis-army-of-expats-at-Jio.html (Accessed 19 May 20204)

PTI, 'Mukesh Ambani got Rs 1.4 cr as compensation from BofA in 2011', *Economic Times*, 16 April 2012, https://economictimes.indiatimes.com/news/company/corporate-trends/mukesh-ambani-got-rs-1-4-cr-as-compensation-from-bofa-in-2011/articleshow/12674259.cms?utm_source=contentofinterest&utm_medium=text&utm_campaign=cppst (Accessed 7 June 2024)

PTI, 'Reliance Communications pays Rs 5,383.84 crore as spectrum', *Times of India*, 20 January 2016, http://timesofindia.indiatimes.com/articleshow/50658820.cms?utm_source=contentofinterest&utm_medium=text&utm_campaign=cppst (Accessed 7 June 2024)

Gupta, Deepali, 'Reliance Jio MD Sandip Das to quit executive role', *Economic Times*, 13 January 2015, https://economictimes.indiatimes.com/industry/telecom/reliance-jio-md-sandip-das-to-quit-executive-role/articleshow/45867542.cms?utm_source=contentofinterest&utm_medium=text&utm_campaign=cppst (Accessed 19 May 2024)

Vodafone Story

O'Brien, Kevin J, 'Sarin leaves Vodafone after 5 turbulent years', *New York Times*, 27 May 2008, https://www.nytimes.com/2008/05/27/technology/27iht-voda.4.13254645.html (Accessed 20 April 2020)

—, 'Arun Sarin biography - 1954', Reference for Business, https://www.referenceforbusiness.com/biography/S-Z/Sarin-Arun-1954.html (Accessed 20 April 2020)

—, 'Max Telecom Ventures to Divest its Stake in Hutchison Essar Telecom', Max India, 30 August 2005, https://www.maxindia.com/press-release/max-telecom-ventures-to-divest-its-stake-in-hutchison-essar-telecom/ (Accessed 22 April 2020)

—, 'Asim Ghosh' , Bloomberg, https://www.bloomberg.com/profile/person/3277711 (Accessed 23 April 2020)

—, 'Annual Reports Hutchison Whampoa' FY05, FY06, FY07. https://www.ckh.com.hk/en/ir/annual.php?cat=hwl&year= https://doc.irasia.com/listco/hk/hutchison/annual/2004/telecom.pdf https://doc.irasia.com/listco/hk/hutchison/annual/2005/telecom.pdf https://doc.irasia.com/listco/hk/hutchison/annual/2003/telecom.pdf https://doc.irasia.com/listco/hk/hutchison/annual/2006/ar2006.pdf https://doc.irasia.com/listco/hk/hutchison/annual/2007/ar2007.pdf (Accessed 23 April 2020)

—, 'Our Journey', Max India, https://www.maxindia.com/our-journey/ (Accessed 23 April 2020)

Wearden, Graeme, 'Vodafone chief executive in shock exit', Guardian, https://www.theguardian.com/business/2008/may/27/vodafonegroup.telecoms (Accessed 20 April 2020)

Pratap, Rashmi, 'Sarin seeks to repeat success story', Economic Times, 22 January 2007, https://m.economictimes.com/industry/telecom/sarin-seeks-to-repeat-success-story/articleshow/1361921.cms?-from=desktop (Accessed 22 April 2020)

—, 'Motivational Story: Analjit Singh', Mbrandezvous, https://www.mbarendezvous.com/motivational-story/mr-analjit-singh/ (Accessed 23 April 2020)

Dixon, Hugo & Mike Verdin, 'Hutch Essar battle: Odds favour Vodafone, Reliance Comm', Mint, 9 February 2007, https://www.livemint.com/Companies/tzzW1VLs3vU3CeHEotgjPM/HutchEssar-battle-Odds-favour-Vodafone-Reliance-Comm.html (Accessed 23 April 2020)

Time News Network, 'Hinduja's begin due diligence for Hutch-Essar bid', Economic Times, 5 February 2007, https://economictimes.indiatimes.com/industry/telecom/hindujas-begin-due-diligence-for-hutch-essar-bid/articleshow/1560587.cms?from=mdr (Accessed 23 April 2020)

John, Satish, 'Reliance Communications to raise $1 bln via FCCB', DNA, 10 January 2007, https://www.dnaindia.com/business/report-reliance-communications-to-raise-1-bn-via-fccbs-1073751 (Accessed 23 April 2020)

—, 'Ashwani Windlass', Max India, https://www.maxindia.com/leadership-board-member/mr-ashwani-windlass/ (Accessed 24 April 2020)

Pratap, Rashmi, 'Hutch to ditch pink for Vodafone's red', *Economic Times*, 6 July 2007, https://economictimes.indiatimes.com/industry/telecom/hutch-to-ditch-pink-for-vodafones-red/articleshow/2179761.cms (Accessed 24 April 2020)

Special Correspondent, 'Kotak helps Max in Hutch comeback', Telegraph India, 1 March 2006, https://www.telegraphindia.com/business/kotak-helps-max-in-hutch-comeback/cid/809871 (Accessed 24 April 2020)

—, 'Circlewise List of India's Telecom Licenses', Medianama, 31 December 2012, https://www.medianama.com/circlewise-list-of-indias-telecom-licencees/ (Accessed 27 April 2020)

Vaish, Nandini, '1995-Telecom licensing begins: The call of change', *India Today*, 24 December 2009, https://www.indiatoday.in/magazine/cover-story/story/20091228-1995-telecom-licensing-begins-the-call-of-change-741625-2009-12-24. (Accessed 29 April 2020)

Wang, Julie, 'Hutchison Unit Widens India Network', *Wall Street Journal*, 30 August 2005, https://www.wsj.com/articles/SB112534638218525900 (Accessed 30 April 2020)

—, 'Essar and Vodafone: US$5.46 billion deal', Essar, 1995, https://www.essar.com/about/essar-and-vodafone-us5-46-billion-deal/ (Accessed 29 April 2020)

—, 'Hutchison to buy Hinduja stake in JV', *Hindustan Times*, 16 June 2006, https://www.hindustantimes.com/india/hutchison-to-buy-hinduja-stake-in-jv/story-YBoSmCA1fmxmF5jMz2PQEK.html (Accessed 29 April 2020)

Chhaya, M., 'Hutch-Essar mull merger', CIOL, 15 March 2004, https://www.ciol.com/hutch-essar-mull-merger/ (Accessed 23 April 2020)

Dasgupta, Shamik, 'BPL's Nambiar drags son-in-law to CLB', *Economic Times*, 28 September 2004, https://economictimes.indiatimes.com/bpls-nambiar-drags-son-in-law-to-clb/articleshow/865946.cms?from=mdr (Accessed 9 November 2022)

Times News Network, 'Hutchison to consolidate Indian operations', *Times of India*, 4 February 2005, http://timesofindia.indiatimes.com/articleshow/1011967.cms?utm_source=contentofinterest&utm_medium=text&utm_campaign=cppst (Accessed 29 June 2023)

Idea Story

Press Release, 'Birla-Tata-AT&T and BPL team up to form India's premier mobile services Company', Aditya Birla, 28 June 2001, https://www.adityabirla.com/media/media-releases/bpl-team-up-to-form-india-premier-mobile-services-company (Accessed 30 April 2020)

Correspondent, 'Batata, BPL in $2 Bn Mobile Merger', *Telegraph India*, 28 June 2001, https://www.telegraphindia.com/business/batata-bpl-in-2-bn-mobile-merger/cid/928040 (Accessed 30 April 2020)

—, 'Passing the baton', Aditya Birla, 27 May 2005, https://web.archive.org/web/20071012131001/http://www.adityabirla.com/media/press_reports/passing_the_baton.htm. (Accessed 16 May 2020)

—, 'Birla, Tata clash over Idea holding', Business Standard, 24 February 2006, https://www.business-standard.com/article/companies/birla-tata-clash-over-idea-holding-106022401152_1.html (Accessed 27 May 2020)

Bureau, 'Birla to buy out Tata, sell 33% in Idea', *Business Standard*, 11 April 2006, https://www.business-standard.com/article/companies/birla-to-buy-out-tata-sell-33-in-idea-106041101165_1.html (Accessed 27 May 2020)

Agencies, 'Tata's 'Idea' of Arbitration Frivolous: Birla', *Financial Express*, 22 August 2007, https://www.financialexpress.com/archive/tatas-idea-of-arbitration-frivolous-birlas/211931/ (Accessed 27 May 2020)

Gupta, Surajeet Das, 'C Sivasankaran: A maverick prone to courting controversy and the CBI', *Business Standard*, 28 April 2018, https://www.business-standard.com/article/companies/c-sivasankaran-a-maverick-prone-to-courting-controversy-and-the-cbi-118042700853_1.html (Accessed 27 May 2020)

Ravindranath, Sushila, 'Tracing the journey of Aircel Sivasankaran: The maverick entrepreneur who went bankrupt', *News Minute*, 26 September 2016, https://www.thenewsminute.com/article/tracing-journey-aircel-sivasankaran-maverick-entrepreneur-who-went-bankrupt-50405 (Accessed 27 May 2020)

Gupta, Seetha and Sharda, *The Brink: Turning Escorts Around*, 2020, New Delhi, HarperCollins India

Bureau, 'Idea Buys Escotel for Rs 350 crore', *Business Standard*, 16 January 2004, https://www.business-standard.com/article/

companies/idea-buys-escotel-for-rs-350-crore-104011601013_1.
html (Accessed 27 May 2020)

Kalesh, Baiju, 'Birla-AT&T-Tata acquires RPG Cell', *Times of India*, 22 December 2000, http://timesofindia.indiatimes.com/articleshow/822697091.cms?utm_source=contentofinterest&utm_medium=text&utm_campaign=cppst (Accessed 7 November 2022)

Bureau, 'Birla-At & T-Tata, Bpl Begin Integration Process', *Business Standard*, 16 October 2001, https://www.business-standard.com/article/companies/birla-at-t-tata-bpl-begin-integration-process-101101601013_1.html (Accessed 8 November 2022)

Press Release, 'Aditya Birla Nuvo to merge with Grasim Industries', Aditya Birla, 12 August 2016, https://www.adityabirla.com/media/press-reports/aditya-birla-nuvo-to-merge-with-grasim-industries#:~:text=Aditya%20Birla%20Nuvo%20Ltd%20(ABNL,which%20will%20be%20listed%20later. (Accessed 8 June 2024)

Ownerships

Narayan, Chitra, 'Brand Campa Cola bubbles in North', *The Hindu Business Line*, 17 November 2011, https://www.thehindubusinessline.com/companies/Brand-Campa-Cola-bubbles-in-North/article20371328.ece (Accessed 2 May 2020)

—, 'Report No 20 of 2015, Chapter II Department of Telecommunications', CAG, 2015, https://cag.gov.in/sites/default/files/audit_report_files/Union_Compliance_Communication_IT_20_2015_chapter_5.pdf (Accessed 6 May 2020)

Raj, Rishi, 'My scam vs your scam', *Financial Express*, 30 December 2010, https://www.financialexpress.com/archive/my-scam-versus-your-scam/730922/ (Accessed 16 May 2020)

—, *India Telecom Vol 4: Overview of the Indian Market 1999–2000*, Information Gatekeepers Inc, https://books.google.co.in/books?id=vzv02dJXhtwC&pg=PA166&lpg=PA166&dq=jt+-mobile+gets+karnataka+andhra+pradesh&source=bl&ots=lM-kUXrjCfk&sig=ACfU3U1YrLvwT6eoDnFejLhi5AQQN-favfw&hl=en&sa=X&ved=2ahUKEwjd4KKS1rfpAhW38XMB-HUh9CAkQ6AEwBXoECAwQAQ#v=onepage&q=jt%20mobile%20gets%20karnataka%20andhra%20pradesh&f=false (Accessed 16 May 2020)

—, 'Telia Nominee quits as MD of JT Mobile', *Business Standard*, 12 February 1997, https://www.business-standard.com/article/specials/telia-nominee-quits-as-md-of-jt-mobile-197021201046_1.html (Accessed 16 May 2020)

Chandramouli, Rajesh, 'Siva Sells Aircel Makes $800M', *Times of India*, 31 December 2005, https://timesofindia.indiatimes.com/business/india-business/Siva-sells-Aircel-makes-800-million/articleshow/1353486.cms (Accessed 27 May 2020)

Bureau, 'Mobilink Joins Hands with Beltron Paging', *Business Standard*, 21 April 1998, https://www.business-standard.com/article/specials/mobilink-joins-hands-with-beltron-paging-198042101078_1.html (Accessed 17 August 2020)

Bureau, 'Vodafone wins AirTouch', CNN, 15 January 1999, https://money.cnn.com/1999/01/15/deals/bellatlantic/ (Accessed 10 November 2022)

Rajya Sabha Questions: QUESTION NO23.08.1995

Airtel Story

Johnson, Jo 'Profile: Sunil Mittal', *Financial Times*, 27 November 2006, https://www.ft.com/content/4a4dcbbc-7dee-11db-84bb-0000779e2340 (Accessed 16 May 2020)

Ghatak, Aditi Roy and Parajoy Guha Thakur, 'What lies behind the incredible rise and rise of Bharti Airtel' 6 August, 2015, https://thewire.in/economy/what-lies-behind-the-incredible-rise-and-rise-of-bharti-airtel (Accessed 16 May 2020)

Tyagi, Chavi, 'How Bharti Airtel's Sunil Mittal was once in financial crisis for the want of Rs 5000', *Economic Times*, 16 December 2017, https://economictimes.indiatimes.com/small-biz/startups/newsbuzz/how-bharti-airtels-sunil-mittal-was-once-in-financial-crisis-for-the-want-of-rs-5000/articleshow/62093302.cms?from=mdr (Accessed 29 June 2020)

Bhandari, Bhupesh, '40 years ago... And now: Sunil Mittal - One step ahead of reforms', *Business Standard*, https://www.business-standard.com/article/companies/40-years-ago-and-now-sunil-mittal-one-step-ahead-of-reforms-115021800032_1.html (Accessed 9 May 2022)

Chandler, Clay, 'Wireless Wonder: India's Sunil Mittal', CNN, https://money.cnn.com/magazines/fortune/fortune_archive/2007/01/22/8397979/index3.htm (Accessed 5 May 2022)

Sachs, Goldman, 'Interview with Alison Mass', https://www. goldmansachs.com/insights/talks-at-gs/chip-kaye-f/transcript.pdf (Accessed 11 May 2022)

Geary John, Johan Martin-Löf, Claes-Göran Sundelius, and Bertil Thorngren, *Telia's History*, Telia Company, https://www. teliacompany.com/globalassets/telia-company/documents/about-telia-company/history/telias-history-1993-2002.pdf. (Accessed 17 July 2022)

Sanotra, Hardev S. and Dakshesh Parikh, 'First meeting we had with any politician was with Rajiv Gandhi: Harshad Mehta', *India Today*, 15 July 1993, https://www.indiatoday.in/magazine/cover-story/story/19930715-first-meeting-we-had-with-any-politician-was-with-rajiv-gandhi-says-harshad-mehta-812069-1993-07-15 (Accessed 1 August 2022)

Voice and Data Bureau, 'TATA-BIRLA AT&T MERGER: The Titans Meet', Voice and Data, 31 March 2000, https://www. voicendata.com/tata-birla-at-t-merger-the-titans-meet/ (Accessed 15 September 2022)

PTI, 'Bharti completes mobile coverage in 23 circles', *Times of India*, 13 April 2005, http://timesofindia.indiatimes.com/articleshow/1076857. cms?utm_source=contentofinterest&utm_medium=text&utm_campaign=cppst (Accessed 14 June 2023)

PTI, 'TDSAT rejects Bharti's plea for refund', *Times of India*, 9 March 2005, https://timesofindia.indiatimes.com/business/india-business/tdsat-says-no-to-bhartis-refund-plea/articleshow/1046869.cms (Accessed 14 June 2023)

PTI, 'Sunil Bharti Mittal takes over as Executive Chairman of Airtel', *Economic Times*, 1 February 2013, https://economictimes.indiatimes.com/sunil-bharti-mittal-takes-over-as-executive-chairman-of-airtel/article-show/18295645.cms?utm_source=contentofinterest&utm_medium=text&utm_campaign=cppst (Accessed 23 April 2024)

Reuters, 'India's Bharti Airtel completes acquisition of Zain Africa', 8 June 2010, https://www.reuters.com/article/idUS3735096686/ (Accessed 24 April 2024)

PTI, 'Manoj Kohli to take over as Bharti Airtel MD', *Business Today*, 30 January 2013, https://www.businesstoday.in/industry/telecom/story/manoj-kohli-to-take-over-as-bharti-airtel-md-38652-2013-01-30 (Accessed 23 April 2024)

Doke, Shunal, 'Airtel launches 4G LTE services in Pune', Firstpost, 18 October 2012, https://www.firstpost.com/tech/news-analysis/airtel-launches-4g-lte-services-in-pune-3610717.html (Accessed 24 April 2024)

Bureau, 'Bharti Airtel-MTN $ 24 billion deal called off', 1 October 2009, https://economictimes.indiatimes.com/industry/telecom/bharti-airtel-mtn-24-billion-deal-called-off/articleshow/5074181.cms?utm_source=contentofinterest&utm_medium=text&utm_campaign=cppst (Accessed 23 April 2024)

Reuters, 'Bharti and MTN tie-up talks collapse again', 30 September 2009, https://www.reuters.com/article/idUSTRE58T1N6/ (Accessed 23 April 2024)

Mankhotia, Anadita Singh and Chaitali Chakraborty, '8 out of 13 top executives leave Bharti after Gopal Vittal becomes CEO', *Economic Times*, 30 December 2013, https://economictimes.indiatimes.com/industry/telecom/8-out-of-13-top-executives-leave-bharti-after-gopal-vittal-becomes-ceo/articleshow/28116382.cms?utm_source=contentofinterest&utm_medium=text&utm_campaign=cppst (Accessed 23 April 2024)

Philip, Joji, 'Bharti Airtel loses its three top executives ahead of key restructuring', 10 January 2013, https://economictimes.indiatimes.com/bharti-airtel-loses-its-three-top-executives-ahead-of-key-restructuring/articleshow/17961317.cms?utm_source=contentofinterest&utm_medium=text&utm_campaign=cppst (Accessed 23 April 2024)

Philip, Joji and Rashmi Pratap, 'Bharti in talks to acquire South Africa's MTN', *Economic Times*, 6 May 2008, https://economictimes.indiatimes.com/industry/telecom/bharti-in-talks-to-acquire-south-africas-mtn/articleshow/3013389.cms?utm_source=contentofinterest&utm_medium=text&utm_campaign=cppst (Accessed 23 April 2024)

Reuters, 'Bharti and MTN extend exclusive talks to Sept 30', 20 August 2009, https://www.reuters.com/article/idUSBOM516528/ (Accessed 23 April 2024)

Tata

—, 'Siva, what next', *Financial Express*, 7 January 2006, https://www.financialexpress.com/archive/siva-what-next/67689/ (Accessed 8 June 2020)

Press Release, 'DoCoMo Names New CEO', 13 May 2008, https://www.lightreading.com/business-management/docomo-names-new-ceo (Accessed 7 May 2024)

—, 'Tata Tele, Huges in Marriage Talks, Again', *Financial Express*, 18 June 2002, https://www.financialexpress.com/archive/tata-tele-hughes-in-marriage-talks-again/49711/ (Accessed 8 June 2020)

Jain, Sunil, 'The Great Gambler', *Business Standard*, 7 February 2005, https://www.business-standard.com/article/opinion/sunil-jain-the-great-gambler-105020701021_1.html (Accessed 21 March 2023)

Staff, Knowledge at Wharton, 'Arun Shourie: "Reservation Is Not Affirmative Action"', Wharton, 30 November 2006, https://knowledge.wharton.upenn.edu/article/arun-shourie-reservation-is-not-affirmative-action/ (Accessed 21 March 2023)

TNN. 'Shourie: VSNL deal fully above board', *Times of India*, 5 June 2002, http://timesofindia.indiatimes.com/articleshow/12009200.cms?utm_source=contentofinterest&utm_medium=text&utm_campaign=cppst (Accessed 22 March 2023)

Law, Vivek and Rajeev Deshpande, 'VSNL controversy: Tata investment decision triggers corporate rivalry, ministerial spat', *India Today*, 17 June 2002, https://www.indiatoday.in/magazine/economy/story/20020617-vsnl-controversy-tata-investment-decision-triggers-corporate-rivalry-ministerial-spat-795084-2002-06-16 (Accessed 26 March 2023)

Rao, Menaka, 'Get monopoly compensation from Trai, Bombay HC tells VSNL', *DNA*, 15 August 2010, https://www.dnaindia.com/mumbai/report-get-monopoly-compensation-from-trai-bombay-hc-tells-vsnl-1423534 (Accessed 28 March 2023)

Bureau, 'Tatas ahead in VSNL race', *Economic Times*, 5 February 2002, https://economictimes.indiatimes.com/tatas-ahead-in-vsnl-race/articleshow/2137882041.cms?utm_source=contentofinterest&utm_medium=text&utm_campaign=cppst (Accessed 28 March 2023)

Bureau, 'Ratan Tata becomes VSNL chairman', *Times of India*, 14 February 2002, http://timesofindia.indiatimes.com/articleshow/904407.cms?utm_source=contentofinterest&utm_medium=text&utm_campaign=cppst (Accessed 28 March 2023)

Correspondent, 'Shourie Move to Hasten VSNL Selloff', *Telegraph India*, 1 October 2001, https://www.telegraphindia.com/business/shourie-move-to-hasten-vsnl-selloff/cid/914334 (Accessed 28 March 2023)

Times staff, 'AT&T; Spinoff Lucent Makes Historic IPO', *LA Times*, 4 April 1996, https://www.latimes.com/archives/la-xpm-1996-04-04-fi-54949-story.html (Accessed 4 May 2023)

—, 'VSNL Acquires TGN for $130 million', Submarine Networks, 1 July 2005, https://www.submarinenetworks.com/systems/trans-pacific/

tgn-pacific/vsnl-acquires-tgn (Accessed 22 November 2023) https://www.tatacommunications-ts.com/our-heritage.php

—, 'Three Tyco execs indicted for fraud', CNN, 12 September 2002, https://edition.cnn.com/2002/BUSINESS/asia/09/12/us.tyco/ (Accessed 22 November 2023)

Gupta, Deepali, 'Telenor's exit from India to hit Viom Networks revenues', *Economic Times*, 9 May 2012, https://economictimes.indiatimes.com/industry/telecom/telenors-exit-from-india-to-hit-viom-networks-revenues/articleshow/13058850.cms?utm_source=contentofinterest&utm_medium=text&utm_campaign=cppst (Accessed 23 April 2024)

Fujimura, Naoko, 'DoCoMo to Spend 164 Billion Yen on Network After Service Outage', Bloomberg, 27 January 2012, https://www.bloomberg.com/news/articles/2012-01-27/docomo-to-spend-164-billion-yen-on-network-after-service-outage?sref=AaLF1RVh (Accessed 14 May 2024)

Reuters, 'India's Tata Tele sells tower unit stake to Quippo', 5 January 2009, https://www.reuters.com/article/idUSBOM365039/ (Accessed 23 April 2024)

General

Dutta Krishnakoli and Josey Puliyenthuruth, 'Itochu to Pick Up Part Of Ntt Stake In Basic Teleservices', *Business Standard*, 14 March 1997, https://www.business-standard.com/article/specials/itochu-to-pick-up-part-of-ntt-stake-in-basic-teleservices-197031401010_1.html (Accessed 24 July 2020)

Agha, Zafar Shefali Rekhi, 'Telecom scandal: Opposition determined not to let go of juicy election issue', *India Today*, 31 December 1995, (https://www.indiatoday.in/magazine/economy/story/19951231-telecom-scandal-opposition-determined-not-to-let-go-of-juicy-election-issue-808108-1995-12-30 (Accessed 19 August 2020)

Bureau, 'HFCL promoters part ways', *Business Standard*, 13 May 2007, https://www.business-standard.com/article/companies/hfcl-promoters-part-ways-107051301043_1.html (Accessed 28 August 2020)

Gupta, Deepali, 'American Towers sued over Xcel Telecom deal', *Economic Times*, 11 June 2010, https://economictimes.indiatimes.com/industry/telecom/american-towers-sued-over-xcel-telecom-deal/

articleshow/6034762.cms?utm_source=contentofinterest&utm_medium=text&utm_campaign=cppst (Accessed 23 April 2024)

PTI, 'Government issues guidelines to liberalise 2G spectrum', *Economic Times*, 5 November 2015, https://economictimes.indiatimes.com/industry/telecom/government-issues-guidelines-to-liberalise-2g-spectrum/articleshow/49674585.cms?utm_source=contentofinterest&utm_medium=text&utm_campaign=cppst (Accessed 19 May 2024)

PTI, 'Viom Networks denies reports of wrongdoing in company', *Economic Times*, 14 September 2011, https://economictimes.indiatimes.com/industry/telecom/viom-networks-denies-reports-of-wrongdoing-in-company/articleshow/9982503.cms?utm_source=contentofinterest&utm_medium=text&utm_campaign=cppst (Accessed 7 May 2024)

BS Reporter, 'American Tower buys Xcel for Rs 800-850 cr', *Business Standard*, 18 March 2009, https://www.business-standard.com/article/companies/american-tower-buys-xcel-for-rs-800-850-cr-109031800052_1.html (Accessed 23 April 2024)

S. Pallavi, 'Quippo Completes Merger with Tata's Wireless TT Info Services', VC Circle, 25 August 2009, https://www.vccircle.com/quippo-completes-merger-tatas-wireless-tt-info-services (Accessed 7 May 2024)

ET Now, 'Viom Networks Chairman Subodh Bhargava quits', *Economic Times*, 6 February 2012, https://economictimes.indiatimes.com/viom-networks-chairman-subodh-bhargava-quits/articleshow/11780997.cms?utm_source=contentofinterest&utm_medium=text&utm_campaign=cppst (Accessed 7 May 2024)

PTI, 'After govt's exit, Tata Group's holding in Tata Communications rises to 58.87%', *Mint*, 24 March 2001, https://www.livemint.com/companies/news/tata-group-s-holding-in-tata-communications-rises-to-58-87-after-government-sells-stake-divestment-to-panatone-finvest-11616544178084.html (Accessed 7 May 2024)

—, 'DoT panel blames Tatas for delay in demerger of VSNL land', *India Today*, 26 April 2011, https://www.indiatoday.in/india/north/story/dot-panel-blames-tatas-for-delay-in-demerger-of-vsnl-land-132733-2011-04-25 (Accessed 7 May 2024)

Bureau, 'Demerger of VSNL land: Tata Comm blames DoT for delay', 24 March 2011, https://www.thehindubusinessline.com/info-tech/

Demerger-of-VSNL-land-Tata-Comm-blames-DoT-for-delay/
article20112798.ece (Accessed 7 May 2024)

Bureau, 'Telecom Regulator Asserts Independence', *Business Standard*, 26 March 1997, https://www.business-standard.com/article/specials/telecom-regulator-asserts-independence-197032601032_1.html (Accessed 3 September 2020)

Bureau, 'Koshika Equity Rejig Plan Sent to CCFI', *Business Standard*, 29 May 1998, 'https://www.business-standard.com/article/specials/koshika-equity-rejig-plan-sent-to-ccfi-198052901053_1.html

'Cellular Telephony', COAI, https://coai.com/indian-telecom-infocenter/cellular-telephony/cellular-telephony-india-1997

Rekhi, Shefali, 'Telecom once again at centrestage of pre-poll power play', *India Today*, 30 August 1999, https://www.indiatoday.in/magazine/nation/story/19990816-telecom-once-again-at-centrestage-of-pre-poll-power-play-824430-1999-08-30 (Accessed 13 October 2020)

Press Release, 'Qualcomm Announces Mahangar Telephone Nigam Ltd.'s Commencement of FirstCommercial CDMA Wireless Local Loop Network in India', 25 June 1997 (Accessed 17 October 2022)

Chandramouli, Rajesh, 'RPG, Vodafone spat over RPG Cellular stake', *Times of India*, 24 August 2000, http://timesofindia.indiatimes.com/articleshow/144822.cms?utm_source=contentofinterest&utm_medium=text&utm_campaign=cppst (Accessed 14 November 2022)

—, 'GoT report will be final by February 19', Rediff, 11 January 1999, https://www.rediff.com/computer/1999/jan/11policy.htm. (Accessed 28 March 2023)

BSCAL, 'Pagelink Blueprint to Hike Mumbai Subscriber Base', *Business Standard*, 9 September 1997, https://www.business-standard.com/article/specials/pagelink-blueprint-to-hike-mumbai-subscriber-base-197090901053_1.html

BSCAL, 'Telia Nominee Quits as Md Of Jt Mobile', *Business Standard*, 12 February 1997, https://www.business-standard.com/article/specials/telia-nominee-quits-as-md-of-jt-mobile-197021201046_1.html

Special Correspondent, 'Bharti buys out Shyam Tele in Hexacom for Rs 430 crore', *Telegraph India*, 6 April 2024, https://www.telegraphindia.com/business/bharti-buys-out-shyam-tele-in-hexacom-for-rs-430-crore/cid/958701

Datta, Saikat, 'A Land of No Return', *Outlook India*, https://www.outlookindia.com/magazine/story/a-land-of-no-return/271041 (Accessed 28 March 2023)

—, 'Arun Shourie: Minister with a clear mandate but unclear powers', *India Today*, 27 August 2001, https://www.indiatoday.in/magazine/

cover-story/story/20010827-arun-shourie-minister-with-a-clear-mandate-but-unclear-powers-774097-2001-08-26 (Accessed 28 March 2023)

PTI. 'TDSAT chairman questions decision on upholding WLL', *Economic Times*, 8 August 2003, https://economictimes.indiatimes.com/tdsat-chairman-questions-decision-on-upholding-wll/articleshow/120986.cms?utm_source=contentofinterest&utm_medium=text&utm_campaign=cppst (Accessed 28 March 2023)

Anand, Sanjay, 'MTNL doesn't want to be an arm of BSNL', Times of India, 16 February 2005, http://timesofindia.indiatimes.com/articleshow/1022113.cms?utm_source=contentofinterest&utm_medium=text&utm_campaign=cppst (Accessed 29 June 2023)

PTI, 'TRAI serves showcause notice on VSNL', *Times of India*, 27 February 2005, http://timesofindia.indiatimes.com/articleshow/1034588.cms?utm_source=contentofinterest&utm_medium=text&utm_campaign=cppst (Accessed 29 June 2023)

PTI, 'TRAI issues notices to Tata, Reliance, MTNL', *Times of India*, 16 January 2005, http://timesofindia.indiatimes.com/articleshow/991674.cms?utm_source=contentofinterest&utm_medium=text&utm_campaign=cppst (Accessed 30 June 2023)

Times News Network, 'Hutch, Airtel slash STD, ISD rates', *Times of India*, 20 January 2005, http://timesofindia.indiatimes.com/articleshow/997022.cms?utm_source=contentofinterest&utm_medium=text&utm_campaign=cppst (Accessed 30 June 2023)

Pratap, Rashmi, 'Unknown Mauritius entity picks stake in BPL', *Economic Times*, 10 September 2008, https://economictimes.indiatimes.com/industry/telecom/unknown-mauritius-entity-picks-up-stake-in-bpl-mobile/articleshow/3465028.cms?from=mdr (Accessed 31 January 2024)

Mookerji, Nivedita, 'Arbitration Panel on BPL Mobile spat set up', *DNA*, updated on September 14, 2017, https://www.dnaindia.com/business/report-arbitration-panel-on-bpl-mobile-spat-set-up-1081356 (Accessed 5 February 2024)

Bureau, 'GTL Infra acquires Aircel tower business for Rs 8,400 cr', *Economic Times*, 15 January 2010, https://economictimes.indiatimes.com/industry/telecom/gtl-infra-acquires-aircel-tower-business-for-rs-8400-cr/articleshow/5446498.cms?utm_source=contentofinterest&utm_medium=text&utm_campaign=cppst (Accessed 23 April 2024)

Reuters, 'India amends overseas borrowing rules for 3G auction', 25 January 2010, https://www.reuters.com/article/idUSSGE60O0BF/ (Accessed 25 April 2024)

PTI, 'Auction for 3G spectrum begins smoothly', *Economic Times*, 9 April 2010, https://economictimes.indiatimes.com/industry/telecom/auction-for-3g-spectrum-begins-smoothly/articleshow/5776998.cms?utm_source=contentofinterest&utm_medium=text&utm_campaign=cppst (Accessed 25 April 2024)

Adepalli, Srinivas, 'India Spectrum Auctions 101', Medianama, 18 May 2010, https://www.medianama.com/2010/05/223-india-spectrum-auctions-101/ (Accessed 25 April 2024)

Times News Network, 'Money in mind, PMO may force release of spectrum', *Economic Times*, 14 April 2008, https://economictimes.indiatimes.com/spectrum-war/money-in-mind-pmo-may-force-release-of-spectrum/articleshow/2956455.cms?utm_source=contentofinterest&utm_medium=text&utm_campaign=cppst (Accessed 25 April 2024)

Singh, Shalini, Times News Network, 'PM steps in, Defence agrees to vacate spectrum', *Times of India*, 27 September 2007, http://timesofindia.indiatimes.com/articleshow/2366989.cms?utm_source=contentofinterest&utm_medium=text&utm_campaign=cppst (Accessed 25 April 2024)

Kar, Parag, 'The History of Indian Telecom Licensing — A Policy Perspective', Medium, 21 September 2021, https://paragkar.medium.com/the-history-of-indian-telecom-licensing-a-policy-perspective-5011dbfe1741 (Accessed 1 May 2024)

Kar, Parag, '2010 Auction', https://paragkar.com/2010-2/ (Accessed 1 May 2024)

Singh, Shalini, 'Raja backs auctions for 3G spectrum', *Times of India*, 13 November 2007, http://timesofindia.indiatimes.com/articleshow/2536697.cms?utm_source=contentofinterest&utm_medium=text&utm_campaign=cppst (Accessed 1 May 2024)

Philip, Joji, '3G spectrum sale: DoT incorporates significant changes to auction rules', *Economic Times*, 27 September 2012, https://economictimes.indiatimes.com/industry/telecom/3g-spectrum-sale-dot-incorporates-significant-changes-to-auction-rules/articleshow/16559876.cms (Accessed 1 May 2024)

Bureau, '3G spectrum: Govt hits jackpot; gets Rs 67,719 crore', *Economic Times*, 20 May 2010, https://economictimes.indiatimes.com/industry/telecom/3g-spectrum-govt-hits-jackpot-gets-rs-67719-crore/articleshow/5951145.cms?utm_source=contentofinterest&utm_medium=text&utm_campaign=cppst (Accessed 1 May 2024)

Times News Network, 'Virgin Mobile enters India, but not as MVNO', *Economic Times*, 3 March 2008, https://economictimes.indiatimes.com/industry/telecom/virgin-mobile-enters-india-but-not-as-mvno/articleshow/2832231.cms?utm_source=contentofin terest&utm_medium=text&utm_campaign=cppst   (Accessed 1 May 2024)

PTI, 'BSNL, MTNL to make big gains from intra-circle roaming pacts', *Economic Times*, https://economictimes.indiatimes.com/industry/telecom/bsnl-mtnl-to-make-big-gains-from-intra-circle-roaming-pacts/articleshow/5970349.cms?utm_source=contentofinterest&utm_medium=text&utm_campaign=cppst

Philip, Joji, 'BSNL, MTNL to make big gains from intra-circle roaming pacts', *Economic Times*, 25 May 2010, https://economictimes.indiatimes.com/industry/telecom/bsnl-mtnl-to-make-big-gains-from-intra-circle-roaming-pacts/articleshow/5970349.cms?utm_source=contentofinterest&utm_medium=text&utm_campaign=cppst (Accessed 1 May 2024)

Gokhale, Ketki and Alastair Reed, 'Telenor May Leave India as Fee Dispute Prompts Write-Off', Bloomberg, 30 April 2012, https://www.bloomberg.com/news/articles/2012-04-30/telenor-writes-down-681-million-in-remaining-india-assets?embedded-checkout=true&sref=AaLF1RVh (Accessed 3 May 2024)

Gupta, Das Surajeet, 'Who's right, Tata or Mittal?', Rediff, 1 June 2005, https://www.rediff.com/money/2005/jun/01spec.htm   (Accessed 7 May 2024)

Bureau, '2G spectrum auction ends in a damp squib, less than Rs 10,000 crore bids received', *India Today*, 15 November 2012, https://www.indiatoday.in/india/north/story/2g-spectrum-auction-ends-less-than-rs-10k-cr-bids-received-121444-2012-11-14   (Accessed 7 May 2024)

IANS, 'Spectrum is already liberalised since 1999: Vodafone', New *Indian Express*, 17 September 2012, https://www.newindian-express.com/business/2012/Jul/16/spectrum-is-already-liberal-ised-since-1999-vodafone-387513.html (Accessed 19 May 2024)

Judgements

Delhi Science Forum SC, https://main.sci.gov.in/judgment/judis/15970.pdf

—, 'Tata Cellular vs Union Of India', 26 July 1994, https://main.sci.gov.in/judgments. (Accessed 29 April 2020)

Scan QR code to access the
Penguin Random House India website